FREDERICK HOWARD WINES

PUNISHMENT AND REFORMATION

A STUDY OF THE PENITENTIARY SYSTEM

Elibron Classics
www.elibron.com

Elibron Classics series.

ISBN 1-4212-3460-2 (paperback)
ISBN 1-4212-3459-9 (hardcover)

This Elibron Classics Replica Edition is an unabridged facsimile of the edition published in 1919 by Thomas Y. Crowell Company, New York.

PUNISHMENT AND REFORMATION

A STUDY OF THE PENITENTIARY SYSTEM

BY

FREDERICK HOWARD WINES, LL.D.

NEW EDITION

REVISED AND ENLARGED

BY

WINTHROP D. LANE

OF THE "SURVEY" STAFF

NEW YORK

THOMAS Y. CROWELL COMPANY

PUBLISHERS

CONTENTS

CONTENTS

REVISER'S PREFACE

To revise another man's book is like taking his place before a half-finished portrait at the easel, or wresting the conductor's wand from his hand while the orchestra is still playing the *andante*. In each instance, the interloper is likely to be the only person who gets any enjoyment from the change. A book that deals chiefly with facts and deductions from facts, however, like the present one, lends itself more readily to posthumous mutilation of this kind than does, say, a volume of poems or the diary of a man's life. One hardly cares to have another person voice his joy at the stars or the sunrise, or dress up an account of his life to suit himself. Facts, however, are impersonal and may be rearranged and added to with impunity.

There are two ways of revising a book. One is to begin at the first page and go through to the last, meticulously scanning each sentence, toning down a generalization here, enlarging one there, and adding footnotes wherever the spirit moves and new information warrants. This may be called the mosaic, or crazy-quilt method. The other is to omit from the original in chunks whatever is unessential or out of date, and then at the end to pile the Ossa of new material upon the Pelion of old. This may be called the Procrustean method.

A logical reason seemed to exist for the use of the second method in the present revision. Since Dr. Wines revised his own book in 1910, remarkable developments have occurred in both the science of criminology and the treatment of law-breakers. These required, not revision of the text as it stood, but supplemental setting forth. Among them is the closer view that has been obtained of the causal factors of crime by the study of individual offenders. To-day we are far less helpless than a decade ago in answering the question: Who are the criminals? Another development is the new light thrown by this same study upon treatment, and what penal institutions have done to respond to this light. A third is the spread of inmate self-government and the growth of the honor system, and a fourth is Goring's monumental inquiry into the existence of an anthropological criminal type, which was begun in 1902 and came to a close in 1913, so that its results were not available for publication when Dr. Wines wrote.

Each of these subjects has been discussed in the present volume. The historical chapters of the 1910 edition, namely, the first eleven, have been retained in this. The revision begins with the second part of Chapter XI, on Criminal Anthropology. Four chapters were discarded, one on the causes of crime, one on the theory of punishment, one on the prevention of crime and one on the outlook for the future. Two papers comprising an Appendix were also dropped.

The thanks both of the reviser and the reader are due, first, to Dr. William Healy, at present director of the Judge Baker Foundation in Boston, whose reading of much of the manuscript of the new chapters yielded invaluable suggestions. Thanks are due also to Mr. George W. Kirchwey and Mr. Calvin Derrick for very generous assistance.

WINTHROP D. LANE

NEW YORK CITY,
December 27, 1918.

PREFACE TO FIRST EDITION

THIS book must be taken for what it is, not for what is does not claim to be. It does not pretend to be either original or exhaustive.

The author was requested to deliver a course of lectures, in 1893, before the students of the State University of Winconsin, which were given extemporaneously; but afterward written, to be read, in January, 1895, before the Lowell Institute in Boston.

They have been rewritten for publication, in the hope that they may prove not only instructive but interesting. A great frivolous interest in crime is demonstrated by the attention paid to it in the daily journals; why not hope that a serious interest may also be taken in suggestions for its suppression?

This is not a book on prisons, much less on the organization and government of prisons. It is rather designed to be an aid to legislation and to the formation of a correct public opinion, which must in the end control legislation. Its aim is to give to the ordinary reader a clear and connected view of the change in the attitude of the law toward crime and criminals, during the century now drawing to its close, and of the honorable part which the United States has borne in the movement for a better recognition of the rights even of convicted criminals. Looking to the future, the watchword should be: *nulla vestigia retrorsum.*

The authority for each statement in the text is not given in footnotes, because of the great number of citations that would be necessary, and the consequent fatigue to the reader. The principal authorities consulted are:—"A History of the Criminal Law of England," by Sir James Stephen; "History of Crime in England," by Owen Pike; "Chronicles of Newgate," by Arthur Griffiths; "The State of Prisons in England and Wales," by John Howard; "The Punishment and Prevention of Crime," by Colonel Sir Edmund F. DuCane; "Crime and its Causes," by William Douglas Morrison; "The Criminal," by Havelock Ellis; "Strafensystem und Gefängnisswesen in England," von Doctor P. F. Aschrott; "Lesebuch der Gefängnisskunde und Berücksichtigung der Kriminalstatistik und Kriminalpolitik," von K. Krohne; "Handbuch des Gefängnisswesens" (by various authors, but edited by Doctor Franz von Holtzendorff and Doctor Eugen von Jagemann); "Esprit des Lois," par Montesquieu; "Beccaria et le droit pénal," par M. César Cantu; "Mémoire sur les moyens de corriger les malfaiteurs et les fainéants," par Ch. Hippolyte Vilain XIIII.; "Histoire de la législation," par M. le Comte de Pastoret; "Dictionnaire de la pénalité dans toutes les parties du monde connu," par M. B. Saint-Edme; "Les prisons de l'Europe," par MM. Alboize et A. Martino Beltrani-Scalia, and many more. It is imtophe; "Du droit de punir," par Émile de Girardin; "Question des peines," par E. H. Michaux; "Sul governo e sulla riforma delle carceri in Italia," di

Martino Beltrani-Scalia, and many more. It is impossible to mention by name the books, reports, documents, pamphlets, and journals which the author has read or examined, during the quarter of a century in which this subject has claimed more or less of his attention. Much of his acquaintance with it is derived, not from books, but from personal contact with prisons and prisoners. The books here named are histories or contain historical material; books on the theory of punishment have been omitted, also books by American authors.

PUNISHMENT AND REFORMATION

CHAPTER I

THE QUESTION STATED

Of all the perplexing questions which confront the statesman and the publicist, probably the most difficult of solution is that which relates to the proper treatment of crime and criminals. This is true, whether the question is approached from its theoretical or its practical side.

An enlightened criminal jurisprudence must rest upon principles which command the sanction of science and the approval of absolute justice; but these principles are not easy to find or to formulate. In practice it must satisfy certain obvious experimental tests. Does it insure the public peace and security, by reducing the volume of crime and the number of known, habitual offenders? Does it accomplish this result with due regard to the rights and interests of convicted criminals, as well as of the community which it seeks to protect? In other words, does it attain the maximum of efficiency without degenerating into oppression, and with the least possible infliction of pain or loss?

For a correct reply to these inquiries, patient historical research and exact statistical knowledge are essential. Criminal law has been slowly and painfully evolved from human consciousness, in response to the varying historical exigencies of the race. The time has arrived when it must be judged by a higher criticism, which needs to be not merely retrospective and philosophical, but ethical and practical. Through what evolutionary stages has criminal jurisprudence already passed? What are its present tendencies? Are these tendencies such as to commend themselves to the ethical, political, and legal sense of mankind, in an advanced state of Christian civilization? The law is itself upon trial. A mass of evidence has been here accumulated, which must have an influence upon the verdict to be rendered by those who do the present volume the compliment to read it.

Our subject may be defined as the treatment of crime, for its repression and prevention; and of criminals, for their extirpation or rehabilitation; both in the past and in the present, with special reference to improved methods of treatment in the future. To this science, if it is a science, Francis Lieber has given the name of "penology," often confounded by typesetters in printing-offices with phrenology, to which it bears no relation. The term is an awkward one, as most technical terms are apt to be. Prison discipline, which the word is meant to include, is an art, rather than a science; but the termination of the word does not suggest any practical application of science. The Germans call this branch of human knowledge, from the scientific point of view, *Gefängnisswesen;* from that of art, *Gefängnisskunde.* In French, it is *la science pénitentiaire;* the mercurial Gauls have borrowed a phrase from the sedate Quakers of the commonwealth of William Penn.

Call it what we may, the theme which now engages our attention is remote from the ordinary experience, and to many it is repulsive. Rightly regarded, however, it is as interesting as it is important. If any apology is required for its presentation, it may be found in the following quotation from Victor Hugo:—

"The study of social infirmities and deformities, with a view to their cure, is a sacred duty. The mission of the historian of ideas and of morals is not less obligatory than that of the chronicler of events. The latter skims the surface of civilization. He registers royal marriages; the birth of princes, quarrels between kings, battles, convocations, the achievements of men illustrious for their public services, political revolutions. He describes the external aspect of events. But it is a deeper and more arduous task to penetrate beneath the surface; to lay bare the foundations on which the social structure has been reared; to tell of those who labor, who suffer, and who wait—of womanhood staggering under burdens too heavy to be borne; of childhood in its young agony; of the silent secret conflicts which alienate men from their kind; of the obscure ferocities, the prejudices, the intrenched injustice, the subterranean reactions of law; of the hidden evolution of souls; of the formless shuddering of the masses of the starved, the half-clad, the disinherited, the fatherless, the unfortunate, and the infamous; of all the hobgoblins that wander in the dark. He who would lay bare the mysterious springs of human actions must descend—with a heart full at once of charity and of severity, as a brother and as a judge—into those impenetrable casemates where crawl in confusion those who bleed and those who strike, those who weep and those who curse, those who fast and those who devour, the wronged and their oppressors. Have these historians of the heart duties inferior to those which are laid upon the historians of the world's exterior life? Has Dante less to say than Machiavelli? Is the under-world of civilization, because it is deeper and more gloomy, less real and important than the upper? Can we know the mountain, if we know nothing of the caverns?"

The limits of penology are incapable of exact definition. It embraces portions of criminal jurisprudence. It covers everything which relates to prisons and prison discipline. It includes certain aspects of the work of the police, and of the institutional and other agencies by which preventive work is carried on in behalf of children and youth. It has points of contact with nearly every science and art which it is possible to name. It is related to medicine, through the connection which subsists between crime and insanity, and the necessity for a sound prison hygiene. The problem of criminal heredity creates a close affiliation between penology and biology. It is an essential and important branch of law, but it is no less intimately connected with government in the wide sense, or with politics regarded from the point of view of the statesman. It enters into the domain of philosophy and of religion. It has its ethical side. Prison discipline is, as we shall see, largely a question of pedagogics. The causes of crime require for their elucidation an adequate knowledge of political economy and of general sociological conditions. To demonstrate their operation the aid of statistics must be invoked; an art of extreme nicety and precision. The comparative study of crime implies familiarity with geography, anthropology, and history. The practical administration of prisons demands some acquaintance with architecture and engineering, with agriculture, with mechanics and manufactures, with trade and finance, and a deep insight into human nature, joined to experience in the government of men and natural aptitude for it. A competent warden needs to be thoroughly grounded in psychology.

In short, all knowledge which has man for its subject or object, and especially all philosophical inquiries which aim to explain human activity, individual or social, in its origin or in its outcome, lead up to the prison question. It is one of many doors through which one may enter the palace of Minerva. There is no social question at once so profound and so far-reaching, unless it be the labor question, with which the prison question is closely and vitally united.

There are two principal methods by which it may be studied—the philosophical and the historical. These are, however, so blended in practice as to be almost indistinguishable, except when the scalpel of the technical analyst divides them from each other upon the dissecting table in the chamber of speculative science, which is the chamber of death. The ideas and conduct of men are in life so inextricably interwoven, that the historic and the philosophic or logical order, in their parallel evolution, during the slow progress of the race from barbarism to civilization, are substantially the same. History needs to be read in the light of philosophy, and philosophy in the light of history, if we would form a distinct mental image of either—an image which will correspond to the real, and afford a clue to the ideal. The author of this book will have succeeded in his aim, if on every page he succeeds in attaching to a historical fact, which is a picture, an explanatory legend in the form of a philosophical conclusion, and if he can induce the reader to turn from one to the other and back again in quick succession.

A brief outline of the scope and order of the topics

included in the plan of the present volume will be an aid to the comprehension of the argument.

Two principal questions demand our attention: What is crime? and, What is the criminal? The notion of crime is not a fixed, but a variable, notion, growing out of local and temporary conditions, subject to perpetual modification in accordance with the political and religious conceptions peculiar to a given community in a given age. The criminal is the concrete expression of the abstract idea of crime. In his relations to the past, he is a product of antecedent causes, partly individual and partly social. In his relations to the present, he is an anti-social and disturbing element, a protest against existing social conditions and regulations, a menace to the public peace and safety, and in a greater or less degree a public enemy. In his relations to the future, he is a problem, whether soluble or insoluble, the future alone can determine.

These questions are separable only in thought. Since crime exists and can exist only in the criminal, the treatment of crime and that of the criminal are merely two phases of one and the same problem. Logically, however, the mind deals first with the question of the suppression of crime, then with the fate of the criminal, and his conversion or extirpation. This is also the historical order. It is only of late that the fate of the criminal himself has attracted public notice and interest.

There have been four distinct stages in the evolution of criminal law. The first was the era of vengeance, or retribution; the second, that of repression; the third, that of attempted reformation and rehabilitation; the fourth, of which we see as yet but the early dawn, is that of prevention. We shall see, as we proceed, how these must have followed each other in the precise order here indicated.

It is of absorbing interest to trace the successive steps by which each of these conceptions of the function of criminal legislation has faded into that which immediately replaced it. The *lex talionis* was the original and barbarous foundation of the penal code. Retaliation, at first a private right, became, in the lapse of time, a public duty. The penalty of death, once the usual and all but universal form of vengeance, could be avoided by pecuniary compensation; and when the primitive State took into its own hands the regulation of such composition, the foundation of a true criminal jurisprudence was laid. The State and the Church then took upon themselves the task of suppressing crime by measures of severity, designed to intimidate would-be criminals by the terrors of torture, in all its hideous forms. This conception held humanity in its unrelenting grasp, not for centuries, but for thousands of years. Judicial and ecclesiastical murders were for ages regarded as the essential safeguard of social order and private security. Banishment was invented as a humane substitute for capital punishment. Prisons were merely places in which the accused awaited trial, or the condemned awaited execution. Beccaria gave the final blow which resulted in the overthrow of torture, and his influence is largely responsible for the gradual disuse and partial abolition of the death penalty.

John Howard pointed out how imprisonment might

itself be made a legal penalty, and at the same time a means of reformation of law-breakers. These two reformers were contemporaries. The entire movement for the amendment of the criminal law, and for the reform of prisons, is vitally connected with the growth of democratic ideas and institutions. It may almost be said to date from the American and the French Revolutions. It was greatly, and on the whole favorably, influenced by the discovery of Australia, and by the English experiments tried on that distant soil, under the system of transportation, which lasted for eighty years, before its failure was formally acknowledged. With the general acceptance throughout Christendom of imprisonment as practically the only secondary punishment, the criminal has become an object of attentive scientific study. The attempt to reform him has led to the invention of three systems of prison discipline: the Pennsylvania, the Auburn, and the Elmira. Penologists are divided into three camps, as they favor one or the other of these systems. The incomplete success of either has led many to doubt the efficiency of all methods which may be adopted for the renovation of the criminal character and impulses. Their persistence has led to new studies of the criminal, in his heredity and in his biological development, which have taken the name of criminology or criminal anthropology. But all are agreed that the principal hope of any material reduction in the volume of crime lies in its prevention, rather than in its cure. Society now seeks a better knowledge and more effectual enforcement of the laws of moral hygiene.

This record of slow but certain progress is the history of a movement in which the history of the human race is hidden at the core. It is the history of the steps by which the bonds of submission to external authority, indispensable in the infancy of the race, but always liable to become arbitrary and despotic, have gradually been relaxed, as mankind has learned the lesson of self-control. It is a history which contains and is the embodiment of a prophecy. But the current of events has not flowed steadily onward without interruption. It has been a raging stream, dashing against rocky barriers, which have thrown it back upon itself; it has been filled with eddies and counter-currents. In the conflict with crime, society may be compared to a blind giant, dealing furious blows at an unseen but ever-present and irritating foe, sometimes hitting the mark, but, alas, too often missing it.

One central, dominating idea has characterized the entire movement, namely, that the world can only be rid of crime by ridding itself of the criminal; whether by killing him, sending him into exile, shutting him up in prison, intimidating and disabling him, or reforming him. The surest of all plans would be to stop the manufacture of criminals. This is the latest development of the war against crime. The modern police system is of more recent date than prison reform. Police surveillance of discharged convicts has been followed by suspension of sentence and surveillance without commitment to prison. Our institutions for the reformation of juvenile transgressors are an addition to the prison system, intended in large measure to supersede it. The principles and methods on which they are conducted have just begun to affect sensibly the organization and discipline of prisons for adults; they have given birth to the new reformatories for adult first offenders. They are largely supplemented by purely preventive institutions for young children of both sexes, who are thus rescued from an environment favorable to the growth of criminal character.

Still more recently, the best authorities on child-saving tend to dispense, as far as possible, with all institution life for children, and to place them directly in private families, where they will receive the benefit of a home, and their surroundings will be more nearly assimilated to those of other children.

If the centuries before Christ and the first eighteen centuries of the Christian era furnish the dark background, against which the beauty that resides in the salvation of the lost and the rescue of the perishing stands more sharply revealed, on the other hand it may be said that the benevolent work of the nineteenth century, throughout the world, is the outward and visible reaction against the barbarity and brutality which, before this century opened, everywhere characterized the administration of the criminal law. The flower of Christian charity has sprung up and blossomed from roots which struck deep into what seemed to be the most unpromising of soils, but which has been enriched by the blood of numberless victims, and watered by the tears of the pitiful.

CHAPTER II

WHAT IS CRIME?

CRIME needs to be sharply discriminated from vice on the one hand, and from sin on the other. Vices are injuries done to oneself, through the violation of natural law, which affect others only indirectly, if at all. Intemperance is a vice; so is sloth, so is improvidence. Sins are offences against God, whose commandments extend beyond outward acts and reach down into the region of unuttered thoughts and unfulfilled desires, of which human legislation can rightfully take no cognizance. Crimes are wrongful actions, violations of the rights of other men, injuries done to individuals or to society, against which there is a legal prohibition enforced by some appropriate legal penalty.

The distinction just made is real, but these categories of wrong-doing are not necessarily mutually exclusive. There are vices and crimes which are also sins. And any vice or sin becomes a crime when it is declared to be punishable by human law.

Again, actions or omissions contrary to equity, for which the legal remedies are merely civil, and consist in restitution, with or without damages, must be discriminated from actions or omissions in which the disregard shown for the rights of others is so palpably immoral and anti-social as to call for the infliction of some degree of criminal punishment, either by deprivation of life, liberty, or property. Only the latter fall within the strict definition of crimes in the technical phraseology of the law; the former are torts.

Sir James Stephen says:—

"The criminal law is that part of the law which relates to the definition and punishment of acts or omissions which are punished as being—

(1) Attacks upon public order, internal or external; or
(2) Abuses and obstructions of public authority; or
(3) Acts injurious to the public in general; or
(4) Attacks upon the persons of individuals, or upon rights annexed to their persons; or
(5) Attacks upon the property of individuals, or upon rights connected with and similar to rights of property."

To this succinct description of the criminal law he adds:—

"The conditions of criminality consist partly of positive conditions, some of which enter more or less into the definition of nearly all offences; the most important being malice, fraud, negligence, knowledge, intention, will. There are also negative conditions or exceptions tacitly assumed in all definitions of crimes, which may be described collectively as matter of excuse."

Crimes are distinguished as felonies or misdemeanors. By the common law of England, felonies were punishable with death. In the penal codes of the United States, the distinction between a felony and a misdemeanor is mainly statutory, and has lost its original significance. The graver offences are felonies. Felonies are punishable by death or imprisonment in a state prison or penitentiary for a term of years; an offence thus punishable is a felony. Misdemeanors are punishable in a minor prison for a term of months or days; an offence thus punishable is a misdemeanor. A finer example of reasoning in a circle cannot well be imagined. The distinction is purely artificial and arbitrary.

The French criminal code makes a somewhat similar and equally irrational, but still more complicated, subdivision of crimes into three grades: (1) Contraventions; (2) delicts; (3) crimes. Contraventions are violations of police regulations. The penalties for delicts are correctional; for crimes they are afflictive or infamous, or both.

For the purposes of this argument, the one important fact to understand and remember is that nothing is a crime which the law does not so regard and punish. Paul, who was as learned in the law as he was indefatigable in his missionary zeal, quaintly expresses this truth, in saying to the Romans: "Without the law, sin is dead. For I was alive without the law once; but when the commandment came, sin revived, and I died."

The origin of law is shrouded in the mists of antiquity. There must have been a time when there was no law, in the sense of legal enactment, for mankind, any more than there is for the brute creation. The passions of men exploded at the touch of conscious wrong, as a dog snarls and bites when another dog attempts to take away the bone which he is crunching under his teeth. No other mode of self-defence was known or practicable. There was a time when the idea of the State was foreign to human thought. Before the organization of the State, all wrongs fell into the category of torts, that is, purely civil injuries, or of sins, that is, insults to the majesty of the gods. Crimes are acts of disobedience to the State. Where there is no State, there can be no crime.

The sense of wrong must have preceded the sense of right in the individual and common consciousness. We now look upon wrong as the negation of right; but it seems probable that to the primitive man wrong was something positive, and that the notion of rights was slowly evolved, through the instinctive opposition felt to successive and repeated injuries. In Sir Henry Maine's opinion, "It is hazardous to pronounce that the childhood of nations is always a period of ungoverned violence." Nevertheless, the natural state of man without law is one of private and tribal war. Where there is no conflict, no struggle for existence, there is no life. Law in an attempt to regulate this struggle among men upon equitable principles and in the interest of the greatest number. In the primeval state of mankind the struggle was unregulated. The sole measure of the atrocity of an injury was the degree of the passionate reaction which it aroused. Self-defence and the redress of injuries were the affair of the individuals directly affected. The steps by which private war was abolished, crimes legally defined, and their punishment relegated to the judiciary will be recounted in a subsequent chapter.

The definition of crimes has varied from age to age, especially in different states or nations. Offences which are punishable by law may or may not be contrary to morals. Much confusion of thought has been occasioned by the failure to recognize this double sense of the word crime. A corresponding uncertainty attaches to the meaning of the word criminal in the mouth of any one not a lawyer.

Among the crimes of a superstitious age, offences against the prevailing religion occupied a prominent place. The ecclesiastical spirit finds its freest scope among the ignorant; and with savages, the priest is everywhere a personage of consequence, clothed with supernatural power and endued with authority derived directly from the gods. He bows before none but the king, and not always before him. The relation of the priesthood to the throne, whether in a theocracy or in a modern State, where the king is supposed to rule by divine right, and the right to reign is conferred with appropriate ceremonies by the Church, is such as unduly to exalt the ecclesiastical authority. If political power in civil government is derived from the consent of any ecclesiastical prince or hierarchy, then the right of the Church to define and to punish ecclesiastical offences, either by its own courts or by those of the civil power, cannot logically be denied. The Church has always claimed this right, and where the separation between Church and State is not absolute and complete, it must be conceded. The common ecclesiastical offences are heresy, sacrilege, sorcery, witchcraft and enchantments, blasphemy, perjury, and Sabbath-breaking. Everywhere the heretic is one who differs in opinion from the religious party in power. Heresy in one place is orthodoxy in another, and the definition of orthodoxy changes with every alteration in popular beliefs. The Egyptians punished with death any one who should reveal the burial-place of the sacred bull, Apis, or who should even by accident cause the death of a vulture, a cat, or an ichneumon. At Athens sentence of banishment from Attica was pronounced against the profane individual who should pluck a leaf from the trees consecrated to Minerva. It was there regarded as sacrilege to kill a bird consecrated to Esculapius. The early Christians were thrown to wild beasts, crucified, and burned alive by the Roman emperors. In the Middle Ages, the Catholic church persecuted Protestants with fire and sword. The Protestants made similar abuse of power when fortune had placed it in their hands. Even the Puritans of Massachusetts banished Roger Williams, though he was himself a Puritan. The ecclesiastical courts of England, until the year 1640, had the right to punish offences against religion and morals; in other words, to punish sin as such, particularly offences arising out of the relation of sex, including every form of incontinence. This right still exists as to incest, which is not a secular crime by English law. The Court of High Commission, which was a sort of Protestant Inquisition, was authorized to enforce ecclesiastical conformity upon all persons, lay or clerical. The decrees of the ecclesiastical courts were enforced by excommunication and penance. The greater excommunication entailed a variety of civil incapacities: an excommunicated person could not sue, nor testify as a witness, nor come into the possession of an inheritance. They also had power to impose heavy fines, and to commit offenders to prison, though not to inflict torture or the penalty of death.

The list of obsolete crimes is a long one. Possibly the most illustrious is that of lese-majesty. *Laesa majestas,* under the Roman law, included pretty much every form of derogation from the dignity of the Emperor, or, in the days of the Republic, of the people. By the law of the Twelve Tables, it was punished by flogging to death. In England a law of Henry VIII. pronounced any one guilty of this offence who should predict the death of the king; and, the prince having been seized with an illness, his physicians dared not say that his life was in danger.

Sumptuary laws furnish another illustration. The law no longer attempts to prescribe what men shall eat or wear, the number of invited guests who may lawfully sit at the table of their host, the number of courses which may be served at a dinner, or the character and cost of the ornamentation which may enter into the building of a house. In Russia, in Turkey, and in Persia—by a grand duke, by a sultan, and by a shah—the use of tobacco has been prohibited, under penalty of having the nose slit or cut off, and even of death.

So, too, of legislation governing trade and commerce. Forestalling, regrating, and engrossing are now almost forgotten crimes. Yet it is barely fifty years since the political economists succeeded in wiping them off the English statute-books. To forestall was to buy goods or provisions on their way to market, with the purpose of enhancing the price or diminishing the supply. To regrate was to buy in the market-place, in order there to sell again at a higher rate. To engross was to buy grain standing, or generally to buy up sundry kinds of provisions with the intention of selling again. The penalties against these acts were designed to cheapen the cost of living, by reducing the number of middlemen. In the reign of Edward IV. the sale of coin to a foreigner was a felony. Under Lysander, the Lacedæmonians put to death any citizen found to have gold in his house.

Resistance to innovation has often sought ineffectually to place legal barriers in the pathway of human progress. Driving with reins was once a crime in Russia, the immemorial custom having been for the driver to ride or run by the horse's side. The German printers who first brought printed books to Paris were condemned to be burned alive as sorcerers, and only escaped death by flight. Francis I., in 1635, forbade the printing of any book in France, upon pain of the gallows. The fate of Galileo needs only an allusion here. The medical doctrine of the circulation of the blood has also been the object of prohibitory legislation.

Curious instances of absurd criminal laws might be given at tedious length. The Ionians passed a law exiling all men who were never seen to laugh. The Carthaginians killed their generals when they lost a battle. Pliny relates that they condemned Hanno for having tamed a lion, because a man who could tame a lion was dangerous to the liberties of the people. In ancient Rome play-actors were deprived of citizenship. By the Julian law celibacy was a crime. In Sparta confirmed bachelors were stripped in midwinter and publicly scourged in the market-place.

On the other hand, modern civilization has created a formidable catalogue of crimes unknown to former generations. All changes in social organization, in customs, in political control, and in religious beliefs import changes in the criminal law as their consequence; because what is overthrown must be prohibited, and the new needs to be fortified and protected by legal sanction. But the chief source of the additions to the code which have been made in the present century is found in the altered conditions of manufactures and trade, growing out of recent scientific discoveries and their application by inventors to the arts. The business of the world as now conducted requires the protection of the law in all its parts. There are, accordingly, penalties pronounced against interference with the new modes of transportation by steam and electricity; penalties against infringements upon the rights of patentees; penalties against the abuse of power by corporations; penalties against illegal combinations by the employed, and against doubtful methods adopted by them for gaining a victory over their employers, or over their competitors in the labor market; penalties against the malicious and wrongful use of new and destructive chemical compounds, such as dynamite; penalties against the criminal neglect of the rights and safety of workingmen in factories and in mines. The entire body of sanitary law is for the most part new; it is measurably due to the rapid growth of towns and the concentration of population under conditions unfavorable to health, where pestilence is easily bred, if proper precautions are not taken for the destruction of the germs of disease. With improved facilities for travel and an ever increasing number of travellers, the system of quarantine has assumed new importance and has been greatly perfected. Other illustrations of the necessary enlargement of the criminal code, the result of the revolutions which have taken place in modern social life, will occur to every reader.

History, from the sociological point of view, is an account of the variations which have taken place in human relations. Among these relations may be mentioned, by way of illustration, the relation of the sexes; the relation of individuals and communities to the soil; the relations of rank, precedence, and subordination; the relations of capital and labor; corporate relations; government relations; and the like. Such relations exist wherever men are found. But they differ indefinitely in detail and combination, according to local and temporary conditions, especially according to the position of tribes and nations in the scale of civilization. The history of crime and punishment is an index, more or less complete, to these historical changes in social and political organization. It is a reflection in miniature of general history, a convenient and comprehensive introduction to the study of sociology.

The relation of the sexes is the fundamental human relation. The laws which regulate it vary, according as monogamy, polygamy, polyandry, or some other system of permanent or temporary marriage is approved by the prevailing local sentiment, on the ground of its supposed social utility. These laws will be more or less rigidly enforced, as the necessity for the preservation of the institutions of marriage and the family are more or less highly appreciated. The toleration of competing forms of sexual relation is a sure sign of lack of respect for marriage; and a wide gulf separates the social condition of a people among whom inquiry into the paternity of an illegitimate child is forbidden, from that of another people whose laws render such inquiry obligatory.

A circumstance which must exert a controlling influence over all social and political institutions is the mode by which the members of any given community are attached to the soil. There can have been originally no property in land; it was what the Roman lawyers called *res nullius,* a thing without an owner, like the air. The first ownership must have been tribal or communal, and could have had no other basis than occupation. When the Israelites took possession of Canaan, they subdivided the conquered territory, not by individuals or families, but by tribes. Where warring tribes contended for possession, as the herdsmen of Lot did with those of Abraham, the only alternative, unless the strife could be settled by an amicable agreement, was an appeal to the law of might. The allotment of parcels of ground to families or individuals, for their temporary or permanent use, was an afterthought. The lands so allotted were at first arable lands only; large tracts still were owned in common, like the German *marks.* Proprietorship in land has assumed different forms in different countries, at different times. It has been governed by different rules, in a nomadic state, under the feudal system, and in modern times. Persons not land-owners, like the English *villeins,* or the *metayer* tenantry of Southern Europe, or the Russian serfs, or our own African slaves, have nevertheless held certain defined relations to the lands cultivated by them, both in the nature of rights and obligations. Instances of communal ownership are still to be observed in the Russian *mir* and in the village communities of India. Of course these landed rights have been protected by appropriate legislation enforced by penalties, which must have varied, and still vary, with the differences in the nature of the tenure by which land is held.

The relations created by the legal recognition of rank could only be maintained by privileges and penalties, which tend to disappear, even in their surviving rudimentary forms, in a democratic age.

How far is crime justifiable or excusable, when two parties agree and consent to its perpetration; for example, in illicit relations between the sexes? or in gaming, which is a form of robbery? or in the duel, which is a form of murder? The attitude of the criminal law has varied indefinitely as to offences of this description, as public opinion has tolerated or condemned these quasi contracts to abide by the issue of an immoral action. At the present moment the public conscience is grappling with the question of the legitimacy of that form of financial speculation which consists in dealing in futures and in options. The suppression of the Louisiana lottery was a task beyond the ability of the people of that State; it could not be accomplished without federal aid. The change in public sentiment which has taken place since the State of New York thought it expedient to sanction a public lottery by law, as an aid to public education, has made a crime of what was once regarded as a virtuous and patriotic action.

Slavery is the child of war. The first slaves were military captives. It has been said that the institution of slavery, by putting an end to the practice of massacring prisoners in mass, was the first and greatest single step in the evolution of civilization. Slavery was originally profitable. So long as it continued to be profitable, it was protected by law. But the experience of all nations in which it has found a foothold—and there are few which can show a clean record in this regard—proves that everywhere its ultimate tendency has been to destroy the nation which has tolerated it. Whenever this has become apparent, the law has overthrown it, often at the end of a bloody struggle.

The time may yet come when war itself may be branded as a crime; but if so, it will not be until the destruction of life and property which it involves is felt to be too great to be longer endured, for the sake of any incidental advantage which may grow out of it.

In a word, crime is a variable quantity. It is the product of the aggregate social condition and tendencies of a people at a given moment in its history. Actions which in one age are regarded as heroic, and which have elevated their authors to the rank of the gods, in another bring the same daring spirits to a dungeon or the gibbet. The connection between law and ethics is not nearly so close as is commonly imagined. In law nothing is wrong which the law itself does not forbid. Precedent and prejudice wage perpetual war with progress. The conservative instincts of the race, which are allied to authority in Church and State, in the form of established governmental institutions, oppose the radical and revolutionary tendencies of the political and social innovators whose respect for the past is limited by the intensity of their aspirations for the future. That which is permanent and abiding in human nature constitutes its larger part; but there is enough that is evanescent to impart a transitory character to many alleged crimes and many forms of punishment. Progress has been attended by one constant effort to throw off oppression —religious, political, legal, and military; to find room for the exercise and development of individual tastes and capacities. The determination to conquer personal freedom has been indomitable, and it has furnished many martyrs, whom tyrants have branded as criminals.

These observations have a distinct bearing upon the question, much discussed of late, whether crime is a disease. Since what is crime in one age is no crime in another, then, if crime is a disease, disease in one age may be health in another. Where heresy is regarded as a crime, the heretic must, upon that theory, be a person whose physical and mental constitution are more or less abnormal. Christians might be regarded as suffering from disease, or at least as constituting an anthropological type, in Arabia; and Mussulmans must be similarly regarded throughout Christendom. The importance of a distinct understanding of terms, before we enter upon the discussion of biological theories of crime, is thus apparent.

Crime is not a character which attaches to an individual. It is not a simple phenomenon of ethical aberration from a standard type. It is rather a complex relation, which the law creates between itself and the law-breaker. The law creates crime. It therefore creates the criminal, because crime cannot be said to exist apart from the criminal. The criminal is a man who puts himself in an attitude of antagonism to the law. We are discussing here, not the ethical rights and obligations of men in association with each other, but their legal rights and responsibilities. We are discussing, not what ought to be, but what is; and one object of this book is to show how the law has treated what the law has declared to be a crime.

CHAPTER III

RETRIBUTION FOR CRIME

In dealing with crime and criminals, society may proceed upon either of four principles. It may inflict vengeance upon the culprit, as an act of justice, because he merits punishment. Or it may have recourse to severe penalties, not from any vindictive motive, but with a view to intimidate the guilty and to deter others from imitating their bad example. Or it may aim at the reformation and rehabilitation of the offender. Or, finally, it may attempt to prevent the commission of crime, by vigilance, by the moral training of the young, and especially by devising practical checks to the operation of the causes which are known to swell the aggregate of criminality. These four methods are not mutually exclusive. Historically, however, each of them has been made prominent, in the order of succession in which they have here been named: retribution, repression, reformation, prevention.

The primitive man knew nothing of law. There was no law in the garden of Eden, except the divine injunction not to eat of the tree of the knowledge of good and evil. How, then, was social order maintained?

The generally accepted theory of primeval social organization is that it was by families. In other words, it was patriarchal. So it is represented in that ancient record, the book of Genesis. The histories of the families of Abraham, Isaac, and Jacob are not unlike instances which might be cited from other nations of antiquity. The power of control was vested in the father of the household—the *patria potestas,* as it is termed in Roman law. This power was so great, that it extended even to life and death. It was no less absolute over children than over slaves. The original social unit not the individual, but the family. The title of the family to property—to flocks and herbs, to servants, to growing or harvested crops, to such rude money as then circulated for purposes of exchange, to the imperfect tools and implements of peace and war—was vested in the patriarch; in a representative capacity, perhaps, but without any actual restriction upon his discretionary right to dispose of it at his will. He rendered judgment, and from his decision there was no appeal.

Out of the family grew the tribe. When the family became overgrown, there was but one remedy for the inconveniences which resulted from such overgrowth, namely, separation—amicable division. So Lot separated from Abraham. So, after the death of Jacob, the children of Israel grouped themselves according to the nearness of their blood relationship, by tribes. A similar organization was that of the Scottish nation, by clans.

All this is so familiar to the intelligent reader, that it need not be enlarged upon here. It would be foreign to our present purpose to point out the steps by which tribes became united and blended, so as to form inchoate nations, which grew into complete statehood by impulses from within and shocks from without.[1] What concerns us now is to note the original supernatural sanction for the authority vested in the father of a family or a tribal chieftain. The primitive form of religious belief, though it was not and could not be formulated, must have been really pantheistic. The superstitious savage sees in every movement of natural objects the visible manifestation of the power of an in-dwelling spirit. Spirits move the sun, the moon, and the stars across the sky; spirits make the leaves and the grass to wave, and water to ripple, in the wind; spirits make the flame and the smoke to rise, and the rain to fall; spirits are in the growing plants, in the rushing rivers, in the flash of lightning, and the roar of thunder. What more natural than that they should suppose that spirits suggested the thoughts of men? Especially did they believe this of the most powerful of all men, the patriarch. They had no rules by which to order their actions in advance. They simply followed their natural instincts, and the head of the family or of the tribe pronounced *ex post facto* judgment upon them. His judgment, whatever it might be, was a divine judgment, dictated to him by the gods. Homer calls these inspired utterances *themistes,* for this precise reason. It seems hardly necessary to allude, by way of confirmation, to the well-known practice of the early kings of Greece, who were in

[1] The deep pulsations of the world,
Æonian music measuring out
The steps of Time—the shocks of Chance—
The blows of Death.

TENNYSON.

the habit of consulting the oracles, particularly the oracle at Delphos, before rendering judgment; or to the Roman augurs.

Nevertheless, every judgment pronounced formed a precedent. The body of such precedents gradually acquired some measure of consistency. They were remembered and anticipated. Thus grew up customs, which were the prepotency and promise of laws to come, when the invention of letters should enable men to supplement and supplant tradition by written records. Then usages would become fixed, and the maxims in which they were embodied could be collected and combined in the form of codes.

This is precisely what happened. It would not be strictly accurate to call the decalogue a code, since the commandments have no penalties attached to them. But the Twelve Tables of the Romans, which are very fully described in Stephen's "History of the Criminal Law," form an ancient and admirable example of a code. All the offences known to early Roman law are there listed, and the penalty for each of them is stated with precision. Still, we see in those tables only the dawn of legislation. The legislative function began to be imperfectly discriminated from the executive in government. The night of superstition began to flee with reluctant, hesitating step, before the rising light of reason. The genius of Rome was not yet able to distinguish sharply crimes from torts, or to cover the ground which a penal code ought to cover, or to measure guilt and penalty, and adjust them to each other with any approach to a correct estimate of either. Neither had the human intellect yet grasped the conception of the difference between legislative and judicial functions.

The origin of courts is very obscure. Ninus, the founder of the Assyrian empire and the builder of Nineveh, is said to have instituted, in almost prehistoric times, regular and orderly tribunals—one for the trial and punishment of murder, another of theft, and a third of adultery. Whether this be true or false, something like it is discoverable in Roman history. The first courts were merely committees of the legislature, to which the duty was intrusted of making certain investigations and decisions with reference to matters referred to them. They were called *quæstiones,* or inquests. Human nature and human needs do not vary, except within tolerably narrow limits; and it might easily happen that some such division of crimes to be inquired into took place in Rome as that credited to Persia. Such inquests, at first temporary in their jurisdiction, naturally tended to become permanent, as their utility was recognized, and to acquire an authority more or less independent of that by which they were created.

It is curious to observe how the steps in the process of growth of jurisprudence just described with so much brevity, and yet, it is hoped, with sufficient accuracy and clearness, correspond to the Spencerian formula of evolution. Von Baehr, the great German naturalist, observed that the growth of the egg is marked by a change from a state of simplicity or homogeneity to one of complexity or heterogeneity. This was Herbert Spencer's starting point. He added that, along with the change from simplicity to complexity, may also be observed a counterchange from indefiniteness to definiteness, and from incoherence to coherence. Von Baehr had noticed that the change is one of differentiation. Spencer added that it is also one of integration. In other words, Von Baehr called attention to the analytic aspects of the change, but Spencer to its synthetic aspects. Accordingly he defined evolution, which is but another word for growth, as "a continuous change from indefinite, incoherent homogeneity to definite, coherent heterogeneity, through successive differentiations and integrations." This formula, which is as simple as it is symmetrical, applies, so far as we can yet see, to all living organisms; and to the extent that human society is a living, organic thing, capable of growth and development, all history unfolds in accordance with it.

Let us apply it to what has thus far been said about the history of government and of law. The union of all governmental functions in one person, the person of the patriarch, was certainly the acme of simplicity and homogeneity; but it lacked nothing so much as definition. The breaking-up of the family into tribes was a process of disintegration, and the more perfect union of the tribes under the form of a state was an act of integration. By the joint and successive operation of these two processes, the vague and ill-defined power residing in the family or tribal chief continually tended, through analysis, to become more definite; to reveal itself at first as separable into two, the executive and the legislative, but later into three, the executive, legislative, and judicial functions. The conception of crime became correspondingly more definite, and at the same time that of penalty also. The system of legislation and of administration became steadily more complicated and yet more consistent. In proportion as we comprehend and retain in our minds this history, the meaning of the formula becomes plain; and *vice versâ*. History, read in this light, ceases to be a chronicle of events, like a catalogue of words in a dictionary, bearing no organic relation to each other. We begin to see the beauty of the providential purpose which unites and regulates it, so that its varied parts form a distinct pattern, which it is possible to trace out and remember. Besides, the direction of the lines which we have followed to their termination in the present must be the same in the undiscovered future; and so we are able to forecast the ways which progress must take, if the unity of history, which is the unity of truth, is not to be violated, as we know that it cannot be.

But this is a digression. To return to the thread of our story, let us revert to the remark already made, that the primitive state of mankind must have been one of war, both individual and tribal. In the absence of law, there was no way to settle disputes but by the arbitrament of force. To defend one's conception of right, at any risk, was regarded as highly moral; to refuse to do so as an immoral act. The fundamental principle of morality is reciprocity. I must give an equivalent for what I get. My neighbor has no right to take from me that for which he does not render an equivalent. If one term of the equation is a minus quantity, the other must be. The primitive man could not see why, if we are to return benefits, we are not to return injuries, upon the same basis of give and take. Accordingly, the instinct of retaliation is one of the deepest instincts in human nature; it survives even in the civilized man. Where there is no possibility of obtaining satisfaction or indemnity without violence, violence no longer presents itself to the imagination as an act of vengeance, but of self-defence. The *lex talionis,* therefore, is the most ancient of all laws. When Cain had killed his brother, he realized in an instant (with no experience to give his thought the form which it assumed), that every man who saw the blood upon his hands would seek his life in Abel's name; and God set a mark upon him for his protection—which the apologists for capital punishment upon religious grounds can explain as they are best able. There is no reason to accept the theory of some scholars that the *lex talionis* originated in Egypt. Rhadamanthus, the wise, just, and (for his age) humane lawgiver of Crete, whom the ancients held in such estimation that the mythologists made him a judge in the lower world, is said to have introduced it into Crete. But it is as old as human nature, as universal as mankind, and as enduring as this present evil world. It was never better stated than in the Mosaic law: "Thou shalt give life for life, eye for eye, tooth for tooth, foot for foot, burning for burning, wound for wound, and stripe for stripe."

I have too sincere an admiration for Moses (who must, I think, be admitted to be the greatest man of all ages, in view of what he did as a lawgiver, not for the Jews only, but for all nations as well), to let this quotation pass without a single apologetic remark, little as Moses needs defence. To be sure, the milder and gentler spirit of the gospel shines by contrast in our Lord's doctrine of non-resistance, which, however, men are not disposed to accept in its literal fulness. Moses is expressly said to have tolerated divorce on account of the hardness of heart of his contemporaries. In the same way he tolerated retaliation for injuries, but sought to restrain the vengeful impulses of men by limiting the degree of reciprocal injury to an exact equivalent; an eye for an eye, but no more—not one wound or stripe in excess of the exact tale of indebtedness. He recognizes and enjoins upon the wrong-doer the sacred obligation to render satisfaction to the party injured, but, with Portia, cries to the latter:—

> "Shed thou no blood; nor cut thou less, nor more,
> But just a pound of flesh."

Given these two conditions—the family or tribe as the social unit, and the right and duty of retaliation supposed to be an ethical axiom—and there could be no avoidance on the part of all the members of a family or tribe to take part in the quarrel of every injured member. Organized revenge became a social institution, under the title of the "blood-feud." In a rudimentary form, ever tending to become obsolete, this institution survives in our own country, at the South, where the vendetta is more dreaded than a pestilence; the vendetta of which Mark Twain has drawn so exact a picture in that delightful book for boys, "Huckleberry Finn." It is the Southern sense of the solidarity of the family, in opposition to extreme Northern individualism, which is the explanation of its survival, in connection with the more or less patriarchal institution of African slavery, not yet extinct in an age when it had become an anachronism.

There were, however, two efficient checks upon private vengeance, of which the first was the right of sanctuary. It may surprise some readers of this book to observe the extent to which the author recognizes the Bible as a sort of elementary text-book of sociology; but this is one of its legitimate uses. The children in our Sunday-schools have been made acquainted with pretty much all the leading features of primitive society, in so far as they bear directly upon the question of the order of social evolution, of which this is an instance in point. They know that Moses instituted cities of refuge, in which a homicide was safe from the avenger of blood, pending a judicial investigation of his criminal responsibility. Similar sanctuaries have been established by the customary or statutory law of most nations. At first they were the temples, and later the churches. The frightened refugee fled to some sacred place, the peace of which could not be lawfully violated, and there he had a right to remain for a certain specified period, until the affair could be arranged by intermediation and mutual concession. When we come to discuss the history of English transportation, we shall see how exile grew out of sanctuary; the peace of the gods was replaced, in the modern state, by the king's peace; the man who left sanctuary usually fled the country; and, when sanctuary was abolished, the criminal was driven from the country.

The other check upon the tendency of retaliation to

run to excess was the system of composition for injuries, out of which has grown the use of pecuniary fines as a form of legal punishment. We have remarked in substance that the historical basis of all criminal codes is found in the original acceptance of retribution as the sole remedy for wrongs, and the ethical justification of private and tribal war. When, in the course of time, the conception of the State as an entity arose from the chaotic earlier political thinking of primeval man, and it was seen that the State as such could itself be wronged, by disobedience to its mandates and defiance of its authority, the State was compelled to assume that it had the same right to inflict vengeance which inhered in a natural person. But, beyond that, the State at a very early stage in its own evolution assumed the *rôle* of an arbitrator and mediator in private controversies, as an obvious safeguard against the peril of a return to a condition of tyrannical exercise of arbitrary power, or a lapse into anarchy. It can hardly be too strongly insisted upon, that crime was originally nothing else than war. It is still war, but in a qualified sense. The plaintiff and defendant in a suit were therefore regarded as combatants in a new and compulsory arena; the State was the referee, with power to prescribe the rules governing the struggle, to enforce them, and to award the victory. It was virtually a public and official peacemaker.

Some historical instances will illustrate this relation. Burckhardt describes in an amusing way a settlement made by a Persian cadi between two men named Bokhyt and Djolan. Bokhyt called Djolan a dog, which in the Orient is a deadly insult, worse than if you should call a Frenchman a pig; and perhaps the character of the curs of the East warrants its being so regarded. There is not in the Hebrew Scriptures a single good word for a dog, and an unappreciated touch in the description of the New Jerusalem, with which the new Testament closes, is the declaration that there will be no dogs in it. Very well. Bokhyt called Djolan a dog, whereupon Djolan promptly hit him. Bokhyt then whipped out a knife and cut Djolan in the shoulder. After hearing the facts in the case, the cadi decided that there was due to Djolan from Bokhyt for the insulting expression a sheep, and for the wound inflicted with a knife three camels; but to Bokhyt from Djolan for the blow upon the arm one camel. The balance of the account was in Djolan's favor, and, upon the payment to him by his antagonist of one sheep and two camels, peace was restored.

Sir Henry Maine has called attention to the trial scene upon the shield of Achilles, in Homer, where the question at issue was the amount to be paid in composition for a murder. One of the parties claimed that such payment was due, but the other denied the obligation. In the centre, between the disputants, lay two talents of gold, which were to be given to the spectator who should give the shrewdest opinion and the best reasons for it, the crowd to be the judge and award the prize to the winner.

Composition of injuries was no less common among the Romans than among the Greeks. Reference may here be made to the famous description by Gaius of the *legis actio sacramenti,* an action very similar to the incident depicted upon the shield of Achilles. One of the parties claimed that the other was his slave; the other denied the claim. This quarrel was referred to the prætor for decision. You need not be reminded of the great importance which attaches to ceremonial among people more or less incapable of abstract thinking. In all ancient legal proceedings due regard to ceremony was essential to the validity of transactions. The gestures in this case were as follows: First, the plaintiff, taking a wand, which represented a spear, advanced and touched the alleged slave with the point, after which he laid his hand upon him, thus asserting in expressive pantomime his right to him. The slave replied by taking a similar wand and repeating every motion of his pretended master. The prætor ordered both to release their hold of each other, and said that he would give a decision of the point at issue. The plaintiff then produced a sum of money, which he offered to wager that he could substantiate his claim. The defendant wagered an equal amount. When the case had been heard and an opinion rendered, the prætor took the money of both as compensation for his services, which goes to show that law has been an expensive luxury from a very remote date.

Our laws are not founded so much upon Roman law as upon the common law of England, which was a development of the practices and maxims of our Teutonic forefathers. Of the Germans, the Romans said that their business in life was bloodshed and acquisition by bloodshed. The Anglo-Saxons had three words to designate money paid in compensation for injuries. *Bot* was paid, if the injury was accidental or trifling; in compensation for a crime the aggressor paid *wite;*

the word *wer* meant the valuation of a man according to his rank, which was payable in some cases to the party wronged, as *bot,* but in others, as *wite,* to the king. *Wergeld,* or blood-money, was the only penalty known to the ancient Salic law. Under Alfred the Great, minute regulations as to compensation of injuries were drawn up at considerable length, according to which, if a man cut off his enemy's thumb, he had to pay *bot* to the amount of twenty-five shillings; for cutting off the first finger fifteen shillings, the middle finger nine, the fourth finger six, and the little finger five. These are given merely as illustrations of the fundamental principle of early criminal law. Moses, on the contrary, strictly forbade the payment or acceptance of blood-money.

That principle in its essence was the substitution of penalties. The *lex talionis,* as stated in the Mosaic code, was so modified as to admit of an agreement between the parties, or an adjustment by intervention of some legally constituted authority, which would dispense with the literally exact observance of the rule, "eye for eye, tooth for tooth, wound for wound, stripe for stripe," and require the aggressor to submit to some other substantially equivalent damage by way of expiation for an injury done, which would at the same time be more satisfactory to the injured party. The principle just stated underlay, of course, the doctrine of penance taught and practised by the mediæval Church. It was easy, after advancing from the thought of crime as a personal injury calling for personal retaliation to that of corporate injury calling for corporate retribution, to take the further step involved in the conception of the violation of justice in the abstract, an injury to the gods, a disturbance of the ethical balance of the universe. Indeed, it might be difficult to prove that the claim of the Church to inflict spiritual penalties for crime did not antedate the claim of the State to deal with it, as the depositary of civil and political sovereignty; since belief in spirits and the supernatural long preceded the acceptance of the notion of the State. As an offence against the majesty of heaven, crime assumes an immeasurable importance, and calls for reactionary penalties proportionate to the distance between the gods and men. Hence the Church, in the exercise of criminal justice, tends to greater severity than the civil power. It also enjoys a freedom from restraint, in the matter of substitution of artificial for natural expiatory punishments, to which the State can lay no claim. It has even been said that the prohibition of private vengeance was in its origin sacerdotal.

However that may be, the State gained control of the punishment of crime, in the first instance, as the natural consequence of the perception of the solidarity of families and communities. The recognition of this solidarity, on both sides of the line which separated the parties who inflicted and who bore the injury, was tolerably impartial. In Rome, when a master had been murdered by a slave, the law authorized the execution of the entire body of slaves of the murdered man. Similarly in Greece, at least in Athens, three persons, from the household where a murder had been committed, could be held until the murderer was delivered to justice, and, in default of his delivery, they could be adjudged guilty in his stead. On the other hand, if a man killed without premeditation had no relatives to claim compensation on his account, ten citizens of the *curia* could make pecuniary settlement with the homicide.

The seizure by the State of the exclusive right to inflict retributory punishments was in the interest of peace, but not necessarily of justice, for the reason that, if crime is an offence against justice regarded in the abstract, a small offence, if its magnitude is measured by the resulting damage, may be thought by the State to merit a disproportionate penalty; and this will tend to be the case, in proportion as the power of the State is vested in an oligarchy as its absolute prerogative. Theoretically, an injury to any citizen is an injury to the social whole of which that citizen is a member; but, under the feudal system (when the king of France dared to say that he was the State), the grand *seigneurs* disposed of the property and persons of the common people, on the pretext of their criminality, almost at discretion. They had power, under the guise of composition of public injuries, to fine their dependants, until the administration of justice became an act of blackmail and of confiscation. The robber barons of the Middle Ages were plunderers, who demanded ransom in proportion to the wealth and rank of their victims. They enjoyed private and personal jurisdiction apart from the sovereign, and had their own dungeons, and erected their own gibbets, a privilege which they highly prized. Under this system, the number and severity of punishments greatly increased. By Roman law, the person of a citizen was inviolable; before corporal punishment could be administered to him, he was, by a legal fiction, reduced to the status of a slave, and declared to be *servus pœnæ*. In France, in the Middle Ages, a noble could not be punished without first being reduced from his rank. But the abolition of slavery in Europe had for its first effect simply the extension of the penalties formerly reserved for slaves to the free-born. The inviolability of the aristocracy continued until the triumph of democracy, in England, France, and the United States, accompanied as it was by bloodshed, which did not spare even crowned heads, virtually extinguished class privileges.

CHAPTER IV

EARLY JUDICIAL PROCEDURE

Before proceeding to discuss the treatment of crime for its repression, it seems necessary, in order to the continuity of the narrative, and as a sidelight upon questions that are likely to arise, at any rate in the mind of the reader, to turn for a moment to consider early judicial procedure, in its relation to more modern methods.

The creation of courts was an indispensable step in the effort to abolish private war. So long as private war was tolerated as a lawful mode of redressing wrong, the only measure of justifiable retaliation was the degree of passionate anger aroused in the injured person. With the delay in the exercise of summary vengeance, this anger tended to subside. The civil power, in intervening for the plaintiff, was bound to regard and reflect as nearly as possible his state of feeling. Hence the distinction in the treatment of offenders caught in the act and those not so caught.

The law of *infangthef* (from the German *infangen,* to seize and hold by the fangs) authorized the aggrieved party, or any other person, to follow a thief caught in the act, and kill him wherever found. A corresponding distinction was made, by the Twelve Tables, between manifest and non-manifest theft. Manifest theft was punishable, as in England under the law of *infangthef*, by death; but non-manifest theft was punishable by a simple fine, equivalent to double the amount stolen.

If the State was to assume the duty of arresting wrong-doers, a systematic organization of arrests had to be devised, which was accomplished by means of the division of the population of England into shires, hundreds, and tithings.

Allusion has been made to the institution of the king's peace, by which brawls in the presence of the king, or in places likely to be frequented by him, were forbidden and severely punished. Certain streets of London were thus set apart. There was also the Church's peace; and even some of the great lords temporal enjoyed, in an age of tumult and disorder, this privilege of a quiet life. Since the transfer of political power to the people, the king's peace has become the public peace; and fighting in public is now everywhere a breach of the statutes, since the majesty of the community, as a whole, is equal to that of any individual exercising rule by divine right vested in himself alone.

The institution of the king's peace suggests another ancient institution, that of peace-pledge, as it was called. It was also called frank-pledge. The tithing was a group of ten men organized as a guild. A guild was in some sense an artificial family, held together by a common interest, and governed by rules which had the sanction of long-established usage in their favor. Guilds played a great part in the development of the trades and industries of our modern life. The tithing was a political or governmental guild. Ten guilds constituted a hundred, and every shire was subdivided into hundreds. The principle of solidarity, of which mention has several times been made, applied to it, since all the members of any tithing were held responsible for the actions of each and every member. This mutual responsibility constituted peace-pledge. It was the original form of police protection. When it was necessary to pursue a fugitive from justice, a hue and cry was raised, and all the members of the tithings, the hundreds, and the shires were compelled to join in it. A criminal could be followed from one shire to another; but, at the boundary line dividing two adjoining shires, the sheriff and posse of the new shire took up the chase, and the members of the posse which had driven him out of their own shire were relieved, and at liberty to disperse to their own homes. The inhabitants of any shire, who could not show that they had tracked any man against whom a hue and cry had been raised, as far as their own boundary, and forced him over it, became liable for the payment of any damages which could be legally collected on account of the wrong done. Warrants of arrest were a later invention, and, when first invented, they were known as warrants of hue and cry.

Let us suppose the thief caught. How was he tried? In Oriental lands, and to a limited extent in Germany, by a popular assembly or an assembly of the elders. But in England, and generally in the north of Europe, by one of two obsolete proceedings, ecclesiastical in form and superstitious in fact, namely, by ordeal or by compurgation.

Ordeal (*urtheil*) was nothing more or less than an

appeal to the Almighty to perform a miracle in vindication of the innocence of the accused.

I will endeavor to describe one form of the ordeal of water. Imagine a church with an earthen floor. Upon the ground, in the centre of the church, a fire has been kindled, the smoke of which rises to the roof, obscuring the altar and the sacred images. Not even the pitying Christ upon his wooden cross can see what is about to happen in his name. Over the fire is an iron kettle with water in it. The company present and taking part in the ceremony is ranged in two divisions, on the two sides of the church, one party being the party of the accuser, and the other of the accused. The priest, bearing the Bible and the rood, and carrying holy water, passes around among them, sprinkling them with holy water and making them kiss the rood and the book. When the water boils, he asks them to join with him in prayer that the truth may be made known. The accused comes forward, his arms swathed in linen, and is ordered to pick up a stone at the bottom of the kettle. There were two forms of the ordeal, single and triple. In the single ordeal he immersed his hand to the wrist, but in the triple ordeal he immersed his arm to the elbow. After picking up the stone, three days were allowed for the scald to heal, when his arm was unwrapped, and, if any sign of the scald appeared, he was held to be guilty.

The ordeal by iron was substantially the same, except that the accused, instead of dipping his hand into boiling water, was required to pick up a piece of red-hot iron—one pound in the single, and three pounds in the triple, ordeal.

By this device the power of the priests was augmented to a highly dangerous degree. Practically, they had the opportunity to destroy their enemies without risk to their friends, since they could swathe the arm more or less heavily, and even apply in advance chemical preparations which would protect the flesh from burning.

For priests under accusation no such chances were taken. All they had to do was to eat a piece of bread called *corsnæd.* It could be poisoned at the suggestion of malice, but if not, the danger of conviction was nothing.

Ordeal could be escaped in but one way, by compurgation. The accused might bring his friends, naturally members of his own tithing, to swear that they believed that the oath to his own innocence which he had taken was a true oath. If the number of compurgators was insufficient, he had to undergo the ordeal. The required number was usually twelve. This practice was no doubt conducive to wholesale perjury, but it was the precursor of trial by jury.

William the Conqueror introduced into England the wager of battle. Each party chose a champion, and the two selected fought to the death in the presence of the constituted authorities; the one who was beaten was declared to be recreant, a judgment which rendered him infamous, if he did not lose his life. This was merely regulated, limited private war.

In the wager of law, the accused appealed to a jury. The jurors could at the same time be witnesses. Indeed, if there were not enough men who already knew enough about the case to pass upon it without further evidence, the tale of jurors was completed by afforcement. The chances of the alleged culprit were rather slim, under a system which knew nothing of any jury but the grand jury, the members of which were not merely witnesses and accusers, but also judges of his guilt or innocence, concerning which their minds were made up when they were summoned to act. The first grand assize took place under Henry II. The creation of a distinct petit jury was an afterthought, when the injustice of the original jury system forced itself upon the notice of men.

If a prisoner refused to plead to the charge brought against him, he was said to stand mute. Refusal to plead subjected him in the first instance to the *prison fort et dure,* where he was given nothing to eat, or at best only bread and water, so that he starved to death, if he continued obstinate. Subsequently for the hard and strong prison was substituted the *peine fort et dure,* which consists in pressing a man to death by placing him upon his back upon the floor, with a platform resting upon his breast, on which was piled iron until the life was crushed out of him. Dreadful as was the suffering, many men endured it without flinching to the bitter end, rather than impoverish their families by pleading and then being found guilty, which involved the confiscation of the prisoner's estate.

But it is no part of the author's intention to describe in detail the evolution of the courts in England, which has been done by Sir James Stephen, and is not germane to the special topic under discussion—the history of punishment.

CHAPTER V

INTIMIDATION AND TORTURE

THE second of the four methods of dealing with crime is repression by intimidation. The motive of retributory punishment is the desire to obtain indemnity for the past; that of deterrent punishment is the wish to gain security for the future. Retributory punishment is supposed to be an effort to adjust and close an account, on a mathematical basis; it is the equation of guilt and suffering—the suffering of the wrong-doer against that of the party wronged, including the state with the individual. Or if guilt is measured, not by the resulting damage, but by the intention of the culprit, there is still, in the minds of those who justify the infliction of pain and loss upon a fellow-man on the ground of the satisfaction of abstract justice, a vague notion that some ascertainable or non-ascertainable amount of sorrow or agony, endured voluntarily or under compulsion by the guilty, will exactly balance the selfishness and malice which prompt any criminal action. Many men, looking at the question from its purely ethical side, imagine that punishment on any other basis is immoral. Others think that man has neither the power to read the heart and estimate guilt, nor the right to avenge it, but that such power and right are the prerogative of Deity. Instead of seeking to restore the lost equilibrium of two hostile individuals in their relation to each other, or the equilibrium between any individual and the community, they have in view the sole end of protecting the community against a repetition of the offence; and, to secure this end, they are ready to sacrifice any number of individuals. As against the social whole, in their opinion, the individual has no rights. That is to say, he has no rights which society is bound to respect, in comparison with its own real or fancied safety. The suffering inflicted upon the criminal may be more or less than he deserves, from the point of view of strict equity; but it does not matter, if the deterrent influence of the example is not lost upon others, who might otherwise be tempted to break the law after the same fashion. It would be idle to cherish the hope that the time will ever come when mankind will accept one of these theories to the exclusion of the other. Historically, they have coexisted; and they find by turns an echo in the approving thought of all intelligent men. On either theory, there is practically no limit to the degree of pain which may lawfully be visited upon victims of the law's displeasure.

In entering upon the painful task of recounting the history of inhumanity by which the administration of the criminal law has been disfigured and disgraced, in all ages and in every quarter of the globe, I shall not, therefore, endeavor to analyze the precise motive which prompted each of the several acts of cruelty which it is necessary to describe. The reason for entering upon this branch of the general subject is that it really forms the larger part of the history of the treatment of crime, extending from the dawn of civilization to a very recent period; and that it is the dark and bloody background against which modern theories of the purpose and methods of treatment stand out in shining relief. The reader who shrinks from the thought of physical and mental agony as too painful for him can pass this chapter without reading.

All possible cruelties fall into two great divisions, according as they do or do not terminate in the death of the victim.

CAPITAL PUNISHMENT

Death is the most ancient of all penalties, and the most common in antiquity, as it still is among savages. It is the most effectual mode of getting rid of troublesome or offensive characters; and the feeling of revenge, when in active operation and unrestrained by the considerations which appeal to the intellect and conscience of civilized men, is an impulse which grows by what it feeds upon, and very easily runs to excess, nor stops short until the extreme limit of possible agony has been inflicted upon the sufferer.

Among the modes of taking human life which are or have been practised by conquerors and rulers, may be mentioned: burning, beheading, hanging, drawing and quartering, breaking on the wheel, crucifixion, strangulation, suffocation, drowning, precipitation from a height, stoning, sawing asunder, flaying alive, crushing beneath wheels or the feet of animals, throwing to the wild beasts, compulsory combat in the arena, burying alive, boiling, empaling, pressing, piercing with javelins, shooting, starving, poison, the troughs, melted lead, serpents, blowing from the mouth of a cannon, and electrocution. I have named about thirty different ways of taking life, under some of which a number of sub-varieties may be specified.

Burning, for instance, is a very ancient method. It is mentioned in the book of Genesis; Judah proposed to burn Tamar, his daughter-in-law, when she was found to have lapsed from virtue. Moses ordained burning as the penalty of incest. Achan was burned. The three Hebrew children, captives in Babylon, were cast alive into a furnace of fire. In the worship of Moloch, a hollow image of the god, of brass, with folded arms, was erected; babes were laid, as living sacrifices, in the idol's arms, and killed by the heat of the flames from a fire kindled within. Cæsar tells us that the Gauls and Britons of his day thrust captives in mass into a wicker image of gigantic stature, then piled wood around, lighted it, and, in the midst of the smoke which concealed the god and his victims from sight, the image and its living contents tumbled together into the fire, where they were consumed. In the early history of England, slaves were burned for theft; female slaves were burned by women—eighty other female slaves were compelled to assist at the ceremony. Burning was the mode of execution of slaves also in Rome. The Theodosian code prescribed this punishment for witchcraft. In the Middle Ages, burning was the usual punishment for sacrilege, parricide, poisoning, arson, and the crime against nature. Under the term sacrilege were included heresy, witchcraft, atheism, blasphemy, and the like. It was customary to drive a stake in the ground, build a platform around it, set straw and fagots in order under or upon this platform, leaving an opening for the introduction of the condemned, then bind him to the stake by iron bands about the neck and waist, and light the bonfire. If it was desired to abbreviate the agony of the victim, a cord passed around his neck was secretly tightened from behind, before setting fire to the pile; or his heart was pierced, through the flames, by an iron dart at the end of a long hooked pole used to stir the fire. A handful of ashes was thrown in the air at the conclusion of the ceremony. In the *auto-da-fé,* or act of faith, the accused was given an opportunity to recant, upon the platform, in the hearing of the spectators; and, if he failed to avail himself of the opportunity mercifully given him to save his life, the ceremony proceeded. In London the ordinary place for kindling the sacred flame was at Smithfield; and the frequency of this punishment under one of the English queens has fastened upon her the title of Bloody Mary.

England, to her everlasting shame be it spoken, demanded the death of Joan of Arc, who was burned at the stake as a heretic. Under Henry IV., of England, a law was enacted which authorized sheriffs to burn heretics without a writ; for this reason no estimate can be formed of the number burned in that country. Burning was also the penalty of treason. Even women were thus punished, under English law; and it is only about a hundred years ago that burning for treason was abolished. Other modes of burning have been in vogue in other parts of the world. Nero smeared the bodies of the early Christians with pitch, and, it is said, used them to light the streets of Rome. In Persia, the punishment invented by Sefi II., known as the illuminated body, consisted in piercing the body with numberless holes, in which burning wicks were inserted. In China a woman is credited with the invention of *pao-lo,* which was a tall metal tube, to the top of which the victim was bound, with arms and legs encircling the tube, and a fire kindled at the bottom was kept up until his remains were reduced to ashes.

So, too, there have been many ways of beheading men sentenced to die. The Romans used a short sword called the glaive, with which, no doubt, John the Baptist was beheaded in prison. The method followed in China and Japan is described as follows:—

The criminal is carried to the place of execution in a bamboo cage, and by his side is a basket in which his head will drop when removed. He is pinioned in a very effective manner. The middle of a long thin rope is passed across the back of his neck, and the ends crossed on his chest and brought under the arms; they are then twisted around the arms, the wrists are tied together behind the back, and the ends are fastened to the portion of the rope on his back. A slip of paper containing his name, crime, and sentence is fixed to a reed and fastened at the back of his head. On arriving at the place of execution, the officials remove the paper and take it to the presiding mandarin, who writes on it in red ink the warrant for execution. The paper is then replaced, a rope loop is passed over the head of the culprit, and the end given to an assistant, who draws the head forward, so as to stretch the neck, while a second assistant holds the body from behind, and in a moment the head is severed from the body. The instrument is a sword made expressly for that purpose.

It is a two-handed weapon, very heavy, and has a very broad blade. The executioners pride themselves on their dexterity in its management. After the execution, the culprit's head is taken away, and generally hung up in a bamboo cage near the scene of the crime, with a label bearing the name and the offence of the criminal.

Beheading was not practised in England before the year 1035. Prisoners sentenced to lose their heads had them taken off, in the Tower, upon a block, with an axe. Macaulay, in commenting upon the blundering and tragic execution of the Duke of Monmouth, says:

"Within four years the pavement of the chancel was again disturbed, and hard by the remains of Monmouth were laid the remains of Jeffreys. In truth, there is no sadder spot on the earth than that little cemetery. Death is there associated, not, as in Westminster Abbey and St. Paul's, with genius and virtue, with public veneration and imperishable renown; not, as in our humblest churches and churchyards, with everything that is most endearing in social and domestic charities; but with whatever is darkest in human nature and in human destiny, with the savage triumph of implacable enemies, with the inconstancy, the ingratitude, the cowardice of friends, with all the miseries of fallen greatness and of blighted fame. Thither have been carried, through successive ages, by the rude hands of jailers, without one mourner following, the bleeding relics of men who had been the captains of armies, the leaders of parties, the oracles of senates, and the ornaments of courts. Thither was borne, before the window where Jane Grey was praying, the mangled corpse of Guilford Dudley. Edward Seymour, Duke of Somerset and Protector of the Realm, reposes there by the brother whom he murdered. There has mouldered the headless trunk of John Fisher, Cardinal of Saint Vitalis, a man worthy to have lived in a better age, and to have died in a better cause. There are laid John Dudley, Duke of Northumberland, Lord High Admiral, and Thomas Cromwell, Earl of Essex, Lord High Treasurer. There, too, is another Essex, on whom nature and fortune had lavished all their bounties in vain, and whom valor, grace, genius, royal favor, popular applause, conducted to an early and ignominious doom. Not far off sleep two chiefs of the great house of Howard—Thomas, fourth Duke of Norfolk, and Philip, eleventh Earl of Arundel. Here and there, among the thick graves of unquiet and aspiring statesmen, lie more delicate sufferers: Margaret of Salisbury, the last of the proud name of Plantagenet, and those two fair queens who perished by the jealous rage of Henry. Such was the dust with which the dust of Monmouth mingled."

Sonorous and pathetic as is this passage, it makes no mention of Sir Thomas More, Sir Walter Raleigh, Algernon Sidney, Archbishop Laud, and the unfortunate Charles I.; names which, for one reason or another, interest us more than some of those with ponderous titles, which the brilliant historian has selected to adorn his pages.

Beheading in France has been reduced to high art, by the adoption and use of the guillotine. In its primitive form, this is a very ancient instrument of decapitation, by which Manlius, the Roman, is said to have lost his life. There are numerous mediæval engravings representing the execution of Manlius, one of which is by Albert Dürer. It was called, in the criminal statutes of the Netherlands, in 1233, the *Panke* or *Diele;* in France, in the fifteenth century, *la doloire;* in Italy, in the sixteenth, the *mannaia.* Beatrice Cenci was beheaded after this fashion. Jean d'Autun, the contemporary and biographer of Louis XII., relates that in 1507, Demetrius Giustiniani, of Genoa, for sedition, was condemned to kneel upon the scaffold and lay his neck upon a block, when it was cut in two by a falling bascule, operated by a cord in the hand of the executioner. At Florence, Sept. 7,

1629, by a similar device, Lorenzo Zei had his head severed from his body. The nature of the instrument is well indicated by the old German name for it, the *fall-beil,* or falling axe. Marshal Montmorency of France was guillotined at Toulouse, in 1652. The "gibbet of Halifax," in use before and during the Commonwealth, and last used in 1650, consisted of two parallel upright beams, and a transverse beam, the latter heavily weighted with lead, and having a sharp, cutting edge in the form of a chopping-knife about a foot square, attached to the lower side; this cross-beam was upheld at a height of about ten feet, by a pulley; when the rope was cut by the stroke of a sword, it fell upon the victim's neck, which was securely held in place between them. Lord Morton, Regent of Scotland, having seen it, was so taken with it, that he introduced it at home, where, on the third of June, 1587, he was the first to test its efficacy in practice. For this reason, the Scotch gave it the name of the "Maiden." It is preserved in the Antiquarian Museum of Edinburgh.

The guillotine is so called after its reputed inventor, Dr. Guillotin, who was, during the French Revolution, a member of the Assembly.[1] A motion offered by him to abolish the immemorial distinction in penalties for the same offences committed by the aristocracy and the common people was agreed to, Dec. 1, 1789, four months and a half after the overthrow of the Bastille. On the 25th of September, 1791, in the penal code that day adopted, it was further provided that the only mode of execution should thenceforth be by be-

[1] The curious reader interested in trifles may like to see the

heading, a privilege which formerly pertained to the nobles, vulgar criminals having to put up with hanging. The motive of both these innovations was humane. Louis XVI. had already abolished preliminary torture. The assembly put an end to all torture, and to the confiscation of estates, as well as to the practice of declaring the posterity of offenders infamous. Equally humane was the intention of Dr. Guillotin in the invention of a machine, still in use in France, by which he designed to reduce the pain of death "to a shiver,"

words of a song which appeared in the *Actes des Apôtres,* a royalist journal, in which the new word was first used:

GUILLOTIN,

MÉDICIN POLITIQUE,

Imagine un beau matin
Que pendre est inhumain
Et peu patriotique.
Aussitôt
Il lui faut
Un supplice,
Qui sans corde ni pôteau
Supprime du bourreau
L'office.
C'est en vain que l'on publie
Que c'est par la jalousie
D'un suppôt
Du tripot
D' Hippocrate,
Qui d'occire impunément
Même exclusivément,
Se flatte.
Le Romain
Guillotin
Qui s'apprête,
Consulte gens du métier
Barnabe et Chapelier,
Meme le coupe-tête,
Et sa main
Fait soudain
La machine
Qui simplement nous tuera
Et que l'on nommera
Guillotine.

as, in his enthusiasm, he explained to his colleagues. It is an instrument substantially like a pile-driver, with grooved posts, between which a heavy axe falls with sufficient force to cut off a human head. The criminal, tightly bound, is laid with his face downward and his neck resting in a curved depression in the block which receives the knife; the blade strikes him from behind, and his head falls into a basket. It was first tried upon three cadavers conveyed from the hospital to the prison at Bicêtre, in Paris, for that purpose. The son of Samson, the notorious executioner, said to his father, at this preliminary trial, that it would interfere with their business; to which the old man responded (with prophetic vision, alas!) that it would make cutting heads off so easy, that the trade would be brisker than ever. This was on the 17th of April, 1792; a week later, it was set up on the Place de Grêve. Originally the blade was at right angles with the upright standards between which it moved, but the king suggested that it would work better, if set diagonally; and, nine months afterward, he benefited by his own suggestion. The reception of the new invention by the mercurial people of France was shocking in its levity. It was the theme of numberless songs and jests. Models of it were made in wood, in ivory, in silver, and in gold, and sold as parlor ornaments and toys for children. A somewhat fashionable closing ceremony with which to wind up a dinner in an aristocratic house was for the noble hostess to produce a *figurante* supposed to represent Danton, Robespierre, or Marat, and with a toy guillotine cut off his head, when, instead of blood, a tiny stream of crimson perfume flowed from the neck, in which the ladies at the table hastened to dip their dainty lace handkerchiefs. The revolutionists, on the other hand, adopted it as a seal.

Hanging is another very ancient method of execution. Haman, you remember, was hanged on the gallows which he erected for Mordecai. Constantine the Great practised it. In France the criminal was conveyed to the gibbet seated in a cart, with his back to the horse, his confessor at his side, and his executioner before or behind him. In this order he was taken through the crowded streets. On arrival at the place of execution, he was made to ascend a ladder leading up to the gallows; the executioner preceded him, mounting backwards, so as to assist the prisoner. The confessor followed. After he had confessed him upon the scaffold, three ropes were attached to the prisoner's neck, two of them knotted, and the third intended to swing him off the ladder. The confessor then descended to the ground, leaving the culprit standing on the ladder, and the executioner upon the platform above him. The latter pushed away the ladder with his foot, swung the prisoner off, and then, horrible to relate, taking hold of the rope in order to steady himself, he jumped upon the prisoner and kicked him to death. In England, however, the cart was driven out from under, and the man's neck was broken by the fall. Executions in France are public. In England the law now requires them to be private; and in Newgate prison not even the official witnesses required to certify the death see the contortions of the expiring convict, whose body falls into a sort of well, out of sight of all but the executioner and the attending physician. When the physician announces that death has taken place, the witnesses come forward, identify the corpse, and sign the necessary attestation.

Drawing was a mediæval punishment by which a man was dragged to death by horses. Brunehilda is said to have been executed in this manner.

When a prisoner was drawn and quartered, he was attached to a platform facing the sky, by two iron bands, one around his chest and arms, the other around his thighs. The weapon with which he had killed his murdered victim was placed in his hand, which was filled with sulphur, tied, and the sulphur fired, so that his hand was burned off him. Next, he was torn with hooks upon the breast and legs, and a composition of melted lead, rosin, wax, and sulphur poured into the wounds. After that, ropes fastened to whippletrees were attached to his arms and legs, each rope secured by two sailor-knots, and the horses attached to the whippletrees pulled him to pieces. A paling was erected around the spot to keep off the eager, curious crowd. The mangled remains were burned in a fire. This mode of execution was reserved for offenders guilty of lese-majesty. One of the most terrible executions upon record was that of Damiens, a poor fool who attempted, it was said, to assassinate Louis XV. He pierced his side slightly with a knife. The king received the attack with courage. Damiens, when questioned as to his motive, said that he did not want to kill Louis, but to give him a warning—to prick him a little, because he was a great tyrant, in order to show him what might happen. All of the parliaments of France were invited to make suggestions as to the manner in which the assassin should be tortured. It would torture the reader to quote the many recommendations gravely submitted in response to this royal request. Pending a decision, in order to prevent his escape, he was tied to an iron bed. The boot was finally agreed to be the most terrible form of suffering, and he was subjected to it for an hour and a half, then taken away to be drawn and quartered, but his sinews were so tough, that he was drawn for an hour, without avail, and a knife had to be used with which to quarter him, while still alive. A woman who was looking on, seeing, from the balcony where she stood, the frantic efforts of the horses to pull harder, exclaimed, "Oh, the poor horses!"

Breaking on the wheel, authorized by Francis the First in 1534, was really a way of pounding a man to death. The wheel was in the form of a cross of Saint Andrew, with four arms of equal length sloping slightly toward the point of intersection, upon which the prisoner was laid, with his face upward. Supports were nailed to the arms of the cross, so as to come half way between the shoulder and the elbow, the elbow and the wrist, the hips and the knees, and the knees and the ankles. With a heavy iron bar the upper and forearms, the thighs and shinbones, could each be broken into three pieces. After being thus rudely disjointed, the body was bent backward, until the head and heels met, when it was attached to a wheel, with the hubs sawed off, which was rapidly revolved on a pivot, until the sufferer was relieved by death. John Calvin is sometimes reproached with theological asperity for having burned Servetus at the stake, as if his religious opinions had prompted that inexcusable cruelty, instead of its being a custom of the age in which Calvin lived. But, as an offset, it may be mentioned that, less than a century and a half ago, Voltaire, who represents the opposite pole of religious thought, in one of his private letters, expresses his gratitude to God for the breaking of the priest Malacreda upon the wheel, and in another the comfort which it was to him to hear that three Jesuits had been burned alive at Lisbon. This form of punishment was known in Greece, where it was applied to slaves. In Athens it was proposed to break Phocion. This was really a form of beating to death, accomplished by the natives of South Africa in a more primitive way, with clubs. By the law of the Twelve Tables *laesa majestas* was punished by flogging to death.

As to crucifixion, Darius is said to have crucified, on one occasion, two thousand Assyrians, and, upon another, three thousand Babylonians at once. Regulus was crucified, but not until he had been rolled down hill in a barrel driven through from the outside with iron spikes. On the cross his eyelids were removed, that his eyes might be exposed continuously to the sun.

There are two modes of empaling, one by forcing a stake or spear through the prisoner's body and pinning him to the ground, the other by forcing his body upon a sharpened point. The latter is closely allied to crucifixion. In Siam a stake is driven longitudinally through the criminal's body, and the body is then elevated upon this stake, which is firmly driven into the ground. Suspension on hooks has been practised in the West Indies; also, for abjuring the Mohammedan religion, in Algeria and in India.

Strangulation, as described in Homer's "Odyssey," appears to have been by hanging. In Sparta it was effected by two executioners, who pulled at the opposite ends of a rope which encircled the victim's neck. Different modes of execution are looked upon as more or less infamous in different countries; in Turkey the bow-string is reserved for the nobility. In China, too, strangulation is regarded as more honorable than decapitation. The Spanish garrote is a mode of strangulation, no longer accomplished, as formerly, by ropes and cords, but by enclosing the neck in an iron ring, which can be tightened from behind by a screw, which is turned until the point of it pierces the spinal column. Strangulation before burning was an act of mercy.

Death by suffocation is mentioned in the Old Testament; Hazael the Syrian murdered Benhadad by dipping a thick cloth in water and spreading it over the king's face. Also in the Apocrypha, where it is said that Antiochus Eupator put Menelaus to death, at Berea, " as the manner is in that place." The Bereans had built a tower fifty cubits high, full of ashes, which could be stirred by some round instrument, possibly a wheel, "hanging down on every side into the ashes." Into this ash-heap Menelaus was thrown, as a punishment for sacrilege. Prisoners have also been suffocated by smoke, especially that given off by burning sulphur. Marshal Pelissier destroyed a force of Algerians who had taken refuge in a cave by smoking them to death.

Drowning is, of course, a mode of suffocation. Jesus Christ possibly alludes to the legal punishment of drowning in Matthew 18 : 6. The story of the drowning of the Duke of Clarence is thus quaintly told by Sir Thomas More in "The Pitiful Life of King Edward the Fifth."

"George, Duke of Clarence, was a goodly and well-featured prince, in all things fortunate, if either his own ambition had not set him against his brother, or the envy of his enemies had not set his brother against him; for were it by the Queen or the nobles of her blood, which highly maligned the King's kindred (as women commonly, not of malice, but of nature, hate such as their husbands love), or were it a proud appetite of the Duke himself intending to be King, at the leastwise, heinous treason was laid to his charge, and finally, were he in fault, or were he faultless, attainted was he by Parliament, and judged to death; and thereupon hastily drowned in a butt of Malmsey within the Tower of London. Whose death King Edward (although he commanded it), when he wist it was done, piteously he bewailed and sorrowfully repented it."

The manorial pits for drowning or half drowning women, like the manorial gibbets for hanging men, were highly prized prerogatives of the early English nobility.

Burying is the terrene equivalent of drowning. When the Third Crusade started from Europe for the Holy Land, certain rules for the government of its members were adopted, and it was announced that their violation would be punished, if at sea, by throwing the offender into the water, but if on land, by interring him alive. In Rome vestal virgins guilty of a breach of the vow of chastity were thus buried.

Sefi, the eighth Shah of Persia, whose name is a synonym for cruelty, believing that an unsuccessful attempt had been made to poison him, buried forty of the women of his seraglio, including his mother. Tacitus records the fact that lewd women were buried alive, by the Gauls, in swamps. Jews were buried by Pepin of France. In some parts of Germany, even since the beginning of the last century, this was the penalty for infanticide.

In 1347, two counterfeiters were boiled alive at Paris. This penalty for counterfeiting was in force in the sixteenth century. The boiling was sometimes done in oil. French law tolerated it until 1791, though it had long fallen into practical disuse. Under Henry VIII., of England, poisoning was for ten years regarded by law as treason, and it was punishable in this manner. The Bishop of Rochester's cook, a man named Rose, was publicly boiled at Smithfield, in 1630, for throwing poison into the yeast-tub in the kitchen of the episcopal palace. His occupation may have suggested the mode of his death.

Stoning, common among the ancient Hebrews, was regarded by them as the most infamous of punishments. The execution took place outside of the camp or city, and the witnesses were required to throw the first stone, but all the people took part in the ceremony. Æschylus was condemned to suffer death by stoning for having written a tragedy which was thought to be irreverent, but the sentence was not executed. Among the Romans this was a military punishment. Stoning was forbidden by Constantine. A law of Æthelstan, in the tenth century, prescribed it as the punishment of male slaves for theft; the thief was stoned by eighty fellow-slaves, and if any of them missed the mark three times he was thrice whipped.

Pressing to death was a mode of execution known to the Carthaginians. The instrument of torture known as the scavenger's daughter, in use in the Tower of London, will be described below, under "Torture." The judgment of penance, referred to at the close of the last chapter, was in these words: "That you be taken back to the prison whence you came, to a low dungeon into which no light can enter; that you be laid on your back on the bare floor, with a cloth around your loins, but elsewhere naked; that there be set upon your body a weight of iron as great as you can bear—and greater; that you have no sustenance, save, on the first day three morsels of the coarsest bread, on the second day three draughts of stagnant water from the pool nearest to the prison door, on the third day again three morsels of bread as before, and such bread and such water alternately from day to day until you die."

Among the punishments mentioned in the Epistle to the Hebrews is sawing asunder, or "dichotomy," which is the penalty for horse-stealing in Tartary, for poisoning in Persia, and was formerly, with obvious fitness, inflicted for bigamy in Switzerland. The *bodoveresta,* prescribed by Zoroaster, the Persian lawgiver, against incompetent physicians and mothers who killed their offspring, was very similar to the Chinese penalty entitled *ling-chee* or "cutting into a thousand pieces," while still alive.

Compare with the horrible torture just mentioned the sentence pronounced, in the reign of Edward the Second, against the Earl of Carlisle, for high treason: "The award of the court is that you be drawn, and hanged, and beheaded; that your heart, and bowels, and entrails, whence came your traitorous thoughts, be torn out, and burnt to ashes, and that the ashes be scattered to the winds; that your body be cut into four quarters, and that one of them be hanged upon the Tower of Carlisle, another upon the Tower of Newcastle, a third upon the Bridge of York, and the fourth at Shrewsbury; and that your head be set upon London Bridge, for an example to others that they may never presume to be guilty of such treason as yours against their liege lord."

Precipitation from a height, another of the punishments forbidden by Constantine, was the form of death inflicted upon Æsop, the writer of fables. Pygmalion, King of Tyre, visited it upon two priests guilty of having eaten the flesh of human sacrifices. In the history of the Maccabees it is written that Jewish mothers, with their infants in their arms, were thrown from the walls of Jerusalem. The Tarpeian rock at Rome was a place set apart for this mode of execution, chiefly practised upon slaves guilty of theft.

The Carthaginian general, Hasdrubal, before throwing his Roman prisoners from a rock, flayed them alive. Excoriation is named as a penalty in the laws of Henry the First of England. The general reader will observe occasional references in historical and other works to the ancient practice of nailing up human skins where they could be seen by the public, and the minds of those predisposed to crime be stricken with terror at the hideous spectacle.

Deserters from the army are, since the invention of fire-arms, usually shot to death. The fact is perhaps not generally known that, in some at least of the Western territories, convicts sentenced to endure capital punishment are given their choice whether they will be hung or shot. The author was shown, in a territorial prison, the location of the convict against the wall, and the spot where the tent is pitched in which the armed guards are concealed; to one or more of them are given guns loaded with blank cartridges. The spot where the Paris communists shot Archbishop Darboy, within prison walls, is shown to visitors, and excites much interest; the marks made by the bullets are still visible. The ancient equivalent form of death was by piercing the victims with javelins, which was also a military punishment.

Prisoners have sometimes been starved to death, either by withholding from them all food, or by feeding them on bread and water, or other provisions known to be inadequate to sustain life.

The Athenians forced Socrates, Phocion, and many others, to drink a poisonous decoction, and so to end their own lives. Years afterward, statues were erected to both these heroes; and the remains of Phocion were brought back from Megara and interred in Athens, at the expense of the public treasury.

Somewhat similar was the ancient Moslem punishment for wine-drinking, namely, pouring melted lead down the offender's throat.

Daniel was thrown, by Darius the Mede, into a den of lions. In Siam prisoners are sometimes thrown to crocodiles. The Roman arena was the place of martyrdom of thousands of the early Christians; the remains of Roman amphitheatres may still be traced in

Great Britain. In China faithless wives are given to elephants to be by them trampled under foot. This was the mode of punishment of deserters adopted by Hamilcar, the Carthaginian general.

Criminals have also been thrown into dens of serpents, or tied down in forests where it was certain that they would be bitten by serpents. The Roman penalty for parricide at one time consisted in sewing up the rebellious child in a leather sack, together with a live serpent, a cock, and a goat, and throwing the sack and its contents into the sea.

Plutarch, in his memoir of Artaxerxes, describes one of the most terrible of all recorded punishments, which was inflicted upon Mithridates, by order of the Persian monarch, for boasting, when overcome with wine, that he, and not Artaxerxes, had in truth slain the mighty Cyrus. He was encased in a coffin-like box, from which his head, hands, and feet protruded, through holes made for that purpose; he was fed with milk and honey, which he was forced to take, and his face was smeared with the same mixture; he was exposed to the sun, and in this state he remained for seventeen days, until he had been devoured alive by insects and vermin, which swarmed about him and bred within him.

Barbarous as are these tales of cruelty and hatred, was the blowing of the sepoys from the mouths of British cannon in India any less shocking?

Many travellers have seen, in the torture chamber at Nuremberg, the figure of a woman constructed in such a manner as to embrace a victim thrust into her arms, and pierce him to death with knives. A similar instrument was invented by Nabis, a Spartan tyrant, who named it the *Apega,* after his wife.

SECONDARY PUNISHMENTS

Mutilation of the body is an ancient penalty known to the Egyptians, who cut out the tongues of those who betrayed the secrets of the state, and cut off the hands of forgers and counterfeiters, with an apparent purpose in both cases to make the punishment fit the crime, and, at the same time, effectually to prevent its repetition; the Egyptian penalty for rape was of a similar nature. When Judah and Simeon cut off the thumbs and great toes of Adoni-bezek, he said, "Threescore and ten kings, having their thumbs and their great toes cut off, gathered their meat under my table: as I have done, so God hath requited me." The Philistines, before setting Samson to grind in the prison, put out his eyes. Mutilation was common among the Persians. Eight hundred Greek captives presented themselves before the victorious Alexander, with a petition that he would avenge their wrongs: some of them had lost their hands, others their feet, others their noses and their ears; their faces had then been marked with hot irons, and in that pitiful condition they had been delivered to the scorn of the Persian people. The Emperor Constantine forbade this practice, characterizing it as one of "the cruelties of the ruthless barbarians." A law of Canute, the Danish king of England, evidently designed to provide a humane substitute for capital punishment, ordained: "Let his [the offender's] hands be cut off, or his feet, or both, according as the deed may be. And if he have wrought yet greater wrong, then let his eyes be put out and his nose and his ears and his upper lip be cut off, or let him be scalped, whichever of these shall counsel those whose duty it is to counsel thereupon, so that punishment be inflicted, and also the soul preserved." Mr. Pike says that William the Conqueror or his council "enunciated the principle that malefactors so debased as those of England should not suffer death, because it was better that they should, as cripples, serve for a warning to the ill-disposed," but that the Synod of London, in 1075, under Lanfranc, the wise and gentle Italian archbishop of Canterbury, expressed disapproval of this maxim. Under Henry I., "the chief moneyers throughout the whole of England were convicted of making pence in which there was base metal illegally alloyed with the silver. By the king's command they were all brought to Winchester, and there suffered in one day the loss of their right hands and of their manhood." The spectacle of maimed offenders at large did not have the deterrent effect expected of it; on the contrary, it provoked imitation. "The brutalizing effect which it had upon the whole population can hardly be conceived, in this modern age of refinement. In the midst of the general lawlessness every man was, when he had the power, a law unto himself, and inflicted upon his enemy the punishment which the law of the land destined for the evil-doer. Maiming, that is to say, depriving a human being of a member, was consequently one of the commonest of offences—for which the law provided a wholly inadequate remedy in the appeal of mayhem." Mayhem was a simple trespass until the reign of Henry IV., who "assented to a statute which, for the first time, declared that it was a felony to cut out the tongue or put out the eyes of the king's subjects, of malice aforethought. It was not, for many a generation afterward, a felony to slit the nose, to cut off the nose or lip, or to cut off or disable any of the limbs." Not until the passage of the "Coventry Act" in the reign of Charles II., was all mayhem made felonious. Mr. Pike, from whom the foregoing quotations are taken, gives the following highly pictorial description of the ceremonial attending the loss of the right hand, under Henry VIII.:—

"For merely striking, so as to shed blood, the loss of the right hand was the penalty, as it had been for many crimes before the Conquest. The offender, as in cases of murder in the court, was tried before the Lord Great Master, or the Lord Steward of the Household, and when found guilty, suffered according to a most remarkable and carefully devised ceremony. He was brought in by the Marshal, and every stage of the proceedings was under the direction of some member of the royal household. The first whose services were required was the Serjeant of the Woodyard, who brought in a block and cord, and bound the condemned hand in a convenient position. The Master Cook was there with a dressing knife, which he handed to the Serjeant of the Larder, who adjusted it and held it 'till execution was done.' The Serjeant of the Poultry was close by with a cock, which was to have its head cut off on the block by the knife used for the amputation of the hand, and the body of which was afterward to be used to 'wrap about the stump.' The Yeoman of the Scullery stood near, watching a fire of coals, and the Serjeant Farrier at his elbow to deliver the searing-irons to the surgeon. The Chief Surgeon seared the stump, and the Groom of the Salcery held vinegar and cold water, to be used, perhaps, if the patient should faint. The Serjeant of the Ewry and the Yeoman of the Chandry attended with basin, cloths, and towels for the surgeon's use. After the hand had been struck off and the stump seared, the Serjeant of the Pantry offered bread, and the Serjeant of the Cellar offered a pot of red wine, of which the sufferer was to partake with what appetite he might."

The following account of the case of William Prynne, a barrister of Lincoln's Inn, in the time of Charles I., is borrowed from Hallam:—

"Prynne, a lawyer of uncommon erudition, and a zealous puritan, had printed a bulky volume, called 'Histriomastix,' full of invectives against the theatre, which he sustained by a profusion of learning. In the course of this he adverted to the appearance of courtesans on the Roman stage, and by a satirical reference in his index (women actors notorious whores), seemed to range all female actors in this class. The Queen, unfortunately, six weeks after the publication of Prynne's book, had performed a part in a mask at Court. Prynne was already obnoxious, and the Star Chamber adjudged him to stand twice in the pillory, to be branded in the forehead, to lose both his ears, to pay a fine of £5,000, and to suffer perpetual imprisonment."

Timothy Penredd, who was in 1570 convicted of counterfeiting the seal of the court of Queen's Bench, and forging writs of arrest, was sentenced to be placed in the pillory in Cheapside, on two successive market-days, with one ear nailed each day to the post, in such a manner that he would have to tear it off to get away.[1]

[1] James Howell, in his "Familiar Letters," written in the first half of the seventeenth century, relates an anecdote which well illustrates the general fear of this form of mutilation. He says: "As I remember, some years since there was a very abusive satire in verse brought to our King; and, as the passages were a reading before him, he often said, 'That if there were no more men in England, the rogue should hang for it.' At last, being come to the conclusion, which was (after all his railing),—

'Now God preserve the King, the Queen, the peers,
And grant the Author long may wear his ears;'

this pleased his Majesty so well, that he broke into a laughter, and said, 'By my soul, so thou shalt, for me. Thou art a bitter, but thou art a witty knave!'"

Louis XV. of France placarded the camp at Compiègne in 1765 with the announcement, that any soldier who should blaspheme the name of God, the Virgin, or any of the saints, should have his tongue pierced with a hot iron.

Another form of disgraceful marking was by branding. In Athens, slaves were branded with the names of their masters; soldiers, with those of their generals. The Athenians branded their prisoners of war. In the war with Samos, the Samians, having gained a victory, retaliated by branding their captive adversaries with an owl, the bird sacred to Minerva, with the effigy of which the coins of Athens were stamped. Under Roman law the brand was placed upon the forehead; but Constantine, who was a humane ruler, and introduced many reforms in criminal jurisprudence, ordained that it should be upon the hand or leg, in order that it might be less conspicuous. In France, the shoulder was the spot selected. The ancient brand was the *fleur-de-lis*, the royal emblem; but afterward it was the initial of the crime committed, as "V" for *voleur* (thief). That the mark made by the branding-iron might be plainer and more permanent, the skin was first scraped, so as to insure the burning of the blood which collected on the surface of the wound. The English brutality in this, as in many other forms of punishment, is shown in the treatment of the Patarines, a heretical sect of the twelfth century, whose foreheads were seared with a hot iron. They were publicly whipped, and every Englishman was forbidden to give them food or shelter, so that they perished of cold and hunger. Under

Edward VI. it was ordered that vagabonds should be branded "V." A vagabond thus marked was to be adjudged the slave, for two years, of any one who would take him. If he ran away, he was to be branded "S," and adjudged a slave for life; if he ran away again, he was to be hanged. If no one would take him, he was to be branded "V" upon the breast, and sent to his native place, there to be compelled to labor upon the highways, or at other public work, or as a common slave from man to man. If he misrepresented the place of his birth, he was to be branded in the face. Brawlers in churchyards were branded "F" on the cheek. During several generations, persons who had taken benefit of clergy were burned on the brawn of the thumb with the initial of the offence with which they were charged, in order that they might not plead clergy a second time; but in 1698 such persons were, by a new statute (which was repealed eight years later) directed to be burned in the left cheek. Persons having in possession filings or clippings of current coin were branded "R" on the right cheek. Branding was abolished in England under George III.

Flogging was authorized by the Mosaic code. "The judge shall cause him to lie down, and to be beaten before his face, according to his fault, by a certain number. Forty stripes he may give him, and not exceed; lest if he should exceed, and beat him above these with many stripes, then thy brother should seem vile unto thee." Under Roman law, a freeman could not be beaten with stripes; yet flogging was authorized as a punishment for aggravated theft; but the thief had first to be declared *servus pœnæ* — the slave of the penalty. Paul's indignant protest, "They have beaten us openly, uncondemned, being Romans," will here recur to many readers. This was also a punishment under Anglo-Saxon law. Petty thieves were flogged in the reign of George III.; men in public, women in private. Whipping for common law misdemeanors has never been formally abolished, though it is not administered where it is not authorized by statute. The lash is now regarded less as a retributive penalty than as a means of enforcing discipline. Some persons have confidence in its deterrent influence, approve of the retention of the whipping-post in Delaware, and advocate the enactment of laws reviving it elsewhere for certain offences, especially for wife-beating. As to this point, the following observations of Mr. Pike are well worthy of consideration:—

"There is, no doubt, a dramatic fitness in punishing the deliberate infliction of bodily pain by the deliberate infliction of bodily pain in return. And if the maxim 'An eye for an eye and a tooth for a tooth' is a proper guide for lawgivers in a Christian country in the nineteenth century, there remains nothing more to be said, except that the 'cat' is, in many cases, too merciful an instrument. If, however, the object of punishment is not vengeance, but the prevention of breaches of the law, it seems useless, so far as example is concerned, to flog a prisoner within the prison walls. The whole power of such a deterrent as flogging (if it is to be regarded as a general deterrent) must be in the vividness with which it can be presented to the imagination of persons who have a tendency to commit, but who have not yet committed, the offences for which flogging may be legally inflicted. But the most ready manner of bringing it home to the mind of the populace is by exhibiting it in public, which, as has already been shown, has the very opposite effect from that which is desired. The fact that the lash has been administered to a convict is now and again brought to the knowledge of the public by the press, and sometimes with the aid of illustrations. But the impressions made, so to speak, by such exhibition at second-hand, cannot be so forcible as that made by the old form of exhibition at first-hand; and in proportion as it becomes effectual at all, it must be attended by the effects which are produced by all brutal punishments inflicted *coram populo.* It is far from an agreeable task to watch the face and figure of the flogger as he executes the sentence; and few would deny that the moral effect upon him must be as great as upon the criminal, whom it is his duty to whip. The state, when it sanctions the use of the lash, causes a human being to do just such an act of violence as it desires to check; it must either recognize the use of the 'cat' as an art of which it is prepared to employ the professors, or it must, on each particular occasion, offer a reward to some one to come into prison and commit a violent assault. It follows, therefore, that even if every criminal who is flogged is deterred from repeating his offence, the gain, small as it is, has been purchased at a very high price—indeed, at the expense of consistency."

The *knut* and the bastinado are savage forms of flogging. The *knut* in Russia has been abolished, but its place has been taken by the *plet,* a sort of heavy cat.

The status of a prisoner is in many respects analogous to that of a slave. War may be carried on in the open field, *vi et armis,* or it may be reduced to a purely legal contest in the courts. In either case the vanquished party has to bear the costs and the consequences. From the condition of a prisoner of war to that of a slave is but a step; why should the condition of a convict be exempt from the liabilities incident to a captive in battle? The conqueror can dispose of the conquered at his pleasure. Compulsory labor is therefore a natural sequel of the condition of servitude, whether military or penal. The Israelites in Egypt were neither convicts nor captives, yet Pharaoh set them to making brick under cruel taskmasters. To be sent to the mines was the severest of Egyptian penalties, except that of death. Mines and quarries were worked by convicts in Greece and in Rome. The conquered Lesbians were compelled to dig deep ditches around the walls of Samos. Sabacos substituted for the penalty of death, compulsory labor for life. Sesostris made prisoners of war dig canals and haul stones for the construction of the temples. Prisoners of war were by the Athenians compelled to serve as rowers in vessels of war. This is perhaps the first indication in history of the use of the galleys for punishment, which in the Middle Ages was so common, that countries without seacoast of their own sold prisoners to countries which had. Venice was naturally a principal buyer in this unique slave-market. Maria Theresa, that noble woman who put an end to so many of the barbarities prevalent before her day, has the honor of having, in 1762, forbidden this practice also. A modified form of slavery survives wherever prison labor is sold to private persons for their pecuniary profit.

Interdiction and civic degradation are other incidents of the loss of personal liberty. In modern times and in civilized nations they go no farther than the temporary or permanent denial to a convict of his proper rank, or of the right to vote, to hold office, to serve on a jury, to carry arms, and (in France) to wear a decoration or be employed as a teacher. But, as in the case of the Patarines cited above, the denial might extend to rights essential to the preservation of life. In the early history of Rome, a citizen might be interdicted the use of fire and water. The purpose of this was to compel him to exile himself, since he could not legally be banished. Draco, the Athenian law-giver, excluded murderers from the temples, the games, from public banquets and assemblies. The bills of attainder for treason with which the records of the English Parliament are stained (of which there was probably not one which was not the offspring of partisan hatred) worked corruption of blood, the effect of which was that descent could not be traced through the person whose blood was corrupted; and thus the innocent offspring of men guilty of none but political crimes were deprived of the hereditary right to their ancestral estates. Attainder and corruption of blood followed sentence of death in all cases of treason or felony. But Parliament could try alleged offenders in their absence, and condemn them upon any evidence which they chose to accept as sufficient. The great Act of Attainder passed by the Irish Commons, to which James II. attached his signature, contained between two and three thousand names, at the top of which was half the peerage of Ireland. Macaulay says of it, that "Any member who wished to rid himself of a creditor, a rival, a private enemy, gave in the name to the clerk at the table, and it was generally inserted without discussion." Even dead men were attainted; Oliver Cromwell, for instance. Parliament resolved, under Charles II., in 1660, that "the carcasses of Oliver Cromwell, Ireton, Bradshaw, and Pride should be taken up, drawn on a hurdle to Tyburn, and there hanged up in their coffins for some time, and after that buried under the gallows."

The confiscation of estates was not merely an act of manifest injustice to heirs, living and yet unborn, but an obvious inducement to judicial murder. Men accused and convicted of treason, by their rivals for royal favor, were robbed of their property for the enrichment of their political enemies. The same result was reached by the heavy fines imposed by the Star Chamber, where, as Hallam says, "Those who inflicted the punishment reaped the gain, and sat, like famished birds of prey, with keen eyes and bended talons, eager to supply for a moment, by some wretch's ruin, the craving emptiness of the exchequer." He further observes that "The strong interest of the court in these fines must not only have had a tendency to aggravate the punishment, but to induce sentences of condemnation on inadequate proof." Under the feudal system, escheats to the crown constituted a large portion of the revenues of the Norman kings of England. Whatever else may be said of feudalism, it was a gigantic scheme of extortion in return for very imperfect protection, by which the powerful and the rapacious built up their fortunes at the expense of their dependants; and the king was the chief extortioner, against whose demands not even the grand seigneurs could protect themselves. Thus the system contained within itself the providential seed of its own destruction. The rapacious of our time rob their victims by other methods, but their ultimate overthrow is probably involved in the very audacity of the means by which their temporary power to despoil their fellowmen has been attained.

Closely connected with civic degradation were the insults heaped upon offenders, in their public exposure both before and after death. The pillory and the stocks are the forms of exposure best known to us, and need no description. The continental equivalent for them was the *carcan,* a ring closed by a lock, by means of which a criminal was attached by the neck to a chain, and so fastened to a post. This is the Latin echo of an ancient Persian device; namely, an acute triangle, in the narrow angle of which the prisoner's neck was confined, while his hands were extended and attached to the opposite side; in this position he could walk about. The special objection to the pillory and the *carcan* was that the populace had the right to pelt victims thus exposed with decayed eggs and fruit, which was unpleasant, and with stones, which was dangerous. The *carcan* was abolished in France in 1832, and the pillory in England in 1837.

The Spanish mantle (of which there is an engraving in John Howard's book) was a cask, with holes cut through the sides for the prisoner's arms, and through the top for his head; he wore it like a coat, and in this ridiculous costume was marched around the town at a cart's tail. Scolds were formerly ducked in a pond by means of a ducking-stool, of which there were various patterns, the essential thing being a seat, to which the woman was strapped, at the end of a long lever operated from the bank, to the rude delight of the spectators.[1] They were also forced to wear the brank,

[1] In "The Little Manx Nation," by Hall Caine, a tale is told of Bishop Thomas Wilson, "half angel, only half man, the serenest of saints and yet almost the bitterest of tyrants." Katherine Kinrade was a poor ruin of a woman, who, being mentally defective, gave birth in succession to three illegitimate children. For the first, the Bishop made her do penance in a white sheet at the church doors. For the second, he committed her for twenty-one days to his prison at the Peel. "It is a crypt of the cathedral church. You enter it by a little door in the choir, leading to a tortuous flight of steep steps going down. It is a chamber cut

which was a cage-like helmet or mask of iron, with a triangular piece entering the mouth and pressing upon the tongue, as a delicate reminder of the proper use of that unruly member. In the Middle Ages a favorite punishment for adulteresses was to scourge them naked through the streets. There were many ways of exposing the dead to derision. Sometimes their bodies were thrown into the streets to be devoured by dogs. Oftener their heads were elevated upon poles. The head of the unfortunate Princess of Lamballe, the

out of the rock of the little island, dark, damp, and noisome. A small aperture lets in the light, as well as the sound of the sea beating on the rocks below. The roof, if you could see it in the gloom, is groined and ribbed, and above it is the mould of many graves, for in the old days bodies were buried in the choir." The third time, he ordered her to be dragged through the sea by a rope tied to the stern of a boat. "After undergoing the punishment the miserable soul was apparently penitent, 'according to her capacity,' took the communion, and was 'received into the peace of the church.' Poor human ruin, defaced image of a woman, begrimed and buried soul, unchaste, misshapen, incorrigible, no 'juice of God's distilling' ever 'dropped into the core of her life;' to such punishment was she doomed by the tribunal of that saintly man, Bishop Thomas Wilson! She has met him at another tribunal since then; not where she has crouched before him, but where she has stood by his side. She has carried her account against him to Him before whom the proudest are as chaff.

"None spake, when Wilson stood before
The Throne;
And He that sat thereon
Spake not; and all the presence-floor
Burnt deep with blushes, and the angels cast
Their faces downward.—Then, at last,
Awe-stricken, he was ware
How on the emerald stair
A woman sat divinely clothed in white,
And at her knees four cherubs bright
That laid
Their heads within her lap. Then, trembling, he essayed
To speak—'Christ's mother, pity me!'
Then answered she,
'Sir, I am Katherine Kinrade.'"

favorite of Marie Antoinette, was carried by a mob about the streets of Paris, placed on the counter of a *cabaret*, where wine was poured down the throat, and the Queen was loudly called to the window of her cell in the Temple to gaze with horror upon the bloody spectacle, but was humanely prevented from responding to the call. Exposure in chains after death was once common. Bunyan saw, in his dream, Simple, Sloth, and Presumption "hanged up in irons a little way off on the other side." These irons were frames rudely corresponding to the shape of the body, so contrived as to hold it until decomposition was complete, and only the skeleton remained bleaching in the sun.[1] The last man to hang in England was a bookbinder named Cook, in 1834, at Leicester. That year, by William IV., hanging in chains was forbidden. A singular tale is related by Plutarch of the beneficial

[1] The following description of chains still preserved at Rye, England, is borrowed from *Notes and Queries* (sixth series, v. 8, p. 183). "To begin at the top, we have a swivel loop. This is obviously for giving a rotatory as well as a swinging motion to the carcass. This swivel is fixed into a frame formed of two pieces of hoop iron bent over, like the wooden frame of a funeral garland, and of sufficient depth to reach from the top of a man's head to his shoulders; the four ends are then riveted into a band encircling his neck. At opposite sides coarse chains are riveted on to the neck band and descend on either side, with four links, to about the middle of the chest. A second and much larger band is then passed through the fifth link and riveted in front. Then come three more links in the same continuous chains, and a third band, which, passing through a fourth link, is similarly riveted in front. The chains continue with three more links, a band is passed through a fourth and final link, and, being riveted in front like the others, nearly completes the framework for the body. At the back a strip of iron starts from the neck band and, bifurcating above the shoulders, descends in parallel lines; it is successively riveted to the three body bands, and being again united into a single strip, ends in a loop immediately below the bottom hoop. Thus the body framing is rendered rigid and complete. Suspended by a chain from the loop behind, and from the

effect of exposure in Ionia, where an epidemic of suicide on the part of young girls was stopped by the passage of a law, directing the dead bodies of those who perished by their own hand to be hung naked on the public gallows; the fear of infamy proved stronger than the fear of death.

It remains only to mention exile, which is essentially an alternative for the death sentence, and has the same effect, so far as the community which desires to rid itself of a culprit is in question. Banishment may, however, be temporary or for life. It may also be compulsory, or, by a legal fiction, it may be voluntary, the criminal being liable to execution if he remains at home. It was by this subterfuge that transportation was instituted, as we shall see in a subsequent chapter. Transportation always involves the dilemma that the persons exiled are either good or bad citizens; if good,

lowest band in front, are separate frames for the legs, consisting of circular bands of different sizes for the knees and ankles, connected by vertical side strips riveted to them. These leg frames are so arranged, with extra length in the side pieces, that they can be taken up or let down, according to the length of the legs of a body within the chains. It should also be noted that the body bands are punched with holes, like a leather strap, so that they can be tightened or let out, according to the size required. This seems to indicate that the same chains were used over and over again, but that it was necessary, for other reasons, that the chains should fit."

Another correspondent of the same periodical thinks that the first instance of an executed person hanging in chains must have been in 1381, and he quotes Sir H. Chauncey's "Hist. Antiq. of Hertfordshire": "Soon after the King came to Easthamsted, to recreate himself with hunting, where he heard that the Bodies which were hanged here were taken down from the Gallowes and removed a great way from the same; this so incensed the King, that he sent a writ, tested the 3d of August, Anno 1381, to the Bailiffs of this Borrough, commanding them upon sight thereof to cause chains to be made, and to hang the Bodies in them upon the same Gallowes, there to remain so long as one Piece might stick to another, according to the Judgment."

they are a loss to their native country; but if bad, that country has no right to impose the burden of their presence upon an unwilling community. Every community is unwilling which has reached a stage of development at which it is self-sustaining without convict labor. The Romans divided banishment into deportation and relegation; deportation was exile to a place specified, from which the banished were not allowed to depart; but relegation was simple exile, and did not involve loss of citizenship. A form of banishment called ostracism (from the Greek word for a shell, because shells were used for balloting) existed at Athens, to which Aristides, Alcibiades, Themistocles, Xenophon, Thucydides, and Demosthenes were subjected. It was inflicted by popular suffrage at a special election, at which not less than six thousand votes must be cast, of which a majority must be in favor of the exile of the candidate from Athens for a period of ten years. Ostracism did not involve the confiscation of the exile's estate, as the ordinary form of banishment did.

Outlawry may also be regarded as a sub-variety of exile.

The mind dislikes to dwell upon acts of violence, such as have been described in this dark chapter of human nature at its worst. It is necessary, however, to know from what we have been delivered, in order to appreciate what we enjoy; and what has been tried and failed, in order to realize the folly of repeating useless experiments. It may seem to the young and inexperienced reader that human nature has changed and is no longer what it was, when these outrages were perpetrated in the name of law and of religion. It is, alas, not true, as the veterans of our own Civil War could testify, or the residents upon or near the theatre of the conflict, if they chose to do so. And yet the self-restraint of both the great armies therein engaged is the pride of every American, one of the wonders of history, and a tribute to the ethical influence of democratic institutions. Our social and political relations have changed, and therein is the secret of the growth of a humane and brotherly feeling among men, which is reflected in our laws and in their administration. The great lesson to be derived from the contemplation of the past is the obligation to vigilance and exertion, in order that what has been won at such fearful cost may not, at the dictation of civil or ecclesiastical tyrants, be wrested from our grasp.

Among the victories to which allusion is here made must be accounted the inclusion in the French Declaration of Rights (1789), of the statement that "the right to punish is limited by the law of necessity"; also the declaration by the Revolutionary Assembly in 1791, that "penalties should be proportioned to the crimes for which they are inflicted, and that they are intended, not merely to punish, but to reform the culprit." That Assembly relegated to oblivion the antiquated notion that imprisonment was merely a preventive measure, by which the prisoner was to be securely held until he could be suitably punished; and it substituted for it the principle that imprisonment, in varying forms and degrees, is itself a penalty of crime.[1] It therefore dis-

[1] "The Ordinance of Louis XIV., August, 1670, is the latest criminal code prior to the Revolution of 1789. The only penalties then permitted (and which are mentioned in the Ordinance) were: (1) Death; (2) torture; (3) the galleys for life, or for a

pensed with all the corporal punishments which the Monarchy had cherished and so fearfully abused. Credit must also be given it for having been the first governmental body to recognize police surveillance without imprisonment, as an adequate remedy, in many cases, for social disorder.

TORTURE

The real use of torture was not to punish a criminal, though it was sometimes employed for that purpose. (The Julian law, for instance, prescribed it for lese-majesty). It was intended, first, to extort from a person accused a confession of guilt, and second, to force him to disclose the names of his accomplices. It was an incident in judicial procedure. The theory of its

term of years; (4) banishment for life, or for a specified term; (5) flogging; (6) the *amende honorable;* (7) reprimand. Besides these principal penalties there were others which were accessory, such as branding, the *carcan,* the pillory, dragging in the mud, and confiscation; also lighter punishments, like fines, etc. But nowhere is imprisonment mentioned in the light of a punishment; never was it so inflicted. The prison was simply a place where the accused was held for trial, and convicts were held until the execution of sentence. The Constituent Assembly adopted imprisonment as the principal, though not the sole, basis of the criminal code. It made of this form of punishment, which was never to be for life, a new feature in criminal jurisprudence. It created the penitentiary system in France; that is, a system founded upon the amendment and rehabilitation of the prisoner. In the penalty of *la gêne* (absolute solitude), authorized by the 14th section of the Code, may be seen the germ of "solitary confinement" practised, later, at Philadelphia. The National Convention made but slight changes in the Code. The Empire, however, overthrew it bodily, by reestablishing imprisonment for life, confiscation, and branding, and by replacing *la gêne* by relegation or exile. The Code of 1810, nevertheless, contains a more advanced provision than does the Code of 1791, in giving to judges discretionary power to determine the duration of sentence within minimum and maximum limits. It also contains a provision for the surveillance of discharged convicts, which did not occur to the Assembly or the Convention."—*Moreau-Christophe.*

advocates was that the knowledge of one's own guilt is guilty knowledge, and to compel him to give it up was only an act of justice; while any evidence which he might have in his possession touching the misdeeds of others was the property of the state, which it had the right to recover by any and all means at its command. This is indicated by the Latin word for torture, *quæstio;* and even the English word in its etymological derivation suggests the same thought—torture is the twisting (*torsion*) from its subject of his guilty secrets. Traces of this theory survive in the French practice of interrogation of the accused by the judge. English law is more humane, since it admits the right of the accused to refuse to answer questions which tend to his incrimination; but there is reason to believe that what the courts are forbidden to do, the police, especially the detective branch of it, does not scruple to attempt, in the United States, without warrant of law.

Like flogging and other corporal chastisements, torture was originally applicable exclusively to slaves. A slave had no rights superior to those of a military captive. Parrhasius, when about to paint his picture of "Prometheus Bound," purchased a captive, whom he subjected to torture, in order that he might the better serve as a model, by his contortions and facial expression. A story is told of a Roman noble, whose lampreys were greatly praised at a dinner given by him; he explained that they have been fed on the flesh of slaves, killed and thrown into the water for that purpose. The testimony of a slave was valueless in Rome and in Athens, unless extracted from him by torture. Paul escaped scourging, to make him confess his crimes, at the hands of the chief captain in Jerusalem, only because he could substantiate his claim to be a freeborn Roman citizen.

Torture is an institution at least as old as Egypt. A passage in the book of Esther makes it probable that it was in use in ancient Persia. Moses forbade it, in the injunction that no proof of guilt should be accepted by the Hebrew courts, except the concurrent testimony of two witnesses. But it was practised in Greece. A rescript of the Emperor Augustus authorized it in Rome, on the express ground that it was useful as an agency for the discovery of truth, *ad veritatem requirendam.* Tacitus relates an anecdote of Tiberius worth reproduction here. A nephew of Pompey was accused of magic, but protested his innocence. With a view to ascertaining the fact, his accusers demanded that his slaves, who were familiar with his habits, should be put to the question, in order to induce them to tell what they knew. A Roman law, however, forbade the testifying of slaves against their master. Thereupon the Emperor freed these slaves, at the cost of the public treasury, in order to enable them to appear as witnesses in the case. The only criticism which it occurs to Tacitus to make upon this transaction is that the Emperor was not justifiable in thus circumventing the law. Since torture cannot well be practised in public, it was not suited to the Teutonic nations, whose tribunals were popular assemblies. It did not find its way, therefore, into Northern Europe, or at least was not expressly recognized as legal, before the reign of Charles V., who, with his successor, Francis I., is credited with the revival of the old Roman jurisprudence. These monarchs established by law, in the sixteenth century, all that is included under the general title of torture. They recognized and adopted the Roman distinction between ordinary and extraordinary penalties; the former were named in the code, and could be ordered by judges upon the testimony of witnesses or upon the plea of guilt by the accused; but, if these were wanting, they could proceed to the question, and, if the sufferer confessed under duress, a larger discretion as to the punishment to be adjudged against him was vested in them.

The right to put accused persons to the question was a prerogative of the grand seigneurs; like other nameless privileges which they enjoyed, it was for them an appanage of rank, a means of vengeance, and an agency for extorting tribute.

There is much evidence that the resort to this more than questionable method of proof was never in England common as it was upon the continent. Hallam, the constitutional historian of England, says that "the common law neither admits of torture to extort confession, nor of any penal infliction not warranted by a judicial sentence;" but adds, "This law, though still sacred in the courts of justice, was set aside by the Privy Council under the Tudor line. The rack seldom stood idle in the Tower, for all the latter part of Elizabeth's reign." As some of the investigations made into prison management prove, jailers sometimes made unlawful use of torture to extract information from prisoners.

There were in the Tower two chambers, both of which were regarded as excellent places in which to seclude a man, in order to stimulate him to serious reflection. One of them was called "Little Ease," because it was too small to admit of his standing, sitting, or lying in it with any comfort to himself; the other was the "Dungeon of Rats."

The principal forms of torture were as follows: First, the cord, which was sometimes applied simply by tying the thumbs together as tightly as possible with whipcord. Generally, however, by the cord is meant the violent jerking of which there is an illustrative engraving in John Howard's book on the "State of Prisons." It is sometimes called the strappado (French *estrapade*).[1] The victim, having submitted to have his hands firmly tied behind his back, was raised by a rope and pulley to a height, then suddenly dropped and caught, so that his joints snapped like a whip. To render it more excruciating, weights were sometimes attached to his feet; Howard saw five different weights in the prison at Zurich, the heaviest of which was one hundred and twenty pounds. Savanarola and Machiavelli were both subjected to this test. The common time for continuing it was an hour, and very few who endured it that long ever regained the use of their limbs.

The thumbscrew I need not describe. A model of it may be seen in the Tower. It was occasionally used, as we use handcuffs, for securely holding prisoners.

In the boot and wedge, the legs were tied and wedges driven between them. The boot was sometimes made

[1] Francis the First, that bloody tyrant, with diabolical ingenuity, combined the strappado with burning alive, in the execution of Protestants, at a place in Paris formerly known as the Estrapade.

of parchment, put on the feet wet, and then dried before a fire.

The rack was introduced into England by the Duke of Exeter, and for that reason was popularly known as "Exeter's Daughter." It was a machine for stretching all the limbs at once, until there was danger of their giving way at the weakest joint, whatever that might be.

The "Scavenger's Daughter" was named after the Lieutenant of the Tower, its inventor, whose name was Skevington. By its use the knees were drawn up to the breast and the feet to the thighs, where they were held by iron bars; the sufferer was practically rolled up like a ball; the blood was forced from his nose and mouth, and not infrequently the ribs and breastbone were broken.

Burning with heated pincers was called the hooks.

A form of torture peculiar to Italy was the *veglia,* by which the point of a diamond was made to press against the end of the spinal cord of a prisoner seated upon a plank in which the diamond was securely imbedded; the result was convulsions.

All the various pains which have been described under this head were borne, it must be remembered, not necessarily by the guilty, but by the innocent. The question preparatory was designed to make its subject commit himself; the question preliminary to make him commit some one else. The former was applied before, and the latter after, judgment. Attempts were made to guard so powerful an engine of oppression against abuse, by restricting the number of persons who could put it in operation, the conditions of its application, the extent to which it could be used in individual cases, and the crimes for whose discovery, proof, or punishment it was lawful to make use of it. But it was placed in the hands of both the civil and the ecclesiastical courts, in an age of ignorance, superstition, and tyrannical abuse of class privilege.

That torture is contrary to humanity and religion, as well as to sound principles of law, is now apparent enough. But the controversy over it lasted for centuries, and at times raged with fury. The great Roman lawyer, Ulpian, opposed it as unsatisfactory and dangerous. The Christian Fathers, Tertullian and Augustine, denounced it. The early Christians persuaded the Emperors not to inflict it during Lent. Many of the Popes condemned it; so did the Protestant sect of the Waldenses; so did the Encyclopædists. Clement V. said that the withholding the sacraments from persons under torture was a damnable outrage. Montaigne said that torture was both cruel and useless. Nevertheless, so deeply engrained in the thought of men were the conceptions which underlay it and gave it vitality, that no writer could give it a death-blow, until Beccaria published his little tractate on "Crimes and Punishments," at Milan, in 1764.

His book was the sensation of the day. It was translated into all the modern languages; he was invited to Paris; but the best of all was that his views were adopted by governments, and that he lived to see torture abolished in France, in Austria, in Russia, and to a large degree in Italy. It lingered in some of the petty Italian states until 1831. We are apt to accord the palm to Howard of England as the greatest of prison reformers. Beccaria did not, like Howard, spend his life and his fortune for the amelioration of the unhappy state of those in bonds. But he perhaps did even more for the world, in winning its ear and altering the whole current of its criminal jurisprudence.

THE INQUISITION

Torture was so preeminently an ecclesiastical weapon with which to combat heresy, for the glory of God and the eternal welfare of human souls, that it would be to give but an imperfect idea of the change which has come over the spirit of the race, if no mention were made of the Inquisition. There were two very distinct periods in the history of the Inquisition, one of which covered two hundred years, from the close of the twelfth to the close of the fourteenth century, and the other began with the creation of the Spanish Inquisition, ten or a dozen years before the discovery of America by Columbus. The first of these periods need not detain us long. The Council of Verona in 1184 condemned the tenets of the heretical sects called the Albigenses and Waldenses, found in the south of France. Peter of Castelnau and Raoul, two Cistercian monks, were sent thither to compel them to abjure their errors. They associated with themselves the great Saint Dominic, founder, in 1215, of the Dominican order. Innocent III. was his friend and patron. They invaded France on their sacred mission in 1204. At the memorable siege of Alby, July 22, 1209 (which made forever infamous the name of Simon de Montfort, the general who conducted the siege and permitted the massacre which followed), the soldiers asked Dominic by what sign they could distinguish the heretics from the faithful; he replied, "Spare none! the Lord will know his own." The church could not itself put its enemies to death, without despite to the spirit of forgiveness by which it was supposed to be animated; but the Emperor Frederic II., under the menace of excommunication by Pope Honorius III., assumed the protectorate of the Inquisition, and ordained that heretics condemned by it should be put to death or otherwise punished, according to their crimes, by the secular power. The Emperor, when it was too late, repented of his weakness, but Innocent IV. had by that time given it permanent life and united it to the Holy See. It was during this period of our story, that the Templars were suppressed, and De Molay, the grand master, burned alive, near the spot where now stands the statue of Henry IV., in Paris. The old Inquisition, however, existed largely in name; its pretensions were resisted; and, although it obtained a foothold in Italy, Spain, France, and Germany, it had, when Ferdinand and Isabella were married, become dormant everywhere except in the Papal States.

About the middle of the fifteenth century, a young man, a student in the University of Salamanca, had the misfortune to fall violently in love with a beautiful Spanish girl named Cazilda, who had engaged herself to a Moor. In a street brawl which ensued, the Moor disarmed the Spaniard, who took a solemn vow to be revenged, not only upon the Moor and his lady-love, but upon the accursed race to which his successful rival belonged. They fled to Granada, where for a time they were safe. This passionate student subsequently made the acquaintance of Father Lopez, the Superior of the Dominican order in Spain, who perceived the brilliancy of his talents, his inordinate ambition, the ardor of his spirit, the intensity and tenacity of his will, and determined if possible to secure him for the church. Becoming intimate, the secret of his undying hostility to the Moor was revealed to his new friend. Lopez, failing in the effort to cure him of a hopeless attachment and to seek peace of mind in a monastic career, suggested to him that possibly, not being of noble blood, he might gratify his longing for vengeance even more effectually in the priesthood than as a simple layman. The young man became a Dominican friar. In the convent library he discovered the ancient records of the former Inquisition. At the risk of his health and his life, he devoted his days and nights to poring over them. They excited his admiration, aroused his ambition, fed the spirit of persecution by which he was consumed, and decided him to become an inquisitor.

But how to arrive at his end? He went to Toledo, where he distinguished himself as a pulpit orator, attracted the attention of the Court, and finally became the tutor and confessor of the young Isabella, the future Queen of Spain. He instilled into her infant mind his own fanatical intolerance. On the day of her first communion, he extorted from her an oath upon the crucifix, that she would, on coming to the throne, either convert the heretics within her kingdom or exterminate them.

In 1481 Isabella, whose marriage with Ferdinand had united the crowns of Aragon and Castile, received a visit, after her coronation, from Lopez, the confessor of Ferdinand, in company with her own confessor, the celebrated Torquemada, the student of whom I have spoken. The war with the Moors had just terminated with the conquest of Granada. The conspirators persuaded the youthful royal pair to make formal application to Sixtus IV., then Pope, for the reestablishment of the Inquisition in Spain, and for the appointment of Torquemada as grand inquisitor. A bull to that effect was granted, and the principal seat of the tribunal was fixed at Seville, in the château of Triana. Torquemada aspired to be a Cardinal. Ferdinand desired to enrich the crown by the confiscation of the immense wealth of the Moors and the Jews. Thus avarice and the love of power, those fatal human passions, were the foundation of the modern Inquisition.

Torquemada lost no time in beginning his bloody work. During his first year, he burned nearly three hundred heretics in Seville alone, and two thousand more in the other cities and provinces of the kingdom. Outside of the walls of Seville he caused to be erected a stone scaffold called the *Quamadero;* at the four corners of the base were four hollow statues, representing the four great Hebrew prophets, into which the condemned were forced, when fires were kindled around them, which were kept up until their bones were reduced to ashes. It is not very many years ago that the remains of this scaffold were still visible.

The work of Torquemada was effectively seconded by Ximenes, the Prime Minister of Ferdinand and confessor of the Queen, who saw in the Holy Office the means of creating, through intimidation, a party which would, in case of conflict, support the Minister against the throne. Purely personal and political motives were enough to make him the protector of the Inquisition.

The Jews, the Moors, and even many Christians began to fly in terror from Spain. Thereupon, emigration was declared to be a crime, and the emigrants were burned in effigy. In 1492, however, the King issued a decree banishing the Jews.

In 1483 the Inquisition was made a permanent institution. The sole power over it reserved to the Pope was that of confirming or rejecting the nominations of the grand inquisitor.

The grand inquisitor presided over the supreme council, composed of five members, one of whom must be a Dominican. The fiscal procurer formulated the charges for trial; the qualificator passed theological judgment upon them; the sergeant-major or marshal of the court was called the alguazil; and there were secretaries, a receiver, and two relators. The familiars of the Inquisition were spies. Their number was beyond computation, their names were unknown; they were called familiars, because they were looked upon as members of one great family. The Inquisition was supported from the outside by two lay societies, one of which, the Brotherhood of the Cross, was composed of nobles; the other, the Holy Hermandad, of the commonalty. They constituted a sort of authorized ecclesiastical police or militia.

The jurisdiction of the Inquisition over ecclesiastical offences was unlimited; it could try some civil offences;

no religious faith was a bar to its jurisdiction. It took jurisdiction of individuals in four ways; by common fame, the reports of spies, secret delation, and open accusation. The tribunal had the right to make arrests everywhere, even in churches. Its prisoners were instantly lost to the world; their friends were forbidden to utter an inquiry as to their fate. Immured in cells till summoned to appear, when they asked of what they were accused, the cold and formal reply was, "You ought to know." Before being put to the question, they were granted three "audiences of monition," in which the arts of finesse and cajolery were exhausted, to entrap them into some admission which might be used against them or against others. At the first audience, they were threatened; at the second, seduced by promises; at the third, interrogated as to their genealogy, family history, and knowledge of theology. The pretended counsel assigned them rarely brought to the attention of the court any evidence in their favor, but did his best to coax them to make confession.

There were three grades of prisons of the Inquisition, all under one roof. The public prisons were for those not charged with any crime against the faith; the intermediate for the discipline of employees of the holy office not charged with heresy. Both of these were open to visitors. The secret dungeons were subterranean; they lay beneath the marble floor of the palace, were both dark and damp, and not a word was permitted to be spoken in them, either by the prisoners or by their jailers.

In the torture chamber, the three principal forms of coercion were by the cord, by water, and by fire. In the second of these, which has not been described, the body was extended at full length upon a frame so constructed as to bend it slightly backward and to elevate the feet above the head; the face was covered with a wet cloth, kept wet by constantly falling drops of water which had to be swallowed, in order to prevent suffocation. At the same time, the cords by which they were bound were continually drawn tighter by a tourniquet, so as to cut into the flesh until it bled. Torture by fire was both with hot irons and by slow roasting in front of flames. If a prisoner confessed, he was burned alive and his property confiscated. This torture chamber was removed from sight and hearing, and hung with black or with crimson. On the wall of the one at Nuremberg, when Howard visited it, was inscribed what he justly calls the "jingling verse:"—

"Ad mala patrata hæc sunt atra theatra parata."

A crucifix hung behind the inquisitor's seat. The executioners were masked. All the proceedings were surrounded with mystery, more deeply to impress the imagination of the ignorant.

Llorente, the historian of the Inquisition, who was its chief secretary, records that the number of its victims amounted, in the two centuries during which it lasted to 341,021, of whom 31,912 were burned alive, and 17,659 were burned in effigy, or their dead bodies exhumed and committed to the flames; for the Inquisition claimed jurisdiction beyond the tomb.

In a history of the Inquisition published at Madrid in 1598, its author, Louis de Perama, an inquisitor, traces its origin to the creation. He claimed that Adam and

Eve were the first heretics and God the first inquisitor. God was alone in the garden with Adam, when he asked him what he had done; this is the warrant for secret interrogation. Adam's punishment was threefold: exile from Eden, deprivation of his former right of property in Paradise, and loss of dominion over the brute creation; thus he justified the claim of the Inquisition to pronounce judgment of banishment, confiscation of goods, and loss of rank. That the *auto-da-fé* is a divine institution, is proved by the flood and by the rain of fire which destroyed Sodom. Inquisitors have existed in all ages; Sarah banished Hagar and Ishmael, Isaac deprived Esau of his inheritance, the Levites were the first inquisitorial council, and Jesus Christ himself caused the death of Herod.

The Emperor Napoleon abolished the Inquisition in 1808, as an infringement upon his own imperial prerogative and upon the authority of the secular courts. A graphic account of the destruction of the Inquisition at Madrid in 1809 was published in an obscure Chicago newspaper, the *Western Citizen,* by Colonel Lemanouski, a Polish officer in the Imperial Army, who was an eye-witness of the scene which he describes. The soldiers of the Inquisition made a desperate resistance, and the walls had to be battered down with the trunks of trees. An entrance having been effected, the inquisitors denied the existence of the secret torture chambers; but, on flooding the marble floor with water, a crack was discovered, through which the water ran in a stream. Repeated thrusts with bayonets in the neighborhood of this crack resulted at last in touching a concealed spring, the flying open of a marble slab, and the revelation of a stairway. In the dungeons reserved for prisoners for life many prisoners were found, of both sexes, all in a complete state of nudity, some of them reduced to a state of imbecility, and in various stages of starvation. Powder was placed under the palace, the walls and towers were thrown down, and the Inquisition of Madrid came to a perpetual end.

The Congregation of the Holy Office still exists in Rome, but, although the canon law asserts the power of inquisitors to constrain even civil magistrates to cause the statutes against heretics to be observed, and to compel the execution of sentence, the Catholic Dictionary states that "nowhere does the State assist the Church in putting down heresy; it is therefore superfluous to describe regulations controlling a jurisdiction which has lost the medium in which it could work and live."

CHAPTER VI

DAWN OF THE REACTION

THE view given, in the last chapter, of the forms of cruelty practised by mankind in dealing with military captives, slaves, and criminal offenders (between all of whom there was a great resemblance in legal status), would be incomplete without some figures tending to show also the extent of the evil. In the nature of the case, no complete or exact statement is possible. A few figures culled almost at random from various sources may be submitted, without expressing any opinion as to their trustworthiness, further than that they presumably give a truthful but inadequate idea of the recklessness of human rights displayed in past ages. Llorente's statement as to the Inquisition has been already quoted. The ancient laws of France authorized the infliction of the death penalty for more than one hundred distinct offences. A French judge, named Rémy, at Nancy, boasted that he had burned eight hundred in sixteen years, and that sixteen committed suicide in one year rather than run the risk of falling into his hands. In the first quarter of the sixteenth century, the public executioner of Nuremberg put to death eleven hundred and fifty-nine persons. In the seventeenth century, it is said, the Parliament of Bordeaux burned more than six hundred sorcerers in a single year. Seventy thousand executions took place in England during the reign of Henry VIII. These are merely sample instances.

At last the world became weary of shedding blood. It was not possible, in view of the growth of human knowledge, the progress of invention, and increased facilities for travel, to say nothing of the multiplication of books and newspapers, that the atrocities of former generations should longer be regarded with popular indifference. The old legislation pushed its blind fury to the point of confounding the innocent with the guilty. Wives and children perished with their husbands and fathers; posterity was robbed for the enrichment of titled and clerical oppressors; if a slave was guilty of theft or murder, hundreds were sometimes slain for the offence of one. Revenge stopped not with the human species; animals, and even inanimate objects, were formally accused, tried, convicted, and sentenced. Punishment assumed *post mortem* and hereditary forms. Men were executed in effigy. In its administration the grossest inequality was sanctioned by law. There was one penalty for the rich, another for the poor; one for the slave, another for the freeman; one for the noble, another for the commoner. Crimes which were known to the law were said to be ordinary; but judges could add to the list others which were extraordinary and unprovided for, in the punishment of which they had large discretionary powers.

The truth of the adage that "crime thrives upon severe penalties" is demonstrated by the experience of mankind, before the genius of Christianty and of modern science taught the lesson of greater tolerance, so imperfectly learned, that even now rash and ill-informed men often express the opinion that what is needed for the repression of crime is severer penalties;

as if we could hope ever to rival what has already been tried in this direction.

Among the distinctions recognized by European criminal law in the Middle Ages was that between the clergy and laity. By benefit of clergy is meant the exemption of priests from trial by the civil courts. The right of appeal to the ecclesiastical courts, however, existed only in case of a capital charge; but so many offences were capital, that this was equivalent to exemption from civil jurisdiction in a large majority of instances. The ordinary demanded the delivery of the clerk by the civil authorities, who at first surrendered him before trial; but later, the ordinary could take him even after trial, and he had the right to clear himself by compurgation. A jury of twelve, all of them priests, was impanelled; he took a solemn oath in their presence that he was innocent; and they solemnly swore that they believed him. This was the easy process by which he escaped punishment for his crimes, if it was not for the interest of the church that he should suffer. Originally, the evidence that he was a clergyman consisted in his tonsure and his habit; but, in an age when the only persons who knew how to read were those in holy orders, or studying for the same, the practice gradually grew up of allowing anyone who could read to plead benefit of clergy. Thus an institution than which nothing can be imagined more unfair, came, in the providence of God, or in the order of nature, to be the occasion of the overthrow of the very injustice of which it was a manifestation. Teaching letters to a prisoner by his jailer, in order to qualify him to claim benefit of clergy, was a punishable act. A man who had once been released upon this plea was not entitled to offer it a second time; and, as has been stated in order to make sure that he should not do so without being recognized, it was the custom to brand him on the fleshy part of his thumb. But an act approved in 1706 admitted all persons to benefit of clergy, upon their own application, which was the virtual repeal of this distinction.

The abolition of branding was one of the first indications of the dawn of a more humane spirit in society. It was due to the recognition of the fact that a thief branded with the letter "T" was thereby wholly debarred from all subsequent opportunity to make an honest living.

Attention has been called to the distinction between felonies and misdemeanors, the former including all capital offences. At the common law, felonies were few in number: the entire list included, probably, no more than homicide, rape, burglary, arson, larceny, robbery, and mayhem. But others were made capital, from time to time, by statute; and those thus added were made felonies "without benefit of clergy." By that was meant that persons convicted of them could not appeal to an ecclesiastical court and so escape death. The result was a great increase in the number of executions. The human mind finally revolted against such indiscriminate and useless slaughter. Magna Charta forbade the compulsory exile of any Englishman. But multitudes of prisoners under sentence of death were given the alternative, of which they hastened to take advantage, of voluntarily leaving the realm, if pardoned. Herein was the germ of English transportation.

On the other hand, the increase in the number of capital crimes rendered it certain that the severity of punishment of misdemeanors would be gradually relaxed.

Little thought had yet been given to the possibility of making simple incarceration, without torture or any form of physical suffering, serve as a penalty of crime. Prisons existed from time immemorial. They are mentioned in the Old Testament. Joseph was thrust into Potiphar's prison, Samson into that of the Philistines, and Jeremiah's dungeon into which he was let down by ropes is never to be forgotten. But the ancient prison was only a place of confinement in which men were kept waiting the final disposition to be made of them. Samson, for instance, had been blinded before his imprisonment, or in the prison, and there he was punished by making him grind corn. Ulpian, the Roman lawyer, expresses this principle in saying, "*Carcer enim ad continendos homines, non ad puniendos haberi debet.*"[1]

The famous Cretan labyrinth was a prison. It was said to have but one inconvenience and but one merit—no one could ever, unassisted, find his way out of it. The Mamertine prison was for many years the only prison in ancient Rome.[2] Afterward, a deep, dark

[1] *Carcer* is by some etymologists supposed to be a derivative of *coërcere*. Others connect it with the Hebrew *carcar*, to bury.

[2] "Felices proavorum atavos, felicia dicas
Sæcula, quæ quondam sub regibus atque tribunis
Viderunt uno contentam carcere Romam."
JUVENAL, Sat. iii.

dungeon was constructed beneath it, called the Tulliana, because it was built by Tullius.[1]

Sir James Stephen is unable to find any mention of imprisonment as a penalty in Anglo-Saxon law, though a friendless man or a stranger who could give no surety, at his first accusation, was required to go to prison "and there abide till he goes to God's ordeal." The first English prisons were merely wooden cages commonly constructed in the king's castles. The barons, however, had private prisons for offenders sentenced in the manorial courts, and the bishops had ecclesiastical prisons.

The dungeons of the Middle Ages were situated either at the top of a tower or in a cellar or subcellar. They were not separate structures, but were apartments in a castle, fortress, palace, hospital, or convent. The habit of despots is to cover up tyranny by the use of euphemisms, which is illustrated by the fact that the ancient prisons were rarely given that name, but were called by some other.

The history of famous prisons and the lives of famous prisoners fill many books. It is not possible to go very deeply into that.

The Tower of London was originally a fortified palace, erected by William I. and used as an arsenal. Except the historical reminiscences which it suggests, the most interesting thing about it to-day is the won-

[1] "Est in carcere locus quod Tullianum appellatur, ubi paullulum ascenderis ad lævam circiter duodecim pedes humi depressus. Eum muniunt undique parietes atque insuper camera lapideis fornicibus juncta sed inculta tenebris, odore fœda atque terribilis ejus facies est. In eum locum postquam demissus est Lentulus vindices rerum capitalium quibus præceptum erat laqueo gulam fregere."—SALLUST, *Catil.*, cap. 55.

derful collection of old arms and armor which it contains. It really consists of several separate structures, the White Tower, the Bloody Tower, and the like.

The Bastille was originally one of the city gates of Paris—a fortified gate, flanked by two towers. It was known as the Porte Saint Antoine. The fortress which replaced it was erected in the fourteenth century, although the last two towers of the eight of which it was composed were not completed until the middle of the sixteenth century. Hugo Aubriau was the first superintendent of construction, and he was also its first prisoner. It was made a prison of state in 1417. When the boundaries of Paris were enlarged, to include the Faubourg Saint Antoine, the Bastille ceased to be of further value as a fortress and became purely a prison. It was here that the Man with the Iron Mask was confined. The French kings in the seventeenth and eighteenth centuries were in the habit of signing letters of *cachet,* by which men and women could be sent to prison without trial and there held during the royal pleasure. Many of these letters were signed in blank and distributed to the nobles at their request—a very handy thing to have, if one wished to dispose of a troublesome friend or enemy. This prison witnessed the death of many such, forgotten by all but their nearest friends. It was captured by the mob and destroyed, July 14, 1789. The commander in charge defended it with great bravery, and wished to blow it up rather than surrender, but the Swiss guards would not let him do so. It was taken only after eight cannon had been brought to bear upon it. This was the beginning of the French Revolution. Most of the apartments were octagonal in form: there were five grades of them, the worst being underground and the next worst at the top. Some of the dungeons contained iron cages, which were looked upon then with greater horror than now. They were invented by the Bishop of Verdun, who subsequently, by an act of poetic justice, occupied one of them. The *oubliettes* (so called from the verb *oublier,* to forget, because the prisoners consigned to them were meant to be forever forgotten) had deep pits in them concealed by a trapdoor, through which a prisoner fell into mud and starved, or into water and drowned, or upon a wheel set with knives which cut him to pieces. Louis XI. is said to have killed not less than four thousand victims in these *oubliettes.*

Another famous French prison was the Conciergerie, which is still used as a prison. It was an appendage of the Palace of Paris, and its name denotes that it was the abode of the *concierge* or royal porter and doorkeeper, whose office was to keep people in as well as to keep them out. Its origin is lost in antiquity. From one of its towers was given the signal for the Massacre of Saint Bartholomew. It has twice been burned, the last time in 1776. The cell from which the ill-fated Marie Antoinette went to execution is here shown to visitors. From this prison went also the man who was the soul of the Reign of Terror, with whose own death it came to an end: Robespierre, who, strange to say, in the Convention had proposed the abolition of capital punishment, and thus allied himself to Marat, who had written a book against it.

Before being transferred to the Conciergerie, Marie

Antoinette, with Louis XVI. and their two children and the children's saintly aunt, had occupied a tower of the Temple, during their long martyrdom. This was the strongest of all the Parisian prisons. It was once the palace and treasure-house of the Templars. After their dissolution in 1312 by order of Pope Clement V., it had been turned over to the Knights of Malta, whose priory it became, on condition that the towers should be used as a prison of state, which was the case until the founding of the Bastille in 1370. It was a prison under the Directory, and under Napoleon till June, 1808; it was torn down by order of the Emperor in 1811.

For-l'Évêque (*forum episcopi*) was, as its name suggests, an episcopal or ecclesiastical prison. It was built about the year 1161, with dungeons and *oubliettes* under the towers. There was in it also a torture chamber. It was several times rebuilt, during the six or seven centuries that it was used. In 1674, after a long struggle between the Bishop and Louis XIV. over the question of secular or ecclesiastical jurisdiction, Louis seized it and converted it into a secular prison, specially devoted to the retention of prisoners *de cachet.* It ceased to be employed as a prison in 1780, and has since been destroyed.

Bicêtre, now a lunatic asylum, once the residence of a bishop, with a long and curious history of changes of owners and of functions, was, at the date of the Revolution, a mixed establishment, partly a prison, partly a hospital, partly an almshouse. From here it was that convicts were sent to the galleys. Their departure was a sight much frequented by the great, who enjoyed the spectacle. About noon, they were brought from their cells to be chained, an operation which occupied the blacksmiths until dark. Twenty-six men were attached to each chain by triangular collars riveted around their necks. The spectators, moved by compassion, made them presents of money. They lay all night upon the straw in the court of the prison, because, being chained, they could not be taken back to their cells; and in the morning they started for the coast in great wagons which held the whole twenty-six, placed in two rows of thirteen each (unlucky number!) back to back. The last convoy of this character left Bicêtre in 1835.

The word Salpêtrière, the name of another French prison, suggests saltpetre, and in truth it was so named because Louis XIII. built it for the manufacture of gunpowder, though he called it the Little Arsenal. After it had ceased to be used as an arsenal, it became for a time a hospital for beggars—a sort of mediæval wayfarers' lodge without the labor test. Louis XIV. converted it into a prison for women. On the 4th of September, 1789, a committee of the Assembly appointed to empty the prison of its inmates entered it for that purpose. The poor creatures there confined were rejoicing at the prospect of liberty, and all the more since a few were in fact set free. But presently a woman was brought before the committee, sitting as an irregular court of justice, who was branded on the shoulder with the letter "V" for *voleur* or thief. She was at once taken into the yard, where a company detailed for that purpose fell upon her and massacred her. Thirty-three women were thus murdered that day in cold blood. The last of them, who had no suspicion (as none of them had) of the fate of those who had preceded her, had dressed herself with care in the clothes she wore when she was committed—a red gown, silver buckles in her shoes, gold earrings—and, when they undertook to carry her down the stairs, she made such a desperate resistance, that she was killed on the staircase. The massacre of the inmates of the prisons of Paris by the revolutionists is one of the bloodiest pages in history. What happened here occurred at many other prisons, with added circumstances of horror.

These were a few of the famous prisons of Europe in former centuries. Others were the Castle of Spielberg, in Austria, where Frederick the Great made such fearful efforts to crush the indomitable Baron Trenck, whose escapes and varying fortunes constitute one of the most exciting romances in the annals of tyranny; the Leads of Venice; and the Seven Towers of Constantinople. In the latter there was a cell called the bloody cell, with a pit under it called the well of blood.

English literature has familiarized us with English prisons of the olden times, especially with the Marshalsea, the Fleet, and the Newgate. It was the custom of those days for every court to have a prison of its own: thus the Fleet pertained to the jurisdiction of the Star Chamber, and the Marshalsea to the King's Bench.

In the sixteenth century there began to be erected here and there houses of correction or workhouses, not punitive nor reformatory, but rather repressive in their character and purpose, designed for the detention not of criminals so much as vagabonds. They were more common on the Continent than in England.

There was in England a palace near Blackfriars called St. Bridget's Well, which was given to the city of London by Edward VI., as a lodging-house for tramps and was converted into a house of correction. It is from the corruption of this title in the mouths of the common people, that the word Bridewell now applied to a city workhouse has been evolved.

Parliament, in the reign of Elizabeth, ordained that there should be a house of correction in every county for persons described by Mr. Pike in the following words:—

> "There were the practisers of unlawful games—the forerunners of our modern skittle-sharpers, welshers, and gaming-house keepers. There were persons who 'used physiognomy, palmistry, or other abused sciences, tellers of destinies, deaths or fortunes. There were 'minstrels not belonging to any honorable person of great degree,' unlicensed buyers of rabbit-skins, sellers of aqua vitæ, petty chapmen, tinkers, pedlers, jugglers, bear wards, fencers, unlicensed players in interludes. There were begging sailors pretending losses at sea, and unable to show a license from two justices living near the place where they landed. There were Irish men and Irish women 'of the sorts aforesaid,' who lived by begging. There were hedge-breakers and petty pilferers of wood. There, too, were scholars of Oxford or Cambridge that went about begging, 'not being licensed by the chancellor or commissary.'"

Begging in old times was a licensed avocation. The example was set by the begging friars; but the privilege allowed them was gradually extended to persons not in religious orders. I quote again from Mr. Pike:—

> "Before the Norman Conquest a man who had no lord was to be accounted a thief: in the reign of Elizabeth a man who had no lord and no master was to be accounted a vagabond. In

addition to the classes already mentioned, the houses of correction were filled with 'idle laborers that would not work for the wages taxed, rated and assessed by the justicès of the peace,' and 'strong, idle persons having no land, money, or lawful occupation.'"

The gypsies, or Egyptians, as they were formerly entitled, were treated as felons; and so were all persons seen in their company.

Still more mixed was the collection of criminals, vagabonds, and unfortunates in the workhouses of the Continent. At Bruchsal, as late as the year 1750, there were gathered under one roof not only felons and misdemeanants, but lepers, lunatics, orphans and even unemployed handicraftsmen. The workhouse system, which was the middle term between the ancient and modern prison, required for its full development about a century and a half—say from 1550 to 1700. This period was marked by the creation of workhouses or houses of correction (the terms are interchangeable) in London in 1550; in Amsterdam in 1588, and in the same year a hospital in Nuremberg was changed into a spin-house; in Lübeck and Bremen in 1613; in Berne in 1615; in Hamburg about 1620; in Basle in 1667; in Vienna and Breslau in 1670; in Lüneburg in 1676; in Florence in 1677, and in Munich in 1687. Nearly all of them were in Northern Europe, and in the Germanic states. That in Munich was intended for disobedient children, frivolous and insolent men, lazy boys and girls, stupid and refractory apprentices, day laborers who shirked their work—in a word, for such as would otherwise loaf and beg, or at least do nothing useful—in order that they might be brought to a better life, or, if that was beyond hope, placed where they could not mislead and injure others. The spin-house founded by Peter Rentzel in Hamburg in 1669 deserves special mention, because, "having observed that the exposure of petty thieves and prostitutes in the pillory tended to make them worse instead of better," he built this establishment "at his own cost, to the glory of God and for the salvation of souls, where they might by labor and religious instruction be reclaimed both for time and for eternity." He thus anticipated the benevolent intentions of Pope Clement XI. in founding the hospital of St. Michael at Rome.

John Howard, in his record of his travels, has much to say of this new system. Among other things he mentions many of the occupations in which prisoners were engaged. In Holland the men were rasping log-wood in the rasp-houses; the women in the spin-houses he found carding, spinning, knitting, and weaving; all of them being set to work, as he says, upon the principle, "Make men diligent, and you will make them honest." When the invention of mills for grinding log-wood rendered this form of handwork no longer profitable, the manufacture of woollen cloth was substituted for it. Other Dutch prisoners were seen by him making fishing-nets, or sorting coffee-berries, or weaving coarse carpets, or sacks for the East India trade. In Germany the felons, called galley-slaves (though without water there could be in fact no galleys) were at work upon the streets or the fortifications, or in the chalk quarries. At Nuremberg, they polished lenses for spectacles; at Bayreuth, they polished marble. In Belgium he observed the manufacture, in the prison at Brussels, of wall-paper; in Portugal, of rope and of lace; in Spain he saw convicts burning lime. At Naples, they were making shoes. At Milan, the prison was noteworthy for the variety of trades taught: shoemaking, tailoring, blacksmithing, cabinet-work, wagon-making, wood-turning, leather-dressing, rope-spinning, nail-making, hand-painting on gauze, and many others. At Zürich, some prisoners, of the trusty sort, were hired out to private citizens by the day.

A not uncommon bas-relief placed over the entrance to a workhouse in Germany he describes, which can only be taken as an indication of the rise of the conception of a new and better use of prisons in the centuries to come. At Mayence, there was such a design, which represented a wagon drawn by two stags, two lions, and two wild boars, with an inscription to the effect that, if wild beasts can be tamed and induced to submit to the yoke, we must not despair of reclaiming the vicious and teaching them habits of industry. In a similar bas-relief at Amsterdam, tigers were substituted for stags, and the wagon was loaded with logwood.

With the creation and multiplication of workhouses, the foundation of the modern prison system was firmly laid. The motive that gave birth to them was humane; they were really a more or less unconscious protest against the undue severity with which minor offences had been pursued. It was but a step to the belief that the punishment of felonies was also excessive. It was not possible to employ prisoners in profitable labor without regular hours and a code of rules; thus was laid the basis of prison discipline. The classification of prisoners was a necessity, at their work and at other times, because of the admixture of classes, of ages and of sexes. Separate quarters had to be provided for women, for debtors, and for the sick. This led to the adoption by degrees of better structural arrangements, and prison architecture began to assume a distinct form. Imprisonment, which the writers of the first half of the seventeenth century characterized as of all known punishments the most wretched and the most injurious, a form of slavery and a living sepulchre, changed its aspect, wherever the new ideas found a congenial soil in which to take root and germinate.

It would be an injustice to human nature, however, not to recognize the fact that in all ages, even the darkest, there were voices raised in angry protest against cruelty even to the guilty, and hearts and hands which were at the service of the unfortunate, even where their misfortunes were the direct result of their own misconduct. It is a duty and a pleasure to emphasize this thought. The Church has always insisted upon the obligation to visit those in prison and to remember those in bonds as if bound with them. The Council of Orleans, in 549, declared it to be the duty of all archdeacons to visit prisoners every Sunday, regardless of their crimes. The Confraternity of Saint John the Beheaded, better known as the *Misericordia*, the origin of which is shrouded in the impenetrable mist of antiquity, the Confraternity of Saint Mary at the Cross, which was founded at the time of the plague in Italy, in 1348, and the Confraternity of Death, created at Modena, in 1372, were religious brotherhoods organized for the amelioration of the sad fate of the imprisoned and the tortured, by a variety of charitable ministrations, but chiefly by attending them on the scaffold, seeing that their dead bodies were given Christian burial, and offering masses for the repose of their souls. At first, the visitation of prisoners was almost exclusively an act of mercy to those under sentence of death, possibly because the greater part of those under arrest were in truth sent to the stake or the gallows. But when the new day dawned, of hope for the hopeless and help for the helpless, prison catechumens and chaplains were appointed, who ministered to all prisoners; they were provided with necessary medical attendance; and skilled artisans were employed to teach them the trades at which they were required to work.

With the classification of prisoners in prison came also, without much delay, the classification of prisons. Thus the first workhouses, rude and imperfect as they were, miserable as was their construction and government, yet marked the point of transition from that now obsolete system of criminal jurisprudence to one which, imperfect as it is, and much as it retains of indefensible theories, at least gives promise of something vastly better in the near future. May Heaven speed the day!

CHAPTER VII

THE REFORMATION OF THE CRIMINAL

When the reaction took place against retribution and repression, it was inevitable that the thoughts of men should turn to the reformation of the offender. There has never been a time when this duty has not been insisted upon by sages and moralists. The Hebrew prophet ascribed to the Almighty the question: "Have I any pleasure at all that the wicked should die?" Seneca said that punishment is designed to protect society by removing the offender, to reform its subjects, and to render others more obedient. Plato held that the proper end of punishment is not merely to render to the guilty their due, but at the same time to make them better. He so far anticipated the course of modern reform in his dream of an ideal as to propose the construction of three grades of prisons—one for persons under arrest, one for minor offenders, and one for great criminals. The intermediate prison he would have named *Sophronisterion,* because it was to be a place for teaching wisdom and continence. Aristotle defined punishment to be "the specific of the soul," and said that law should be "wisdom without passion." Saint Augustine, the venerable bishop of Hippo, in pleading for mercy to certain heretics, who had murdered two priests, declared that, however atrocious crime may be, it should not awaken anger and the desire for revenge, but should rather be looked upon as an inward malady which it is our duty to heal. Pope Boniface VIII. anticipated the famous dilemma of Mr. Frederick Hill, "reformation or incapacitation," in one of his edicts, in which he said that, while the prison is to be regarded as a place of detention rather than of retribution, yet the Church would not disapprove the incarceration of confessed or convicted clerical offenders for life or until they should give evidence of repentance.

But these were the utterances of individuals. They were in direct opposition to the heathen spirit; and the Christian spirit has never made more than a partial impress upon social and legislative institutions, even in so-called Christian lands. Yet it is the reformatory idea which distinguishes the penitentiary era of criminal jurisprudence.

The honor of having inaugurated that era is generally accorded to Pope Clement XI., who, when he founded the Hospital of Saint Michael, at Rome, in 1704, inscribed over the door: "For the correction and instruction of profligate youth, that they who when idle were injurious, may when taught become useful, to the State." And in the hall where the boys were at work he placed the inscription, "*Parum est coërcere improbos pœnâ nisi probos efficias disciplinâ,*" which Howard thus renders: "It is of little advantage to restrain the bad by punishment unless you render them good by discipline." This was a formal and official admission, by the highest authority, that the entire system of retribution and repression had proved a practical failure. The erection of this juvenile reformatory institution, therefore, is the landmark which divides two civilizations or two historical epochs. But Saint Michael's was not a prison pure and simple. It contained a department for two hundred orphan boys, and other departments for aged and infirm men and women, of whom there were over five hundred, while the number of criminal boys was only fifty. For the latter the plan of the institution provided sixty single cells, in three tiers, one above the other, ten cells in each row, on the two sides of a spacious hall lighted by three large windows, one at the end and one at each side. This corridor was used as a common workroom by day; in the centre hung a placard with one word, "Silence!" These were the essential features of what, a century later, was called the Auburn system.

The reformatory idea made but slight progress until the day of John Howard, whose name shines illustrious in the annals of humanity and blazes like a star upon the roll of the saints in heaven. The best biography of him is by Hepworth Dixon. He was born at Hackney, now a suburb of London, Sept. 2, 1726. The humbleness of his origin should be an encouragement to every young man possessed of the apostolic spirit, that enthusiasm for humanity which supplies the place of noble birth and even of distinguished talents, if joined to the capacity for persistent and thankless toil. Howard's father was in trade, a dissenter, and, though he retired from business on a competency, he was not what would even then be regarded as a man of large wealth. The great prison reformer was but a dull scholar: he never succeeded in acquiring much education, and to the day of his death he was unable to spell the English language correctly. Two friends assisted him in the preparation of his book on the "State of Prison." One of them reduced his mass of memoranda to order, and the other gave them the requisite literary form. While still a boy he was for a time apprenticed to a grocer. His mind was narrow, his health infirm, but he was intense, religious, firm but kind, somewhat eccentric, and, above all, single-minded and devoted. His first visit to the Continent was as a valetudinarian, seeking for health, before his first marriage. He was twice married and twice a widower. In 1755, after the death of his first wife, he sailed for Lisbon in a vessel named the Hanover, having conceived in his mind a project for the relief of the sufferers by the great earthquake in Portugal that year. The Hanover was captured by a privateer, and he was for a week a prisoner in a horrible dungeon at Brest. This was no doubt the place where the seed of interest in prisons and prisoners was sown in his philanthropic soul. For fifteen years it lay dormant. During that period he married again, built model cottages for the tenants upon his estate at Cardington, near Bedford; his only son was born (who afterward died a lunatic); he buried his second wife, with whom he had lived seven years, and made another journey for his health. Soon after his return, he was made Sheriff of Bedford and placed in charge of the jail in which a hundred years before John Bunyan had written the "Pilgrim's Progress." This was in 1773. While we were fighting for national independence, he carried on, single-handed, a war against the oppression of the guilty and the innocent, against precedent, prejudice and self-interest, in which he laid down his life.

As Sheriff of Bedford, his attention was soon drawn to the fact that prisoners who had not been indicted, whose accusers had failed to appear against them, and also some who had been acquitted, were detained for want of money to pay the fees allowed by law to the jailer and other officials. He asked the county justices of the peace to make an allowance to the jailer in lieu of fees. They demanded a precedent for charging the county with this expense. Thereupon he rode into several of the adjoining counties in search of one, but learned that the same injustice was practised there as at home; and, looking into the prisons, he witnessed scenes of sorrow which daily he burned with intenser zeal to alleviate. In order to become more thoroughly informed as to its nature and extent, he visited most of the county jails in England. Seeing in two or three of them some forlorn creatures whose aspect was more than ordinarily deplorable, he inquired why this was so, and was informed that they had recently come from the Bridewells. This furnished him a new subject for investigation, and he made a second tour of England. The worst evil he encountered was jail fever, concerning the prevalence of which he was examined at the bar of the House of Commons in March, 1774, and the speaker publicly thanked him for his evidence. From this time forward his journeys in the interest of prison reform lasted almost without intermission until his death, of the plague, Jan. 12, 1790, at Cherson, in Russia, where he is buried.

During these sixteen years of public service at his

private expense, he visited almost every known country then accessible to European travellers. The first foreign prison that he sought to inspect was the Bastille, to which he could not gain admission. He passed through an attack of jail fever in France. In Spain, he requested to be confined for a month in the prison of the Inquisition at Madrid, but was told by one of the secretaries that "None come out under three years, and not then without taking the oath of secrecy." He sailed from Smyrna to Venice in a plague-infected ship, that he might learn by personal experience all about the lazarettos, in which he felt as deep an interest as in the prisons. The vessel was attacked by Mediterranean pirates, and with his own hand Howard fired the gun which put them to flight. His death occurred on his sixth tour of the Continental prisons and hospitals, when he was on his way for the first time to Turkey and the Orient. His statue was the first that was erected in the Cathedral of Saint Paul in London.

In the history of prison reform, the two greatest names are those of Howard and Beccaria; one an Englishman, one an Italian; one a Protestant, the other a Catholic; one a commoner, the other a nobleman. Beccaria was younger than Howard by about ten years, but he launched his book against torture ten years before Howard's first publication. Beccaria was a thinker, a student, who worked among his books; and, though not a lawyer, his attack was directed against criminal law. Howard left his home and his native land, to pursue his studies in the field; his knowledge of the subject was gained by original observation, and his attack was aimed at the practical abuses in the administration of the law. Howard's personal vanity led him to suppose himself much more of a physician than he really was; but the vanity of Beccaria lay in the direction of political economy. Beccaria was seduced from the strict orthodoxy of a devout Catholic by the brilliant speculation of the Encyclopædists, and he accepted the illusive and fallacious doctrine of the social contract. Howard never swerved from the simple faith of an evangelical Christian; religious speculation had no attraction for him; and his unconscious philosophy was that of Bacon, for he followed, without knowing it, the inductive method. His spirit was less philosophic but more scientific than that of Beccaria, more patient, more laborious, more indefatigable. Beccaria had the languid, indolent temperament of a Southerner; he lacked the lifelong consecration to a single purpose which distinguished his Anglo-Saxon contemporary; he was animated more by ambition and less by a sense of duty. Both were sincere, courageous, and undaunted by danger or opposition. They had many views and sentiments in common. Both condemned the needless infliction of pain, and disapproved of the death penalty, of life imprisonment, of imprisonment for debt, and of long imprisonment awaiting trial. Both saw the utility and necessity for labor and of education for convicts. But the genius of one was destructive, his eyes were turned toward the historic past, and he dealt to a dying outrage the finishing stroke of the gladiator. The eyes of the other were prophetically directed to the future, his genius was constructive, and he laid with skill the enduring foundations upon which the modern world has erected the prison system of the nineteenth century. They never met. Howard knew of Beccaria's book, for he quotes it; whether Beccaria was aware of Howard's existence I do not know. But both were the product of the revolutionary age in which they lived, when thrones were tottering and despotism was giving way to political freedom and equality; and both were chosen instruments in the hand of God for the elevation of the race by the better recognition of universal human rights.[1]

A fitting close to this chapter will be a brief account of the evils in prison construction and management, in England, at the end of the eighteenth century.

Howard complained of the private ownership of prisons by the Lords of Manors and by the Bishops. Private pecuniary interest has always been a fruitful source of oppression, whether this interest has taken the form of blackmail or of profits upon convict labor.

[1] Beccaria was a thinker, Howard an actor; hence Howard more impressed the popular imagination, and has been more frequently idealized in a literary way, as in the following poetical panegyric:

"From realm to realm, with cross or crescent crowned,
Where'er mankind in misery are found,
O'er burning sands, deep waves, or wilds of snow,
Mild Howard journeying seeks the house of woe.
Down many a winding step to dungeons dank,
Where anguish wails aloud, and fetters clank,
To caves bestrewed with many a mould'ring bone,
And cells whose echoes only learn to groan,
Where no kind bars a whispering friend disclose,
No sunbeam enters, and no zephyr blows,
He treads, inemulous of fame or wealth,
Profuse of toil, and prodigal of health;
Leads stern-eyed Justice to the dark domains,
If not to sever, to relax their chains;
Gives to the babes the self-devoted wife,
To her fond husband liberty and life.
Onward he moves; disease and death retire;
While murmuring demons hate, they still admire."

In the Bishop of Ely's prison, the luckless captives lay upon their backs, upon the floor, with spiked iron collars around their necks, and heavy iron bars across their legs. (A similar account is given of an ancient castle in Transylvania, where, as late as 1840, prisoners were laid upon their backs every night, with their feet fast in stocks, so that they could not move.) He reprobated the toleration of the practice of garnish, footing, or chummage, as it was variously called, the nature of which can be inferred from the command given by the jailer to each new arrival, "Pay or strip." He saw, in the rules which authorized the collection of fees from prisoners, on sundry pretexts, a fruitful occasion of wrong; and he desired the abolition of the fee system and the payment of fixed salaries instead. He found men and women not only ragged but actually dying of starvation. In some Bridewells no food was furnished. The keepers, on applying to the magistrates for an order to supply it, had been silenced by the brutal answer, "Let them work or starve." In many jails food was not given to debtors, who were dependent on charity for the continuation of their existence. Prisoners who had money were required to buy supplies from the jailer, who kept a tap, where not only food but drink was sold, at an exorbitant price. The sale of beer by jailers was prohibited, under George III., but the statute was evaded by giving permission to debtors to sell. The profits of the tap, together with the fees and garnish money, enabled the jailer to pay rent to the owner of the prison, if it was a private prison. The Duke of Portland charged eighteen guineas a year for a prison of one room, with a cellar under it. The office of Warden of the Fleet was granted by Elizabeth to Sir Jeremy Whichcot and his heirs forever. Later, the patent was set aside, on the ground of its descent to persons not qualified to execute the duties of the position, and a grant of life was made of it to Baldwin Leighton. After his death, it was given to one Huggins and his son, for the term of their lives, in consideration of £5000 paid to Clarendon, the Lord Chancellor. Huggins & Son sold out to Bambridge & Corbett, whose cruelty to prisoners for the sake of extorting money from them resulted in a Parliamentary inquiry and their having to stand seven trials for murder and another for theft. The Warden of the Marshalsea rejoiced in an income of £3000 or £4000 a year. One method of extortion was to iron prisoners heavily and make them pay to have their fetters removed or lightened. The bedding furnished without charge was as scanty as the food; prisoners often lay upon the straw, which was not changed and finally wore into fine dust. Outsiders were freely admitted, even loose women to spend the night, if money could be thus made by the jailer. There was no privacy which was not bought. All mingled freely, of both sexes; and poor debtors, like the Vicar of Wakefield, had their families with them as permanent residents of an abode the atmosphere of which was as foul and obscene as any upon earth. Even in the Bridewells, the object of whose establishment seems in many instances to have been forgotten, it often happened that no occupation was provided. The time was spent in gaming, fighting, dawdling, recounting real or fancied criminal exploits, planning fresh depredations, and horse-play. A favorite amusement was the holding of a mock court.[1] The sanitary condition of the prisons was worse, if possible, than their moral state. They lacked ventilation and drainage, there was usually no water supply, they were poorly lighted, and they were abominably filthy. Some of them were badly overcrowded. In the majority, there was no medical attendance; in some there was medical care of felons, but not of debtors. Malignant typhus fever, called jail fever or ship fever, since those were the places in which it was most likely to originate, was generally prevalent. Howard affirmed that more prisoners were destroyed by this fever than were put to death by all the public executioners in the kingdom. The disease was not confined to prisons, but was propagated by contagion in the courts. The "Bloody Assize" was held in Oxford Castle in 1577. All who were present, including the Lord Chief Baron, the

[1] Mr. Buxton, in his "Inquiry" (1818) describes the trials in Newgate, as follows: "Their code is a subject of some curiosity. When any prisoner commits an offence against the community, or against an individual, he is tried. Some one, generally the oldest and most dexterous thief, is appointed judge; a towel tied in knots is hung on each side of his head, in imitation of a wig. He takes his seat, if he can find one, with all form and decorum; and to call him anything but 'my lord' is a high misdemeanor. A jury is then appointed, and regularly *sworn,* and the culprit is brought up. Unhappily, justice is not administered with quite the same integrity within the prison as without it. The most trifling bribe to the judge will secure an acquittal, but the neglect of this formality is a sure prelude to condemnation. The punishments are various; standing in the pillory is the heaviest. The criminal's head is placed between the legs of a chair, and his arms stretched out are attached to it; he then carries about this machine; but any punishment, however heinous the offence, may be commuted into a fine, to be spent in gin, for the use of the judge and jury."

A somewhat similar moot court was tolerated by the local authorities in the county jail at Denver, Colorado, some years ago, and the United States court was obliged to put an end to it.

Sheriff, and about three hundred more, died within forty hours. In 1730, at Taunton, several hundred, among whom were the Chief Baron and the Sheriff, died from jail fever contracted at the Lent Assize there held. The odor in some of the prisons that he visited was so fetid and so clinging, that he had to travel on horseback on account of it, not being able to endure the scent of his clothing in the confined atmosphere of a coach. It is greatly to his credit, that, with no medical education, he should have divined the cause of this fever and the remedy for it, and that his representations with reference to it resulted in its entire suppression in England within seven or eight years from the time that he entered upon his labors.

His strictures upon the non-residence of jailers and the infrequency of jail deliveries were also well-deserved; and he fearlessly held up to the English people the superiority in so many particulars of the Continental prisons, especially in those of cleanliness and of industrial employment of prisoners. The prisons of Holland, he said, were so clean that one would scarcely believe them to be prisons. But one advantage the English prisons could congratulate themselves upon; there was no chamber of torture in any of them.

It is evident that the reformation of prisons had to precede, in the logical and historical order, the reformation of prisoners. Probably the same is true, at the present time, of the slums in our great cities; their physical must precede their spiritual transformation.

CHAPTER VIII

THE PENNSYLVANIA AND AUBURN SYSTEMS

A PRELIMINARY hint as to prison architecture had been afforded in the cellular construction of the Hospital of Saint Michael at Rome. But the real beginning of that art, in its influence upon prison construction in our time, was the building, by Vilain XIIII., of the prison of Ghent. Vilain was a man of extraordinary capacity and character: a gentleman by birth, who was Burgomaster first of the town of Alost and afterward of the town of Ghent. A Deputy of Flanders, the Empress Maria Theresa made him a Viscount, in recognition of the great work he had done in the reform of the Flemish fiscal system.

There is a natural connection between mendicity and crime. Habitual hunger develops and fixes the criminal character. All men must recognize the similarity between the characteristics of a petty criminal and those of a vagrant. There are men who beg when they cannot steal, and who steal when they cannot beg. The beggar and the thief are alike lacking in foresight, in the power of application, in continuity of thought, in personal, moral responsibility. Both are constitutional liars. Both feel that the world owes them a living. Neither sustains any permanent relation to society at large, except one of antagonism to social order; and often, in the case of both, there is wanting any attachment to the soil.

After the breaking-up of the feudal system, mendicity was very prevalent in Europe. The Crusades

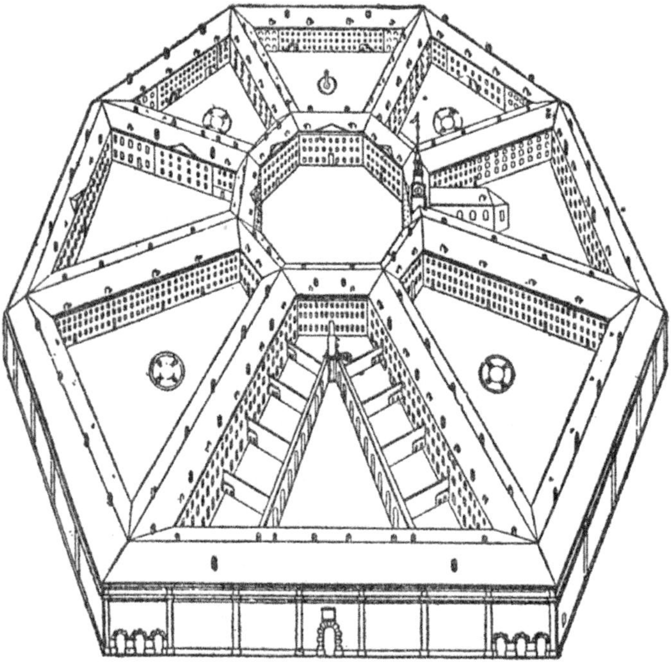

THE PRISON OF GHENT

General Perspective View (from a Model by Braemt).

helped materially to develop it. It received a fresh and mighty impulse, on the return of the Crusaders. The Church did not frown upon it; the mendicant friars were a familiar mediæval sight, and they set a bad example for imitation by men who needed not to take any vow of poverty and who would not take the vow of chastity or of obedience. At the close of the eighteenth century, Flanders was overrun by an idle and vicious horde of supposed paupers, more than half of whom were impostors, who devastated the country, cutting and burning timber, robbing the peasants, and committing depredations which called for severe chastisement. But severe measures are rarely adopted anywhere for dealing with tramps; and still more rarely are they enforced. In 1771 the Deputies of the Estates of Flanders prayed Vilain to formulate and submit for their adoption a plan of relief. In April he responded to this appeal in a memoir which bore as its motto two familiar scriptural quotations: "If any man will not work, neither let him eat," and "In the sweat of thy brow shalt thou eat bread." He suggested the erection of a *maison de force* or workhouse, the cost of which he estimated at six hundred thousand florins. This proposition was discussed by the Provincial Assembly, adopted in July, approved by the Empress of Austria in January, the necessary tax was levied, and in 1773 the prison was partially finished and occupied. The dates are important, for the period of the American Revolution was that of so many of the movements which, in their entirety, formed the beginning of prison reform.

Before submitting a drawing of the outline of this famous structure, the remark is in place at this point, that the elements of prison architecture are very simple. The first prison was a single cell, usually at the top or bottom of a tower, lighted by a narrow window if at all. It may have been square, circular or octagonal, but is fairly represented by a square, as follows:—

Two cells would look thus:—

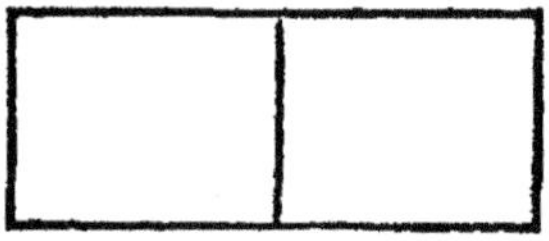

Suppose a corridor added, on one side:—

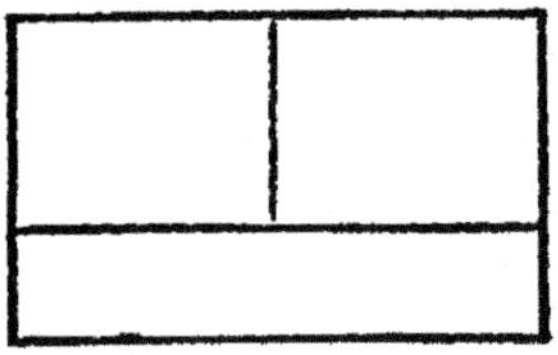

Or placed in the centre:—

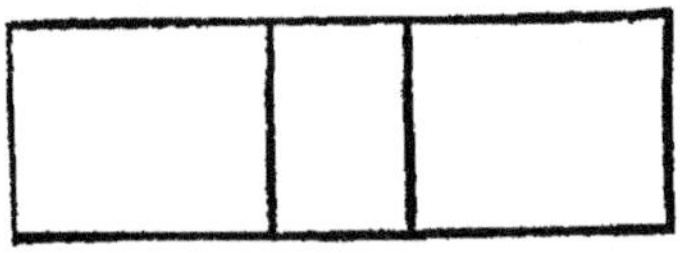

These are the elementary principles of cellular construction. There will be a corridor or there will be none; if there is a corridor, it will be in the centre or on one side. If on one side, it may be on two or three or four—the principle is the same. If the corridor is in the centre, the cells will have outside windows, and the corridor will be lighted from the roof or by one or two end windows. If the cells are in the centre, the corridors will be lighted, and the cells will not. The arrangement of cells in long rows, or in tiers

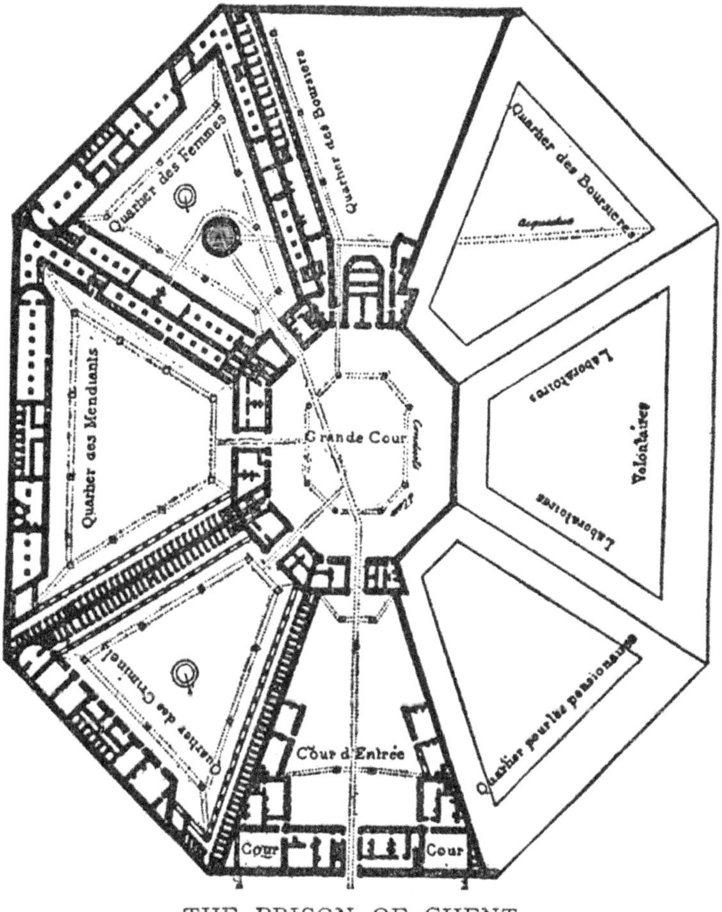

THE PRISON OF GHENT

Ground Plan (from the Memoir by Vilain xiiii).

one above the other, does not change the principle; neither does the size of the cells, nor the manner in which they are furnished.

In the Hospital of Saint Michael, at Rome, the corridor was in the centre, as at Philadelphia; but in the prison of Ghent, the cells were in the centre, and the corridors next the outer walls, as at Auburn. This is, I think, the oldest historical example of that mode of construction. Another novelty in its plan was the arrangement of the departments or wings. The outline of the building was octagonal, with eight trapezoidal courts between eight wings radiating from an octagonal centre, enclosing an octagonal central court, making nine courts in all; the wings were connected at the extremities. The stellar form given to this prison may have influenced the architecture of the penitentiary at Philadelphia,[1] and the placing of the cells that of the prison at Auburn, so affecting the direction of the movement for prison reform in two ways at once, as we shall see.

From the book in which Vilain gives an elaborate account of the prison at Ghent, its aim and spirit, its organization and rules, and the organization of labor in it (with many interesting observations on the nascent

[1] Sir Edmund F. DuCane, in "The Punishment and Prevention of Crime," following no doubt other writers in whose accuracy he supposed that he could have confidence, asserts that the radiating plan of prison construction was first adopted at Rome, in the erection of *San Michele.* That the distinguished head of the English prison system has not himself carefully studied the subject at first-hand is evident, because he expresses a doubt whether John Howard had seen *San Michele,* though the great prison reformer gives a description and partial drawings of it in his work "On the State of Prisons." Howard does not intimate that it was built on the radiating plan. Nor does Signor M. Beltrani Scalia, in his book "Sul Governo e sulla Riforma delle Carceri in Italia"; the latter, on the contrary, says that *San Michele* was "all under a single roof." What evidence is there that the plan of the Prison of Ghent was borrowed from Rome? None, so far as the author knows. If there is any, he would be glad to have his attention drawn to it.

manufactures of his day, in a state which has ever occupied an honorable preeminence as an industrial

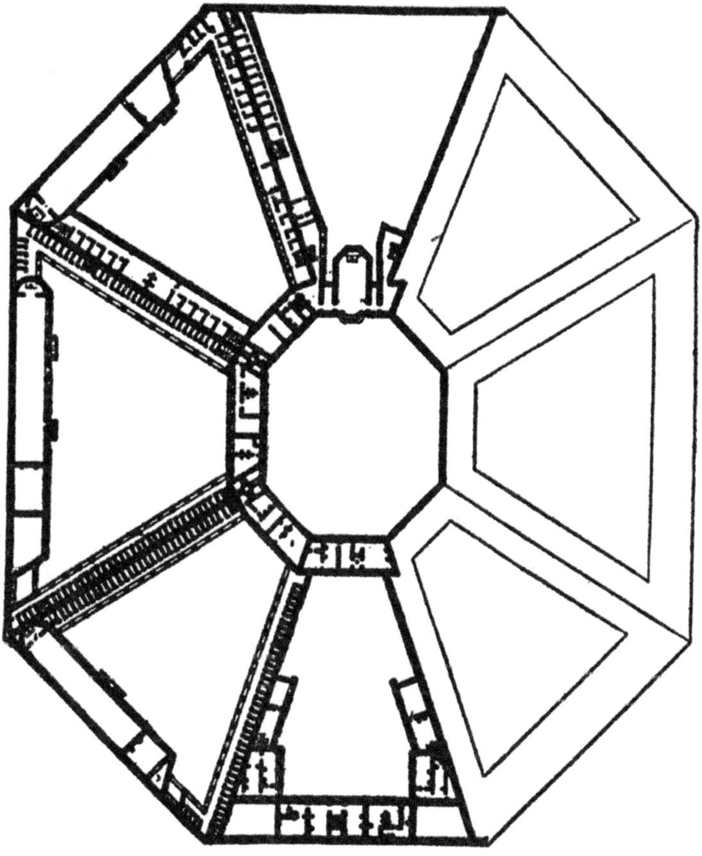

THE PRISON OF GHENT
First and Second Story Plan (from the Memoir by Vilain xiiii).

centre, which throw more or less light upon the origin of the factory system), it is clear that the architectural merits of the prison constitute its smallest claim upon our attention. It was remarkable, however, for the intelligent appreciation which it exhibited of the essential correspondence between structure and function, and for the skill with which the mutual adaptations of the two were experimentally wrought out. The design seems not to have been fully executed; one-half of it was never built.

Vilain has been justly entitled "the father of modern penitentiary science." In the first place, his prison had for its avowed aim the reformation of those committed to it. Then he believed in industry as the primary agency for reformation of the criminal character. The labor which he regarded as reformatory was not, like the English crank and treadmill and shotdrill, perfunctory physical exercise of a semi-punitive, semi-sanitary sort; nor was it, like picking oakum, as nearly unproductive as can well be imagined. Furthermore, he recognized and insisted upon the importance of trade instruction, with a view to putting the prisoner in condition to earn an honest living, when discharged. Finally, he appreciated the importance, in the selection of prison industries, of choosing, as far as practicable, such as would come least into competition with free labor on the outside. For this reason he rejected several excellent business offers to introduce certain lines of manufacture into the prison, one of which was the manufacture of tobacco, which, besides, he regarded as demoralizing to the inmates. He sought to find trades not followed in Flanders, but which, if adopted, might prove profitable to the Flemish people. In fact, there was a great diversity of avocations followed in the prison, among which may be mentioned: carding, spinning, weaving, shoemaking, tailoring, carpenter-work, and the manufacture of wool and cotton cards. To encourage prisoners to work, he allowed them a percentage of their earnings, and the opportunity to do overwork. Part of their earnings was their own, to expend in the prison; part was retained, to be given to them at their discharge, so that they might not be penniless and on that account relapse into crime. The rasping of logwood was reserved as a penal pursuit.

Few men have ever better expressed the nature and end of discipline than he, in the first of sixty-three police regulations framed for the government of prisoners: "Discipline consists in the exact execution of every order given by a superior officer, without question or remark; and in the punishment of every act of disobedience, in order to achieve what the sentiments of honor and probity are insufficient to accomplish." This he expected to secure by constant vigilance on the part of guards, and by the gradation of disciplinary punishments, according to the degree of offences and the amenability of the thoughtless or unruly to admonitions and warnings, culminating in the lash, solitary imprisonment, and the prolongation of the term of incarceration, at the rate of a week of added detention for each day in the dungeon.

Every prisoner had a cell to himself at night, the work-shops were in common, and meals were served at a common table.

He provided a resident physician and a resident chaplain.

Proper attention was paid to the classification of

prisoners. Felons were separated from misdemeanants and vagabonds, there was a distinct quarter for women, and he designed to make special provision for children also. His purpose being to combat mendicity, he allowed the commitment of children of the very poor by their parents, at a moderate charge; the directors subscribed a fund at their own expense, the interest of which was to be applied to the payment of a schoolmaster.

Commitments for grave offences were by commutation of sentence from corporal or capital punishment to simple imprisonment. Vilain objected to life sentences, as tending to produce despair and therefore insubmission; and to short sentences, as not sufficient to teach the prisoner a trade, and therefore not reformatory. He wanted a minimum sentence of at least a year. He thought it unfair to authorize by law the detention of a convict after the expiration of his term of sentence, by way of penalty for misconduct in prison, and not to admit of a reduction of sentence as a reward for good conduct; but remarked that, since the right of pardon and commutation of sentence is a royal prerogative, the prison authorities ought to be empowered and required to recommend convicts for pardon from time to time, at their discretion. This was a sort of prophetic approval of what is now known as the indeterminate sentence, or at least of our "good time" laws.

Such enlightenment in advance of his age is truly wonderful. It is not surprising that the prison at Ghent excited Howard's warm admiration. On the occasion of his third visit, in 1783, he observes:—

"I found a great alteration for the worse; the flourishing and useful manufactory destroyed; and the looms and utensils all sold, in consequence of the Emperor's too hasty attention to a petition from a few interested persons. That which ought to be the leading view in all such houses is now lost in this house."

Maria Theresa of Austria, whose noble ambition was to reform every part of the imperial administration, had been succeeded by her son, Joseph the Second, who was also a reformer, but in whose mind the pecuniary interest of court favorites or the friends of such favorites outweighed all considerations of the welfare of prisoners and of the advantage to society to be expected from their reformation. A few years later, Flanders was occupied by the French, who inaugurated the system of contract labor in this prison, so that it never fully recovered its former prestige as a reformatory institution.

Nevertheless, it was the birthplace of the new penitentiary dispensation. The first signal instance of its influence upon human thought was the publication, in 1787, of a series of letters by Jeremy Bentham, then in Russia, to a friend in England, entitled "Panopticon, or the Inspection House." The Panopticon seems to have been the joint invention of himself and his brother, who was an architect, employed to build a Russian prison (which was not erected, because of the war which just then broke out between Russia and Turkey); and the distinguished English publicists, seeing an advertisement that a house of correction was about to be erected somewhere in England, thought that a modification of the Russian plan would answer for that. A comparison of the drawings for the

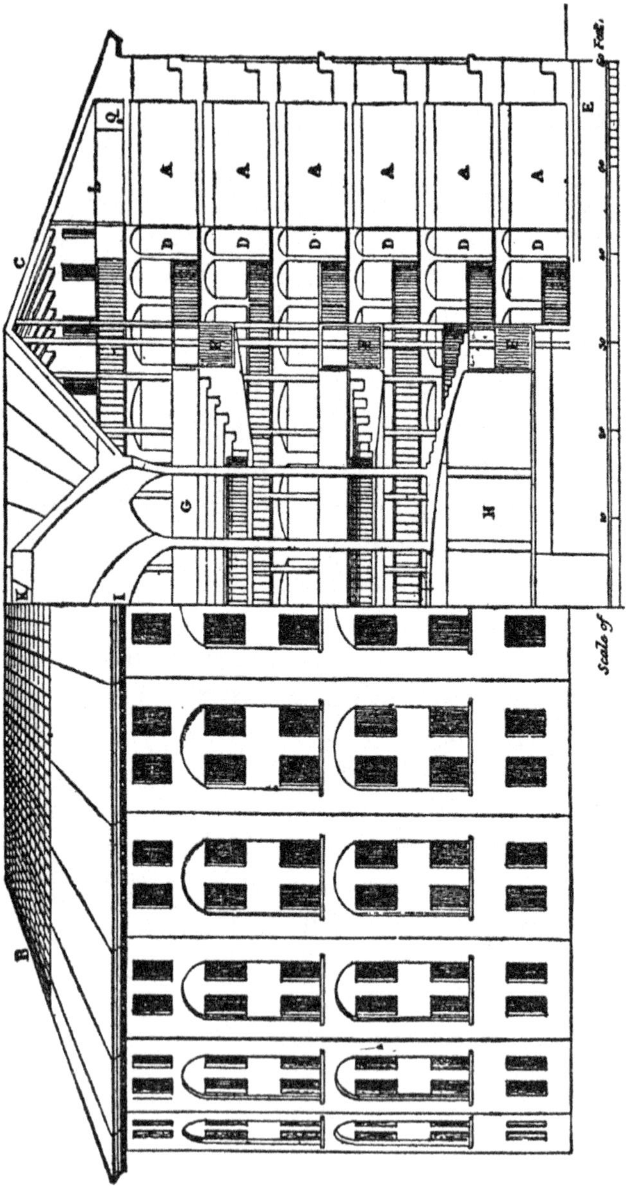
Scale of
60 Feet

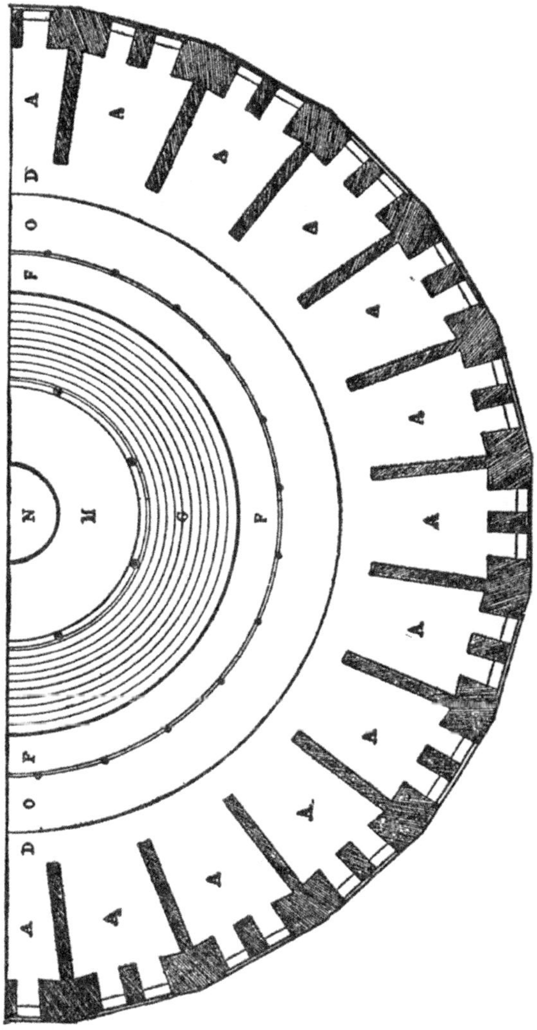

THE PANOPTICON

Jeremy Bentham's Design for a Penitentiary. (Ground Plan, Elevation and Cross Section.)

Panopticon with those for the prison of Ghent will show that they have little in common, except the general form of a circular structure. The Panopticon was to be in effect a gigantic lantern, lighted by a glass roof, with cells next the outer wall, facing the centre, and an apartment for the Inspector in the middle, so that the interior of each cell would be at all times visible from a single point. The scheme had little merit, in comparison with its defects; and, although efforts were successively made to have it adopted in Ireland, England, France, and the United States, it was everywhere rejected. A committee reported adversely upon it in New York, in 1811. It can be regarded in no other light than as one of the curiosities of prison history.

There is, however, little doubt that the design of the Eastern Penitentiary of Pennsylvania was suggested by that of the prison of Ghent.[1] Both are radiating prisons, with wings extending in various directions from a common centre, like the spokes of a wheel or the arm of a windmill. In the Philadelphia prison, the cells are next the outer walls, instead of in the centre, as at Ghent; and the connecting structures at

[1] When the idea of the penitentiary system dawned upon the world, there were no precedents by which to be directed in its development. In the matter of architectural construction, the friends of an improved prison discipline were divided between the "radiating" and the "circular" plans. The Panopticon was strictly circular; the Eastern Penitentiary at Philadelphia was strictly stellar. Between the two were the Prison of Ghent, built before either of them, and the Millbank Penitentiary, in London, built after them both. Ghent was an octagon, with eight surrounding triangles; Millbank was a hexagon, with six surrounding pentagons. The arrangement of cells, however, at Ghent, was predominantly radiating; at Millbank it was predominantly circular in principle, though not really circular in

the extremities are lacking, as if the felloes of a wheel had not yet been fitted to the spokes. The resemblance in other respects is quite striking.

William Penn, the founder of the colony which bears his name, had been a prisoner in England, because of his religious belief; he had, as a Quaker preacher, visited Holland, and had been greatly impressed by the Dutch workhouses. The denomination to which he belonged has always been noted for its benevolent spirit; the Friends condemn war and slavery and capital punishment. When Penn framed a criminal code, he reduced the number of capital crimes (which in his native country aggregated between one and two hundred) to one, namely, wilful murder. The Quakers took up the cause of prison reform, and made a religion of it. The Philadelphia Society for Relieving Distressed Prisoners was the parent of all modern prison associations. It was organized in 1776, suspended operations during the War of Independence, and was reorganized in 1787, when the war had ended, under the new title of "The Philadelphia Society for Alleviating the Miseries of Public Prisons."

There was at that time a jail in Philadelphia, called

form—each of the pentagons was, so to speak, a modified circle, that is, in the words of Mr. Holford, the prison was "so built as to enclose its courtyards within its perimeter." Archbishop Whately said, as late as 1832, "I do not think there is any one system which, in the present state of our knowledge, we are authorized to fix on as decidedly preferable to all others; it would certainly be the most modest, and I think it would also be the wisest, procedure, to give a fair trial to each of several different ones, which have been well recommended." He was not speaking of architecture, but the remark illustrates the uncertainty which prevailed as to the best course to pursue. In fact, the radiating system of construction is still highly esteemed, after trial; the circular plan has been abandoned.

the Walnut Street Jail,[1] the condition of which was wellnigh intolerable. It was a congregate prison, without discipline. The first time that any clergyman attempted to conduct religious services in the yard, the jailer, as a precaution against riot and to insure the preacher's personal safety, had a cannon brought into the yard, and placed beside it a man with a lighted match. It is possible that the evils of promiscuous association as here seen were one of the inciting causes of the advocacy by the Quakers of separate imprisonment.

The idea of strictly cellular isolation by day as well as by night was not original with them; at least it was not new in the world. The *oubliettes* and the dungeons of the Inquisition were made for solitary confinement of prisoners—but with a view to hastening their death. The Church had a motto, *Ecclesia abhorrent a sanguine,* which it construed literally, but had ways of putting its victims to death, in some instances, without the shedding of blood; for example, in the horrible dungeons, named *Vade in pace,* which means "Depart in peace." They are said to have been invented by a Prior of Saint Martin-in-the-Fields, named Matthew, and were places where men were allowed to starve to death. But the first mention of solitary incarceration as a means of bringing an offender to repentance

[1] The old jail at the corner of Third and Market Streets having become insufficient, the Legislature, in 1773, authorized the county commissioners to build a new prison at the southeast corner of Sixth and Walnut Streets, a description of which may be consulted in the *United States Gazette* for October, 1835. A new prison in Arch Street was provided for in 1803. In 1831 both the Walnut and Arch Street prisons were sold, and the Moyamensing County Prison erected instead.

(which was the Quaker idea) that I have been able to discover, is in the following extract from the posthumous works of Mabillon, a Benedictine of the Abbey of Saint Germain, in Paris, one of the most learned men of the age of Louis XIV.:—

> "Penitents might be secluded in cells like those of the Carthusian monks, and there employed in various sorts of labor. To each cell might be joined a little garden, where, at appointed hours, they might take an airing and cultivate the ground. They might, when assisting in public worship, be placed in separate stalls. Their food should be coarse, and their fasts frequent. No visitors from the outside should be admitted; but the solitude of prisoners' lives should be unbroken, except by the visits of the Superior or some person deputed by him to exhort and console them."

Other references to the separate system as an ideal are scattered along the byways of literature. The Christian Knowledge Society of London, organized in 1699, appointed a committee on prisons, of which Dr. Thomas Bray was the chairman. He made a report in 1700, followed, in 1710, by an "Essay toward the Reformation of Newgate and the Other Prisons in and about London," which is reprinted in Dixon's life of Howard. In these publications he proposed separate confinement for prisoners under sentence of death, but limited it to them. In 1740 or 1750 (different authorities give different dates) Bishop Butler preached a sermon before the Lord Mayor, in which he advocated separate cells for all prisoners; he said that he considered preparation for life even more important than preparation for death. A clergyman named Denne took the same position, in 1772, in a letter to Sir Howard Ladbrooke. Howard himself favored it, but not without reservation. He had seen separation practised in Europe. Of Holland he reports that "in most of the prisons, there are so many rooms, that each prisoner is kept separate; they never go out." In Switzerland, in every canton visited by him, felons each had a room to themselves, "that they might not tutor one another." In his chapter on permanent improvements, he expresses his own opinion:—

> "I wish to have so many small rooms or cabins, that each criminal may sleep alone. If it be difficult to prevent their being together in the daytime, they should by all means be separated at night. Solitude and silence are favorable to reflection, and may possibly lead them to repentance."

Elsewhere he has said that he wished "all prisoners to have separate rooms, for hours of thoughtfulness and reflection are necessary"; and added that he meant by day as well as by night, but yet "not absolute solitude." That he dreaded the effect of too protracted isolation is apparent from the following quotation:—

> "It should be considered by those who are ready to commit for a long term petty offenders to absolute solitude, that such a state is more than human nature can bear without the hazard of distraction or despair."

The earliest prisons built upon the separate system in England were built, one of them at least, under Howard's eye, or after consultation with him, the jail at Gloucester, built by Sir G. O. Paul, an eminent magistrate, about 1785, and opened in 1791, under a special Act of Parliament for the regulation of the Gloucestershire prisons. A separate cell for each prisoner was also provided in the jail at Horsham, built in 1779, six years before that of Gloucester, but there is no evidence that the separation of prisoners by night and by day was there enforced.

Solitary imprisonment was prescribed by the revolutionary penal code of France, adopted in 1791, in the following words:—

> "Every convict sentenced to *la gêne* shall be incarcerated alone in a light cell, and shall not be put in irons nor be branded; but he shall be interdicted from all communication, during the term of his sentence, with other convicts or with persons from the outside." [1]

This was almost a literal transcript from the Austrian code published by Joseph II. in 1785; but the Austrian original contained a clause forbidding the giving to any prisoner, at public expense, of any food other than bread and water, which was substantially equivalent to slow starvation. The purpose of the Austrian code was the immemorial wish to suppress crime by severity; but the French modification of it was animated by a half formed thought of the possibility that the prisoner might be benefited by seclusion.

Notwithstanding these various premonitions of the

[1] This reminds one of the dreadful inscription which the great and humane Edward Livingston proposed, in his "System of Penal Law for the State of Louisiana," to have inscribed on every murderer's cell: "In this cell is confined, to pass his life in solitude and sorrow, A. B., convicted of the murder of C. D.; his food is bread of the coarsest kind, his drink is water, mingled with his tears; he is dead to the world; this cell is his grave; his existence is prolonged, that he may remember his crime and repent it, and that the continuance of his punishment may deter others from the indulgence of hatred, avarice, sensuality, and the passions which led to the crime he has committed. When the Almighty, in his due time, shall exercise toward him that dispensation which he himself arrogantly and wickedly usurped toward another, his body is to be dissected, and his soul will abide that judgment which Divine Justice shall decree." There is no doubt that this was meant as an inducement to the Legislature to be content with the abolition of the death penalty, for which it was designed to be a substitute.

coming revolution in prison construction and management, the real foundation of the separate system can hardly be said to have been laid until, in April, 1790, the Legislature of Pennsylvania directed the County Commissioners of the county of Philadelphia to erect, in the yard of the Walnut Street Jail, "a suitable number of cells six feet in width, eight feet in length, and nine feet in height," which, "without unnecessary exclusion of air and light, will prevent all external communication, for the purpose of confining there the more hardened and atrocious offenders, who have been sentenced to hard labor for a term of years, or who shall be sentenced thereto by virtue of this act."

Unfortunately, no labor was provided for convicts thus separately confined. The old Quakers, sensitive as they were to the infliction of bodily pain, seem to have been unable to form in their minds an image of the fearful mental torture of solitude in idleness, as they did not foresee the inevitable affect upon the prisoner's physical and mental health.

The condition of prisons in America, previous to this beginning of prison reform, and in many places for years afterward, was about as bad as in England and elsewhere in Europe. In the State of Connecticut, there was at Simsbury,[1] for fifty years or more (1773

[1] The Simsbury copper mines were worked at intervals for about seventy years prior to the American Revolution, then abandoned and used by the Colony of Connecticut in 1773 as a permanent prison. The first prisoner was committed Dec. 2, 1773. Congress applied in 1781 for the use of these mines as a military prison, but, before the completion of the negotiation, the war closed. For a time mining was followed, but given up on account of the use made of the mining tools by the prisoners in digging out. Afterward they were employed in making wrought nails. This was the Connecticut State Prison from 1774 to 1827.

to 1827) an underground prison which was merely an abandoned mine, into which prisoners were thrust at night with their feet fast to iron bars and their bodies attached by chains around the neck to a great beam above. It was, notwithstanding this severity, a place where revelry ran riot, and at times pandemonium reigned. The cells in the Maine State Prison certainly as late as 1828 were in the form of pits, entered by a small ladder, through a grated iron door, from the top; for at that time the intention of the authorities was to make enough more cells just like them to admit of the solitary confinement of every inmate.

In 1817, the Pennsylvania Legislature authorized the construction of two penitentiaries, one in Philadelphia and the other at Pittsburgh. Both were planned by an architect to whom the world is under a permanent obligation—Edward Haviland. That at Pittsburgh was first built and occupied; the arrangement of the cells in a circle was bad, and has not been imitated. That in Philadelphia has served as a model which has been copied in all parts of the world, with variations, but preserving its main characteristics, the radiating wings, with cells next the outer walls and a corridor in the centre. The drawing shows the original design, which has been departed from and greatly injured by the construction of additional wings, for which there was really no available space; but the more recent cells are an improvement upon those first built.

The construction of individual cells was a natural and very praiseworthy reaction against the recognized evils of confinement in association, especially in idleness and without much attempt at discipline. The preamble to the Act of Parliament adopted in 1779, at the persistent instance of Blackstone, Howard and Eden (afterward Lord Auckland), defined the object of the penitentiary system to be: "to seclude the criminals from their former associates, to separate those for whom hopes might be entertained from those who were desperate, to teach them useful trades, to give them religious instruction, and to provide them with recommendation to the world and the means of obtaining an honest livelihood after the expiration of the terms of their punishment." The questions to be decided were, first, how far the classification of prisoners required to be carried, whether they should be grouped or isolated; and second, whether, if isolation were to be the rule, it should be by night only or both by day and night.

At the same time that the people of Pennsylvania were grappling with these problems, the people of New York were doing the same, but finding a different solution. There new laws and a new system had been approved in 1797, but the Auburn State Prison was not created until 1816. It was designed for separation by night only; the convicts were employed during the day in large workshops, in which, under the superintendency of Elam Lynds, formerly a captain in the army, the rule of absolute silence was enforced with unflinching sternness. Captain Lynds said that he regarded flogging as the most effective, and at the same time the most humane, of all punishments, since it did no injury to the prisoner's health and in no wise impaired his physical strength; he did not believe that a large prison could be governed without it. This be-

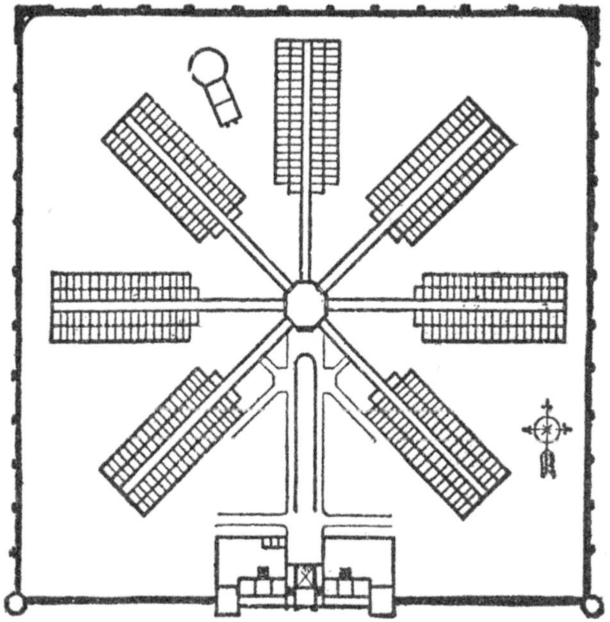

lief actuated his conduct. He had little or no faith in the possibility of reformation of convicts; he believed them all to be arrant cowards, and encouraged in the sub-officers the disposition to treat them with contempt. A tale is related of him, that, having heard that the prison barber had threatened to cut his throat, he seated himself in the chair, demanded to be shaved by him, and, at the conclusion of the ceremony, remarked to the abashed and intimidated man, "I am stronger without a weapon than you are when armed." Accordingly, corporal punishment was frequent at Auburn; it was inflicted upon the spot, the moment that a man was detected in communication with a fellow-prisoner. Captain Lynds proved to be such a successful disciplinarian, that he was selected to build the new State Prison at Sing Sing, created by act of 1825, which he did with convict labor, to the astonishment of mankind, who did not suppose such an achievement within the bounds of possibility. Now that the nature of prisoners is better understood, it is so common as to excite no remark.

Silence was, of course, so far as it could be enforced, in itself a form of separation of prisoners.

In 1819, the New York Legislature authorized and directed the building of a wing at Auburn with cells like those in the Walnut Street Jail at Philadelphia, for trying the effect of cellular isolation upon prisoners. The block, which contained eighty cells, was occupied in 1821; but the results, in the direction of insanity and impaired health, were reported to be such, that the experiment was abandoned in 1823. The men confined to it were given no work; five of them died within a year, and one of them went furiously mad.

In 1827, the Pittsburgh prison was ready for the reception of convicts. There was no provision for the employment of convicts committed to it. A committee of the Legislature of Pennsylvania, appointed in December of that year, to report whether solitary confinement should be the rule in the Eastern Penitentiary, advised the introduction into it of the Auburn system; but, under the influence of Roberts Vaux and others, the recommendation of the committee was rejected. It was determined, however, no longer to confine prisoners in solitary cells in complete idleness; and, in 1829, the legislature prescribed employment for all prisoners.

Between the Pennsylvania and Auburn systems, so-called, a fierce rivalry sprang up. On the one hand, it was insisted that the remedy for the mutual corruption engendered by contact of convicts in association can only be prevented by putting an end to all communication between them. To this it was replied that there can be no such contamination under the rule of silence. The solitary or separate system was admitted to be the more costly. Its opponents declared that it was cruel and dangerous; its friends denied the charge. Lafayette was not favorable to it, because, he said, he remembered that when he was incarcerated in the fortress of Olmutz, he was forever planning new revolutions, from which he inferred that an ordinary criminal would in like manner plan, in the solitude of his cell, fresh depredations upon society; and also because he had seen the wretched inmates of the Bastille released from their dungeons, and he knew that many of them had been reduced to a condition of complete imbecility. Edward Livingston, on the other hand, was its admirer and advocate.

The Boston Prison Society, founded in 1826, and the New York Prison Association, organized in 1845, waged a long and bitter controversy over the question at issue, with the Pennsylvania Society. The necessity for prison reform societies was, in the formative state of the penitentiary system, very great. Our forefathers, who had emigrated to secure for themselves the blessings of civil and religious freedom (to say nothing of making their fortunes in the New World) were capable of as arbitrary and cruel acts as any of their Old World oppressors, as is witnessed not only by the insane persecution in New England of old women and young girls as witches, but by various other facts less familiar. In New York, for example, negro slaves were sometimes burned alive, and, in order that they might be the longer in burning, green wood was used in making the fire. Worse even than that, they were sometimes hung up in a sort of frame and left to starve to death and their bodies to be eaten by the birds. The state of sentiment in Massachusetts may be inferred from a declaration adopted by the directors of the Massachusetts State Prison in 1815, in which the doctrine was laid down that the discipline should be as severe as the law of humanity will by any means tolerate; that a prisoner's mind requires to be reduced to a state of humiliation; that all intercourse of prisoners with each other, and still more with the outer world, ought to be suppressed; that no newspaper should be allowed inside the walls; that a prison is a world by itself, whose inhabitants are not supposed to know anything of what is passing without its orbit; that the rules should be rigidly enforced, and the smallest deviation from duty severely punished; that the punishment of a convict is incomplete, so long as his mind is not conquered—convicts should be brought to the condition of clay in the hands of the potter, subject to be moulded into any form which the government of the prison might regard as necessary. The guards were exhorted to think of the prison as a volcano filled with burning lava, which, if not restrained, would destroy both friends and foes; therefore they were always to be on their watch against a possible eruption. I dare say that the fact is almost wholly forgotten that the ancient practice of tattooing Massachusetts prisoners on the arm with the words "Massachusetts State Prison" was not abolished by law until June 12, 1829.

The example set in the Walnut Street Jail was followed here and there, in the United States, for a longer or shorter period, and with some limitations and reservations; but it failed to produce a permanent impression upon the American prison system. Solitary confinement for some proportional part of the term of sentence was authorized in Maryland in 1809, and in New Jersey in 1820. Solitary confinement as a disciplinary punishment in a State prison or penitentiary, with or without prescribed limits, is not uncommon; and the general opinion of American experts in penology is favorable to the complete isolation of prisoners under arrest and awaiting trial. But the only States,

I think, which have experimented with it, except Pennsylvania, as the principle of a prison system, are Virginia, where it can hardly be said to have had a fair trial—it was in 1822—the cells were in a basement, never warmed, where the water stood in drops upon the wall; New Jersey, which adopted it in 1833 and abandoned it in 1838, and Rhode Island, which adopted it in 1838 and abandoned it in 1842 or 1843. It was given up in the Western Penitentiary of Pennsylvania in 1869; and the model prison erected on the bank of the Ohio River, at Allegheny, is on the congregate plan.

Even at Philadelphia, the modifications introduced into the system have been great: its harsher features have been gradually eliminated, and the failure of the legislature to provide funds for the proper enlargement of the establishment has compelled a partial abandonment of the attempt to carry it out in full, according to its original intention. The number of cells is so much less than that of the convicts who occupy them, that "doubling up" was inevitable. In some instances, however, particularly in the female wing, the association of prisoners is allowed, in the cells or at work, from motives of humanity, and it is admitted to be needless and unprofitable to insist upon the absolute isolation of all convicts, of every class.

The conflict between the Pennsylvania and Auburn systems attracted the notice of the civilized world, and various European commissions crossed the Atlantic, to examine and report upon them; of these reports four are conspicuous by their thoroughness. Messrs. Beaumont and De Tocqueville came first, in 1831, at their own expense, but accredited as the representatives of the French Government. Sir William Crawford was sent here, the same year, by the English Government, which made the liberal allowance of £5,000 for his expenses, which enabled him to provide himself with many illustrative drawings and other valuable material for an elaborate report, which was the basis of the English Act of 1835. He said of the Eastern Penitentiary at Philadelphia, that it was "in fact, with some trifling difference in the arrangements, but a counterpart of the Bridewell at Glasgow,[1] which was in operation five years before the erection of this prison." In 1835, Dr. Julius was commissioned by the King of Prussia to make a similar investigation and report. At a later date, we were favored with a visit from Messrs. Demetz and Blouet, two other Frenchmen.

From America the controversy passed over into Europe, where it has not yet ceased. The two rival systems are known all over the world as the Pennsyl-

[1] Mr. J. J. Gurney, who visited the Glasgow Bridewell, Sept. 10, 1818, says of it in his "Notes" that its principle was solitary confinement—one cell for every prisoner, but that Mrs. Fry and he found two persons in every cell. "The prisoners are able to communicate with one another out of their respective cells by day and by night. As their windows look over a small plain on the public road or street, every little noise and every fresh object on the outside divert their attention from their regular duties. As we approached the prison, we observed a great majority of these windows crowded with spectators." At Aberdeen, where there was also a Bridewell, which was inspected by them, August 29, 1818, the separate system appears to have been better enforced, for Mr. Gurney says: "The several stories of this building consist respectively of a long gallery, with small but commodious and airy cells on each side. Every gallery is divided in the middle by the central stone staircase, the men prisoners being confined on one side [at one end?] of the house, the women on the other. The cells on one side of the galleries are for sleeping, those on the other for working. Every prisoner occupies a sleeping and a working cell, the Bridewell being intended only for solitary confinement."

vania and Auburn systems, though the first did not originate in Pennsylvania, nor the second in Auburn, and though neither is now followed, at least in its entirety, as conceived by its originators, either there or here. The general adoption of these distinctive names is nevertheless an admission, honorable to the American nation, that it was on the free soil of the United States, under the influence of democratic ideas, that the penitentiary system received its earliest and best expression, as a humane reaction against former tyranny and oppression in the name of criminal justice. The Pennsylvania system was better thought of abroad than at home. It was adopted in Belgium in 1838; Oscar, of Sweden, authorized its introduction into Sweden in 1840; it found its way into Denmark in 1846, and into Norway and Holland in 1851; the French Republic, in 1875, approved it for the Departmental Prisons, but the cost of the change has prevented it being fully effected. Many of the very best prisons of Europe, in these and other countries, are constructed, organized and managed on the separate system.

That it has great merits is indisputable. One of them is the ease with which a prison can be governed, when the whole force of the administration, augmented by the architectural resources of the prison, can be opposed to the will of each individual undergoing sentence. Another is the opportunity which it offers for individual discrimination between prisoners in their treatment, according to their personal needs. The absence of almost all occasion for disciplinary punishments is another; the prisoner is certain to demand work, and there is little in the way of disorder or insubordination which he can do by himself. Then, such reformatory influence as may be brought to bear upon him by the prison officers or by the authorized prison visitors is not liable to be counteracted by the public sentiment of evil associates operating in the direction of combined resistance to admonition and counsel. On his discharge, moreover, he is free from the peril of being recognized by some companion in punishment and seduced or blackmailed by him. The motive which prompted it and which sustains it is the belief that solitary reflection has a tendency to bring evil-doers to repentance for their misdeeds; that seclusion protects them from the deterioration of character resulting from evil communications in prison; and that the reformatory agencies employed for their amendment will have freer scope and a more certainly favorable issue, if resistance to such agencies is not countenanced by the precept and example of the incorrigible. These principles seem, to the advocates of the system, so self-evident, that they are dogmatically sure that nothing half so pertinent and weighty can be said on the other side.

There is, however, the objection that the prisoner, though relieved from the presence of evil companions, is not and cannot be delivered from the company of his own thoughts; that he is still free to indulge in solitary vice; that the natural effect of solitude is to enfeeble both body and mind; and that habits contracted during a long term of confinement unfit their subject for the return to the temptations of ordinary life. It is said that the solitude is not complete; that the prisoner is visited by officials of various grades.

True, but if any one will take the trouble to divide the number of prisoners by the number of officers and employees who do in fact visit convicts in their cells, he will easily satisfy himself that the number of minutes, on the average, during which the prisoner is not alone can be but small.[1] Of course, his education in the elements of knowledge is hindered by the want of class instruction. The difficulty of imparting religious instruction, and of overseeing the work of prisoners, and of giving them needed physical exercise, is enhanced. Finally, the claim that communication between prisoners is suppressed cannot be conceded. Vibrations in a solid wall separating adjoining cells are easily produced by tapping, and the signals so conveyed are readily understood and answered. It is a proverb that sound will travel wherever air can go: the pipes in every prison upon the separate plan serve, if the prisoner knows how to make use of them, as speaking tubes. All devices invented to prevent communication in one or the other of these two ways are ineffectual or too costly for adoption.[2] Prisoners seem

[1] The physician of the Eastern Penitentiary of Pennsylvania, in his report for 1850, observed: "I have heard various estimates of the amount of intercourse afforded to our prisoners, but they were all very much exaggerated. My own observation and the opinion of our most intelligent officers satisfy me that the average daily conversation of each prisoner does not exceed, if indeed it equals, ten minutes." If this was the average, how much intercourse with their fellow-men did those have who enjoyed less than the average? They probably constituted the majority. Remember, too, that this average was administered not all at one time, but in broken doses.

[2] In the solitary cells of the Russian fortress of Saint Peter and Saint Paul, the floors are covered with painted felt. The walls are also covered with felt, and at a distance of five inches from the wall is a wire netting covered with linen and with yellow paper. The object of this contrivance is to prevent communication between prisoners by knocking on the wall.

to have ways of passing word from one to another which are too subtle for detection: they know as if by instinct what the authorities in charge fancied to be an impenetrable secret. Mr. George Kennan has given an interesting account of the manner in which the Russian prisoners have developed out of the "knock" alphabet a highly ingenious cipher, the use of which even in communicating by taps upon the wall diminishes the number of taps which are necessary.[1]

[1] This is accomplished by a highly ingenious arrangement of the alphabet in five vertical columns, as shown on the following page.

Instead of counting the number of each letter from the beginning of the alphabet (which would require, for the letter T, twenty knocks),

	1	2	3	4	5
1	A	B	C	D	E
2	F	G	H	I	J
3	K	L	M	N	O
4	P	Q	R	S	T
5	U	V	W	X	Y
6	Z				

the number of the line is to be given in which the letter is found, followed by that of the column, so that, for T, four raps are followed almost immediately by five more, making nine in all—a saving of eleven, or more than half. The saving on each letter in the second line is three raps, seven for each letter in the fifth line, eleven in the fourth, fifteen in the fifth, and in the last nineteen; against which there is a loss, on each letter in the first line, of one. The total saving, therefore, is 194 out of 351 raps, which would otherwise be required in repeating the whole alphabet, or an average of 55 per cent. If the square had no other value, this would be enough to recommend it. But Mr. Kennan shows how it can be converted into a cipher almost or quite inscrutable, by using a key word, and adding its value to that of the other words in a sentence. The example which he gives is as follows, in which the keyword is "prison":

N	i	c	h	o	l	a	s	a	r	r	e	s	t	e	d
P	r	i	s	o	n	p	r	i	s	o	n	p	r	i	s
34	24	13	23	35	32	11	44	11	43	43	15	44	45	15	14
41	43	24	44	35	34	41	43	24	44	35	34	41	43	24	44
75	67	37	67	70	66	52	87	35	87	78	49	85	88	39	58

The peculiar merit which he sees in this cipher is that the

If the separate system has not proved as successful as was hoped, the same may be said of the Auburn system also. In most American prisons the rule of strict silence is not only not enforced, but no attempt is made to enforce it. Congregate prisons are, nevertheless, popular, largely because the employment of prisoners in shops, in connection with machinery operated by steam, renders their labor more profitable, whether they are at work upon contract or on public account. The reformatory influence of labor is perhaps less, where its primary purpose is the profit to be derived from it; and the presence of a prison contractor, while it relieves the warden of a responsibility always burdensome, to which he may, moreover, be unequal, and while it is recommended by its greater certainty to save to the State a part, if not the whole, of the cost of maintenance of the prison, is yet an obstacle in many ways to the establishment of a reformatory discipline. The reformatory end in view in the creation of the penitentiary system, has through the growth of a disposition to connect our prisons with the political machinery of elections, been measurably lost sight of;

same letter may at one time be represented by one number and at another by another, while the same number may at different times represent different letters. A cryptograph of this kind cannot be deciphered by any of the ordinary methods. In deciphering a communication thus disguised, the numerical equivalents of the key word are, of course, to be subtracted from the cipher numbers, and then the letters which correspond with the figures in the remainder, are to be sought in the alphabetical square.

The cipher numbers are sometimes written, sometimes called aloud, sometimes communicated by waving the hand, or alternately showing and concealing a light. If a prisoner has access to a window, communications can thus be carried on with persons at a distance—with friends outside, or with other prisoners.

All of which suggests the question, does isolation isolate?

though it has been made more prominent, since the organization of the National Prison Association and the holding of annual Prison Congresses.

The real test of the excellence of a prison system is its adaptation to develop in its subjects the power of self-control. Like the lunatic and the idiot, the criminal, if he ever had normal power of self-control, has lost it by disease or disuse. It is therefore not only necessary to restore or to create it, but to demonstrate the precise degree to which it has been developed. This the Pennsylvania system does not do, since it sedulously guards its subject from external temptation. Neither does the Auburn system accomplish this end; for it is not enough to know by observation how a man will act in prison under guidance and restraint, but we need also, before releasing the grasp of the law upon him, to know how he will act when the restraints of prison life are removed. A new system has therefore been evolved out of the failure of these two, as they were evolved out of the failures which preceded them.

The general influence which gave rise to the new or graded system may be traced to Australia, as will be shown in the next chapter.

CHAPTER IX

TRANSPORTATION AND THE PENITENTIARY SYSTEM

THE provision of Magna Charta which protects Englishmen from compulsory exile was evaded, before the abolition of the right of sanctuary, by the offer, in certain cases, of a free pardon to criminals, on condition of their abjuring the realm, and by threatening them with hanging, should they ever return. A statute passed in the thirty-fifth year of Elizabeth authorized the administration of the oath of abjuration to Roman Catholics and to Protestant dissenters; in 1596, by a similar act, rogues and vagabonds were given the same privilege of voluntarily leaving the country for their country's good. Abjuration and the right of sanctuary were abolished under James I. The Act 18, Charles II., c. 3, authorized the transportation "to any of his Majesty's dominions in North America" of felons under sentence of death: they were given their choice between hanging and transportation, so that the latter was in effect a conditional pardon. In 1718, by Act 4, George I., c. 2, the penalty (or privilege) of transportation was extended to all felons sentenced to a term of imprisonment not less than three years; to return prior to the expiration of sentence was an offence punishable by death. Contracts were made with private persons to convey the transported across the sea; the contractors and their assigns were given the right to their labor during the term of sentence, which they sold to the criminal himself or to his colonial purchaser. Sometimes he was released before he passed the mouth of the river Thames; oftener, on his arrival in Jamaica, Barbadoes, Maryland, or elsewhere on the American coast. For a time, four or five hundred were shipped to Maryland annually; others were sent to Virginia. The planters bought them. In effect, they were slaves, for a term of years; and the traffic in convicts was a form of competition with the African slave-trade. Reputable American colonists freely expressed their disgust with the system, but it suited the Mother Country, and the practice only ceased with the War of the American Revolution. When this outlet for English rogues was forcibly stopped, the number of convicts in England increased so rapidly as to constitute for twelve years a serious embarrassment to the Government, which had not prisons enough to hold them. The surplus convict population was therefore confined in hulks, of which more will be said by and by. Not knowing what to do, the Government made an effort to establish a penal colony at Sierra Leone. In consequence of the mortality resulting from the intense heat; this experiment proved a failure and had to be abandoned. Thus the American War was the unexpected occasion of the birth of the penitentiary system, and of modern prison reform, as the sequence of the discussion in England to which the embarrassments growing out of that war gave rise.

The voyages of Captain Cook, in 1770, 1773 and 1777 (in all of which he visited Australia, formerly called New Holland), attracted the attention of the

English Government to that quarter of the globe. Europe was distracted by the events which preceded the French Revolution, and had its eyes turned elsewhere. England profited by this circumstance, and took possession of a new world.

By an order in council, dated Dec. 6, 1786, Commodore Alfred Phillip was appointed Governor of New South Wales. Eleven vessels, two of them ships of war, were loaded with seven hundred and fifty-seven convicts (part of whom were women), a limited number of troops, provisions and other necessaries, and finally set sail from Spithead for Australia, May 13, 1787.

The voyage lasted eight long months; the emigrants disembarked January 18, 1788, at Botany Bay—a ridiculous misnomer, since the place proved to be a desert. Leaving there a few of the sick, Commodore Phillip pushed toward the north and landed, a week later, at Port Jackson, where the foundations were laid of the now flourishing city of Sydney. Eleven of the colonists, with their wives, under the guard of two soldiers, settled on Norfolk Island, a veritable Eden, afterward famous as a hell on earth.

By the close of the year, the provisions on hand began to fail; no fresh supplies were received from the Mother Country; scurvy broke out; and the settlers suffered both from famine and pestilence. Even the natives were afflicted with small-pox, a disease of which they had previously no knowledge, but which the English attributed to contagion from a French sailor. To the other troubles of the colonists were added hostilities on the part of the aborigines. Within twenty months of the first landing, out of eight or nine hundred souls, one hundred and fifteen were already dead. No relief came until the third of June, 1790, when a vessel arrived, with some provisions and a cargo of women, which was soon followed by two more; but several vessels with supplies were lost at sea.

The task assigned to Commodore Phillip was no easy one. He set himself with all his might to organize an element of honesty in the midst of abounding rascality and profligacy, and to teach his men to become self-supporting, as well as in a degree self-governing. His authority was greatly augmented by the bestowal upon him by the Crown of the right of conditional pardon. But the moment arrived, when the terms of sentence of the transported convicts began to expire; a terrible moment for him and for the colony. There was nothing for them to do, and no place to which they could go. He offered them concessions of land, employment, government aid, and warned them that the alternative would be a return to England at their own cost. The majority spurned his offers. He could neither imprison them, nor attach them to the soil as free men. They returned home as best they could, as seamen before the mast or as stowaways; any way to get back to their former haunts, and there resume a life of crime. To add to his perplexities, many unconvicted emigrants (chiefly Irish) arrived in search of an easy fortune in the new Eldorado, as they supposed it to be, most of whom landed in a state of destitution. A glamour of romance surrounded new countries, a century ago, which was enhanced by such books as Paul and Virginia, that idyl of love and innocence in the tropics. Then he had tremendous difficulties to encounter, in consequence of the overwhelming preponderance of the male sex. With the dawn of commerce, ardent spirits were smuggled into the settlement; enforced abstinence had aggravated the appetite for drink; what could one expect? In short, by the end of 1792, Commodore Phillip was exhausted, and he applied to be relieved of a responsibility which was beyond the powers of any living man.

He was succeeded, provisionally, for a year and a half, by Major Grose, the Lieutenant Governor, under whom originated the system of hiring convicts to free colonists, also the breeding of live stock; the latter was largely due to the exertions of an officer named McArthur.

The Government then sent out Captain Hunter. When he arrived, the most flourishing business in the colony was the distillation and sale of liquor, which could not be suppressed; it was therefore authorized and the privilege conferred upon favored individuals. The convicts had, too, in some unknown way, managed to arm themselves, but were held in check by an armed police composed of convicts who were well disposed. A census, taken Sept. 1, 1796, showed that there were then 361 self-supporting convicts, 3,638 who were not self-sustaining, and that nearly a thousand of the more turbulent and dangerous were on Norfolk Island. The fact that convicts will not become colonists, until all hope of a return to the land from which they came is extinguished within them, became more and more evident; and the presence of those whose terms of sentence had expired, besides being a pecuniary burden, was a constant menace to social order and security. By the year 1800, the necessity for a prison was so urgent, that private and voluntary subscriptions of money were freely made, to defray the cost of its construction.

Captain King, the Commandant of Norfolk Island, followed Captain Hunter. One of his first acts was to found an orphan asylum for girls, eighteen miles from Sydney, who were there to be trained for wives, married off, and provided with homesteads at the public expense. In 1804, he started a settlement, under Colonel Collins (in Van Diemen's Land, now Tasmania, then recently discovered), and founded Hobart Town. Norfolk Island had become such a nest of brigands, that an attempt was made to break it up, by the offer of free transportation to the new penal colony, and a double concession of land; but the majority preferred to remain where they were.

Captain Bligh, who succeeded King in 1806, was a tyrant; the colony rose against him and held him a prisoner in his own house, until he could be sent to England.

Colonel Macquarie, the next Governor, was an able and popular ruler, who began his administration by appointing an ex-convict to a seat upon the bench. The number of convicts who had then been transported to Australia, during the twenty years which had elapsed since the landing of Commodore Phillip, was 13,000 men and 3,265 women, of whom about 5,500 had died, leaving a population of 10,000 or more. The number of children born to them was about 9,000. Macquarie founded a bank. He secured gratuitous passage from

England of the families of convicts, and the sending of young girls who professed penitence from female reformatories at home to be married in Australia. His reign lasted for twelve years, but it was embittered by attacks made upon him in Parliament, which led to an investigation, resulting in nothing except the division of Australian society into two hostile factions, the "emancipists" and the "exclusionists"; the former wished to give the convicts a voice in the Government, but the latter were radically opposed to convict colonies.

This division of feeling, which was very marked under General Brisbane, was the first symptom of the ultimate failure of the entire system. The adaptation of Australia to sheep husbandry and the growing of wool attracted English free settlers. Brisbane, by concessions in land, induced them to assume the charge and maintenance of convicts, and this gave rise to the troublesome and dangerous system of assignments, which closely resembled the lessee system now in vogue in some of the Southern States of the American Union. It was the cause of immense irritation in the colonies. The parties assigned to a planter were known as a "clearing gang." The money paid for their labor was paid to the Government. Since a higher price could be obtained for the better class of convicts as mechanics, only the worst of them went to the clearings and the sheep farms. Without following the history of the successive colonial administrations in detail, it is enough to say that in 1837, at a time when the English Government was in love with a novelty recently imported from America—the cellular or separate system of imprisonment, a select Parliamentary Committee, which included Lord John Russell and Sir Robert Peel, was appointed to inquire into the justice of the complaints made by the colonists. The upshot of this investigation was the adoption of a new system, that of probation.

At first, the period of probation was served in Australia. The convict, on his arrival, was placed in a probation gang, and employed in felling timber or in other public work. These gangs worked in chains, lived in barracks, and moved about from place to place. From the probation gang the prisoner rose by good conduct to a state of comparative freedom, in which he worked for private individuals, but the Government appropriated the money paid for his services. In Van Diemen's Land, there were three grades or classes of convicts, between the probation gang and conditional liberation on ticket-of-leave; and each prisoner passed through all of them in succession. The ticket-of-leave was followed by a complete pardon, but, by the Act of 1847, the term of probation was ordered to be served in England; at its expiration, the criminal was transported; on his arrival in Australia, he was given a ticket-of-leave and was at liberty to hire himself to a free settler. Thus for assignment was substituted freedom of contract.

It would be foreign to our immediate purpose, to trace the history of Australian transportation farther than is necessary to show its connection with the development of the prison system, first in England, then in Ireland, and at last in the United States. The experiment finally broke down, as it was inevitable from the beginning that it would. The difficulties in the way of success were chiefly three: (1) the inequality of the sexes; (2) the want of work for discharged prisoners in an unsettled country, where there are no employers; and (3) the dissensions which arose, after the advent of innocent settlers in numbers sufficient to enable them to demand that no more convicts be sent into the country. Besides, the accompaniments of this form of punishment were truly horrible. On the convict ships, the discipline was much the same as upon a slaver; men and women, separately chained in pairs, were imprisoned in the hold, where blasphemy and obscenity reigned, with little or no effort to put a stop to them. Ship-fever was common and fatal; in a ship which sailed in 1799, with three hundred convicts, one hundred and one died on the voyage. On land, the difficulty of enforcing discipline was the occasion of great brutality; the main reliance for order was the lash, and in 1838, with 16,000 convicts, the number of floggings administered was 160,000, or an average of ten to each man. From 1793 to 1836, the death-rate among the transported was forty per cent, but among the free colonists only five per cent.[1]

Transportation to New South Wales was suspended in 1840. Mr. Gladstone suspended all transportation, during 1847 and part of 1848. Just at this crisis, gold

[1] "Sir William Molesworth's committee of 1837-8, after a laborious investigation, concluded their report by condemning the punishment of transportation, as being unequal, without terror to the criminal class, corrupting to both convicts and colonists, and extravagant in point of expense. This committee recommended the institution of penitentiaries, at home and abroad, in place of it. These resolutions, together with the report of the Duke of Richmond's committee in the preceding year, produced a great effect upon public opinion, and the whole subject came seriously under the consideration of the Government."—Sir Joshua Jebb, at the Social Science Congress, London, 1862.

was discovered, in 1850, in New South Wales and Victoria. The Government had agreed to send out as many free colonists as convicts. Western Australia had been erected into a new penal colony; but the free colonists were flocking to the gold fields. With the passage of the Act of 1857, the word transportation disappeared from the statutes. The thing itself lasted, under the name of probation, until 1867, when the last shipload of convicts sailed for the antipodes, thus bringing to an end an experiment which lasted for precisely eighty years, and had at last to be abandoned.[1]

A word in passing as to French and Russian transportation will divert us but a moment from the course of the argument.

France made an unsuccessful attempt to establish transportation, about a hundred years ago. By a provision of the penal code of 1791, criminals convicted a second time were ordered to be transported for life. By an act of the 24th Vendémiaire, in the year II., the Convention extended this order to include vagrants; and by the law of the 11th Brumaire, in the same year, the island of Madagascar was designated as the site of the proposed penal colony. The naval war between

[1] The convict life of Australia and the effect of the brutalities practised by some of those to whom the administration of the transportation system was there confided are well described in a work of fiction, "For the Term of His Natural Life," by Marcus Clarke, which occupies in Australian literature a place somewhat analogous to that of "Uncle Tom's Cabin" in our own. It has been dramatized, and the play founded upon it is a stock piece, which can be put upon the boards at Sydney in any dull theatrical season. The warden of an American penitentiary, after reading this novel, purchased a number of copies for the prison library, with the double motive, as may be supposed, of contrasting his own mild but firm discipline with a harsher system, and of explaining his motive in adopting it, which was not moral weakness, but the reverse.

France and England prevented the execution of this design. In 1810, the project having remained in abeyance, the Code Napoléon abrogated the former code and so put an end to the project. In 1851, it was revived, during the reign of terror that succeeded the *coup d'état* of December 2, and by an unconstitutional ministerial decree, transportation was established. The decree named Guiana and Algiers as colonies to which prisoners might be sent; but it was modified, the year following, so as to apply only to Guiana. In May, 1854, an act legalizing transportation was passed, and this penalty was substituted for hard labor in the *bagnes*, which were suppressed, though that at Toulon continued to exist, until nearly twenty years later, as a depot for convicts awaiting passage across the sea. New Caledonia, an island in the South Pacific Ocean, about seven hundred miles east of Australia, was made a penal colony in 1863, at first merely as an experiment. Guiana and New Caledonia are now the only French penal settlements, though some military prisoners are still sent to Algiers.

The history of the attempt to colonize Guiana is inexpressibly sad. The country lies too near the equator, to be inhabited by Europeans; the coast is marshy, the temperature always high, and rain falls one hundred and eighty days in the year. It is devastated by yellow fever (which is said, however, not to be epidemic), by marsh fevers, by dysentery, and by a fatal anæmia. In face of the depressing climate, marriages tend to become sterile. Count d'Haussonville has reported that, during the first period in the history of this colony, the average mortality was twenty-five per cent., and at some places it reached thirty-two per cent. In consequence of the terrible mortality, the Government, in 1867, relinquished the purpose to send European convicts thither, and Guiana is now reserved for negro convicts sentenced by the courts of Guiana, Martinique and Guadeloupe, and for Arabs shipped from Algiers.

The first shipload of two hundred and fifty convicts sailed from Toulon for New Caledonia, Jan. 2, 1864, and arrived in the roadstead of Nouméa on the 9th of May, after a voyage lasting a little more than three months. Nouméa is the seat of government. The prisoners are divided into four grades. They disembark on the island of Nou, which presents from the water the appearance of a great manufacturing establishment, with its workshops, its tall chimney, and its prison barracks, built of stone, in which the men sleep, in groups of fifty to each barrack. The most incorrigible are here. The moral atmosphere of this island is identical with that of the old *bagne* at Toulon, of unsavory memory, which has in effect been removed bodily to Oceanica. From Nou they are conveyed by the "penitentiary flotilla,"—a tow of barges drawn by a wheezy steam-launch,—to Nouméa, which is a beautiful port, but destitute of easy means of entry, without wharves or lighthouses, much less fortifications, the streets of which are said to be open ditches. From Nouméa they are sent to the camp of Montravel, and given a ten days' rest from the fatigue of the voyage. Thence they are distributed to various points to work; only, as M. Denis, formerly assistant director of the colony, dryly remarks, they need not work unless they choose, for they cannot be punished for not working.

The lighter punishments they do not fear; and although the law authorizes their confinement in a dungeon, the architect of the prison quarters on the island of Nou kindly omitted to provide any dungeon. New Caledonia consists of a wooded mountain range, of volcanic origin, pushing its head above the level of the sea to a height, in some places, of eight thousand feet. The greater part of the surface is rocky; here and there are plateaus of rock covered with a few inches of soil. The celebrated farm of Bourail, the pride of the colony, produced, in 1880, with three hundred farm hands and one hundred factory hands three and a half tons of sugar, while the annual product of the farm of Koe brings forty thousand dollars less than its cost.

French transportation is sustained by two powerful motives, the desire to be rid of dangerous criminals, and the wish to found colonies. But the difficulties encountered have proved to be the same as in Australia, with some others superadded. There is the initial difficulty of determining what class of criminals shall be transported, and at what stage of their punishment and for how long a period. Then arise legal questions as to the character of this penalty. What is it? an original sentence, a supplemental sentence, or a commutation sentence? If transportation is to follow imprisonment, where shall the preliminary term of incarceration be served? In the colony or in the Mother Country? Another vexed question. There is also the difficulty of supervision of criminals at so great a distance from the home office, to say nothing of the increased expense of maintaining and guarding them.

How are they to be prevented from escaping and returning home, or from leading the life of outlaws in the uninhabited portions of the colony? Either the convicts must be surrounded by free population made up of honest emigrants, which will in time absorb them, and these honest citizens rebel against the practice of thrusting upon them convicts as associates; or, if not so surrounded, the convict population preys upon itself and becomes a moral cesspool. In the absence of free settlers, the Government is put to great expense for the repression of crime and the relief of destitution among the transports whose term of service has expired.

The earliest mention of transportation in the penal laws of Russia was in 1648, when it was regarded less as a punishment than as a means of getting rid of crippled and mutilated criminals. Mr. George Kennan says:—

"The amelioration, however, of the Russian criminal code, which began in the latter part of the seventeenth century, and the progressive development of Siberia itself gradually brought about a change in the view taken of Siberian exile. Instead of regarding it, as before, as a means of getting rid of disabled criminals, the Government began to look upon it as a means of populating and developing a new and promising part of its Asiatic territory."

And again:—

"In the eighteenth century, the great mineral and agricultural resources of Siberia began to attract to it the serious and earnest attention of the Russian Government. The discovery of the Daurski silver mines, and the rich mines of Nertchinsk in the territory of the Trans-Baikal, created a sudden demand for labor, which led the Government to promulgate a new series of *ukazes* providing for the transportation thither of convicts from the Russian prisons. In 1762, permission was given to all individuals and corporations owning serfs, to hand the latter over to the local authorities for banishment to Siberia, whenever they thought they had good reason for so doing. With the abolition of capital punishment in 1753, all criminals that, under the old law, would have been put to death, were condemned to perpetual exile in Siberia, with hard labor."

The exiles may be divided into three groups: (1) those sentenced by a court, of whom nearly all are criminals, who must remain in Siberia for life; (2) those banished by administrative process, without trial; (3) voluntary exiles, comprising members of the families of the banished. Of those banished by order of the Minister of the Interior, two-thirds are sent away at the request of the *mir* or village community to which they belong, and are simply vagabonds or discharged misdemeanants. The political prisoners, of whom the number exiled annually is almost insignificant, are not separated from the rest, in the above classification.

Mr. De Windt says:—

"There are two kinds of criminal prisoners in Siberia, namely, those who have forfeited all civil rights, and those who, though undergoing long terms of penal servitude, have retained them. An exile of the first category is, from the date of his sentence, practically dead to the world. He can never hope to return to Europe, his property goes to his heirs, he loses everything he has, even to his wife and name; for the former is at liberty to remarry, while the latter, as a legal signature, is worthless. This class is distinguished by the head being half-shaven. The second-grade convicts lose no family or property rights, but are destined, their imprisonment over, for colonization. Of this class, many find their way back to European Russia, and the majority serve but a short term of penal servitude, though their sentence be a severe one. If well conducted, they are generally permitted to live outside the prison with their families, earning their own livelihood, but devoting a portion of their time to Government work. Many of the women become domestic servants."

The number banished each year, which used to average about eighteen thousand, has declined of late, and is now less than fifteen thousand. Many ameliorations in the lot of the exiles have also been brought about. The following account of the route by which they arrive at their destination is taken from De Windt:—

"The Great Forwarding Prison of Moscow forms the rendezvous whence, in summer, gangs of about seven hundred exiles each are despatched two or three times a week by rail to Nijni-Nóvgorod. Here they are embarked upon prison barges and towed by steamer to Perm. From Perm well-appointed and specially built railway cars convey them across the Ourals (mountains only in name) to Tiumén, and from Tiumén a river journey of about nine days (upon similar barges to those aforementioned) lands them at Tomsk. At Tomsk the march (for those sentenced to remote districts) commences. Many, however, convicted of minor offences, are landed at Tobolsk, Sourgout, or other settlements far nearer Europe. From Tomsk the great post road (the only one) leads to Irkútsk. Two days beyond the latter city lies Lake Baikál, across which prisoners are conveyed in large wooden hulks, towed, as on the Obi, by cargo steamers. The post road is then taken once more, and three or four weeks later, according to circumstances, the mines of Siberia (Kará and Nertchinsk) are reached. The voyage from Moscow to the latter is usually made by ordinary travellers in a little under three months; but the time varies considerably with prison convoys, who may be detained by sickness, floods, impassable rivers, etc. No travelling is done in winter."

The road is lined with stations called *étapes,* built of logs or of planks, for the accommodation of prisoners *en route.* They have large chambers with double rows of sleeping platforms through the centre of each, and closely resemble the barracks[1] in which leased pris-

[1] "In Mr. George Kennan's celebrated papers upon the Russian exile system, he fully describes the *'kameras'* or cell-houses in use in Siberia, and his articles are accompanied by numerous illustrations. I will venture the assertion that, if any Floridian con-

oners are so often housed in the Southern States of the American Union. They are not large enough to furnish proper care of so many convicts as frequently occupy them for the night, and are at times badly overcrowded. It is easy to believe that their sanitary condition is not always satisfactory.

The evils of the exile system are well known to the Russian officials and have been freely commented upon by them. Count Sollohub declared himself "an implacable enemy of transportation," and said that in Siberia "recidivism exists perpetually, on a colossal scale;" it was his intention to have given to the public the official information in his possession upon this subject; but the time never came when he thought it expedient to carry out this purpose. The report of Governor-General Anúchin to the Emperor, in 1880, on the state of

vict was shown these pictures without the accompanying text, he would be prepared to swear that they were ruins of the camp in this State. It is not merely a slight resemblance, nor even a marked resemblance, but the two are absolutely identical in every essential detail. The main difference is that there is no building-chain used in the Siberian cell-houses, the prisoners being given the liberty of the room, after they are locked in. The sleeping platforms, called '*nares*' in Russia, and those in use here are exactly alike; such scanty arrangements as exist for personal cleanliness are similar, and the general arrangement and construction of the building and the stockade are the same. The lowest order of Russian prisoners are fastened with stride and waist chains exactly like those used in Florida, and there is a coincidence of little details that is perfectly amazing to one familiar with both systems. Mr. Kennan states that, when he visited one of the *kameras,* he was horrified to observe that the whitewashed walls were stained a dusky red for some distance above the sleeping platforms, and was told that the stain was made by the prisoners, who crushed there the innumerable vermin that infested their beds. Mr. Kennan need not have gone so far away from home. In summer time these insect pests are almost impossible to exterminate, and it takes only a few weeks for the convicts at the camps to paint a dado on the walls exactly similar to that which Mr. Kennan observed."—"The American Siberia," by J. C. Powell, Captain of the Florida Convict Camp.

affairs in Eastern Siberia, as quoted by Mr. Kennan, proves that the Australian experience has been partially duplicated there. Russian convicts are sentenced to imprisonment with hard labor, or to forced colonization without labor. The latter are, upon their arrival at the place of their enrolment, given their entire freedom and expected to maintain themselves.

"Only the least spoiled part of them, and those accustomed to work, establish themselves in the places to which they are assigned, or seek employment in the gold placers. The rest abandon their places of enrolment and wander about the country, giving themselves up to laziness, and imposing themselves as a heavy burden upon the local population, at whose expense they are fed. The influence of these exiles upon the people of the country is very pernicious, since they carry into the villages and towns the seeds of depravity. As the Siberian population grows more and more prosperous, it manifestly feels more and more the heavy burden of these criminal colonists, and submits to their presence only as to an evil that is inevitable, protesting loudly, however, in the meantime, against such an order of things."

Two of the greatest difficulties experienced by the Government are the impossibility of adequate supervision, so that at Kará very nearly ten per cent. of the prisoners at work in the mines escaped in one year, and the lack of sufficient facilities for the industrial employment of convicts, so that more than half of them are idle.

Since 1869, the island of Sághalin, in the gulf of Tartary, has been used as a penal colony. Prince Krapotkine describes it as a spot unsurpassed in desolation except by Nova Zembla and New Siberia. This island is something less than seven hundred miles in length, and one hundred and fifty miles in extreme width, with coal mines and some arable land of poor quality. The aboriginal population, a tribe of savage hunters and fishermen, numbers five thousand. The country is "shrouded, summer and winter, by dense fogs, the sun is seldom seen, and even in the month of June snow lies upon the hills, and the ground is frozen two feet deep." To the extent that this barren region is made a seat of penal servitude, Siberia will be freed from the presence of the undesirable class of colonists, but at what a cost to the victims of the hateful system!

Alaska has sometimes been talked about as a desirable penal colony for the United States. But, apart from the warning contained in the experience of other nations there are reasons founded in our political system why the establishment of such a colony would be impossible. In America crime is a local affair, since every State has its own code; the only federal offences are offences against the Federal Government, or offences committed upon federal territory. The Federal Government would not have enough prisoners of its own to render it worth while to transport them, while the States have no jurisdiction over Alaska, and could not send their prisoners there, even if they wished.

After this digression, we return to the question of the influence of Australian experience upon the course of prison evolution in England.

When the American War of Independence closed the colonial outlet for felons (of whom Mr. Eden estimated that England sent abroad one thousand a year), Parliament, in 1779, directed that the county Bridewells should be enlarged, which, however, the local justices neglected to do, and proposed the erection of penitentiaries on the separate system, but with labor.

As a measure of purely temporary relief, two old hulks at Woolwich were converted into prisons, though they were never so called, or treated as such in any statute; other hulks were afterward provided, at other royal dockyards. These hulks were not adapted to occupation by convicts, and they became not only death-traps, by reason of their unsanitary condition and the prevalence in them of typhus fever, but cess-pools of moral contagion. They were leased out to a contractor, at a fixed price per head for prisoners committed to them, and the contractor was made overseer, so that his accountability must have been very slight, and the opportunity for abuses to grow up was proportionally great. The hulks were in use in England until 1857, and at Gibraltar until 1875.

In consequence of the inadequate accommodation which they supplied, the erection of Millbank prison, for twelve hundred prisoners, was determined upon in 1812.[1] It was begun in 1813, opened in 1816, but not completed before 1821, and cost over $2,000,000. It contained provision both for separate and for associated treatment of convicts, in two stages, beginning with the solitary cell; the second stage was abolished

[1] An Act authorizing the construction of a Penitentiary had been agreed to in 1779 (19 George III., c. 74); a site was purchased in Sept., 1782; but the intention of the Government to found a colony at Botany Bay led to the suspension of the project, until Mr. Bentham came forward with his scheme for a Panopticon, which was informally approved and an Act passed in 1794 (34 George III., c. 84), under which fifty-three acres in Tothill Fields were conveyed in 1799 to Mr. Bentham, and a contract with him drafted, which was fortunately never signed. In 1810 Sir Samuel Romilly called the attention of the House to the inaction of the Government. Two more years elapsed before the enactment of 52 George III., providing for the erection of a Penitentiary for the Counties of London and Middlesex on the land reconveyed by Mr. Bentham to the Supervisors.

in 1832. Millbank, after the abolition of the hulks, was the depot from which convicts sentenced to transportation took their departure for Australia. It ceased

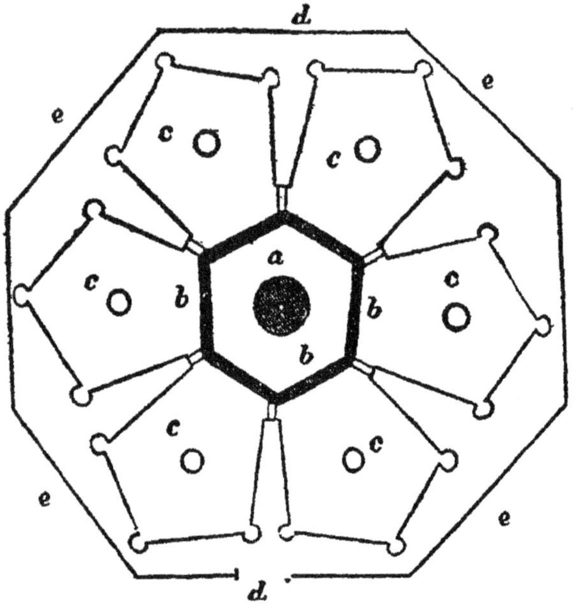

GROUND PLAN OF MILLBANK PENITENTIARY

a Chapel. *b* Hexagon.
c Pentagons. *d* Entrance.
e Boundary Wall.

to be a convict prison in 1886, and has since been destroyed.

The report of Sir William Crawford on the penitentiaries of the United States, made in August, 1834, led to the creation of the metropolitan prison at Pentonville, for five hundred prisoners. This was meant to be a model prison, on the separate system, with the reformation of offenders as its avowed aim. It was begun April 10, 1842, and in its construction the radiating plan of the Eastern Penitentiary at Philadelphia was followed. The hulks and Millbank had been used as substitutes for transportation; Pentonville was meant to be a preparation for transportation.

At this time, two distinct stages of punishment were recognized, namely: eighteen months of separate confinement at Pentonville, followed by exile to Australia. Tickets-of-leave were not granted in England, but could be granted in the colony. Eighteen months was found to be too long a term of isolation, and the time was subsequently reduced to nine months; afterward, an intermediate stage of imprisonment was introduced, which was served in a different prison, organized on the principle of separation by night and associated labor by day, on the Auburn plan; and transportation with a ticket-of-leave was made a reward for good conduct in the prison.

Penal servitude, established in 1847, as a preparation for transportation, was, in 1857, when transportation was by law formally abandoned as a punishment, made a substitute for it. Then began the erection of great public works prisons. Portland was opened in 1847, Dartmoor in 1850, and to these have now been added Chatham and Portsmouth, where convicts are employed in enlarging the docks. The original theory of English criminal law was that, of all secondary punishments (by which are meant punishments not capital), transportation was the most severe; but it came to be believed that servitude in a public works prison was more severe than transportation, as is proved by the fact that four years in such a prison was made the equivalent of seven years' service in Australia.

So much for the English prisons. The necessity for building prisons in England would have been avoided, if the people, first of the United States and then of Australia, had not absolutely refused to allow the deportation of convicted felons to those countries.

The next point to be considered is the reaction of Australian methods of dealing with convicts upon the prison system at home. Commodore Phillip, as has been shown, was given the right of conditional pardon, as Governor of the Colony. The lack of any prison structure made it necessary to work the men in gangs; hence arose the system of progressive classification, which was developed in Australia to a high degree of perfection. The final stage of penal servitude was that of conditional liberation on a ticket-of-leave, which was an Australian invention. The effect upon English criminal legislation is very apparent. The Act of 1847 created four stages of imprisonment, namely: (1) cellular confinement in complete isolation, not exceeding nine months; (2) probation, in England, in a public works prison; (3) transportation to Australia, with a ticket-of-leave or the promise of one upon arrival; (4) absolute liberation, at a period to be determined by the amount earned by the convict while on ticket-of-leave. Thus transportation, which had at first been considered the most dreadful of punishments except that of death, came to be regarded as a reward for good conduct while in prison. The period of probation in public works prisons was given the title of penal servitude, which is equivalent to the French *travaux forcés* or the

American "imprisonment at hard labor." At Portland, prisoners were divided into several classes, distinguished by different dress, and promotion from one to another was earned by good conduct. The labor, which was in the open air, was in common. Here we have many of the characteristic features of the graded prisons of our own day, barring that of marks, which was also an Australian invention, the history of which must now be recounted.

Norfolk Island, four miles long by three miles in width, was the principal penal settlement, to which the worst convicts were sent. Of about fifteen hundred on the island, probably two-thirds had been "doubly convicted," that is, convicted in Australia of some criminal offence there committed, while under sentence of transportation. In point of natural beauty, the island was a Paradise, but the conduct of the men banished to it was indescribably bad; they were given up to murder and all unnatural crimes. Upon one occasion, a witness in a murder trial professed to have seen so many murders on the island, that he could not remember the one in question; he said that he had seen men "cut up like hogs by a butcher." The punishments were so severe, that men would sometimes commit murder, for the sake of being transferred to Sydney, for trial, in the hope that the chance might present itself of escape on the voyage, or that the witnesses might so escape. It was not uncommon for small parties to escape to the woods; and once a number of prisoners, who had so effectually hidden themselves as to be undiscoverable, on being reduced to starvation, ate six of their comrades, rather than return and give themselves up.

Mutinies were frequent. It was testified before the Parliamentary Committee that, after one of these mutinies, seven men sentenced to death, on account of their part in it, dropped upon their knees and thanked God that they were at last to be delivered from the sufferings of life on Norfolk Island.

Hither, in 1840, came, as superintendent, Captain Alexander Maconochie, of the Royal Navy. In Van Diemen's Land, according to his own sworn statement, he "had witnessed the dreadful state of depravity in which the men in the public gangs were sunk," and the idea occurred to him, that "it arose from the state of slavery to which they were reduced," which led him to "think of the expedient of marks as a form of wages, by which the state of slavery might be obviated, and still the act of punishment not lost." This plan of managing prisoners had been brought by him to the notice of the Transportation Committee of the House of Commons, in 1837.

The first voice raised against time sentences was that of Archbishop Whately, of Dublin, in 1832, who suggested that the convict, instead of being imprisoned for a certain length of time, should be sentenced to perform a certain amount of work; he would substitute, for time sentences, labor sentences, in the belief that the change would be an improvement.[1] Whether the writings of

[1] "The plan which, as far as I am competent to judge, seems to me, on the whole, to promise the most favorably, is that which is suggested in the *London Review,* but which has not, that I know of, been hitherto anywhere tried; viz., that of requiring, of such criminals as are sentenced to hard labor, a *certain amount of work;* compelling them indeed to a certain moderate quantity of daily labor, but permitting them to exceed this as much as they please; and thus to shorten the term of their imprisonment, by accomplishing the total amount of their task in a less time than

Whately had fallen under Maconochie's eye is not known; but his suggestion was in the same direction.

Maconochie proposed to the Committee "that the duration of sentences be measured by labor and good conduct, with a minimum of time but no maximum; that the labor thus required, being represented by marks, a certain number of these, proportioned to the original offence, be required to be earned in a penal condition, before discharge; and that, according to the amount of work rendered, a proportion of them should be credited day by day to the convict, and a moderate charge be made, enough for all provisions and other supplies issued to him; should he misconduct himself, a moderate fine be then imposed on him—only the clear surplus, after all similar deductions, to count toward his liberation." By this means he "sought to place the prisoner's fate in his own hands, to give him a form of wages, to impose on him a form of pecuniary fines for his prison offences, to make him feel the burden and obligation of his own maintenance, and to train him,

that to which they had been sentenced. I would also allow them, for a certain portion of the work done, a payment in money; not to be expended during their continuance in prison, but to be paid over to them at their discharge; so that they should never be turned loose into the world entirely destitute. Instead of being sentenced to confinement for a fixed time, they should be sentenced to earn, at a certain specified employment, such a sum of money as may be judged sufficient to preserve them, on their release, from the pressure of immediate distress; and orderly, decent, submissive behavior during the time of their being thus employed should be enforced, under the penalty (besides others, if found necessary) of a proportionate deduction from their wages, and consequent prolongation of their confinement."—Letter to Earl Grey, 1832.

The article in the *London Review,* to which Archbishop Whately refers, was written by himself, and appeared in 1829. It is quoted in "Suggestions for the Repression of Crime," by Matthew Davenport Hill, p. 474.

while yet in bondage, to those habits of prudent accumulation which after discharge would best preserve him from again falling." On assuming the charge of Norfolk Island, he introduced, apparently on his own responsibility, and as an aid to good government, the mark system which he had devised, and which had received from the Parliamentary Committee a qualified approval. It was absolutely new and untried.

The story of his achievement, with its aid and by his personal power and tact, in reducing a turbulent population to comparative order, in four years, is interesting and instructive, but is omitted, in order that the attention of the reader may be concentrated upon the mark system and Maconochie's relation to it. Every convict was debited by him with a certain number of marks, according to the character of his offence, which he must redeem, before being recommended for conditional liberation. Instead of issuing the prescribed quantity and kind of government rations, he credited each man with a certain number of marks per day, for his subsistence, to which he assigned an arbitrary pecuniary value, and the prisoner was at liberty to exchange them at their nominal face value for food and other supplies, at the Government Depot. Marks were earned by good conduct and by labor; intellectual marks were also given to those engaged in the prosecution of their studies; and the surplus above the amount charged for maintenance went toward the purchase of more speedy liberation. The effect upon discipline was so extraordinary, that Maconochie himself said, "I found Norfolk Island a hell, but left it an orderly and well-regulated community."

He was afterward for a time Governor of the Birmingham Jail, in England, where he put the same system in operation; but, inasmuch as the law did not recognize task sentences, the difficulties in his way were insuperable, and he appears to have been officially looked upon as a failure—apparently with little justice. He seems to be one of England's unappreciated and partially forgotten worthies.

The mark system, however, went into the English code, after Sir Walter Crofton had first experimented with it in Ireland. Crofton borrowed it from Maconochie.

In the mark system now in use in England, the highest number of marks that can be earned is eight per day. The first year is regarded as a period of probation, and is spent in a solitary cell. The minimum number of marks which will entitle the prisoner to pass into the next stage, which is called the third or lowest grade, is seven hundred and twenty. Eight marks per day, or two thousand nine hundred and twenty in the year, earned in the third grade, entitle him to promotion to the second or intermediate grade; and the same number there earned advance him to the first grade, in which there is a higher sub-class called "special." Should he fail to earn the full tale of marks demanded for promotion within the year, he remains in the lower grade until they have in fact been acquired. During the year of probation, the convict earns no money; in the lowest grade, he earns one shilling per month; in the intermediate grade, a shilling and sixpence; in the highest grade, half a crown. In the lowest grade, prisoners are allowed to receive visits from their friends but twice during the year; other distinctions in privileges are made as to diet, exercise, and correspondence. The convicts in each grade wear a different uniform dress. There is a "star class," selected entirely from first offenders, in which a red star is worn on the breast. The provisions as to grades in the local jails are similar, but the number of marks required for promotion is there only two hundred and twenty-four. During the first stage, the prisoner sleeps on a plank, without a mattress; in the next, he has a mattress five nights in the week; then six; and in the highest grade, every night.

The Irish or Crofton system was somewhat different. The English graded system recognized three stages, solitary imprisonment, labor in association, and transportation; when transportation was abolished, the third stage was altered to release, in England, on a ticket-of-leave. Sir Walter Crofton, the Director of Irish Convict Prisons, who was made a baronet for his services as such, and who certainly exhibited great talent as an organizer and governor of prisons, introduced a fourth stage. The period of cellular incarceration was served at Mountjoy, where there was a prison in two departments, one for men and one for women. The second stage was that of "progressive classification," a phrase of which he was the author. His male prisoners were transferred from Mountjoy to Spike Island, where they were divided into five classes; the probation class, third, second, and first classes, and the advanced class. The probation class could be skipped by prisoners who had made a good record at Mountjoy. The majority of those transferred were placed in the third class, where they had to earn nine marks per month for six months, or fifty-four marks in all, as the condition of promotion. The number of marks to be earned in the second class was the same; and in the first class, twice as many, so that they could not pass from the first to the advanced class in less than one year. Under the English system, they would then have been entitled to a ticket-of-leave, but Sir Walter would not grant it until after a test had been applied, in a condition of comparative freedom, at a third prison, called an intermediate prison, at Lusk, where they slept in movable iron huts and were occupied almost precisely as freemen would have been, in farming and manufacturing. The prison at Lusk had neither bars, bolts, nor walls. Its aim was to make practical proof of the prisoner's reformation, his power of self-control, his ability to resist temptation, and to train him for a considerable period—never less than six months—under natural conditions, and so to prepare him for full freedom by the enjoyment of partial freedom as a preliminary step. The success of Lusk was largely due to the extraordinary capacity of the teacher there employed, Mr. Organ, whose name is famous in prison annals. The female prisoners served the second stage of progressive classification at Mountjoy; but were transferred, for the third or intermediate stage, to Golden Bridge, three miles from Dublin, which was a Refuge, presided over by a Sister of Charity. Since Sir Walter Crofton ceased to be the Director of Irish Convict Prisons, the English Government has abolished the intermediate stage.

The only place where the Irish system can now be found in its entirety is at Lepoglava, in Hungary, where it has been organized under Mr. Tauffer, who there conducts one of the great and successful prisons of the world. The convicts are divided into three grades. Those in the first grade are subjected to a strictly cellular *régime.* In the second grade, they work in association. On reaching the third (or intermediate) grade, they occupy cottages, at a considerable distance from the main prison, resembling those inhabited by the Croatian peasants. These cottages have neither bars nor bolts, and there are no guards other than the overseers of the work of the prisoners. The fourth and final stage is one of conditional liberation.

The mark system has of course been imitated in the English Colonies. It is also found in the prisons of Denmark, Hungary, and Croatia.

CHAPTER X

THE ELMIRA SYSTEM

THE state of American prisons, twenty-five years ago, was far from satisfactory. The discipline in most of them was either severe to the verge of cruelty, or lax to the point of weakness, according to the ideas and sentiments of the wardens in charge. The wardens were appointed almost wholly for political reasons, and were subject to change with every alteration in the political complexion of the State governments. Comparatively few of them were really competent for their position, and they did not, as a rule, remain in office long enough to become thoroughly acquainted with their duties and qualified to perform them. The majority of them openly professed a disbelief in the possibility of convict reformation. The prisons were great manufacturing establishments, operated by prison contractors for personal profit. The State took little interest in the fate of the sentenced, except to insist that they must be made to pay, as nearly as possible, for their own support by their labor. The best warden, in the popular estimation, was the man who could show the best balance-sheet at the end of the year; and the financial test was the principal test of the excellence of prison management.

The change which has taken place is largely due to the exertions and influence of the Rev. Dr. E. C. Wines, the able and devoted secretary of the New

York Prison Association, by whom the National Prison Association was organized, at a Congress held in Cincinnati, in 1870, from which the era of recent prison reform in America may be fairly dated. Associated with Dr. Wines was a noble group of men and women, among whom it might be regarded as invidious to name individuals, with one or two exceptions, notably Dr. Theodore Dwight of New York, Mr. F. B. Sanborn of Boston, and Mr. Z. R. Brockway, then of Detroit but later of Elmira. The gentlemen named were all partisans of the Irish system, which they wished to see transplanted, and which they believed it possible to modify so as to adapt it to our political conditions. The creation of the New York State Reformatory at Elmira, in 1869, afforded them the opportunity which they coveted, and it was there that the new prison system about to be described (apparently the coming system of modern civilization) was virtually created.

Dr. Wines had been much impressed by the published accounts of the results of the reformatory experiments made by Montesinos in Spain, and Obermaier in Bavaria.

Colonel Montesinos was appointed, in 1835, Governor of the prison at Valencia, which was an old Augustinian convent containing from a thousand to fifteen hundred convicts. He organized it on the military system, dividing the population into companies, and appointing prisoners to be inferior company officers. He encouraged convicts to learn trades, of which he had at one time fully forty in operation at once; they did all the prison work besides. The workshops cost the government nothing, and one-half the earnings were appropriated to the support of the prison. There was in this prison a school, which boys under twenty were obliged to attend for one hour daily; and any prisoner above that age, who desired to do so, might join the classes. With no guards, except a dozen old soldiers, there were nevertheless few escapes. The great hold which Montesinos had upon his men, apart from his personal character and ability, consisted in the fact that they could, by good behavior, reduce the term of their sentence by one-third. The number of recommitments, while he was Governor, fell from thirty-five per cent. to a figure which it would be imprudent to name, lest it should not be believed. The law was subsequently changed, so as to require all prisoners to serve their full time, and in an instant the system collapsed. Montesinos resigned; he was subsequently made Inspector-General of all the prisons in Spain, but he was powerless to reform them. In a pamphlet which he published in 1846, he said:—

"What neither severity of punishments nor constancy in inflicting them can secure, the slightest personal interest will obtain. In different ways, therefore, during my command, I have applied this powerful stimulant; and the excellent results it has always yielded, and the powerful germs of reform which are constantly developed under its influence, have at length fully convinced me that the most inefficacious methods in the prison—the most pernicious and fatal to every chance of reform—are punishments carried the length of harshness. The maxim should be constant and of universal application in such places, not to degrade further those who come to them already degraded by their crimes. Self-respect is one of the most powerful sentiments of the human mind, since it is the most personal; and he who will not condescend, in some degree, according to circumstances, to flattery of it, will never attain his object by any amount of chastisement; the effect of ill-treatment being to irritate rather than to correct, and thus turn from reform instead of attracting to it. The moral object of penal establishments should be not so much to inflict punishment as to correct, to receive men idle and ill-intentioned and return them to society, if possible, honest and industrious citizens."

Obermaier was made Governor of the prison at Kaiserslautern, in Bavaria, in 1830; in 1842, he was transferred to Munich, where he found between six and seven hundred prisoners chained together, dragging heavy weights, in a state of riotous insubordination, and kept in order by about one hundred soldiers, who were distributed not only on the walls, but in the passages, in the shops, and in the dormitories. In a very short time this wonderful man had gained the confidence of his men, taken off their chains, discharged nearly all the guards, and appointed a convict superintendent of each of the shops. His success in reforming prisoners was so great, that only about seven per cent. of those at Kaiserslautern, and ten per cent. of those at Munich, relapsed into crime after their discharge. He was aided by two favoring circumstances, of which the first was that many of the men were sentenced, at that early date in Bavaria, to simple imprisonment for no fixed term; and the second, that there was a thorough supervision of discharged convicts, supplemented by the labors of numerous active prisoners' aid societies.

The aim of Sir Walter Crofton in creating the Irish prison system was the reformation of prisoners; he thus placed himself historically by the side of Montesinos and Obermaier. England, in adopting it, laid too little stress upon its reformatory influence: the main idea of the English penal system is that of repression by exemplary punishments. The Irish system was much admired by students of penology in various parts of the world, and nowhere more than in the United States. Messrs. Wines and Dwight, in a historically important report made by them to the Legislature of New York, Jan. 8, 1867, on the Prisons and Reformatories of the United States and Canada, said:—

"We have no hesitation in expressing the opinion that what is known and has become famous as the Irish system of convict prisons is, upon the whole, the best model of which we have any knowledge; and it has stood the test of experience in yielding the most abundant as well as the best fruits. We believe that in its broad, general principles—not certainly in all its details—it may be applied, with entire effect, in our own country and in our own State. What, then, is the Irish system? In one word, it may be defined as an adult reformatory, where the object is to teach and train the prisoner in such a manner that, on his discharge, he may be able to resist temptation and inclined to lead an upright, worthy life. Reformation, in other words, is made the actual as well as the declared object. This is done by placing the prisoner's fate, as far as possible, in his own hands, by enabling him, through industry and good conduct, to raise himself, step by step, to a position of less restraint; while idleness and bad conduct, on the other hand, keep him in a state of coercion and restraint."

It was under the inspiration of this thought, that the New York Prison Association urged the creation, in that State, of an intermediate prison on the reformatory plan.

Mr. Brockway furnished a paper[1] for the Twenty-

[1] Mr. Brockway's utterances, in this paper, of a desire for the abolition of term sentences, it will be observed, is subsequent to the Report of Messrs. Wines and Dwight, in which they had already said: "This whole question of prison sentences is, in our judgment, one which requires careful revision. Not a few of the best minds in Europe and America have, by their investigations and reflections, reached the conclusion that time sentences are wrong in principle; that they should be abandoned, and that reformation sentences should be substituted in their place."

fourth Annual Report of that Association (1868), in which he said: "Legislation is needed, to abolish the peremptory character of the sentences imposed upon persons committed to these establishments." And again, "Persons whose moral depravity makes them a public offence should be committed to properly organized institutions until they are cured." The Legislature of New York, in 1868, provided for the appointment of a Commission to select a site for a new State Prison. At the suggestion of the New York Prison Association, the bill was so amended as to designate the new institution a Reformatory. The Commission reported in 1869:—

"We propose to make the sentences (to the Reformatory) substantially reformation sentences. It has been a favorite theory of that distinguished criminal judge and philanthropist, Mr. Recorder Hill, that criminals should be sentenced until they are reformed, which may, of course, turn out to be for life. While we do not propose to recommend this rule in full, we think that it may be safely tried in a modified form. We propose that, when the sentence of a criminal is regularly less than five years, the sentence to the Reformatory shall be until reformation, not exceeding five years."

The act establishing the Elmira Reformatory was passed in 1869, one year before the assembling of the Cincinnati Congress, at the call of Dr. Wines, where Mr. Brockway read a paper (somewhat famous in the annals of American prison history) on the proper organization of a prison system for a State, in which he presented in germ nearly all the theories as to the nature and needs of the criminal, which he has since wrought into the spirit and life of that institution. In particular he planted himself upon the proposition that "sentences should not be determinate, but indeterminate." Dr. Byers, of Ohio, at the same Congress, spoke in favor of the establishment of intermediate prisons; and Mr. Sanborn discussed the possibility of introducing the Irish system in America.[1] The Elmira

[1] The Cincinnati Congress adopted a Declaration of Principles, in thirty-seven paragraphs. In the first, punishment is defined to be "suffering inflicted on the criminal for the wrong done by him, with a special view to secure his reformation;" and in the second, it is said that "the supreme aim of prison discipline is the reformation of criminals, not the infliction of vindictive suffering." Other paragraphs are as follows:

"III. The progressive classification of prisoners, based on character and worked on some well-adjusted mark system should be established in all prisons above the common jail.

"IV. Since hope is a more potent agent than fear, it should be made an ever-present force in the minds of prisoners, by a well-devised and skilfully applied system of rewards for good conduct, industry, and attention to learning. Rewards, more than punishments, are essential to every good prison system.

"V. The prisoner's destiny should be placed, measurably, in his own hands; he must be put into circumstances where he will be able, through his own exertions, to continually better his own condition. A regulated self-interest must be brought into play, and made constantly operative.

"VIII. Peremptory sentences ought to be replaced by those of indeterminate length. Sentences limited only by satisfactory proof of reformation should be substituted for those measured by mere lapse of time."

In other paragraphs of this remarkable paper, the doctrine is laid down that "In order to accomplish the reformation of criminals, there must be not only a sincere desire and intention to that end, but a serious conviction, in the minds of the prison officers, that they are capable of being reformed;" that "a system of prison discipline, to be truly reformatory, must gain the will of the convict;" that "the prisoner's self-respect should be cultivated to the utmost, and every effort made to give back to him his manhood;" that "in prison administration moral forces should be relied upon, with as little admixture of physical force as possible;" that "the most valuable parts of the Irish prison system are believed to be as applicable to the United States as to Ireland;" that "reformation is a work of time, and a benevolent regard to the good of the criminal himself, as well as to the protection of society, requires that his sentence be long enough for reformatory processes to take effect."

It was at this Congress that President Rutherford B. Hayes, then Governor of Ohio, enlisted for life in the cause of prison reform. Here, too, the steps were taken which resulted in the organization of the National Prison Association and the International Penitentiary Congress.

Prison was built under an act passed in 1870, and subsequent acts, but was not ready for the reception of prisoners before 1876, when a board of managers was appointed, who elected Mr. Brockway superintendent. The first inmates were transferred to it, from the State Prison at Auburn, in July of that year.[1]

There is in the organization of this Reformatory, and in the laws by which it is governed, nothing that

[1] In a work purporting to aim at historical accuracy, and in which an effort is made to show the genesis of the Elmira idea and how many individuals unconsciously cooperated to a common end, due credit should also be given to the Warden of Sing Sing Prison, Mr. Gaylord B. Hubbell, who, in 1865, at his own cost, made a thorough study abroad of the English and Irish prisons. An extended account of his observations and conclusions is printed in the Twenty-second Annual Report of the New York Prison Association, in which he said: "Can the Irish system be adopted to advantage in our own country? For my own part, I have no hesitation in returning an affirmative answer, with emphasis, to this question." He proceeded to sketch his conception of the best method of procedure in the attempt to introduce it, and proposed the purchase of a farm of two or three hundred acres *on the line of the Erie railroad,* and the erection upon the site selected of *a new prison,* to be organized *in three divisions*—each of which should have a special discipline. His first division he would have in solitary or separate confinement; the second division should work in association through the day, but be separated by night—in that the mark system should be in force; in the third division, with associated dormitories and no wall, all the arrangements should be such as to give the largest possible freedom to the inmates. He said: *"A careful system of classification of prisoners should be made, based on marks,* honestly given according to their character, conduct, industry, and obedience. For it must be remembered, that a classified system of association without marks, and without impressing on the prisoner's mind the necessity for *progressive improvement,* is of little value." Again: "All prisoners sent to the proposed establishment should, under proper restrictions, be *allowed to work their way out."* Once more: "The Maconochie mark system, the gratuities, *the school teaching, the library, the course of lectures, competitive examinations, debates,* etc., etc., could all be introduced here as well, at least, and in my opinion much better than in Ireland." (The italics are not in the original, but are introduced to show how far Mr. Hubbell anticipated the methods followed at Elmira.)

Mr. Hubbell had been influenced by the brothers Hill, who

is absolutely new. The novelty consists rather in the combination of principles whose validity had been separately recognized, and in the intense earnestness with which they have been here applied by a man whose enthusiasm for the reformation of convicts has in it a quality closely allied to genius. Somewhat unconsciously, perhaps, the methods adopted closely resembled those which had been long in use in institutions for

also exerted an influence on the mind of Dr. Wines. They had been influenced by Captain Maconochie, who was Governor of the Birmingham Jail while Matthew Davenport Hill was Recorder of Birmingham. The connection is clear. Mr. Hubbell was in charge of the leading prison of the State of New York. Dr. Dwight was vice-president and Dr. Wines secretary, of the New York Prison Association. Mr. Brockway was not a resident of that State, but Superintendent of the House of Correction in Detroit, Michigan. This was ten years before he was called to take charge of the completed prison at Elmira. In the light of facts like these, the opening sentence of Alexander Winter's book, "The New York State Reformatory at Elmira," is not warranted: "In the year 1876 Mr. Brockway, who, up to that date, had been for many years accumulating a wide and comprehensive experience in the administration of prisons, laid before the State Commission appointed for their management and inspection a plan of organization *worked out entirely by himself,* for the improvement and reform of criminals." The statement, a few lines below, *"Thus arose* the Elmira institution," is not true.

Mr. Havelock Ellis does not fall into this error, in his introduction to Mr. Winter's book, but speaks of "the founders of Elmira," in the plural. He is mistaken, however, in saying, as he does, that they "had no knowledge of the scientific movement that was arising in Europe." (See the critique upon Prosper Despine's "Psychologie Naturelle" and "De la folie au point de vue philosophique ou plus spécialement psychologique," by Dr. Wines in the *Princeton Review,* May, 1878, reprinted in "The State of Prisons," pp. 641-660.) It is true that the founders of Elmira were not criminal anthropologists in the technical and narrow sense of that phrase; and Elmira was not, as Mr. Ellis claims, "the practical outcome of their studies." All that is fundamental in the Elmira system is wholly independent of the acceptance or rejection of their speculations as to nervous and mental action, heredity, evolution, or the existence and proof of a distinct anthropological type. The attempt to identify the two is an injury and not a benefit to the cause of prison reform, because it awakens prejudice against it in the minds of many who would otherwise be its friends. It is, moreover, wholly needless.

the reformation of juvenile offenders. Indeed, it could not well be otherwise, since men are but children of a larger growth, and the methods which succeed at a youthful age ought, with the necessary modification, to succeed, though probably not to the same degree with older men. The Australian inventions of marks, grades, and the ticket-of-leave, had been accepted by the English Government, which also borrowed from the United States her Pennsylvania system of cellular imprisonment by day and night for the first stage of penal servitude, and her Auburn system of separation by night only and employment in workshops by day, for the intermediate stage. In Ireland, Sir Walter Crofton went a step further, and applied a practical test of the fitness of his men for conditional liberation, before granting them a ticket-of-leave. This consisted in employment in a condition approximating complete freedom. All of these ideas were imported from Australia and Great Britain into the Elmira system. They constituted, in fact, its base; but there was added to them another, which gave to the whole a wonderful vitality, and which is really the distinguishing feature of the system, namely, the so-called indeterminate sentence.

At this point, it is necessary to interject into the argument some observations concerning reformation and the means by which it can be effected.

What constitutes reformation? Not necessarily religious conversion. Reformation may stop far short of that, and yet be such a change of habits and character as to satisfy all reasonable legal or sociological expectation. On this point, the Reverend Mr. Burt,

Chaplain of the Pentonville prison, has pertinently remarked:—

"The result aimed at by a penal code is attained when, by whatever motive, the criminal is induced to restrain his vicious propensities within the limits which the law prescribes. Three influences, more or less distinct, may operate in producing this result. It may be one effect of religious conversion; it may arise from a general amelioration of the moral character; or it may be the result of prudential consideration, of intimidation, or of forethought. It is not often, I apprehend, that actual reformation can be exclusively referred to any one of these causes. The several influences usually cooperate, and one passes insensibly into another, though in different cases different motives predominate. In any case, however, the result is reformation."

He adds:—

"In the reformed criminal it would be unreasonable to expect impeccable piety or stoical fortitude; enough will have been effected to merit the title of reformation, when the once habitual offender exhibits an average standard of virtue, under an average pressure of temptation."

For the purposes of the government, a criminal is reformed who does not require to be rearrested, retried, and again incarcerated for some new violation of the criminal law.

The agencies by which this result is attained are three, namely, labor, education, and religion; and they correspond to the analysis of human nature as physical, intellectual, and moral. But the unity of human nature is such, that any influence which affects an individual in any part of his being affects directly or indirectly the whole man. And the relation between religion, labor, and education is so intimate, that they almost seem at times to be different names for the same thing. Labor and religion are both educational agencies; neither intellectual nor ethical development is possible without labor, and religion demands of every man, that by training and effort he shall make the most of himself, and do the most for the world, that the extent of his talents will permit.

Of these three, it is probable that the most certain to secure from every prisoner some measure of response is labor. Labor, if real and productive, is not only a means of bodily health and strength, but it compels thought, thus awakening and moulding the mind, and in many ways it reacts favorably upon the moral character of the workman. The abolition of prison labor, which, in their ignorance and greed, largely at the instigation of their employers, so many members of the trades unions demand (on the double ground that convict and free labor are antagonistic, and that competition with the former is a degradation to the unconvicted), would throw our prisons back to the state in which they were, three or four centuries ago. The laboring class (if it is proper to speak of working-men as a class) would gain nothing by the change, since they would then have to support prisoners in idleness, at the cost of the public treasury. Prisoners, if unconvicted, would be compelled to enter the labor market; how does conviction for crime deprive them of the natural right to live by their own exertions? And what excuse has the government to offer for preventing them from earning their own support, and for levying contributions upon the innocent, to keep the guilty from starving? It has been repeatedly shown, by actual computation, that the competition of convict labor in the market is so small, in comparison, as to exert no appreciable effect upon the demand for labor or upon wages. It may affect certain trades; and the policy of the authorities should be to select industries in which such competition is least, and to diversify to the largest practicable extent the industries pursued in prisons. But some degree of rivalry of interest is inevitable, whatever we may do; for anything that prisoners do might be done by outside labor,—even roadmaking or the manufacture of supplies for public institutions, both of which are just now rather popular fads. It is a strong phrase, but the consequences to the public of the forcible stoppage of labor in prisons must sooner or later be of such a serious nature, that it is not too much to say that the man who favors so violent a measure is an unconscious enemy of mankind. The reformatory influence of labor, even in prisons which are managed for profit, and where the profits inure largely to contractors and not to the State, is so potent, that of men committed to an ordinary American penitentiary it is safe to estimate that one-half do not, after their discharge, relapse into crime.

Labor needs, however, to be supplemented by education in the common acceptation of that word, meaning development by educational processes skilfully applied to the training both of the head and the hand. Statistics prove that the number of prisoners without any trade education is greater than of those without a common school education. Some prisoners are highly educated men, but their number is relatively small. Owing to the division of labor in manufactories, a trade education is not necessarily obtained in the shops, hence the establishment of trade-schools in prison is desirable, on account of the opportunity which it affords of giving to prisoners such a knowledge of the use of tools as will quality them for useful and profitable employment upon their discharge. The utility of literary and scientific teaching in prison, by lectures, books, and classes, consists not merely in the improvement of the mind, but in its occupation and diversion, that it may not be given over to introspection, vain regrets, impure imaginations, bitterness, and the planning of fresh criminal enterprises. It should not, therefore, be confined to elementary instruction in reading, writing, and arithmetic, but mental food should be provided for all tastes and capacities represented in the prison population at any given time. The old story is here in point of the Quaker visitor who said to an embittered convict, "Friend, thee should have better thoughts," to which the prisoner replied, "Where shall I get them?" The positive value of education to the prisoner must not, however, be overlooked, especially on subjects concerning which (largely from the want of proper instruction) he is apt to cherish perverted notions. Four topics should be given a prominent place in the prison curriculum, namely: the principles (1) of law, generally, as a rule of conduct, and specifically, in its relation to crime; (2) of civil government, its necessity and utility; (3) of political economy, especially in its bearing upon the labor question and the means by which property is legitimately accumulated; (4) of practical ethics, or the mutual rights and obligations of men living in the social state.

In this connection, the following remarks by Mr.

Michael Davitt are worthy of reproduction here. He expresses the opinion founded on his personal observation as a political prisoner, that "direct Scripture or moral teaching, either through religious works or the labor of prison chaplains, is all but useless with criminals." On the other hand, he believes that "no more efficacious reforming medium—apart, of course, from industrial occupation and habits—could be employed for the reclamation of all that is reclaimable in criminal lives, than a judiciously stocked prison library, in which the moral-teaching and wrong-punishing description of novel should be largely represented." He adds that "it is only what prisoners read, between labor hours in prison, that can come between themselves and their thoughts of crime past and reveries of criminal deeds to come."

No less important, certainly, is it to reach the heart and touch the conscience of all who are susceptible to religious influence. The great Italian poet has shown by appropriate and impressive imagery the truth that there are three spiritual states in one of which must be found every human soul. The first is that in which the soul is in love with evil, does not perceive it to be evil, and attributes the pain which it endures to every cause but the right one—the return of an evil deed upon the doer of it. This is hell. The second is that in which the soul has recognized its sin, seeks to escape, and welcomes the pain of repentance as a purifying, purgatorial fire. Finally, having struggled with itself and gained the victory, having overcome the power of self-love, which creates discord between sister souls and between the soul and God, it accepts the divine order, the human and the divine wills come into sweet accord, and at last it reaches the state of paradisaic rest and everlasting joy. There are multitudes of convicts who, in Dante's sense, are still in hell; how are they to be delivered? Born without moral sense, or having impaired, if not destroyed, the faculty of conscience, by its neglect or abuse, they are spiritually blind to the true nature of their own actions and relations. It seems a hopeless task, to renew in them the faculty of moral insight. Yet it must be undertaken, and for its accomplishment our hope is in God, the creator and the re-creator of the spirit that is in man. Physical and intellectual culture may contribute to the end in view; but without the appeal to conscience, in the name of God, without picturing to the tempted the parting of the ways which lead to death or to life, without holding before their minds judgment and mercy, destruction and forgiveness, and urging them to decision, in the light of eternity and of their personal accountability to the Judge of all the living and of the dead, the central spring of moral activity will not have been reached, and any reformation which may take place will be superficial or evanescent.

An American prison chaplain, comparatively new to the duties of his position, was sneeringly asked by an officer how many of the prisoners he had converted by his ministrations. He replied, "The same percentage, I think, as of the prison officials."

If the relation of the foregoing observations to the indeterminate sentence is not self-evident, it can readily be made apparent. Crime is the measure of the criminal's opposition to social institutions and of his incapacity to adapt himself to them. If the institutions happen to be wrong, he may be right; but he must bear the consequence of his deed. What society demands of him is submission. The discipline of the criminal law is designed to subdue or convert his will, so as to make it conform to the will of the social whole. Subjugation was the old idea; conversion is the new. The effort to break a prisoner's will proceeded on the theory that he was a man of exceptional strength, and dangerous for that reason; the effort to enlighten and persuade it assumes that precisely the contrary is the truth, that the criminal is an exceptionally weak man, incapable of self-direction and self-control, to whom it is necessary to impart power, but power for good, not for evil. He therefore needs to be studied in a state of incarceration, to discover what is his special weakness, whether it is in his physical, mental, or moral constitution, in order that the treatment to be given him may correspond to his actual condition and needs. But no treatment will produce the best result, unless the consent and cooperation of the criminal patient are secured. For this an adequate motive, to which he will be likely to respond, is essential. The average criminal is an egotist, who has more faith in his own perverted instincts than in the advice and assurances of wiser and better men; he is a creature of habits which he cannot easily shake off; he does not want to be morally awakened and renovated; he sets himself in opposition to every influence which will elevate him and make him ashamed of his past and sorry for it. Ordinary persuasion is for the most part thrown away upon him. The only motive which is sure to affect him, in proportion to his intelligence, is the hope of freedom. That hope springs eternal in the convict's breast, but it ordinarily assumes the form of vague expectation of a pardon, or of a favorable chance to escape. If he can be convinced that these anticipations are fallacious, but that he will be released as soon as it shall become apparent to the officers who have him in charge that society has no longer anything to fear from him, and that he can convince them of this fact by his own conduct in prison, from that moment his will is gained, and the rest is comparatively easy. As Maconochie expressed it, "When a man keeps the key of his own prison, he is soon persuaded to fit it to the lock."

The indeterminate sentence, therefore, puts into the hand of a competent and devoted prison superintendent the precise lever that he requires, in order to subvert the criminality of the convict, assuming that it can be subverted. It is merely a tool. It is of no value if not used, or in the hand of a man who does not know how to use it. It has in itself no reformatory power; it is a dead thing. The real power is in the reformatory agencies which have been named—labor, education, and religion. These, if applied, will produce the same effect under a definite as under an indefinite sentence; the difference is that, under the latter, the prisoner ceases to resist their application, and may even be induced to apply them to himself. It puts him in the most favorable attitude to be operated upon, in the condition most favorable to a cure.

The history of the evolution of the conception of the indeterminate sentence is interesting and instructive. Punishment must be admitted to be a natural reaction against wrong. In the early stages of social evolution, when the retributory principle was uppermost in the thoughts of men, retribution meant the return to a private or public enemy of an exact equivalent for the injury suffered at his hands; and in an exact equivalent there was no room for variation within specified limits. When composition of injuries was admitted as an indirect mode of retaliation, more satisfactory on the whole to both parties, the substitute payment to be made by the offender to the offended party was a matter of bargain between them, and the sum to be paid a fixed sum, which could be neither increased nor diminished. When the State took the regulation of private quarrels upon itself, it inflicted upon the guilty the penalty of death, which was a fixed penalty, or usually some other definite amount of loss, like the loss of a finger or an eye, or the infliction of a given number of stripes. Recur for a moment, too, to the slow growth of political institutions, the division of power first between the executive and legislature, then the development of courts out of legislative committees, resulting at last in the separation of the judiciary. Remember that imprisonment was not itself a penalty for crime, until within a very recent period in the history of the world. Imprisonment, like torture, is an elastic penalty, capable of abbreviation or prolongation. Discretionary power to terminate it at some fixed point must be lodged somewhere.

At first, this power was retained and exercised by the legislature. Absolute penalties were the rule—definite terms of imprisonment for specific acts, regardless of extenuating or aggravating circumstances; or an attempt was made in the code to define and estimate at their true value such circumstances. All early criminal codes were fixed codes, with fixed penalties.

The evil of fixed penalties, however, can never be long hidden, even from averted eyes. Especially clear is the impossibility of such foresight on the part of the law-making body as will enable it to apportion punishment adequately and justly, in accordance with the many varying degrees of guilt, estimated by the double standard of the culprit's intention and the amount of the injury done. We find, therefore, the evidence of a certain shrinking, on the part of legislatures, from a task for which they feel themselves incapable, in the attribution by them to the criminal courts of large discretionary powers in the infliction of punishment, within certain prescribed minimum and maximum limits. In this country, at least, the growing tendency of legislatures is to reduce the *maxima* and do away with the *minima*.

The question now arises, how have the courts acquitted themselves, in fact, of this responsibility? The difficulty has not been gotten rid of; it is only removed. It was supposed, no doubt, that judges, with all the evidence before them, could make tolerably correct estimates of guilt and suffering, and that they could apportion the one to the other with sufficient accuracy to insure, in most cases, some degree of approximation to equivalence between the two. Has this expectation been realized? It is susceptible of demonstration that it has not. It was an unreasonable expectation at best. Admitting for the moment that a correct human measurement of guilt or of suffering is possible, was it to be expected that the most protracted and searching criminal trial would reveal all the attending circumstances of each criminal action—the precise degree of the prisoner's legal and moral responsibility, measured by his ability to characterize his own conduct and to control it, or by the peculiar stress of temptation or provocation under which the act was committed? the precise degree of the injury done to individuals and to the community? the exact menace to society involved in a merciful sentence? If not (and still more, if the judge should prove to be impulsive or fickle in his temper, or if the jury and not the judge should be entrusted with the determination of the length of sentence), how could the grossest inequality and even inequity in the apportionment of punishment to different individuals be avoided? It has not been avoided. The experience of all prison officers affords countless illustrations of the glaring contrasts between sentences pronounced for the same or different offences upon prisoners convicted in different courts, or in the same court on different days; contrasts most exasperating to such sense of justice as is found in the breasts of convicts, and calculated greatly to diminish their respect for law and therefore their disposition to obey it. One instance, in the State of Illinois, will serve by way of illustration, instead of thousands, where two juries sat upon the case of two burglars convicted separately of robbing the same store on the same night, in partnership with each other, and one of them was sent to the penitentiary for one year, the other for three years. But more striking still is the evidence accumulated in the Eleventh Census of the United States as to the inequality in sentences in different States, often adjoining each other and alike in all essential political and social conditions. The average sentence in one State, for all offences, has been proved to be more than double that in another; and the want of congruity in sentences for different crimes, in detail, in different localities, is amazing to contemplate. It does not seem to be the fault of the codes, so much as of the courts, if it is a fault. But, upon its face, it is the condemnation of the entire system of fixed sentences for particular criminal acts.

All definite sentences may be assumed to be unjust, either by way of excess or of defect. They are also inexpedient. Short sentences fail, in many cases to make any impression other than one of indifference to imprisonment; they beget a class of minor recidivists known as rounders or repeaters or revolvers, who are continually in and out of prison, which becomes their principal place of abode. A man named "Silly Kelly" died in Edinburgh, in 1872, at the age of eighty-two years, who had been convicted of drunkenness and other petty offences three hundred and fifty times; it was estimated that he had spent more than forty years of his life in prison. Mr. Frederick Hill has officially reported the case of a man in Scotland, who was convicted more than one thousand times. The superintendent of the New York City Workhouse, on Blackwell's Island, once said to the author of this book, "We have prisoners who are repeatedly committed, on the charge of drunkenness, for the uniform term of thirty days. When their term expires, they return to the city, immediately proceed to drink again to intoxication, and are recommitted on the day following. Our guards are allowed, by our rules, one day off each month; and, really, the only difference between the guards and the prisoners, in this respect, is that the latter are locked up, while the guards are not." Long sentences, on the other hand, especially life sentences, depress the convict too much, by depriving him of any well-founded expectation of any end to the weary routine of a life without object or stimulus, except in the grave.

Definite sentences are never reformatory, since they are in fact retributory, and are founded on the character of the act, which is past, having occurred prior to the sentence, and is therefore irrevocable. Reformatory sentences can be based only upon the character of the actor, which it is desired to correct, but the time required to alter it cannot be estimated in advance, any more than we can tell how long it will take for a lunatic to recover from an attack of insanity. There is an analogy between crime and insanity, which may be pushed to an extreme, yet is useful for our present purpose.[1]

[1] The analogy between crime and insanity was the theme of an extemporaneous address made by the author, in 1886, to the inmates of the Elmira Reformatory, of which the following were the heads:—

1. The basis of insanity is physical, its manifestations are physical, mental, and moral. The same is true in large measure of criminal propensities.

2. Insanity and crime are both hereditary—to what extent is not definitely known. The predisposition to both is often congenital.

3. The approach of insanity and the growth of criminal character are alike gradual, in many instances, and unsuspected by the victim of either.

4. The change from innocence to depravity corresponds with the alteration in personal character observable in the insane.

5. The lunatic and the criminal both form theories, to account

Except upon the theory of retribution, why should a criminal be sent to prison for a definite period of time, any more than a lunatic to a hospital for the insane? Is the protection of society more effectually secured by an unsuccessful attempt to satisfy an abstraction, or by the seclusion of a dangerous element in the community until the convict, in the judgment of experts, who have him under constant and prolonged observation, has ceased to be such? As to the retributory theory of criminal law, it need only be said that crime and penalty cannot be adjusted to each other, unless we first find some accurate measure of guilt on the one hand and of suffering on the other, which seems to be impossible.

Regarded in this light, the whole present basis of the criminal law appears to be unsound—ethically, medically, and legally; the verdict of the three learned pro-

for the perversion of which they are more or less conscious, which are very far removed from the truth.

6. The manifestations of insanity assume one of two opposite forms—undue exaltation or undue depression; in either form they present the appearance of a pronounced self-consciousness, amounting to egotism, and often accompanied by hallucination or delusions. In this particular the resemblances between insanity and crime are striking.

7. As insanity tends to make progress and to end in dementia, so does the habitual criminal sink into moral imbecility—the complete loss of moral perception, depravation of moral tastes and inclinations, and paralysis of volition.

8. Insanity and crime are both the occasion of intense pain, succeeded by insensibility or indifference.

9. Both incapacitate their subjects for normal social life; and both are treated by incarceration, if of a dangerous or troublesome type. The motive of such treatment is twofold, the cure of the patient and the protection of the community.

10. The cure of either is difficult; much depends on beginning in time, and, for success in the effort to develop the power of self-restraint or self-direction (which may have been originally lacking, or lost by disuse or abuse), the cooperation of the patient is indispensable.

fessions against it, when finally delivered, will probably be unanimous.

The alternative, if imprisonment is to be retained as the only secondary punishment (or fines, though they are theoretically an alternative form of punishment, are commutable into equivalent terms of imprisonment), is the substitution of indefinite for definite sentences.

Archbishop Whately said, in a letter to Earl Grey, in 1832:—

> "It seems to me entirely reasonable that those who so conduct themselves, that it becomes necessary to confine them in houses of correction, should not be turned loose upon society again, until they give some indication that they are prepared to live without a repetition of their offences."

Maconochie agreed with Whately in his preference for task sentences rather than time sentences, and gave his reason in the following words:—

> "The purpose of this is to make the man's liberation, when he is once convicted of a felony, depend upon the subsequent character and conduct evinced by him, rather than on the original quality of his offence."

The first voice, however, raised in favor of distinctively reformation sentences was that of Mr. Frederick Hill, Inspector of the Prisons of Scotland, in the following words, in a report made by him in 1839:—

> "As regards the question, how are convicts to be disposed of after their release from prison, supposing transportation to be abolished, I would humbly suggest that it is desirable that those whom, from the nature and circumstances of their offences, as shown upon their trial, there can be no reasonable hope of reforming, should be kept in confinement through the remainder

of their lives; the severity of their discipline, however, being relaxed in various ways, which would not be safe, were it intended that they should return again to society." [1]

His brother, Matthew Davenport Hill, the eminent Recorder of Birmingham, reduced this principle to the epigrammatic formula, "Reformation or incapacitation," meaning thereby that if a prisoner fails to reform, under proper influences, and remains a peril to social order and security, he should be held for life.[2] This was in 1846. The same year, at the opening of the Civil Tribunal of Rheims, M. Bonneville de Marsangy delivered a memorable discourse on Preparatory

[1] In Mr. Frederick Hill's book on "Crime" (1853), he refers, in a foot-note to page 150, to "the plan of using a prison as a kind of moral hospital, to which offenders shall be sent until they are cured of their bad habits" as having been "recommended by Mr. Simpson, of Edinburgh, in a paper on the 'Treatment of Criminals,' which appeared in the *Law Magazine* many years ago."

[2] "The school of criminal jurists, to which I belong, have not deserted received opinions on light grounds; or sought for new principles until the failure of the old ones for the production of good practical results had been demonstrated by centuries of experiment, varied until the wit of man had exhausted all the possibilities of permutation. What course then remained for choice? None within the scope of my imagination, save two. First, such treatment as incapacitates the criminal from the commission of offences, leaving at the same time his appetites and passions unsubdued, and his desires unchanged; or, secondly, a treatment which has for its object to reform him, by leading him to yearn after good instead of evil, and by so training his habits as that he shall be able to give effect to his new aspirations. We are reduced, in short, to *Incapacitation* or to *Reformation.* Both these expedients, it must be admitted, are of very humble pretensions, when contrasted with the ambitious aims of deterrent punishment. Incapacitation limits itself to preventing the criminal from repeating his offence; either for a time, as when imprisonment is employed, or forever, as by the infliction of death. But as we are in no wise friendly to capital punishment, we would only use incapacitation as furnishing the opportunity for exercising reformatory action on the criminal; or, in extreme cases, for withholding from society one who has resisted all endeavors to approve him."—*Letter of M. D. Hill to C. B. Adderly, Esq., M.P.* (1856).

Liberation, in which the same thought was elaborated and defended. He defined preparatory or conditional liberation to be "a sort of middle term between an absolute pardon and the execution of the entire sentence; the right conceded to the judiciary, to release provisionally, after a sufficient period of expiatory suffering, a convict who appears to be reformed, reserving the right to return him to the prison, if there is against him any well-founded complaint." He especially pointed out that this was the method of dealing with juvenile offenders already accepted by the French law, and equally applicable to adults.[1]

Mr. Brockway accepted this principle, as did many

[1] In 1847, M. Bonneville (who was *procureur du roi* at Versailles) elaborated his thought in a work entitled "Traité des institutions complémentaires du régime pénitentiaire" (An essay on the institutions complementary to the penitentiary system), in which he discussed the pardoning power, conditional liberation, police surveillance of discharged convicts, patronage (aid to discharged convicts), and rehabilitation. This was distributed by the French Government to the members of both Chambers, as though it had been an official document. In 1864 he published a larger work in two volumes entitled "De l'amélioration de la loi criminelle," of which the twenty-fourth chapter is devoted to the discussion of conditional liberation, which, he says, "is nothing more nor less than the extension to adult convicts of a principle applied with such success to juvenile offenders." He insists that "as a skilful physician gives or withholds remedial treatment according as the patient is or is not cured, so ought the expiatory treatment imposed by law upon the criminal to cease, when his amendment is complete; further detention is inoperative for good, an act of inhumanity, and a needless burden to the state." Society should say to the prisoner: "Whenever you give satisfactory evidence of your genuine reformation, you will be tested, under the operation of a ticket-of-leave; thus the opportunity to abridge the term of your imprisonment is placed in your own hands." This course is, in his opinion, recommended by considerations of the greater deterrent effect of longer sentences by the courts, and of the moral encouragement given to the prisoner by the hope held out to him, as well as of the aid rendered to discipline in the prison; also for economic and sociological reasons. In his second volume he expresses satisfaction with the Irish graded system and the excellent results thereby secured.

other American students; but he did more. He secured its incorporation into American law, first in Michigan, in 1868, in the passage of the so-called Three Years' Law, applying to prostitutes, which authorized their commitment to the Detroit House of Correction for an indefinite term, not exceeding three years, and had for its immediate effect a general exodus of women of that class from that city. Subsequently, in 1876, he drafted the original statute directing the sending of young first offenders to Elmira under an indeterminate sentence, not to exceed the maximum term named in the New York code for each of the offences of which they might be convicted. He then proceeded to show, in the organization and government of the new Reformatory, what could be done, by the aid of this weapon, in the way of making good citizens out of bad. This is the signal service to humanity rendered by him, which has settled his position in the history of criminal reform, despite any errors of judgment on his part in the details of the application of the system.

The principle of the indeterminate sentence, with majority as its maximum, for juvenile offenders, was already familiar to us all. We were also accustomed to the operation of the commutation or good time laws, by which the actual term of imprisonment is abridged, in conformity to a standing rule in force at the time when sentence is pronounced, as a reward for good conduct while in prison. These were helps to the acceptance, as an experiment, of the indeterminate sentence, so-called, though the true indeterminate sentence has neither minimum nor maximum, and no one has had the courage to propose its adoption, as yet.[1]

The Elmira system, in practice, is a combination of marks, grades, and the parole, under the indeterminate sentence. The division of prisoners into grades, and the practice of promoting them from one grade to another, were methods prescribed in Massachusetts by law in 1826, and followed in the Massachusetts State Prison for many years. But, so far as appears, promotion was not offset by any corresponding power of degradation, nor was the sentence shortened as a reward for winning one's way into the third or highest class, neither was the classification determined by marks. Whether this was an original Massachusetts idea or borrowed from Australia is uncertain. It apparently did not give satisfaction, for it was ultimately dropped, and is now pretty much forgotten.

Marks are useful, but possibly not essential, as a means of keeping the record upon which a prisoner's promotion or degradation depends. They should of course be given in the three divisions of his daily life, for obedience to rules of order, work done in the shops

[1] Since the above paragraph was written, my attention has been called to the fact that in New York the maximum limit has been removed. Theoretically, its removal can be justified, and logical consistency probably requires that it should be removed; but prudential and practical arguments can be adduced against pushing a sound principle to this extreme, in advance of its general and decided acceptance by the public at large, on the following grounds: (1) Such action is unnecessary, since, if the maximum is sufficiently high, the same purpose is subserved as if there were no maximum; (2) the public and the courts are reluctant to place in the hands of any man or set of men unlimited power to detain a prisoner for life, regardless of the gravity of the offence of which he is guilty, especially if he is a young man and a first offender; (3) there is danger that a reaction may set in, which will encourage the enemies of the system to move for a return to definite sentences.

or elsewhere, and diligence in study. Their number is a question of pure detail, like marking in school: the highest mark may be three or five or ten, it matters little which. So, too, the number of classes may be varied, according to circumstances. The indispensable feature of the progressive classification scheme is that prisoners shall be raised and lowered in the scale on the basis of their merits. There are, however, instances in which the arbitrary remission of punishment by loss of rank is justified, by the effect upon a discouraged man. The good of each convict and of the body of convicts is the end sought, and anything which tends to secure that is proper.

Conditional liberation or the ticket-of-leave is not to be confounded with the indeterminate sentence. Conditional liberation is the act of the executive, not of the judicial branch of the government. It is the release of a convict, prior to the expiration of sentence, on probation, if, in the judgment of those in the most favorable position for forming a correct opinion, there is good reason to believe that he will henceforth abstain from crime; but he is released with the express understanding that he is still in custody, and that if he disappoints the expectation entertained of him, and relapses into criminal associations or ways, or manifests signs of being about to do so, he can and will be arrested and returned to the prison at any time during the continuance of his ticket-of-leave and before his liability to the criminal law terminates by his absolute discharge. Wherever conditional liberation is practised, except in the United States, this privilege is granted under a definite sentence: this is the case in England, Germany,

Switzerland, France, and Holland. The usual custom abroad is to delay the giving of a parole—in Sweden until the convict has served ten years; and it is regarded more as an act of grace, and not so much as a reward, to which the man who has earned it has a title.[1]

It seems more important to define the principles upon which the Elmira system is founded, than to describe in detail the architectural and other structural arrangements and the general management, however interesting that might be.[2] The great underlying thought in

[1] The first application of the principle of conditional liberation or "ticket-of-leave" to adults was by the English Government, after the failure of the system of transportation. By the law of 1847 this privilege was granted only to convicts shipped to Australia; but by the Act of 1853 tickets-of-leave were authorized to be granted also to convicts incarcerated on English soil. The system of conditional liberation (German, *Erlaubs-pass*) was adopted by the Kingdom of Saxony in 1862; and in the same year by the Grand Duchy of Oldenburg; in 1868, by the Canton of Sargovie, in Switzerland; in 1869, by the Kingdom of Serbia; in 1871, by the German Empire; in 1873, by the Kingdom of Denmark, also by the Canton of Neuchâtel; in 1875, by the Canton of Vaud, also by the Kingdom of Croatia, in Hungary; in 1878 by the Canton of Unterwalden; in 1881, by the Kingdom of Holland; in 1882, by the Empire of Japan; in 1885, by the French Republic. In none of these countries is it connected, as in the United States, with the indeterminate sentence. In all of them it is hedged about with more or less superfluous legal restrictions, which tend to defeat the end in view in its enactment.

[2] An apology seems to be due to the other American institutions founded upon the Elmira principle and in successful operation, for giving what may seem to be undue prominence to the New York Reformatory at Elmira, as if it were the only one worthy of mention or discussion. This is by no means the author's opinion. The Massachusetts Reformatory, at Concord, in particular, should be carefully studied, since it is strong in some of the very particulars in which the New York Reformatory is weak. But Elmira is the mother institution. Its superintendent, Mr. Brockway, was one of the little group of advanced thinkers upon this question who dared to advise the new departure and to elaborate it in imagination, before their ideas were given concrete form and substance. He was its creator, and

that institution is that criminals can be reformed; that reformation is the right of the convict and the duty of the State; that every prisoner must be individualized and given the special treatment adapted to develop him in the point in which he is weak—physical, intellectual, or moral culture, in combination, but in varying proportions, according to the diagnosis of each case; that time must be given for the reformatory process to take effect, before allowing him to be sent away, uncured; that his cure is always facilitated by his cooperation, and often impossible without it; that no other form of rewards and punishments is so effective, in so many instances, as transfer from one class to another, with different privileges in each; but that the supreme agency for gaining the desired cooperation on his part is power lodged in the administration of the prison to lengthen or shorten the duration of his term of incarceration. The other great thought, here insisted upon as nowhere else in the world, is that the whole process of reformation is educational; not meaning by that term the injection of information without assimilation, but the drawing out to its full natural and normal limit of every faculty of the body, mind, and soul of every man who passes through the institution. This is accomplished by all sorts of athletic training; shop work, military drill, gymnastics, Turkish and

was in charge of it, from the day it was opened. It has seemed better to confine the reader's attention to the most striking and original example of the ideal prison than to dissipate his thoughts by dwelling upon possible differences in the spirit and administration of prisons of this class. The application of the Elmira principle to women may be studied in the Massachusetts Prison for Women, at Sherborn, an institution of which all Americans have just reason to be proud.

other baths, massage, and diet; by all sorts of intellectual discipline as well, including not merely class instruction and the hearing of lectures on subjects in which prisoners most need instruction, but also systematic reading under direction, and examination upon the books read;[1] writing for the *Summary*, the prison weekly which circulates instead of the ordinary daily newspaper within the walls; and debate, in the presence of a teacher who guides and moderates the discussion. Trade instruction is made prominent. The aim of the institution is to send no man out who is not prepared to do something well enough to be independent of the temptation to fraud or theft.

If the question is asked, Where does the punishment come in? the answer is: In the discipline, which is unremitting and exacting; in the violence done to the criminal tastes and habits of the prisoners, which they have no opportunity to indulge; in the consciousness that one is held in a net of influence and restraint, which one is powerless to break; in the uncertainty as to one's ability to earn a discharge in time, or without too great a personal sacrifice; in the regularity and monotony of life under a rigid rule. Certain it is, that the worst men prefer to be sent to a prison organized on the old plan, and that there have been moments when the strain of anxiety to win an early parole has been so

[1] "It appears to me that we have a right to believe in the alteration of character of a prisoner, who at the beginning of his term of incarceration took pleasure only in reading of a frivolous sort, but, after having attended school for several months, draws from the library none but scientific or other serious works, and assimilates their contents, as the teacher knows, from his answers to the questions put once a month to all prisoners concerning their reading."—DR. GUILLAUME *of Switzerland.*

ominous of possible mental derangement as to alarm the superintendent and compel him to relax the pressure upon certain sensitive spirits thought to be in danger of eclipse. For the generation of the moral force necessary to carry the mass of prisoners upward and onward in a great reformatory current, association (under necessary restrictions) is indispensable, which is the reply to the criticisms upon this system by the advocates of the Pennsylvania system. Nor is there any point in the observation that association and routine are inseparable, and that individual treatment is impossible without cellular separation by day and night. If that were true, it would be necessary to have a separate class-room for every child in school, and to build our churches with separate stalls, as chapels are constructed in some foreign prisons.[1]

The Elmira system has been adopted in whole or in part, and made applicable to all or a part of the prisoners, in several other states: in Massachusetts, Pennsylvania, Ohio, Michigan, Illinois, Minnesota, Kansas, and South Dakota. One advantage gained from it is that it compels the study of the criminal himself, from all points of view; also the study of the causes and conditions which have made him what he is.

Above all other systems, however, it demands direction by a man of the highest integrity, attainments, and consecration. It has dangers peculiar to itself. The least of these, perhaps, is the liability to bribery and

[1] For a full and detailed account of the administration of the system at Elmira, the reader is referred to "The New York State Reformatory in Elmira," by Alexander Winter, F.S.S. (London, 1891), or to the more recent "Year Books" of the institution itself. The latter are finely and profusely illustrated.

corruption of the warden, if he has the power of release, to secure the earlier discharge of convicts not entitled to consideration on account of their records. It is far more probable that, as the result of our widespread acceptance of the doctrine that office is the reward of partisan service, and that parties can only be held together by the hope of plunder, the position of superintendent of a reformatory prison (and all prisons should be reformatories) will be given to an incompetent man, in payment of a political debt. The art of practical politics has been well defined as "the art of paying your debts at somebody else's expense." On this subject the author may be excused for quoting from himself:—

> "If a warden is given his place as a reward for party service, he is in so far disqualified for the highest success, by the very tastes and aptitudes which fit him to be a party leader. But whatever may be his fitness for the position, it is certain that, under a political administration of prisons, he will be turned out, whenever the control of the government passes into the hands of the opposite party, or even of a different faction of his own party. He has therefore little inducement to master the business entrusted to him. Worse than that, the subordinate positions in his gift are regarded as counters in the game; and unless he has himself the sense and skill to play them for all that they are worth, these minor appointments will be dictated to him, and he will be forced to put up with incompetency, if not with disloyalty. There can be no prison reform in the United States until the divorce of the prison system from practical politics is pronounced with such authority as to prevent any subsequent reunion of the two."

What constitutes competency depends upon what is expected of a public officer. If nothing more than that prisoners shall not escape, a soldier or a policeman will answer. If a pecuniary profit from convict labor is demanded, the warden must be a good business man. If he is to make the prison a factor in caucus and convention politics, he must be a "fine worker." In any event, he must be a judge of human nature, and capable of handling men. Honest he must be, of course, and kind, for if not kind, he is apt to be lacking in personal bravery. But if he is to be the centre and mainspring of educational and reformatory influence, he must be unsurpassed as a teacher and as an example of purity. The work of uplifting the degraded is one which calls for the highest qualities of soul and of brain. It is a work which it would not have shamed Phillips Brooks to have undertaken, at Charlestown or Concord; and, until we have the best men in this position, we cannot look for the best results. Where the personal fate of a thousand or fifteen hundred men depends upon the application to duty, the insight, the moral honesty, of another man clothed with almost despotic power, it will not answer to give that power into the possession of one who does not understand his responsibilities or who is unequal to them. But, if he possesses the requisite characteristics, no imaginable force will add so much to his power for good, as the right to fix the date of graduation of his pupils.

CHAPTER XI

CRIMINAL ANTHROPOLOGY

THE scientific study of the physical and psychical peculiarities of criminals is a new branch of anthropological investigation, to which the name of criminal anthropology has been given. Crime is admitted to be an ethical, social legal fact; is it or is it not also a biological fact? Naturally, biologists are disposed so to regard it, and they look with envy and disgust upon the mass of clinical material for biological and anthropological research which is allowed to go to waste, from the lack of scientific curiosity, in prisons. The conclusion to which such study points, in the estimation of men whose opinions are not to be dismissed without due consideration, is, in the words of Benedikt, that "The brains of criminals exhibit a deviation from the normal type, and criminals are to be viewed as an anthropological variety of their species, at least among the cultured races."

There is always danger in speaking of groups or classes of men, without reservations, such as that a particular observation is meant to apply not to all individuals of the group, but to the majority; or that it is intended as a generalization expressive of an average condition and tendency; or that it is true of all members of the group who fall within certain defined limits, and that the exceptions are outside those limits.

Precisely what constitutes an "anthropological variety" is not quite clear. But certainly it is a group of which the physical, mental, and moral composite, if we could arrive at it, would differ from the corresponding composite which should include all mankind, or all of a given race, or all the members of all other groups exclusive of the one under observation; and it might be assumed that it would also differ from the composite of any other group that can be named. Probably, too, if our knowledge of its history were minute and extensive, it would appear that it had been generated, under the pressure of a special environment, by inheritance; and we might even be warranted in predicting for it that it would continue to exist and grow, as a distinct aggregation of individuals more or less remotely connected with each other by blood, on account of marital unions between its members and the resulting intensification of the hereditary criminal strain. The result of this process of evolution of a separate class in the community would be that, upon the whole, the individuals included in it would bear a certain family resemblance to each other, manifesting itself in the absence or defect of certain physical and psychical traits common to other men, and in the corresponding overgrowth of other organs, functions, or habits.

The question to be answered, therefore, is whether men who have been convicted of crime and sentenced to imprisonment constitute such a group; whether the percentage of known criminal peculiarities of any sort can be ascertained and compared with the corresponding percentage for men not convicted and sentenced; and whether the differences which can be demonstrated by a sufficient number of observations pointing to a common conclusion are due to heredity or environment, or to both, and, if to both, in what relative proportion.

A multitude of medical and other scientific men, with greater or less aptitude for this sort of inquiry, have had their attention directed to this question and are seeking for its solution.

It needs no apparatus for minute and accurate measurements, with rules, scales, callipers, and goniometers —no chemical analysis of blood, tissues, and excretions—no careful experiments to test the degree of nervous susceptibility of different sensory organs—no specially devised psychical tests—to enable a common man, familiar with criminals through his relation to them as an officer of the police or of a court or prison, to describe their most obvious and striking characteristics. As a woman masquerading in male attire can be readily detected by a trained eye, so a thief can be known often by his looks and motions. A "furtive" look (furtive from *fur*, Latin for thief) is the look of a thief. But so can most mechanics, and even professional men. The demand made by every avocation in life upon its votaries for specific exertions on the one hand and sacrifices on the other, never fails to leave its impress upon the figure, the attitude, the entire bearing of the man, and to affect even his dress and gestures. This is not saying, however, that bankers or clergymen or editors or hotel clerks constitute distinct types, or that by anthropological study each of these groups of men engaged in similar pursuits could be shown to constitute a type, that is, "an *en-*

semble of distinctive characters" tending to perpetuate itself by sexual selection.

The criminal anthropologists dissect the criminal, so to speak, while he is still alive; measure every anatomical dimension of skull and trunk and limbs, record the color of his hair and his eyes, take his temperature, test his vitality with the stethoscope and sphygmograph, count his inspirations and expirations, search everywhere for evidence of abnormality of structure or of physiological action—for the pathological; and they extend this search to the internal organs, if the desired opportunity offers itself for an autopsy. It is a tedious process, if thorough, involving as it does, the examination of a multitude of individuals, and the comparison not of isolated phenomena, but of aggregated groups of phenomena.

What have they found? A general answer to this question is all that can properly be given in a work not medical but designed for lay reading, avoiding as far as possible technical terms and omitting observations which are incomprehensible without a minute acquaintance with the anatomy of the human body, particularly of the brain and nervous system.

Among the anatomical peculiarities noticed by students like Lombroso, Ferri, Benedikt, and many others who might be named, are the shape of the skull, including cranial asymmetry, microcephalism and macrocephalism. A very frequent defect is insufficient cranial development, markedly in the anterior portion. A receding forehead is common. Criminals are said to have a disproportionate tendency to the sugar-loaf or pointed head. Lombroso makes much of the unusual depth of the median occipital fossa. This is observable in the skull of Charlotte Corday, belonging to the collection of Prince Roland Bonaparte, which was exhibited at the Second International Congress of Criminal Anthropology at Paris, in 1889, and gave rise to a somewhat heated discussion of the question whether she was in fact a criminal or a patriot.[1] The same authority calls attention to the exaggeration of the orbital arches and frontal sinuses. Thieves are said, by one criminologist, to have small heads, while murderers have large heads; the sufficiency of his data for so daring a generalization is questionable. Beneath the skull, Benedikt claims to have discovered an unusual confluence of the fissures of the brain, and additional convolutions in the frontal lobe. The shape of the skull affects the countenance, in which have been observed certain deformities of the nose and ear, peculiarities in the coloring of the eye, irregularities of the teeth, prominence of the cheek-bones, elongation of the lower jaw, and the like. Another bold generalization is that which declares that the long and square jaw is common among criminals guilty of crimes of

[1] "Lombroso said that the skull of Charlotte Corday demonstrated anatomic characters of the criminal born, such as platycephalic, the occipital fossette, and other characters of the virile skull. Dr. Topinard responded by affirming that the skull of Charlotte Corday was normal, and that it presents all the proper characters of the skull of a woman. The platycephalic was a normal character, and the vermicular fossette was not an anomaly, and there was nothing irregular in the skull, unless it should be its platycephalic: and he said it was rare that a skull was the same in all its parts, and on both its sides. Benedikt said that according to his belief one had as much right to say that the occipital fossette was an indication of predisposition to hemorrhoids as to crime. Ferri and Lombroso replied vigorously to Benedikt, while Senator Moleschott came to his aid."—Dr. Wilson's Report to the Smithsonian Institution.

violence, but a receding chin among petty offenders; this is bold, however, only in the sense that it probably rests upon an inadequate statistical foundation, otherwise it is merely the application to convicts of a hackneyed physiognomical remark. The prominence of the criminal ear has been especially noted. Prisoners are said to have wrinkled faces; male prisoners have often scanty beards; many hairy women are found in prison. Red-haired men and women do not seem to be given to the commission of crime. Similar remarks might be quoted relative to the skeleton, such as that convicts have long arms, pigeon-breasts, and stooping shoulders.

Some of the physiological peculiarities noted are disordered nervous action, insensibility to pain, quick and easy recovery from wounds, defective taste and smell, strength and restlessness of the eye, mobility of the face and hands, left-handedness, excessive temperature, perverted secretions, abnormal sexual appetites, precocity, and so forth. Some medical writers say that the hearing of criminals is defective, others that it is preternaturally acute. Some affirm that color-blindness is prevalent among them, but others that it is rare. They are usually sensitive to climatic and meteorological influences. A very common observation is their freedom from the habit of blushing, but this may be a psychological rather than a physiological phenomenon.

The value of scientific investigation depends upon a variety of considerations, such as the competency of the observer, the number and extent of the observations, and the methods employed. No observations, however numerous, are of any scientific value (except as material for science) until they are reduced to order by classification and comparison. Observations of the abnormal are of no value without comparison with the normal.

The test of the adequacy and accuracy of the observations themselves is the agreement or disagreement of the observers in statements of fact. In the declarations regarding convicts made by criminologists, disagreements like those above cited as to their color-blindness or their hearing prove that the examination made was superficial, on the one side or the other, or else that the groups examined were of insufficient size to insure correspondence in the statistical result. This inquiry of necessity assumes largely a statistical form. The opportunities of police and prison officers to obtain, by means of daily contact with the criminal class, more accurate impressions and a better general notion respecting their appearance and character, exceed those of any scientific enthusiast; but they are apt to be unskilled observers, incapable of conducting an investigation after the systematic methods followed in an anthropological laboratory, or of pursuing it to the point of medical interrogation of the vital organs; and the commonplaces of the prison need statistical verification, for which records are necessary, which it is not usual to keep. Now every statistician knows that the limits of variation in the percentages obtained by the mathematical subdivision of any two corresponding groups of observed facts, if the groups are only large enough, are extremely narrow. Where the groups are large, and the percentages do not closely approximate each other, group for group, the difference is the result of causes operating locally, which are either known or can be searched out. Until a sufficient number of criminological statistical tables shall have been made and compared with each other to demonstrate their substantial agreement, without reference to the personality of the observer or the observed, the elementary facts of criminal anthropology can have no scientific authority, for want of an adequate scientific basis.

In the second place, the comparisons which must be made, in order to have any bearing upon the question of the existence or non-existence of a distinct and recognizable criminal type, must be comparisons not of isolated phenomena, but of groups of phenomena. A type, whatever else it may be, is "an *ensemble* of characters." It is not enough to know that certain characters exist in detail in more abundant measure in the criminal than in the non-criminal class; their tendency to repeat themselves in certain specific combinations must be proved, and the combinations themselves described. The new science, if it is a science, is not yet in position to attempt anything of the sort. The extreme difficulty of such a comparison is probably unsuspected by the great majority of its votaries.

Furthermore, if every criminal in the world were listed, examined, a truthful report made of all his essential peculiarities, and an accurate count made, showing all the important groupings of such peculiarities, so that the result could be tabulated and the percentages calculated, it would still be necessary to have a corresponding report exhibiting the same groupings of the same characters in an equal number of persons never convicted of crime, as a background for comparison, before the assertion that any particular grouping is even *primâ facie* evidence that its subject belongs to a separate anthropological type. The case is here put strongly, in order to impress this point upon the imagination. It would not in fact be necessary to carry the investigation so far. But it is necessary to carry it far enough to secure credibility in the result, and it must be carried as far for the innocent as for the guilty. It is said that red-haired criminals are relatively more rare than honest people with red heads. How is this known? How can it be known, without a statistical inquiry too extended to be attempted by private initiative? Suppose that the reverse were true; would it be allowable to entertain a suspicion of the honesty of all blondes? The peculiarities recorded in the case of convicts are also observable in honest men and women. Much has been made of cranial asymmetry, about which every hatter who uses a *formateur* can give a criminologist points which would possibly correct his estimate of the value of this particular stigma. A photographer could do the same with reference to asymmetry of the countenance; if he knows his business, he makes every subject sit with the worst side of his face in shadow.

Anatomical remarks are of course the most palpable; for this reason the writings of the anthropologists exhibit the greatest affluence of statistics upon the precise points which are of the smallest relative significance. Of greater importance is the study of physiological peculiarities, especially if they are at the same time pathological and reveal a nervous diathesis analogous to that of the insane or epileptic. But, after all, the most important characters demanding investigation are the psychical. If a criminal type in fact exists, it can be discovered and brought to light only by a demonstration of the uniform or approximately uniform coexistence of certain combinations of physical and psychical manifestations, which are rarely if ever found to be dissociated from each other. Such a demonstration would afford a trustworthy basis for scientific prevision and prediction. The perfection of any science is shown by the capacity of those who have mastered it to read the future, as astronomers, for instance, are able to foretell the precise moment of an eclipse, while meteorologists can rarely foretell the weather twenty-four hours in advance. Judged by this standard, criminal anthropology is still in the state of adolescence, if not of infancy.

Finally, what is a type? The word is employed in two very different senses. Popularly, perhaps, it is used to express the fact that certain groups of characters repeat themselves in numbers of individuals, without reference to the question whether they are accidental and due to environment, education, or habit, or whether they are transmissible by inheritance. Every such group of individuals bearing a marked resemblance to each other in appearance, habits, tastes, occupations, and so forth, is said to be a type. Even in this sense a single character does not constitute the type, but an aggregation of characters—an *ensemble*. In the strictly scientific sense, on the contrary, an anthropological type cannot be said to exist, where it does not tend in a high degree to reproduce itself in offspring. The *ensemble* of characters which, taken together, express it, must be recognized in a majority at least of the members of a family, a tribe, or a nation, united by ties of blood. They must be inherited from a common ancestor. In the first of these two senses, the existence of a criminal type is admitted, though it may be difficult to define with precision all the elements of which it is composed. In the more restricted and accurate signification of the term, the existence of an anthropological criminal type has not been proved, and it is doubtful whether it can be proved.

In order to prove it, it will be necessary to push the inquiry a step further, and to ascertain, in a sufficient number of individual instances, whether any special group of peculiarities demonstrably attaching to criminals and more rarely found in combination in virtuous, peaceable, honest citizens, did in fact characterize either or both the parents of the criminals in question; or, if not, whether they characterized some more remote progenitor; and whether they are repeated in any considerable number of the near relations of the aforesaid criminals, who may be supposed to have in their veins a large proportion of the same vicious or degenerated blood. Here we touch upon the vexed question, still in suspense, of the transmissibility of acquired characters, into which we cannot here enter, but which is the vital question of evolution, and the central point of this particular controversy.

From these statements the reader may form an adequate notion of the difficulty, as well as of the importance of the task to which these gentlemen have devoted their talents and their energies. The obstacles to be overcome are enormous, if not insuperable. They are enhanced by the ignorance, stupidity, indifference, suspicion, and inveracity of the convicts, who alone, in many cases, can give the desired family history (which a large percentage of them cannot do), and whose statements regarding themselves require verification, before science can predicate any conclusions from them. When the facts shall have been collected and verified, the work of interpretation will be in order; but it involves so much hypothetical, speculative reasoning, particularly upon the point of the relative importance of heredity and environment in the production of the specific characters included in each type, that the conclusions formulated will differ with the personal convictions and prejudices of the writer. From the description of an anthropological type should be excluded all characters which are not hereditary, or at least transmissible—cuts and scars, for instance, of which there is a fearful percentage among old, habitual convicts; and yet one observer with little notion of perspective gives undue prominence in his picture of typical crime to the wrinkled faces of prisoners.[1]

Among the questions on which students are by no means agreed is that of normality: what is normal? and what is abnormal? At the Rome Congress of Criminal Anthropology, Albrecht entered the controversial arena with the astounding motto emblazoned upon his crest: "The criminal alone is normal—not the

[1] There is indeed a wrinkled face—the face of an idiot child, with a prematurely old look (though this may also be compared to the wrinkled faces of the newly born), which is connected with congenital defect; but there are also wrinkles of remorse and care, of passions indulged, which are purely individual and largely due to environment.

honest man." (David said, in his haste, that all men were liars.) There is also apparent a tendency to division upon the question whether murder or theft is the more truly typical crime; which of the two can be most clearly traced to a prenatal origin. Garofalo thinks that murder is the crime *par excellence* and that the sentiment of probity is, evolutionally speaking, "more recent" and less transmissible by inheritance; that causes external to the thief himself, such as hard times, want of employment, etc., more directly affect the prevalence of crimes against property. Habitual theft, however, is more common in the aggregate and probably also more common relatively to the whole number of crimes of violence or of dishonesty, than habitual murder; so that the late and lamented Mr. Richard Vaux, who was not an anthropologist, but who was for more than half a century connected with the board of management of the Eastern Penitentiary of Philadelphia, would exclude from the "crime-class" all convicts who are not thieves.

Nevertheless, the attempts which have been made to place criminal anthropology in the rank of a true science are worthy of the highest commendation, because they serve preeminently to bring into high relief the truth that criminal jurisprudence has reached a period in the history of civilization, when it can no longer afford to confine its attention to the crime and the penalty for crime, but must take notice of the criminal also. The attack upon the legal profession by the medical profession is justified by the necessity for establishing harmony between statutory and natural law, which has been disturbed by the blind conservatism of the criminal code, clinging to exploded precedents, and refusing to recognize the demand for new foundations and a new superstructure. The actual work of renovation can be effected only by lawyers, since the changes to be made in the law must not contradict the established principles of civil government and of judicial procedure. But reforms in existing institutions are rarely, perhaps never, brought about, except by agitation and pressure from without. It pertains to the medical and clerical professions, acting in concert but from opposite directions, to formulate the demand for the indeterminate sentence and for a reformatory discipline, in prisons, properly guarded, so as fully to protect individual rights, justice and freedom. It pertains to the legal profession, and to the people represented in the legislature, to meet this demand. When the demand shall be met, as it surely will be, the criminal anthropologists will be entitled to their full share of credit for promoting and keeping alive the agitation to which the benign result will be due.

One immediate and practical result has already been accomplished, if no more; the recognition of the value of anthropometry as a means of identification of criminals, and detection of recidivists. Anthropometry is an aid to anatomical study only, and therefore its scientific importance, according to the views expressed in this chapter, is comparatively slight. But the measurements taken of the bony skelton—the height, length of the extended arms, of the limbs and their component parts separately (including the fingers and the feet), and dimensions of the skull and chest—do not precisely correspond in any two human beings, in their totality. Dr. Alphonse Bertillon, of Paris, has grasped this thought, and he has devised a set of instruments for taking these measurements, and a system of recording them upon cards and arranging the cards systematically, so that, under the classification which he has invented, they can be consulted with as much ease as a dictionary, or the card catalogue of a library. His card catalogue of convicts is the best conceivable form of a universal criminal register, upon many accounts; not only because it is practical, accurate, and adequate; but because the habitual convict whose criminal record is needed for any legitimate purpose can be unmistakably identified thereby, without any knowledge of his name; while the accidental or occasional criminal who does not relapse into crime, and is not again arrested, is therein buried out of sight as irrecoverably as if the record had been destroyed in the central fires of the earth. It has been adopted by many nations, states, and municipalities; but for the highest utility in this country the creation of a central registration bureau is a necessity, which should be under the control of the Federal Government, as the only suitable and proper agency for its creation and maintenance.

It is now possible to add to the foregoing analysis the results of an elaborate and painstaking inquiry, based upon the careful measurement of a large number of criminals and intended to determine once for all whether a criminal anthropological type exists. This inquiry was completed after the first edition of the present volume was published. Heretofore, the chief weakness of those who opposed the Italian school has been their lack of trustworthy facts with which to confute the claims of their antagonists. However extravagant these claims might be, they were difficult to upset when put forth in an atmosphere of scientific veracity and repeated with great conviction. A new day dawned, therefore, in the anthropological study of the criminal, when a deputy medical officer of Parkhurst prison in England, Dr. Griffiths, after listening to heated discussions of the Lombrosian theory at a Paris congress of criminologists, decided to go home and discover the truth for himself. Dr. Griffiths' intention was to select a large number of prisoners convicted of certain similar offences, to make accurate physical measurements of them, and to conclude upon the basis of these measurements whether, in fact, the prisoners studied showed any deviation from persons who had not committed crime. The plan was later enlarged to include the general body of convicts without selection, and observations were begun in 1902. Three thousand prisoners consecutively admitted to English convict prisons were studied. So stupendous was the undertaking that not until 1908 were all the data compiled, and not until 1913 were interpretations and conclusions published.[1] Meanwhile, Dr. Griffiths had been replaced early in the inquiry by Dr. Charles Goring, upon whom fell the brunt of the investigation and to whose personality and determination is due the major part of the credit for carrying it through.

All of the prisoners studied were recidivists. They

[1] "The English Convict," published by His Majesty's Stationery Office, London, 1913.

were, thus, the very persons who would most confidently be presumed to constitute a criminal type, if such type there be. Though examinations were made by different medical officers, a uniform procedure was adopted and Professor Karl Pearson, whose applications of the methods of statistical science to large masses of craniometric data have attracted wide attention, gave his personal assistance and granted the use of his biometrical laboratory.

It would be tedious here to describe the elaborate mechanism by which Goring first secured and then "weighed" his facts. Coming at once to his comparisons, the first of these lay between the head-length, head-breadth and cephalic index (ratio of breadth to length of head) of the 3,000 criminals, and the same characteristics of 1,000 undergraduates in Cambridge University, England. (The data concerning the undergraduates had been secured from the Cambridge Anthropometrical Committee.) A difference was found between the two groups of only 1 millimetre in mean head-length and of 3 millimetres in mean head-breadth, the criminals displaying the smaller measurements. These differences are, of course, fairly negligible. Moreover, the criminals were sixteen years older than the Cambridge students on the average, and 3½ inches shorter. When, therefore, corrections were made for these differences, the variation in head-breadth was materially reduced and the variation in head-length entirely disappeared. Then, too, the heads of the convicts were closely cropped of hair, a fact leading, said Goring, to a relative "depreciation of measurements." The difference in skull capacity, thirty-four cubic millimetres, was pronounced by him "practically negligible" when considered in relation to the total magnitude involved.

Similar comparisons were made between prisoners and Oxford undergraduates. Data concerning 959 Oxford students happened to be at hand. When these were set off against the measurements of criminals, the results were the same as in the comparison with Cambridge students. Differences ranging from 1½ to 2 millimeters in the three principal head diameters were revealed. The considerations that tended to diminish these differences in the former study were equally applicable here, so that once again it was demonstrated that the youth who committed England's crimes were in no wise markedly different, so far as general shape and girth of head were concerned, from the youth who achieved her scholastic honors.

Goring did not stop, however, with comparisons with University students. He compared his convicts also with the inmates of a general hospital. Here the contrast lay, not between prisoners and those apt to be the most distantly removed from them in education, intelligence, and physique, but between prisoners and a class not much higher than that from which prisoners are mainly drawn. The result, nevertheless, was much the same: no differentation in head-shape, and only a slight difference in absolute measurements of the head. It was the hospital inmates, moreover, who showed the smaller dimensions in this instance. Goring explained this as due to the "shrinkage" of bone and tissue that illness and defective nourishment are likely to produce. His conclusion was, therefore, that the hospital patients, and not the criminals, constituted a class "physically differentiated" from the general community, if the existence of such a class was indicated by the comparisons.

These studies dealt with length, breadth and circumference of head. Another set of cephalic characters had been largely dwelt upon by the Lombrosoan school, namely height, width and slope of forehead, the projection and slope of the occiput, the relative magnitude of front to back of head, and the general shape and symmetry of the head. These, indeed, are the characters which, in extreme form, have been called "cephalic anomalies" and which produce those low, narrow, receding foreheads, "dome-shaped" heads, "sugar loaf" heads and heads with bulging protuberances that have so often been emphasized as peculiarly characteristic of criminals. Lombroso had even gone so far as to say that he could pick people out of the general population as being either criminal or non-criminal by their possession of these attributes.

Goring compared his prisoners with a group of non-commissioned officers and men of the Royal Engineers (sailors) in order to test the theories of the Lombrosoan school with respect to these characteristics. Various measurements and data were recorded. With the aid of Pearson a method was devised for taking the statistical records of these features, for arriving at the mean contours of the two groups from three angles representing the top, back and profile views, and for superimposing the contours of one group upon those of the other. No "anomalies" were found. The contours practically coincided. The Royal Engineers were no more and no less "bulged" as to the forehead or protruding as to the occiput than the prisoners. Once more, therefore, Goring concluded that physical stigmata were a myth.

Goring announced his conclusion in one highly quotable sentence. After comparing the Cambridge and Oxford students not only with prisoners but *with each other,* and introducing a third University, Aberdeen, he declared that *"prison inmates, as a whole, approximate closer in head-measurements to the Universities generally, than do students of different Universities conform with each other in this regard."* Also, with respect to Lombroso's contention that criminals were "predestined" to do evil and that their future could be predicted with relative certainty, he said that "from a knowledge only of an undergraduate's cephalic measurements, a better judgment could be given as to whether he were studying at an English or Scottish University than a prediction could be made as to whether he would eventually become a University professor or a convicted felon!"

Criminal anthropologists have not relied solely upon measurements of the head. Color of the hair and eyes, shape of the nose, defective hearing, left-handedness —these and other characteristics are said to mark criminals from the rest of mankind. Accordingly, Goring gathering data about them and compared his prisoners with groups from the non-criminal community for whom similar facts existed. One of the most striking results was that revealed by a comparison between the hair and eye color of convicts and of a group of English school boys. Here is the record:

Groups Compared	Eyes Per Cent.		Hair Per Cent.			
	Light	Medium and Dark	Red	Blonde	Light Brown or Fair	Dark Brown and Black, or Medium and Dark
English Convicts......	35.1	64.9	3.4	2.5	29.5	65.5
English School-boys...	38.4	61.4	3.7	?	35.0	61.3

It will be seen at once that the school boys showed only a very slightly lighter shade, in regard both to hair and eyes, than did the convicts. When it is remembered that hair and eyes tend to become darker during the passage to adult life, the significance of this result is apparent. Similar unimportant differences were found with respect to conformation of nose and left-handedness.

So far, the studies mentioned here have dealt only with comparisons between criminals and the general population. They shed no light on possible differences between one group of criminals and another. It might still remain true, for example, that thieves possess physical characteristics setting them off as a class from forgers, assailants from burglars, incendiaries from wife-deserters, persons convicted of damage to property from those convicted of damage to persons, etc. Goring tested this possibility also. He selected thirty-seven different physical characteristics, classified his prisoners on the basis of the crimes they had committed, and then compared the different groups of criminals on the basis of each characteristic.

No evidence was found to indicate that one kind of criminal bears any such striking differences from another as to make it an anthropological variety. The investigation did reveal small differences in head-length, shade of hair, complexion and one or two other characteristics, marking particularly the groups of *fraudulent offenders and incendiaries.* It is impossible here to go fully into the discussion of these differences, but it is enough to say that Goring was fairly able to explain them as due to natural causes. Fraudulent offenders, for example, he said, are drawn for the most part from "the upper middle and middle classes," incendiaries from the opposite end of the social scale. Since "class" differentiation is a widely accepted fact, and since his own data furnished evidence that such differentiation exists even between different types of criminals, he concluded that the differences he had found between criminals as a whole and fraudulent offenders and incendiaries as groups, were far more likely to be due to class distinctions than to crime. Nutritional and environmental circumstances also, he thought, might be contributory causes to these differences.

Brief as this résumé is, it gives some notion of the nature of Goring's data concerning an anthropological type. The reader should not infer that he found *no* differences distinguishing criminals, either from the general population or from each other. What he did *not* find were definite physical anomalies or stigmata, such as would necessarily constitute a physical type. What he did find were certain very general physical traits distinguishing criminals. These he described as *an inferiority in stature and body weight* and summed them up as follows:

"All English criminals, with the exception of those technically convicted of fraud, are markedly differentiated from the general population in stature and body weight; in addition, offenders convicted of violence to the person are characterized by an average degree of strength and of constitutional soundness considerably above the average of other criminals, and of the law-abiding community;[1] finally, thieves and burglars (who constitute, it must be borne in mind, 90 per cent of all criminals), and also incendiaries, as well as being inferior in stature and weight, are also, relatively to other criminals and the population at large, puny in their general bodily habit."

What does this inferiority in stature and body weight mean? It is the same that von Kleinsmid[2] found among 5,680 inmates of the Indiana Reformatory, which led him to draw the conclusion that "these men are physically inferior to the average young man not in prison and presumably normal." Goring interpreted the inferiority as due in the main to a process of selection. Physique, he said, plays an important part in the choice of many occupations; why not in crime also? Soldiers and policemen, for example, must be strong, while clerks and others who follow sedentary occupations need not be. It is easy to imagine, Goring thought, that deficiency of physical stamina may account for the entrance of many persons upon criminal careers. Moreover, since only about 59,000 persons were arrested for 91,000 indictable

[1] A stout, strong, healthy, thick-set individual, if anything rather below the average stature of his class: this, said Goring, is the typical portrait of a person prone to commit criminal violence.

[2] Rufus Bernhard von Kleinsmid: Preliminary Report, Department of Research, Indiana Reformatory, Jeffersonville, 1914.

offences reported to the police in England and Wales in 1906, *some* selection evidently takes place among those caught, and feebleness may be regarded as a factor more conducive to apprehension than strength.

Again, tall and well-built persons, though perhaps equally inclined with others to become pickpockets and burglars, are not as likely to choose these callings in the long run as persons of a more unnoticeable appearance. So with incendiaries; individuals convicted of this offence in England, said Goring, are for the most part farm laborers who, smarting under real or imaginary grievances, fire the stacks of their masters—the "typical revengeful act of a weakling, from whom a physical assault would be ineffective." Finally, there are the fraudulent offenders, persons who have committed crime from motives of material benefit, upon whom it is difficult to understand how physique could exert any selective influence. And it is precisely these offenders whom we find in Goring's study unselected by either stature or body weight—their "mean stature and weight being the same as those of the same social and economic classes in the general non-criminal community."

How, then, does the matter stand? Thus: there is no criminal anthropological type; physical stigmata of crime do not exist; criminals are not differentiated either from the non-criminal population or among themselves by particular attributes. They do, however, constitute a class inferior in respect to stature and body weight. Goring put it in this wise:—

"In the present investigation we have exhaustively compared, with regard to many physical characters, different kinds of criminals with each other, and criminals, as a class, with the law-abiding public. From these comparisons, *no evidence has emerged confirming the existence of a physical criminal type, such as Lombroso and his disciples have described.* Our data do show that physical differences exist between different kinds of criminals: precisely as they exist between different kinds of law-abiding people. But, when allowance is made for a certain range of probable variation, and when they are reduced to a common standard of age, stature, intelligence and class, etc., these differences tend entirely to disappear. Our results nowhere confirm the evidence, nor justify the allegations, of criminal anthropologists. They challenge their evidence at almost every point. In fact, both with regard to measurements and the presence of physical anomalies in criminals, our statistics present a startling conformity with similar statistics of the law-abiding classes. The final conclusion we are bound to accept until further evidence, in the train of long series of statistics, may compel us to reject or to modify an apparent certainty—our inevitable conclusion must be that *there is no such thing as a physical criminal type.*"

To this statement of his conclusions Goring added expressions of severe condemnation for the methods and ideas by which Lombroso and his followers had so long held the center of the criminological stage. The Lombrosian theory he called a "superstition." It if "kith and kin with the misnamed 'sciences' of phrenology, chiromancy, and physiognomy." Behind Lombroso's notion, he said,

"there were positively no facts at all. He had been studying the cadavers and living persons of criminals for months, when, suddenly, at the sight of certain anomalies in the skull of one particular brigand, revelation flashed through the surrounding gloom: the hypothesis was framed. We contend that a notion arrived at in these romantic and emotional conditions could not legitimately be employed as a working hypothesis for directing a disinterested investigation; we maintain that the whole of Lombroso's enterprise was conducted, we do not say with the express purpose, but with the unconscious intention, of stamping a preconceived idea with the hall mark of science."

And again:

"Nor were the adventures of Lombroso confined within prison walls. On one occasion, he pointed out, as an example of the criminal type, a youth who had never appeared in a court of justice; 'he may not be a legal criminal,' was the airy utterance, 'but he is a criminal anthropologically.' At pause before the skull of Gasparonne, a famous nineteenth century brigand, the seeker found many of the stigmata common to the skulls of ordinary prison inmates. Thus, he tells us, there was, in the unfortunate Gasparonne, a wormian bone; microcephaly of the frontal region, erignathism, oxycephaly, dolico-cephaly, and enlarged orbital capacity, were also implacably present. Charlotte Corday's skull inspires this eloquence: 'Not even the purest political crime, that which springs from passion, is exempt from the law which we have laid down.' And, borne onward by the flood of enthusiasm, our intrepid explorer sets foot at last upon the shores of antiquity. Confronting the effigy of Messalina, he sees in triumph the unmistakable criminal stamp—the heavy jaw, the low forehead, the wavy hair; he recognizes them all! . . . Perhaps, however, he is at his best, his happiest, in contemplation before the old woman of Palermo, who poisoned so many people with arseniated vinegar. 'The bust,' writes Lombroso, 'which we possess of this criminal, so full of virile angularity, and, above all, so deeply wrinkled, with its Satanic leer, suffices of itself to prove that the woman in question was born to do evil, and that, if one occasion to commit it had failed, she would have found others.'"

Whatever we may think of this asperity, we must admit that he who uttered it has effectually laid, for the present at least, the views upon which it is heaped. In concluding this chapter, we must consider some of the criticisms that have been made of Goring's inquiry.

In a preface to Goring's work, Sir Evelyn Ruggles-Brise calls it "the first attempt that has been made in this, or in any other country, to arrive at results in criminology by the statistical treatment of facts." The very circumstance that the statistical method did underlie the whole inquiry has been made a point of objection to it. This method, it is said, with its complex, involute and rigid means of passing judgment upon objective facts, is wholly adequate to discover truth in regard to the causes of crime. This criticism is sound in so far as it applies to the more subjective or personal causes of crime, those having to do, for example, with psychological factors, but it is difficult to see how it applies to the matter in hand. How can the existence or non-existence of physical stigmata be proved or disproved except by the exact measurement of human beings and the careful correlation of the data recorded? The whole quarrel with the Indian school is that it did not use sufficiently exact methods of calculation; to object to the opponents of the Lombrosians that they *have* used these methods seems hardly a logical procedure. The statistical method has its limitations, but it is not one of those limitations to deal with measurable quantities.

Criticism has also been directed against the inquiry on the ground that it failed to furnish adequate comparison with the normal population. An ideal inquiry might perhaps have gone further, but when we compare Goring's data with those of his predecessors we are compelled to admit that his disproof is at least stronger than their proof. Another criticism is that the legal conception of the criminal adopted by Goring is too narrow, since "criminals" include many more than just those persons who are caught and sent to

English prisons. Instead of being a weakness, this may be a strength, for the individuals studied were recidivists and if an anthropological type exists, we should expect to find it among those who most often get into jail.

Undoubtedly, however, when Goring left the field of measurable physical characters and entered that of mental attributes and the forces of environment, he stepped onto slippery ground. Neither his methods nor the range of his observations were calculated to discover truth here. He had no definite standards for measuring mental ability (the Binet-Simon tests were translated into English the very year that Goring stopped gathering data), and while his general conclusion, namely, that defective intelligence is one of the vital causes of crime, is in line with present opinion, his own material on this head was not scientifically gathered. Moreover, there is nothing to indicate that he was aware of the many totally different kinds of mental disease that may cause anti-social conduct. His elimination of the "force of circumstances" as having little or no causal relation to crime may be set down as valueless, first, because he did not conduct an intensive study of individuals, and, second, because the very element that gave strength to his inquiry in regard to a physical type—the fact that he was dealing with recidivists—weakened his study of environment, since persons who commit crime repeatedly are much less likely to have been brought to that strait by external circumstances than those who commit it once in a life-time.

To leave Goring's inquiry with these remarks, however, would be to fail to point out the essential difference between his attitude and approach toward the criminal, and the attitude and approach that seem most hopeful to-day of accomplishing beneficial results. Doubtless Goring's insistence upon accurate and careful study is an improvement over the methods of the criminal sociologist, who has been wont to enumerate all manner of chance conditions *associated with criminality* and to call these *causes* of crime. Goring is all for careful, accurate, scientific work. Nevertheless, he does not help us to see that the true method of dealing with the man who has broken society's laws is to discover what has made that particular man a criminal and then to strive to remove the particular cause. He does not deny this, but he does not help to affirm it. He would too loosely substitute one set of general causes for another set, without making us see that no set of general causes is sufficient. The aim of applied criminology is two-fold: first, to discover the specific causes of crime in an individual; second, to base treatment upon everything about the individual that may have a bearing upon reformation —his mental nature, his heredity, his growth from infancy up, his associations and environment, his physical well-being. The cause may be epilepsy, insanity, constitutional mental inferiority, inordinate sex impulses, or any one of many similar or different factors. The remedy may be permanent custodial care, dissolution of a mental complex, a regulated emotional life, or a period of bracing existence in the open air. The thing to remember is that categories of crime and general theories concerning criminals crumble and fall away when one faces the particular man or woman convicted of a criminal act. Goring does not contribute to this discovery; his methods are not the methods to reveal it. What those methods are we must now consider.

CHAPTER XII

THE STUDY OF THE INDIVIDUAL DELINQUENT

I. Diagnosis

No one would attempt to-day to make a sick man well without knowing what was the matter with him. We have passed out of the dark age of medical practice when physicians regarded all disease as of one kind and, acquainted with only a few remedies, applied these in turn until the patient either recovered or died. We know to-day that disease is of many kinds, and that exact knowledge of the specific ailment from which an individual is suffering is not only obtainable but necessary. We are interested in the precise nature of a man's ill health, and we study every part and phase of him in order to learn. We test his organs, we examine his tissues, we take samples of his blood and sputum, we consider the part played by fatigue and nutrition, we enter his very body through the X-ray. All this we do before thought of treatment, for modern treatment presupposes exact knowledge of the nature of disease. A physician who should simply say of every patient who came to him that the patient was *sick,* and should send him and all others to a hospital without further attention to the nature or causes of his sickness, would soon be ostracized professionally.

This process of discovering the exact disease from

which an individual is suffering is called diagnosis. Diagnosis is not the only prerequisite to treatment, however. Having discovered the nature of the disease, one must know what caused it. To know that a patient is the victim of typhoid is not enough. One must know that typhoid is caused by a bacillus and he must know how this bacillus lives and what will kill it. Often he must know, also, the indirect or predisposing causes of the disease. If a condition of anæmia or fatigue is favorable to typhoid, that fact must be known and reckoned with. In other words, the complexity of causation must be considered. Treatment must proceed upon two bases: It must recognize the necessity of individual diagnosis to discover the specific disease being dealt with, and it must recognize the necessity of a knowledge of causes before effective cure can be applied.

These statements are platitudes in regard to disease. They are novel in regard to crime. There is a close analogy between the method to be pursued in curing a man of disease and that to be pursued in checking his criminal tendencies. In each instance the method is diagnosis of the individual, the discovery of the special cause or causes of his malady, and then prescription of the measures best calculated to effect cure. This does not mean that there is any similarity between disease and crime *per se.* The analogy lies between the *scientific method* of approach or attack upon the two things, not between the things themselves. Diagnosis and etiology (study of causes) can be applied to the law-breaker no less directly than to the sick man; it is only because we have not understood the nature of many criminals and criminal acts that we have not heretofore adopted them more generally.

We are coming to do so to-day, however. Diagnosis of individual offenders is an established part of the work of a few courts and an increasing number of correctional institutions. The method is still in its infancy, and even in those places where it is being tried not all offenders, usually, receive study. Moreover, standards of procedure and thoroughness vary greatly. In general, juvenile courts and reformatories have been the first to perceive the advantages of diagnosis, though several prisons have recently established clinics for such study, as well as one or two criminal courts for adults. The county jail of Hudson County, N. J., has attempted diagnosis on a small scale. Private foundations in a number of cities have aided courts in this research, and some private institutions for delinquents, such as Waverly House in New York City, have adopted the method in their work.

As a result of this effort, a new profession has come into existence. It is that of the clinical or diagnosing criminologist. The leaders in the profession are for the most part specialists in psychiatry, with special knowledge also of psychology and medicine. They are peculiarly prepared, therefore, to study offenders on both the mental and physical sides. The most proficient among them are well versed also in the effects and causes of heredity and social adjustment. To do the most effective work, they must be scientifically inclined, capable of pushing investigation back to its ultimate sources. An acquaintance with educational methods and possibilities is obviously of importance in the prognostic and therapeutic aspects of their work. The American Association of Clinical Criminologists, formed in 1913, is largely made up of members of this profession.

These advocates of a new criminology have not as yet won the attention of the general public. Their findings are only slowly seeping through to the popular mind. For the most part their discussions find light at scientific gatherings or in scientific periodicals. Judges, prison wardens, probation officers and others who have to do with the treatment of the criminal do not, except in rare instances, recognize the importance of their contributions; social workers are only beginning to do so. Even when it is conceded that the science of human behavior may throw some light on the nature and causes of crime, it is not always admitted that each individual requires study. Penology, except for the play of humanitarian impulses, which are not always wisely directed, is still groping in its dark age.

Only a moment's reflection is necessary to convince the reader of the preceding chapters that this is true. Penology has remained for the most part a theory. It has concerned itself too much with general categories of criminals and general statements concerning the causes of crime. It has looked, first, at symptoms and has classified men as thieves, murderers, incendiaries, etc., because these words describe the final act by which the criminal reveals himself. It has tried to discover general reasons for the breaking of society's laws, and having found these in ignorance, alcoholism, poverty, insanity, violent temper and the like, has made little effort to trace the operation of these causes in the individual or to discover other and less obvious causes of crime. Its conclusions have been promulgated from the arm chair and it has made slight attempt to "go to the criminal for the facts"; where it has tried to do this, its methods have been impressionistic and based on loose observation. Meanwhile, it has prescribed treatment for criminals *en masse*. It has assumed that a uniform regimen—usually confinement in some odious, high-walled prison—would overcome the evil tendencies of all law-breakers, in so far as these were possible to be overcome. It has attempted a universal specific—incarceration: and incarceration under conditions varying little and based on the uniform possession by prisoners of normal or nearly normal faculties. Even where it has, in recent years, attempted a change from the rigors of prison confinement and, by means of probation, sought a more hopeful way of achieving its ends, it has for the most part been guilty of just as indiscriminate an application of its new remedy as of its old. It has known almost nothing of diagnosis or of the individual's capacities and needs. It has regarded criminals as the chance or inevitable products of forces that did not need to be determined, either to protect society or to cure criminals of their lawless ways.

The criminal has not, of course, been altogether lost sight of as an individual. Trial in court is itself a species of individualization, though its purpose has hstorically been merely to settle the single question of guilt, and the criminal has quickly merged with the general mass—either of his fellow convicts or of society—when the trial was over. One class of irresponsible law-breakers, it is true, has long been recognized—the so-called "criminal insane"; but even here what might have been a promising beginning in the individualization of the criminal was vitiated by the methods pursued in determining insanity—leaving the matter for the jury to decide, and aiding it only by the answers of "specialists" to cleverly worded hypothetical questions—and also by the inadequate treatment usually accorded those who were held to be insane. Modern humanitarian movements, beginning with Beccario and John Howard, have tended to force attention more and more upon the individual, while Lombroso, as we have seen, gave a pseudo-scientific prominence to him.

More recently the use of the indeterminate sentence has both contributed to and resulted from the realization that criminals differ from each other in important respects and that different modes of treatment are necessary to secure reformative results. Finally, intensive studies of individuals begun some two decades ago and carried on by only a few students, notably in Germany, suggested the possible complexities of criminal causation and paved the way for the systematic work that has since been carried on.

For the real beginning of the new science of criminal diagnosis, however, we must look to the Juvenile Psychopathic Institute in Chicago, organized in 1909 in connection with the Juvenile Court of Cook County with Dr. William Healy as director. This was a private organization, established for the express purpose of securing practical and intensive studies of young offenders. Funds for a five-year program were supplied and a notable group of jurists, psychologists and others acted as an advisory council.

From the first the institute chose repeated offenders for study because, by reason of their numbers and the seriousness of their offences, these were believed to have the "greatest significance for society." It chose juvenile offenders partly because prime causative factors stand out more clearly in youth than they do later on, partly because data concerning traits, early characteristics and environment are more easily obtainable then, and partly because "the best results of therapeutic efforts are from working with youth." Since most confirmed criminals begin their delinquent careers in childhood or early youth, it was believed that the inquiry would have a direct value for the study of all offenders.

Dr. Healy tells us that it had repeatedly been thrust upon his attention that there was "astonishingly little in the literature of criminology which is directly helpful to those who have to deal practically with offenders." Of "general theory" there was "no lack," but when one came to "that study of the individual which leads to clear understanding and scientific treatment," there was "almost no guidance." It was for these reasons that he decided to "go to the criminal for the facts." Divesting himself, as far as possible, of all presuppositions, he set out to gather every shred of trustworthy information about each offender that could possibly be expected to have a bearing upon that offender's delinquency. At the end of five years the work had proved so valuable and the success of the undertaking was so well established that the county took over the institute and made it a department of the Juvenile Court, supported from the public treasury.

The results of the work are summarized in Dr. Healy's epoch-making volume, "The Individual Delinquent," published in 1915.[1] There 1,000 repeated offenders are dealt with, clustering around the ages of fifteen and sixteen years. Dr. Healy not only sets forth the methods of diagnosis that were worked out and used in the institute, but analyzes the causes and types of criminality that were found as a result of the study, and offers isolated suggestions for treatment. Case histories are given in abundance. Much of the classification of offenders is tentative and the methods of research need not be regarded as the best that will be ultimately devised. This is not only admitted by Healy but is put forth as one of the major conclusions of his work. "Neither we," he says, "nor other investigators can make such a contribution to the principles of our science as shall ever do away with the necessity for (a) careful personal study of each offender, and (b) testing the value of measures carried out, always by the criteria of future results."[2]

Following the establishment of this institute, other courts and institutions began to make studies of individual offenders. A visit to the institute by Judge A. W. Frater, judge of the Juvenile Court of Seattle, resulted in the employment by that court in 1911 of Dr. Lilburn Merrill in the double capacity of chief

[1] "The Individual Delinquent," by William Healy, A.B., M.D.; published by Little, Brown & Company, Boston, Mass.

[2] *Ibid.*, p. 19.

probation officer and diagnostician. The municipal court of Boston under Judge Wilfred Bolster was the next to take up the matter, Dr. V. V. Anderson being placed in charge of diagnosis. Since then the idea has spread with comparative rapidity. Juvenile courts in San Francisco, Savannah, Boston, Detroit, St. Louis, New York City, Providence, Memphis, and other cities have established some measure of diagnostic work, and institutions for confinement have followed suit. A partial list of clinics for such study will be found in the Appendix.

What is the diagnosis that ought to precede treatment of every delinquent? What facts ought it to include? No better short answer to this can be given than to say that it ought to include every fact that can possibly have a bearing upon conduct. Interpreted in the light of our present knowledge of human behavior, however, this answer would leave no limits to inquiry; there is nothing in the whole realm of the individual's experience that can safely be disregarded, as unaffecting conduct. We must, therefore, call to our aid the knowledge that has been revealed by previous inquiry concerning the causes of anti-social conduct, and, *while always remaining on the lookout for new and unsuspected factors,* devote particular attention to those phases of experience that the past has shown to yield most fruitful results. Two general principles may be enunciated. First, each individual is to be regarded as not only a product but a process. At any given moment, he may be looked upon as "the sum of all of his present constituent parts," and a cross section view of those parts may be taken; he is also to be looked upon, for purposes of criminological inquiry, as the result of a long-continued process of growth, of "conditions and forces which have been forming him from the earliest moment of unicellular life." These conditions must be open to view before causative factors can be announced with assurance.

The second principle is that not only the debit but the credit side of the individual's make-up must be ascertained. The future as well as the past is of interest to the criminologist, for the object of his endeavors is to improve the person under his care. He must, therefore, if possible, discover whatever desirable qualities the individual may possess, for the cultivation of these may aid in the task of improvement. Many a delinquent has been saved by the discovery of some special aptitude, some undeveloped talent, some unfulfilled and creditable desire or ambition. These things are occasionally active causes of wrongdoing, and to put the individual in the way of attaining or fulfilling them is not infrequently the key to successful therapy.

No one has improved upon the detailed statement of facts to be sought by diagnosis that Healy drew up as a result of his experience at the Juvenile Psychopathic Institute. Even this represents an ideal, one that Healy and his associates found far from attainable. Nevertheless, some ideal is desirable, and the closer one approximates to that ideal in practice the better is the chance of making a helpful diagnosis. The desirable facts are classified by Healy under the following eight headings: family history—especially all aspects of heredity; developmental history—including antenatal conditions; environment; mental and moral development; anthropometry—including photography; medical examination—particularly from a neurologic and psychiatric standpoint; psychological examination—(a) mental testing, (b) psychological analysis; and finally, delinquency.[1]

For the sake of clearness, a little further detail concerning each of these must be indicated. Under family history, important facts are those that have to do with the race, marital conditions and work history of the offender's parents; the number of births in the family, with an account of miscarriages and causes of any deaths in infancy; the parents' habits in regard to the use of drugs, alcohol and tobacco. Specific defects or diseases of the father and mother, particularly such as may have debilitated the germ plasm or affected the embryo, and including hereditary diseases, should be noted. Mental aberrations, defects and peculiarities on the part of the forebears are important, as well as mental and physical defects and characteristics of brothers and sisters and ancestral side-lines. Any court or institutional record in the family should be ascertained.

Developmental history includes such facts as a full account of the growth, constitution and early habits of the offender during infancy and childhood. Did he suffer injury through an accident to the mother during pregnancy? What were the antenatal conditions of health, hygiene and occupation of mother during pregnancy? Were there nutritional disturb-

[1] For a full statement of the facts to be sought under each of these headings the reader is referred to Healy's complete schedule, pp. 53-65 of "The Individual Delinquent."

ances or convulsions in infancy? At what age did the offender creep, walk, run, teeth, talk, go to school? Did he develop any adolescent instabilities or peculiarities, either mental or physical? Did he suffer from somnambulism, night terrors and the like? These are some of the questions to be answered.

The story of environment covers family control and other obvious factors in the outside world. The fourth heading, mental and moral development, has to do with more subtle matters, such as school history in detail, associations with the opposite sex, development of special talents, general behavior, and any observable mental traits.

Anthropometry, the measuring of anthropological characteristics, has not proved as helpful, Healy points out, as its advocates had hoped. Nevertheless, certain facts are to be especially noted: time of appearance of menstruation and of hair on the pubes and on the face; time and degree of development of the breasts; time and peculiarity of eruption of the various teeth; and studies of the growth curves of height and weight. Any evidence of degeneracy is also, of course, highly important.

The medical examination includes everything that can throw light on the physical functioning and peculiarities of the offender. Special attention should be paid to convulsions, epilepsy, petit mal, sexual habits and diseases, alcoholism, excess of tobacco, drug taking and sleep. Even mental factors can be here discovered—such as attention, memory, judgment, physical and mental control, association processes, etc.

There should be an examination of cranial nerves, of sensory and motor reactions, and of reflexes.

A more minute discovery of mental elements can be arrived at through the psychological inquiry. The records of psychological tests should for the most part be made at the moment of testing.[1] Not only the actual records of the tests, but the observer's general impressions of the subject's behavior are important. But the psychological examination includes more than tests. Hidden mental worries and conflicts, recurrent imageries and mental attitudes, half-forgotten mental experiences, many of which underlie misconduct, may be studied. Here lies a promising field for investigation.

The final division of facts to be included in diagnosis comprises those having to do with the offender's delinquent career, if he has one. This should include a description of each anti-social act, the cause of delinquency in the opinion of relatives and friends, and the attitude of the offender toward court, probation officer and institution.

When collected, many of these facts will obviously have no bearing on the delinquent behavior. The inquiry should be followed, therefore, by a *diagnostic and prognostic summary,* the purpose of which is to select those facts that do have a bearing upon that behavior. In the light of their significance the outlook under various environmental conditions may be expected to become plain.

According to Healy, the diagnostic and prognostic

[1] A word in regard to the use and interpretation of tests will be given later.

summary should proceed in some such way as this: "Here is the individual with (1) such-and-such physical characteristics, and (2) such-and-such mental abilities and mental traits, who (3) committed such-and-such types of delinquent acts. There are (4) in the background such-and-such conditions of defective heredity, pathological development, injuries, early teachings of immoral conduct, bad personal habits, lack of educational opportunity, or what not. In the light (5) of his being what he is physically and mentally and having this background, we can offer, on the basis of known predictabilities, such-and-such a prognosis if such-and-such treatment is afforded in such-and-such an environment. (Always to be included here are the old environment and other alternatives open.)"

The scope and nature of the diagnostic inquiry have now been suggested. It must also be borne in mind that human beings are highly complex entities. The kind of information concerning them that can be discovered, and that when discovered *is seen to have a bearing on conduct and the capacity for reform,* is so constantly enlarging that no limits can be set to future diagnosis. Even the tools and technique of inquiry may be expected to improve, especially in the detection of psychological and mental factors. Nevertheless, men must use the tools and knowledge they have. Such facts about the individual as can now be seen to be desirable can be set down. The range of these will undoubtedly widen from decade to decade, especially with the growth of psychology and the increase in our knowledge of human nature, but this is no bar to our following now a scheme of inquiry that seems calculated to give the results we are seeking.

A better understanding of the kind of study that results from this mode of inquiry, and of its helpfulness, both in prescribing and administering treatment, will be gained from a typical history of a delinquent individual secured by this method. The following record is that of a recidivist at Sing Sing prison:[1]

"S. R., a nineteen-year-old Italian-American, was admitted to Sing Sing on a sentence of three years and five months after having confessed to burglary in the third degree. The boy is the issue of illiterate and primitive southern Italians, the parents having immigrated to the United States about thirty years ago. The father, whose occupation was that of porter and bootblack, died several years ago of pulmonary tuberculosis. The mother is still living, somewhat invalided from rheumatism. An older brother, a confirmed criminal, has been in frequent conflict with the law, and is also a drug addict. Another brother suffers from chronic headaches, is quite impulsive and explosive in conduct, frequently changes places of occupation, and was arrested once on suspicion. Still another brother has the reputation of being unusually sullen in his general attitude.

"The inmate grew up under very miserable home conditions and without any rational supervision. The family always lived in poor, cramped quarters, in the congested section of the lower East Side of New York. Usually the entire family of parents and eight children occupied two rooms, never more than three. The father's work as porter in a saloon kept him away from home from early morning until late at night, and he had very little opportunity to supervise the children. Home offered no attractions to the children, and from an early age they found unsupervised recreation on the streets of the lower East Side. The mother was attended by a midwife during confinement with inmate; labor normal. His infancy and childhood appears to

[1] From "A Study of 608 Admissions to Sing Sing Prison," by Dr. Bernard Glueck, in *Mental Hygiene* for January, 1918.

have been uneventful. He entered school at the age of six and continued steadily until the age of eleven, when he had reached 5-B grade. For some time before this, however, relatives and neighbors began to notice certain changes in his character. He became disobedient, untruthful, dishonest and secretive. He was easily led by other boys, but his parents had absolutely no control over him, especially since the age of eleven. At this time he became rebellious at school, truant, and finally had to be placed in the truant school.

"Aside from this change in behavior at home and at school, the boy had been associating for some years before, in fact since the age of about seven, with a set of wild and anti-social boys in the neighborhood, and his record with the Society for the Prevention of Cruelty to Children dates from June, 1908, when he was but ten years of age, and when his first arrest for theft took place. He was committed to the Catholic Protectory, where he remained until May 12, 1911, when he was placed on trial with his mother. Several months later it was reported that the boy had given up old companions and that he remained at home most of the time, but was ungovernable, displaying bad temper when brought to task. He yelled at the top of his voice, jumped up and down, and generally created such a disturbance as to have annoyed neighbors who threatened to move. The janitress as well as other tenants accused the boy of going to the roof and throwing stones down on tenants or anyone passing through the yard. The family was threatened with dispossession unless something were done with the boy. The boy was interviewed at this time by a parole officer from the Catholic Protectory and was told that if his misbehavior should lead to a recommitment to that institution, he would have to be kept until the age of twenty-one. He promised to do better, but did not impress the officer as being sincere. In October of the same year, however, the boy was arrested at the instigation of his father, who complained that the boy was wild and beyond control of the family; that he remained away from home most of the time, and was constantly getting into trouble. His school record at this time was very bad. The boy was placed on probation for about a month. Nothing definite of record happened until March 30, 1912, when he was recommitted to the Catholic Protectory for theft, running the streets and fighting. It is noted that his parents lived at this time in two filthy rooms, and could not manage the boy at all, who was already then beginning to terrorize the household. At one time he stabbed his sister in the arm in a fit of rage, and since previous discharge from the Protectory had been arrested three times for theft. The institution physician at that time said that the boy was suffering from trachoma. The boy was again allowed out on trial on July 5, 1913, was given his working papers, and promised to obtain work and behave himself well. The father at this time had become a helpless invalid, and conditions at home were much more distressing, but the boy apparently was but little impressed with the situation, resumed his former habits of a wild, ungovernable street life, and in September of the same year had to return to the Protectory again at the solicitation of parents and neighbors. In February, 1914, he was again released on trial from the Protectory, but after two weeks' steady work, resumed his former habits, began to steal more boldly and excessively, and in June of the same year was sentenced to the State Reformatory at Elmira for burglary. His industrial career up to this time was naturally very defective, irregular, and unproductive, since he had spent most of the time from the age of eleven at the Catholic Protectory.

"It is highly significant that up to the time of his sentence to Elmira at the age of sixteen, no effort had been made to define in any rational or helpful manner the extremely serious problem which this youngster presented. While our field investigator was able to obtain a fairly accurate record of his behavior at home and in his unsupervised street life, no helpful information concerning his difficulties and behavior at school and at the Protectory is at hand. It would seem that at school, at least, this difficult and troublesome boy should have led to a more intelligent attempt to understand the problem he presented than mere transfer to the truant school. It is only as a result of his contact with Elmira that we began to get evidence of an intelligent effort to understand this troublesome personality. Here he is described as a coarse type of Italian, native of New York, weight 122 pounds, 4 feet 2⅛ inches tall, of poor mental capacity, poor susceptibility, and of poor physical condition. He lost ten of the fifteen months of his incarceration there for misconduct involving disobedience of orders, assault, malicious disturbance and damaging state property. A moron with physical stigmata whose extremely low mentality caused him to be placed in their special training class for mental defectives.

Finally his condition gave evidence of the gradual development of mental disorder, and on November 5, 1915, he had to be transferred to the Dannemora State Hospital for the criminal insane. The prognosis rendered at Elmira was, 'Outlook for improvement nil; absolutely no progress in school or labor; a turbulent, vicious degenerate, whose criminal character will probably cause continuous confinement in penal institutions.'

"At Dannemora his behavior was better and he was discharged from that institution at the expiration of his sentence, December 6, 1916, as recovered. The diagnosis was, 'mentally deficient, paranoid trend.' Then, while the subsidence of the acuteness of the medical problem which this boy presented may well have justified the termination of his residence in a hospital for the insane, the woeful lack of appreciation of the serious social problem involved deserves note. Not that the authorities at Dannemora necessarily failed to estimate the gravity of the situation, but that there is still lacking proper legal provision for a more indefinite detention of individuals like this.

"Following his return from Dannemora, relatives noticed a change in his makeup—he was more changeable, seemed nervous, restless, irritable, and quick-tempered. He worked fairly steadily for about one month and a half, then resumed his former habits, and in addition began pugilistic activities, and earned part of his subsistence in this fashion. He resumed, however, his stealing propensities, and about three months after his release from Dannemora was arrested for burglary and sentenced to Sing Sing for a period of three years and five months. His conduct at home during this time was unbearable. The father having died, the mother was quite helpless, and finally was obliged to leave home after a threat to kill her if she didn't supply him with money.

"Our examination of the boy showed him to be rather under-sized and under-developed physically, of coarse features. He was extremely infantile in his makeup, rather contentious and pugnacious. He appeared to have no conception whatever concerning the seriousness of his past mode of life, and did not impress one in the least as having benefited to any extent from previous sojourns in correctional institutions. The boy apparently has, up to this time, acquired no well-defined meaning of life, has no insight whatever into his past difficulties, and does not entertain any idea with reference to his future that might justify the assumption that he will improve in conduct. He entered into the examination rather freely, cooperated well, but gave distinct evidence of conscious deception as well as inability to give a correct account of his past life. He was rather boastful in manner when talking of his past exploits, took the entire situation lightly, and seemed to be distinctly pleased with the fact that he was an inmate of the state prison. He insisted that he was innocent of the crime for which he was sentenced, but that he knew who did the crime, but, of course, would not think of telling the police who did it. He was quite well informed on current events and his general information was quite on a par with his educational advantages. He said that the Mississippi River divided the West from the East in this country, that Grant was a general commanding the Northern army during the Civil War, that the Spanish-American War was due to the sinking of the Maine, named the Great Lakes, states and capitals without difficulty, and according to an examination by the Terman Revision of the Binet Scale, reached the psychological age of fifteen years and six months with an intelligence quotient of .96. His vocabulary was about 9,000 words, and he readily performed the Binet Paper Cutting Test, and the Ingenuity Test under the XVIII series. It is extremely interesting to note that his psychometric examination threw so very little light on the inmate's personality, and that the ultimate estimation of his makeup had to depend upon a study of his past career and type of reactions to daily situations. On the other hand, he showed a distinctly emotional deterioration and indifference. Certainly he had no adequate conception of the meaning of his life up to the present and of the difficulty in which he had been, a deterioration which is probably a sequence of the psychotic episode which necessitated his transfer to Dannemora State Hospital."

This is a relatively full account of a delinquent. After all of the facts have been gathered and the history is well in mind, and after causal connections between parts of the history and the delinquency have been established, the account can be much shortened for practical use in court, in the institution where the offender may be confined or by the probation officer.

Here are several good examples of such shortened accounts, taken from Healy's records:[1]

"John Doe. Age 16. No. 111. Sept. 26, 1908.

Physically: very good general condition. Strong, active boy, slouchy type. Sex development, adult.

Mentally, high-grade feebleminded—moron.

Delinquencies consist in earlier truancy—was once in institution on account of this; general mean behavior earlier at home; recent vicious sex assault upon a boy.

Causative factors: (*a*) mentality as above. The boy has been in an institution for the feebleminded for a couple of years; (*b*) lack of family control. The father was rather an irresponsible character and the family has broken up; (*c*) proportionate sex over-development and (*d*) alcohol. Up to the day of the assault this boy had been doing quite well at work, but he was given whiskey to drink and the offense quickly followed. (The causation of the mental defect was never satisfactorily obtained. The father was previously a drinking man, but now holds a good position. The mother is long since dead. She was said to have had some education.)

The *outlook* is altogether bad in a community where he can get alcohol. He might do well on a farm where he was free from temptation to drink. He has succeeded industrially since leaving the school for the feebleminded over a year ago. Under the circumstances he should be returned."

"Adele B. Age 15. No. 222. March 8, 1907.

This girl is magnificently endowed *physically*. She is strong and well and has a considerable measure of good looks. She had an early puberty and is much over-developed in sex characteristics for her age. We note a rather mask-like expression, typical of some prostitutes.

Mentally, this girl has distinctly good ability and has a very good range of interests. She belongs in our B class. Is rather a suggestible type. Considering her advantages she has read many good books. She has a distinctly refined attitude toward her delinquencies, as shown in her manner of relating them.

Delinquencies: Excessive sex immorality since she was ten years old. She has already been once in a reformatory school.

[1] "The Individual Delinquent," pp. 123-125.

Causative factors: (*a*) heredity. Father alcoholic. Mother immoral. Maternal uncle criminalistic; (*b*) mother's influence. She has been flagrantly immoral herself and has made light of this girl's transgressions, if she has not deliberately urged them; (*c*) early maturity and magnificent physique.

Prognosis: Notwithstanding this girl's bad background in heredity and environmental conditions, she shows certain qualities which speak in favor of her reformation. Her good mental ability and good interests, and her refined behavior are encouraging. Her physical over-development at present rather speaks against her chances, but she may develop self-control. Her suggestibility may be used to her advantage. This is a case in which better environment under good personal influences may produce an entirely different result from that of the past. She is probably worth doing much for."

"Mary Doe. Age 18. No. 333. Sept. 26, 1911.

Physical: Very well developed and nourished. Pleasant features and expression. No sensory defects of importance. Examination otherwise negative.

Mental: Notwithstanding the fact that this girl never got beyond third grade, we find her to have quite fair mental ability. We were astonished to see her good performance on some tests. She has good mental control and is well oriented in all ways. She has much motor dexterity. Not the slightest evidence of aberrancy found, although her relatives say she must be crazy to do what she has done. Mental diagnosis: good ability with exceedingly poor educational advantages.

Delinquencies: Repeated stealing over a considerable period in department stores where she has been employed. At one time she was stealing by a system which she had evolved.

Causative factors: (*a*) heredity. Parents are dead, but from other relatives we gain nothing but negative evidence. The whole family have good reputation; (*b*) developmental history. This, except for ordinary children's ailments, is negative; (*c*) environmental conditions during childhood were not especially good on account of poverty which in turn was caused by much illness in the family. However, we do not know this has direct bearing; (*d*) much more important is the fact that the girl had exceedingly poor educational advantages on account of frequent changes of abode and being kept at home on account of family illness; from this has come (*e*) a dearth of healthy mental interests. The girl is a great reader, but only of the cheapest literature and the sensational daily newspapers; (*f*) probably the most important factor is due to mental conflict over sex affairs. She has had no guiding hand and ever since her childhood has been hearing of these things from bad sources. Many of her occupational acquaintances tell her of the easy money they make in these ways and are able to indulge in dress and pleasures which are beyond her. Apparently she has always rejected the advances which had naturally come to her as an attractive girl among immoral associates, but has thought much about it. (Note her own story.) As a definite reaction to this, she has got to stealing; (*g*) bad companions.

The *outlook* we should consider distinctly good under different environmental conditions and if some good woman will give her a helping hand. The mental mechanism back of her misconduct has been frequently observed by us, and the best of results have been obtained when constructive measures have been offered under probation. Change of occupation, friendship with some woman competent to become her confidant, adviser and helper, and development of healthy mental interests, we feel sure, will do what is needed."

To summarize what has been said in this chapter, diagnosis is the discovery of those elements in the individual's constitution and history that bear upon his delinquency. It is nothing but a method. It has no value beyond the value of supplying information. With etiology, or the study of causes, it forms the scientific and common-sense approach to a rational and understanding criminology. Its aim is to establish the connection between delinquency and facts or influences in the offender's life, past or present. To do this it must cover a wide range and make use of every resource known to the student of conduct; it must constantly avail itself of new discoveries in behavioristic psychology and in the sciences of mental life. Each offender must be separately and personally diagnosed, without regard to others who have committed similar offences or who may be suspected of having become delinquent from the same causes; factors not appearing on the surface are often uncovered in the study of a given case. Finally, diagnosis and etiology supply a basis for prognosis and treatment and are valuable only in so far as they (a) lead to an improved method of handling the individual studied, or (b) add to the sum total of our information concerning the causes of crime.

II. Mental Factors and Delinquency

From the preceding discussion it should be clear that the immediate purpose of the modern scientific method in criminology is to discover, as accurately as possible, the causes of crime in the individual; upon this information to erect a basis of treatment. So recently has this method come into use and so few have been those who have applied it, that generalization in regard to causes has progressed but little. One reason for this is that the science of human behavior is only in its beginnings. We stand upon the threshold of a new era in our exploration of the springs of conduct and are only beginning to know what to look for; we are still in the tool-making stage, devising means of getting facts, rather than actually getting them in any considerable numbers. For every fact that we positively know in regard to the operation of the mind there are scores that we only suspect, and probably hundreds of whose existence we do not even dream.

There is a scientific objection, moreover, to proceeding too hastily with generalization. Long and patient inquiry, and a multiplying of cases, are necessary before trustworthy classification can set in. If studies of offenders have taught one thing, it is that the causation of crime in the individual is intricate and complex. Seldom can one say of a recidivist, for example, that this or that cause was the sole driving force that led him to his offence. A thief may be found to be slightly subnormal mentally, he may have come under the early influence of bad companions, he may have a physical defect that makes association with others painful, he may have been surrounded by a poor home environment and, in addition to all these, he may be the victim of over-developed sex impulses that stimulate his desire for money with which to gratify them. To select any one of these factors as the prime cause of his delinquency is not only to run the risk of error, it is likely to lead to a harmful emphasis in treatment. The full, rounded view must be kept in mind. To take another case: an epileptic may have become an early victim of stimulants; he may have suffered from poor eyesight that caused educational retardation so that he was later unable to get a good position; he may have acquired vagrant tendencies from irregular living conditions; and, particularly, his attacks may cause him to be undesirable in any but the lower grades of society. In diagnosing such a case it must be remembered that not all epileptics are criminals, and that to say that epilepsy was *the* cause of crime in this individual may be to lose sight of other equally important or at least contributing factors.

It is this complexity of causation in the individual that makes generalization difficult. Nevertheless, generalization can be more readily undertaken in regard to *causes of crime* than in regard to offenders. To know that some one condition or circumstance has actually caused crime in any individual is, scientifically, sufficient evidence for denominating that condition or circumstance *a cause* of crime, provided we do not push the statement farther. Thus, epilepsy, feeblemindedness, insanity, abnormal sexualism, the use of narcotics, certain physical peculiarities, etc., may all be set down as causes of crime in the sense that they have been shown to be capable of causing crime if not offset by other and counteracting conditions. To go on from this statement, however, and to say that an offender in whom any one of these things is found is a criminal *because of the presence of that factor* is to take a step that is unjustified by logic and that may later prove to be not in accordance with fact.

One further caution in regard to generalization is necessary. What use is to be made of it? If its effect be to dull the search for causative factors in the individual, then it is to be deprecated, for no general set of causes can take the place of accurate knowledge of the offender. Of what importance is it to know that a certain percentage of crime is caused by mental deficiencies and aberrations, another percentage by faults in our judicial system, another by industrial maladjustments, etc., when the concrete issue, a particular individual who has committed a given offence, is before us for treatment?

Two important uses for classification exist, however.

One is the aid it can render in defining measures of prevention for the community at large, for only by knowing general causes of crime can society attack crime at its source. The other use is in framing systems of treatment. So long as segregation continues to be the necessary way of caring for many offenders, institutions will be required; and these institutions should be adapted to the classes that inhabit them. The mingling of chronic sufferers from mental disease with persons who have committed single offences from accidental causes is one instance of unwise segregation. To avoid this, and to devise a correlated system of institutions that will promote individual treatment to the utmost, classification is most important.

One of the safest methods of classifying causative factors, in the present state of our knowledge, is to enumerate them in the order of frequency. This method was followed by Healy and his co-workers in Chicago; the various factors affecting the individual were first set down in rough chronological order, as they had apparently produced the career of the offender, and were then evaluated so far as possible in regard to their importance. This was the basis of the following table:

SUMMARY OF CAUSATIVE FACTORS BY GROUPS AND TOTALS IN 823 CASES: 560 MALES, 263 FEMALES[1]

Groups of Causative Factors	Number of times appeared to be main factor	Number of times appeared to be minor factor	Total Number of times appeared as factor
Mental abnormalities and peculiarities.	455	135	590
Defective home conditions, including alcoholism	162	394	556
Mental conflict	58	15	73
Improper sex experiences and habits.	46	146	192
Bad companions	44	235	279
Abnormal physical conditions, including excessive development	40	233	273
Defects of heredity	..	502	502
Defective or unsatisfied interests, including misuse or nonuse of special abilities	16	93	109
Defective early developmental conditions	..	214	214
Mental shock	..	3	3
Deliberate choice	1	..	1
Sold by parent	1	..	1
Use of stimulants or narcotics	..	92	92
Experiences under legal detention	..	15	15
Educational defects extreme	..	20	20
	823	2,097	2,920

With these preliminary remarks, we may now turn to consider some of the results that have been achieved by the modern study of individual delinquents. Undoubtedly, one of the most important of these has to do with the dominating part played by mental factors in the etiology of crime. This is a more significant statement than might appear at first sight, if one remembers the wide sway held in the past by social and biological theories of crime. Its implications for treatment are obviously manifold. Already, as we shall

[1] "The Individual Delinquent," pp. 130-131.

see, it is leading to proposals for wholesale revision of our penal systems. Dogmatism in regard to so technical a subject, and one so newly opened to investigation, is unsafe, yet certain conclusions stand out with striking clearness.

The table just quoted gives evidence of the part played by mental factors in causing crime among young people. Mental abnormalities and peculiarities there appear as main factors nearly three times as frequently as any other group. Still more tangible evidence is found in the high degree of correlation that exists between feeblemindedness and crime. Feeblemindedness, as the term is used in this country, includes both imbecility and idiocy, but if we omit these, feebleminded persons may be defined as those who are incapable, because of mental defect existing from birth or from an early age, of competing on equal terms with their normal fellows or of managing themselves and their affairs with ordinary prudence.[1] A feebleminded person is, as Goddard puts it, a "potential criminal"; this means that he lacks those safeguards of self-control and inhibition that enable normal people for the most part to choose their acts in a way to avoid legal retribution.

Every once in a while the general public is startled by the published details of a revolting crime, a murder or other outrage. Perhaps a well-known man has been assassinated or a humble school teacher has been viciously attacked on her way home from school and

[1] Based on the definition of the English Royal Commission on the Care and Control of the Feebleminded, which in turn was suggested by the Royal College of Physicians of London.

left dying by the roadside[1] or a boy in his 'teens has coaxed his companions into a lonely wood and there tortured them to death.[1] The affair is sensationally discussed in the press and the culprit is freely described as a "crime-monster" or "ghoul." An energetic reporter may interview the offender's acquaintances and learn that he has been regarded all his life as "queer" or as not quite "all there." The newspapers thereupon refer to him as a "half wit" or a "lunatic" and grow insistent in their demand for his punishment. Ultimately he is punished by death or life imprisonment, and the public, believing that it has got rid of an exceptionally dangerous character, heaves a sigh of relief and forgets all about the incident.

If the public realized that it had been dealing with a person of feeble mentality, a person with the mind of a child and with a child's appreciation of the seriousness and consequences of its acts, it would perhaps take a different interest in the case. If it realized, further, that one in every five of the inmates of prisons and reformatories in this country is a person of just such feeble mentality, and is a potential perpetrator of precisely similar acts of violence, its interest would undergo a still more radical change. It would perhaps sense the inadequacy of mere punishment as a measure of prevention, and would realize that it is not necessary to wait until such an act has been committed before knowing the danger.

One in five is a conservative estimate of the number of mental defectives among convicted offenders. The

[1] These are instances of actual occurrence.

studies that have led to this conclusion are many and varied. Not all of them, to be sure, are to be accepted as trustworthy. The newness of methods of investigation is in part responsible for this. Then, too, the personal equation among investigators must be allowed for, the expertness with which the investigations have been carried on, and the difference, usually slight, between the standards of mental defectiveness applied. Sometimes so-called "borderline" cases have been classified on one side of the mental level, sometimes on another. Especially important in this connection is the fact that different institutions in which tests have been given have different characters of population, due in part to the neighborhoods from which they draw and in part to varying judgments as to who should be committed. In some institutions mental defectives have been largely weeded out by careful antecedent work in the courts; in others first offenders preponderate; in others there is a disproportionate number of colored inmates, and in still others mental defectives have tended to congregate because of conditions affecting release. Finally, in States where probation is on a high plane, the brighter and more hopeful cases are apt to escape being sent to the institutions, thus leaving only the mentally inert and dull to receive custodial care.

Nevertheless, the evidence of feeblemindedness is overwhelming. One of the most recent and convincing studies on this point is that by Dr. Glueck at Sing Sing, who found that of 608 adult prisoners out of an uninterrupted series of 683 cases admitted to that institution in a period of nine months, 28.1 per cent.

"possessed a degree of intelligence equivalent to that of the average American child of twelve years or under."[1] Another trustworthy study was conducted by Williams and Terman at the Whittier State School for Boys in California, where, out of 215 cases tested, 32 per cent. were found to be feebleminded. At the Indiana Reformatory, at Jeffersonville, 11 per cent. out of 2,000 cases studied were feebleminded, and 20 per cent. "borderline." Numerous other studies have been made. The 1914 annual report of Elmira Reformatory, New York, gives 42 as the percentage of feebleminded inmates there. A study at the Illinois State School for Boys at St. Charles showed 20 per cent. mentally defective.[2] At the New Jersey State Reformatory at Rahway, according to the annual report for 1914, 47 per cent. of the young men there are mentally defective. In estimating the value of these studies one must know, of course, the methods pursued in getting the facts, the care taken in making diagnoses, the percentage of all the inmates studied and the thoroughness with which each individual was tested. Impressionistic methods of observation are not reliable; formal tests for discovering mental ability should at all times be insisted upon. For this reason, many of the earlier studies made before the use of mental tests became general are of doubtful value. Instances are on record where as high as 80 and even 90 per cent. of the inmates of a penal institution have been called feebleminded; obviously the investigator

[1] "A Study of 608 Admissions to Sing Sing Prison," by Dr. Bernard Glueck, published in *Mental Hygiene* for January, 1918.

[2] Many cases of defective delinquents are weeded out at the Chicago Juvenile Court and Psychopathic Institute.

was here dealing with a highly selected group, or his methods were at fault.

Perhaps the whole matter may be summed up in the following words of one careful student of the subject: "At least 25 per cent. of the inmates of our penal institutions are mentally defective and belong to either the feebleminded or to the defective delinquent class."[1] The ratio of one in five has been adopted by the present writer as escaping any charge of overstatement and as at least unlikely to lead the general reader astray. Whatever the actual figures are, they are large enough. It must, of course, be remembered that the figures here quoted refer only to *convicted offenders* and not to offenders in general. It will always be true, doubtless, that the cleverest law-breakers are the ones least likely to be caught, and that institutional populations contain, therefore, disproportionate percentages of feebleminded. This is particularly notable in connection with the crime of prostitution. Studies of convicted prostitutes have shown especially high percentages of mental defectives. Fifty-one per cent. of 300 prostitutes chosen at random from three institutions in Massachusetts were found to be feebleminded,[2] and 49 per cent. of 243 prostitutes studied at the Massachusetts Reformatory for

[1] Dr. Walter E. Fernald, superintendent of the Massachusetts School for the Feebleminded, Waverly, Mass., in a paper read at the Massachusetts State Conference of Charities, Oct. 23, 1912.

[2] "Report of the Commission for the Investigation of the White Slave Traffic, So-called," February, 1914. House Document 2281, State of Massachusetts. The report of this commission declared, with reference to the number rated as feebleminded: "The mental defect of these women was so pronounced and evident as to warrant the legal commitment of each one as a feebleminded person or as a defective delinquent."

Women.[1] These studies were carefully made and while there is no reason to doubt their validity *for the populations investigated,* it would be unscientific to apply the conclusions reached to prostitutes in the world at large.[2]

Mental defectiveness, however, is only one of the abnormal mental traits that enter largely as causative factors into the commission of crime. There are others of a more elusive and subtle nature, in the detection and definition of which investigation has not yet put its foot on such sure ground. The study referred to by Dr. Glueck did not deal alone with feeblemindedness. Dr. Glueck found that of his 608 prisoners 59 per cent. were "classifiable in terms of deviations from average normal mental health." These embraced all of the strange and indefinable psychopathies, aberrations and insanities—the mental twists, deflections and contortions that make up the whole range and scope of mental abnormality. Dr. Glueck was able to break them up into three classes, as follows:

"1. Of the 608 cases, 28.1 per cent. possessed a degree of intelligence equivalent to that of the average American child of twelve years or under. . . .

"2. Of the 608 cases, 18.9 per cent. were constitutionally inferior, or psychopathic, to so pronounced a degree as to have rendered extremely difficult, if not impossible, adaptation to the ordinary requirements of life in modern society. . . .

[1] "Mental and Physical Factors in Prostitution," by Edith R. Spaulding, M.D.; Proceedings of the National Conference of Charities and Correction, 1914.

[2] For much of the information in this discussion of feeblemindedness and crime the author is indebted to an unpublished manuscript by Alexander Johnson and Margaret Lane.

"3. Of the 608 cases, 12 per cent. were found to be suffering from distinct mental diseases or deteriorations, in a considerable number of whom the mental disease was directly or indirectly responsible for the anti-social activities."[1]

Because of the importance of this study, one of the best of an adult group yet made, we quote still further from Dr. Glueck's analysis.

"That a finer differentiation of types will be possible when we come to a purely clinical presentation of the subject cannot be doubted, and in one instance, at least, we are almost certain to be able to add an additional group—the Epileptic Group. As a matter of fact, in the 608 cases studied, only two cases were classifiable as definitely suffering from epilepsy. Even in these two cases, the original mental defect was so prominent that we felt it advisable to include the two with the mentally defective. On the other hand, we have frequently felt, in studying a case, that we were dealing with a temperament or makeup which, if not definitely epileptic in character, certainly was very closely allied to the epileptic constitution.

"Under the Intellectually Defective Group were placed all cases who had shown, as a result of a study of their life histories, a general incapacity to adjust themselves to the ordinary requirements of life, which incapacity appears to have been based largely, if not wholly, upon a general retardation in mental development, and which retardation was capable of definition by means of laboratory study. None of the cases included in this group had reached a degree of intelligence beyond that of the average American child of twelve years, and in a considerable number of cases the intelligence was much lower. It is not easy, as we have already indicated, to define the precise relationship between mental defect and criminal behavior in every instance, but the evidence tends to be cumulative that, inasmuch as criminal behavior is the resultant of the interaction between a particularly constituted individual and a particular environment, environmental factors play a significant rôle in determining criminal behavior, even in the defective. This general opinion may

[1] See *Mental Hygiene* for January, 1918, p. 86.

be expressed with reference to all the psychopathologically classifiable types.

"The Mentally Diseased or Deteriorated Group includes cases in which evidence came to light of a change in personality, as well as of more or less distinct and well-defined delusional formations and hallucinatory experiences, which findings had their basis in either a mental disease or a deteriorating process. As will be seen in the more detailed discussion of this group, dementia præcox and conditions closely allied to it contributed chiefly to the group. A more detailed study of the relationship between the personality changes involved in this disease and criminal behavior is being contemplated.

"The Psychopathic Group—the most difficult to define—constitutes beyond a doubt the most baffling group in our classification. Because it is often so difficult to convince the layman, or even the physician, that one is dealing here with a distinctly abnormal personality, a clearer definition of this form of deviation from normal mental health is very much needed. Our diagnoses were based upon a study of the life history and mode of reaction which these individuals exhibited in their various contacts with society. That we have probably not erred to a very large extent in diagnosing the individuals belonging to this group may be seen, for instance, in the fact that the average number of sentences to penal or reformatory institutions per psychopathic recidivist is 3.9, and that 23.67 per cent. of them have had more or less habitual recourse to the use of narcotic drugs. The industrial careers in most instances were anything but successful, and the entire life picture which the average case in this group presents cannot fail to give one the distinct impression that he is dealing here with a decidedly abnormal type.

"The Unclassified Group embraces all cases which could not be classified within any of the three preceding groups. It does not mean, of course, that we are dealing here with what is generally considered to be a normal human being. It simply means that our knowledge concerning a great many of the individuals embraced in this group is still so deficient as to make it unwise at this time to classify them definitely. It is our belief that a more intensive clinical study of these now unclassifiable cases will throw a good deal of light on the causative factors in criminal behavior."[1]

[1] *Mental Hygiene,* Jan., 1918, pp. 90-91.

Dr. Glueck drew some interesting conclusions from this study in regard to the relation between the seriousness of an offence and the frequency with which it is committed, on the one hand, and between its seriousness and the percentage of psychopathological offenders committing it, on the other. He found that the offences committed by these prisoners, when classified on the basis of motive, fell for the most part into three groups, as follows:

	Number	Per Cent.
Crimes having their impulse in the instinct of acquisitiveness	388	63.8
Crimes having their impulse in the instinct of pugnacity	148	24.3
Crimes having their impulse in the instinct of sex	60	9.9
Other crimes	12	2.0
	608	100.0

Believing that acquisitive crimes are more serious than pugnacious and pugnacious than sex, Glueck drew from this table the conclusion that "the frequency of a given type of offence is in inverse ratio to its seriousness." He further analyzed these three groups in regard to the percentage of psychopathologically classifiable offenders in each, and found:

Number and Per Cent. of Psychopathologically Classifiable Offenders

Nature of Crime	Number	Per Cent.
Acquisitive	222	57.2
Pugnacious	87	58.8
Sex	42	70.0

From this Glueck concluded that "the extent of psychopathological classifiable cases is in direct ratio to the seriousness of the offence." A similar relationship came to light between the degree of delinquency, or recidivism, and the extent of psychopathologically classifiable cases: of the entire 608 cases, 66.8 per cent. were recidivists; in the mentally diseased or deteriorated group this percentage was lower, being only 63, but in the defective and psychopathic groups it was higher, being 80.6 and 76.7 respectively.

Further illustration of the part played by mental factors in the etiology of crime is afforded by the study of 243 inmates of the Massachusetts Reformatory for Women, referred to above. Here, again, not only mental defectiveness was found. Epilepsy, hysteria and psychopathic tendencies abounded, as is shown by the following summary of the cases studied:[1]

	Cases	Per Cent.
Giving history of epilepsy	29	12.0
Giving history of hysteria	28	11.6
Psychopathic personalities	5	
Transferred to hospitals for the insane	3	14.1
Markedly neuropathic	15	
"Control defectives"	12	
Total		37.7

Eighty-four of the 243 cases showed apparent normal mentality, yet further study revealed that forty-seven of these displayed the following characteristics:

	Cases
Hysteria	17
Epilepsy	7
Psychopathic types	5
Neuropathic types	10
"Control defectives"	8

Thus, it will be seen that only thirty-seven cases, or 15 per cent. of the whole, showed normal mentality

[1] See first footnote, p. 297.

or were without marked nervous defect. "Considering that those cases," says Dr. Spaulding, "which show poor mental ability, are not perhaps able to cope fairly with their environment on account of their slight mental defect, we find 85 per cent. of the cases studied showing some underlying defective mental or physical factor. We do not believe that this represents to any extent the cause of prostitution, for there are doubtless large numbers of individuals in the community with the same mental and physical defects who are not leading such a life. Still we feel that this class of women if not sufficiently protected, represents the ones who are first (on account of their weakened resistance) to offer themselves to fill the demand."

This is not the place, nor is the present writer the person, to go into niceties of psychological definition, or to draw the line closely between one group and another of the mentally abnormal and indicate the peculiar characteristics of each. The subject is highly technical and knowledge of mental types is in a state of flux; even terms and classifications in accepted usage to-day drop from favor to-morrow. The purpose here is merely to suggest something of the relation that mental factors bear to delinquency, and to give the reader a general idea of what is afoot in this field. Some of the implications of the subject for treatment will be discussed in a later chapter. Meanwhile we may fairly sum up the position of present students by quoting the conclusion reached by Healy as a result of his work at the Chicago Psychopathic Institute from 1909 to 1914: "Our own case studies have gradually led us to the overwhelming conclusion that for practical purposes, what we particularly want to know about the offender are the immediate mental antecedents of his conduct. . . . With full respect for those who earliest apprehended the problem of the delinquent as an individual, we nevertheless see the utter inadequacy of work which did not, first and foremost, determine the offender's mental content, his mental traits, peculiarities and abilities. Vastly important though social and biological backgrounds are, yet they must take at least second place to these more causative factors of delinquency."[1]

Healy also prepared a list of the mental factors that he found as "bases of delinquency," which because of its inclusiveness, and suggestiveness for the non-technical reader, is worth quoting:

Mental dissatisfactions; those developed from cravings of no special moral significance in themselves, or even from unfulfilled creditable ambitions.

Criminalistic imagery, sometimes fairly obsessional, which persists, and is strong enough to impel misconduct.

Irritative mental reactions to environmental conditions, seeking expression or relief in misdoing.

The development of habits of thought involving persistent criminalistic ideas and reactions.

Adolescent mental instabilities and impulsions.

Mental conflicts, worries or repressions concerning various experiences or matters of mental content. These sometimes interfere with that smooth working of the inner life which fosters socially normal conduct. The misdeed here, too, may be a relief phenomenon.

The chronic attitude of the offender representing himself to himself as one, like Ishmael, whose hand shall be against every man and every man's hand against him. The remarkable phenomenon of anti-social grudge may be included here.

[1] "The Individual Delinquent," pp. 28, 29-30.

Mental peculiarities or twists which are agents in the production of anti-social conduct, but which do not overwhelm the personality enough to warrant us in grading the subject as aberrational.

Aberrational mental states: all the way from fully-developed psychoses to temporary or border-line psychotic conditions.

Mental defect in any of the several forms described in our special chapter on the subject.[1]

Of the methods of research by which mental and psychological factors are discovered, a whole volume might be written. Since special texts and monographs on the subject abound, no attempt will be made to discuss it in detail here. Its relation to the modern study of criminology, however, demands that a few words of explanation be given.

Undoubtedly the science of applied psychology, though yet in its infancy, has grown lustily during the past decade. Criminologists have both benefited from and contributed to this growth. Studies of individuals have brought about an improvement in technique, and have raised standards both of observation and of scientific self-criticism; meanwhile, new instruments of measurements have been forged out of the necessities of criminological inquiry. Not only is it possible now, as has already been suggested, to discover general levels of mental ability, but it is possible also to discover special aptitudes, defects and characteristics. For some of these definite tests have been formulated, for others common-sense methods of inquiry and observation are sufficient. Criminalistic imagery and mental conflicts, for example, can often be discovered through skilful questioning by an experienced exami-

[1] "The Individual Delinquent," p. 32.

ner. More formal attributes and qualities require more formal and exact methods.

The growth of such methods has been attended by one of the most animated disputes in the annals of science. The reverberations of this dispute have not yet ceased. The discussion centered about the use and interpretation of formal tests for measuring mental ability and discovering mental traits. Some of the acrimony of the dispute was undoubtedly caused by the incautious claims of a few early advocates of mental tests. The Binet Measuring Scale for Intelligence was hailed as an instrument of marvellous exactness. Anybody's mentality could be diagnosed by it; anybody could use it. All that was necessary was a few minutes of time, a little attention, and presto! the person tested would be told on just which rung of the mental ladder he stood. The reaction from this attitude was swift. Many people went so far as to discard the tests as entirely worthless. Finally, however, a more scientific attitude set in and as a result of criticism applied both to the tests and to their use, their possibilities and limitations came gradually to be seen with clearness. Meanwhile, adaptations and improvements were made and the Yerkes-Bridges and the Stanford Revision, among others, were added to the available tests. To-day conservative psychologists recognize in these and other carefully worked out measurements, instruments of proved usefulness in diagnosis. In general the tests are now regarded as having no great value for accurate diagnosis beyond the mental age of ten years.

The development of tests for mental ability bears

a close analogy to a similar movement in the more strictly educational field. Workers with school children have also been inventing tests during the past decade. A similar controversy, too, has waged over these. Six years ago a speaker before the Department of Superintendence of the National Education Association was loudly applauded for declaring that "one could no more measure the relation between teacher and child than he could measure the divine afflatus of a mother's love." Yet to-day scales for the measurement of educational products and teaching efficiency are in use throughout the country and in all parts of the world. Progressive educators are able to apply definite, standardized tests to the progress of pupils in spelling, arithmetic, drawing, English composition, the use of vocabulary, geography, handwriting, reading, Latin and other subjects, and are able to measure their own and others' teaching efficiency.[1] Tests for these purposes differ from most of those that we have been considering in that they measure products and achievement rather than qualities and aptitudes. Their object is to supply a basis for criticising the teaching process, while the object of the others is to measure mental capacity and to reveal the subject's degree of educability. Both proceed upon the belief that "whatever people now measure crudely by mere descriptive words, helped out by the comparative and superlative forms, can be measured more precisely and con-

[1] For a full list of tests and scales in the various school subjects see the "Seventeenth Yearbook of the National Society for the Study of Education," Part II; published by the Public School Publishing Company, Bloomington, Ill.

veniently if ingenuity and labor are set at the task."[1] Neither has so far been perfected as to justify blind and indiscriminate use, but both have become valuable tools in the hands of those who know how to apply them.

It was a defect of many of the earlier mental tests, and especially the Binet, that they were based largely on the use or understanding of language. Everybody knows some person whose flow of words gives him the appearance of being bright or well-informed when a little closer acquaintance shows him to be in reality a garrulous dullard; we all know, too, clever people who are extremely slow at expressing themselves. This simply means that language is not the only medium through which people give evidence of their capabilities. Other tests, therefore, have been devised for discovering ability. Many of these are called performance tests, and involve the use of concrete material in such ways as to measure some of the most socially valuable qualities. Certain tests, for example, call for inserting the missing parts of pictures, others for fitting various sized pieces of wood into given spaces, others for solving simple or more complex puzzles requiring a process of reasoning, others for visually memorizing geometrical and other figures, and the like. The game of checkers is sometimes used as a test for foresight, though care must be taken to make sure that the subject has not had an opportunity to acquire skill by learning any of the well-known openings and lines of play.

[1] "The Nature, Purposes and General Methods of Measurements of Educational Products," by Edward L. Thorndike, *ibid.*, p. 16.

Not all mental tests now in use are intended for the discovery of so-called levels of general ability. There are special tests for special aptitudes and functions such as motor coordination, power of memory, attention, ability to learn and profit by experience, judgment, discrimination, planfulness, suggestibility and even will-power. Obvious tests exist for artistic ability and for discovering the nature of one's mental interests. For work with offenders some of these are especially valuable; for example, it may be more important, in getting at the underlying causes of delinquency, to know how an individual grades in self-control, in perceptive power, or in ability to learn from experience than to know the effect of formal education upon him or his language ability.

Undoubtedly, new tests will be devised from time to time and many now in use will be discarded. A profitable field for experimentation now lies open in regard to vocational aptitudes, where an almost virgin soil awaits the experimenter.

In the giving of tests, caution and safeguards are necessary. Conditions must consciously be prepared for the examination; even the room must be got ready. The judge who recently permitted the giving of the Binet tests to a defendant in open court[1] may have contributed dramatically to the enlightenment of the jury and the public in regard to psychological procedure; it is doubtful if he established a valuable precedent in the method of discovering true mental conditions. Nothing is more important than the state of mind of the examinee at the time of the inquiry.

[1] *The Survey* for January 13, 1917, p. 427.

Many conditions may disturb the examination, such as the warmth or closeness of the room, dulness from anemia or recent illness, fatigue, the various mental states supervening in epileptics, the irregular mental states of hystericals, the effects of special sensory defects, etc.; Healy gives a long list of others. Deliberate deception is rare; laziness is occasionally encountered. The ability of the examiner to secure cooperation is all important. A stiff or impatient examiner may secure results that do not reflect the patient's real ability. The examiner should efface himself as far as possible, should bend with the person being examined, should play into his moods. Encouragement is often the key to successful testing. A common error is in thinking that the examiner need not be specially trained or temperamentally fitted for his task. Not only training, but a large experience in giving tests is necessary for good results.

In interpreting the results of tests, trustworthy norms for comparison are essential. To compare the performance of uneducated delinquents from poor environments with that of college-bred sons of wealthy and cultured homes yields little that is suggestive. Not only must standards "be worked up for each given situation or social group in which tests are applied," but "unless there be remarkable uniformity of school training, environmental background and emotional conditions, such as obtain readily in a college laboratory, interpretation of answers, types and times of performance can only, in all fairness, be made within wide limits."[1] When such conditions do exist, in-

[1] "The Individual Delinquent," p. 104.

terpretation by trained psychologists is relatively easy.

In concluding this discussion of mental factors and delinquency, a warning must be sounded against exclusive emphasis of the psychiatric attitude in relation to crime. This attitude does not by any means tell the whole story. Mental factors happen to be the ones most needing emphasis at present because they are the ones most likely to be overlooked; moreover, no matter what the external causes may be, these must produce some psychical effect before crime ensues. Nevertheless, neither psychiatrists nor others should lose sight of the many non-psychological factors that contribute directly or indirectly to anti-social behavior. Glueck says that "the mere establishment of the fact that so many criminals are defective, or insane, or psychopathic, will not aid materially in the solution of the problem of crime, if one remains blind to the various environmental factors, physical as well as social, which are responsible for criminal behavior." And we have already quoted his statement that since criminal behavior is the "resultant of the interaction between a particularly constituted individual and a particular environment, environmental factors play a significant rôle in determining behavior." This general opinion may be expressed, he says, with reference to all the "psychopathologically classifiable types."

Among the environmental factors that may become the starting points, if not the causes, of criminal careers are unintelligent handling in the home or unfortunate home conditions (crowding, poverty, immoral home environment, severity of treatment by the parents, constant irritation, uncongeniality, etc.), bad adjustments at school, unwise social allurements, vocational maladjustment—indeed, misfortune in any one of the many shapes that human flesh is heir to. Here, as in regard to mental factors, knowledge of etiologic relations is becoming greatly broadened by the study of individuals. We must not exclude from the list of environmental factors certain gross defects in the machinery of the criminal law which are undoubtedly responsible not only for the continuance but in some instances for the beginning of lives of misconduct. The commitment of first offenders to an institution, which too often proves to be only a school for learning crime, is one respect in which criminal jurisprudence is still prone to err. Other environmental causes exist. Further attention to these will be given in a later chapter. For the moment we must now consider treatment in its relation to the individual offender.

CHAPTER XIII

TREATMENT

THE treatment of the offender as here discussed is to be carefully distinguished from the prevention of crime. Prevention embraces every measure that seeks to modify or remove conditions favorable to the initial commission of crime; treatment is the reclamation of the actual law-breaker and embraces every measure that seeks to check his waywardness or to render him harmless to society. Prevention may address itself to conditions that extend throughout society or it may centre about a single individual who has not yet committed crime and try to prevent him from taking that step. Treatment, on the other hand, is almost solely concerned with the individual. Prevention may be likened to sanitary measures for the control of disease, treatment to the cure of the sick. Treatment has, however, a more positive side than this. It aims to increase the offender's usefulness to himself and to others. The cure for delinquency not infrequently lies in the development of some admirable trait or talent by which a new interest in normal ways of living is attained.

Treatment, to be successful, must be sharply individualized. We do not cure the sick *en masse;* no more can we change law-breakers into law-keepers so.

What to do with this particular bit of human flesh and emotion is the question put inexorably by every offender to society. Once the causes of misconduct in a particular individual are learned, all the resources of the physician, the educator, the psychiatrist, the religious or moral leader and the disciplinarian should be brought to bear to remove them. Experience in dealing with anti-social behavior is invaluable, too. One should know, for example, when to punish and when to withhold punishment; when an excitable temperament is in danger of outrunning self-control and of becoming abusive or of forming a delusion of persecution; when it is safe to exact a confession for misconduct, and when a confession will bring only humiliation and loss of self-respect. One should be able to distinguish between the various degrees of obstinacy, slowness of comprehension and mental deficiency—and the appropriate measures for each. Insanity can often be averted by restraint in the use of force. The braggadocia and boastfulness of youth are not infrequently best encountered by being permitted to run their course, rather than by being met with punishment or an unforgiving front. With prisoners of fair intelligence and judgment, reason and a straightforward facing of facts are demonstrably superior weapons to bullying and distrust. Many a prisoner has been heard to say that he would "never forgive such-and-such an officer" who had browbeat him, while another was the "first fellow who ever talked things out with me in a square way."

Treatment falls naturally into three parts: that which can be applied before confinement, that which can be applied during confinement and that which can be applied after release.

Treatment Before Confinement

The policeman is society's outpost in the treatment of crime. It is he who usually comes into contact first with the offender. No attempt can be made here to outline a model police system, but one observation grows naturally out of the preceding chapter: It would be well if policemen knew more than they do concerning the nature of delinquency and the causes of crime. Their very position gives them a strategic influence upon the future of law-breakers. They can often make or break the careers of first offenders by sympathy given or withheld, by fair or rough handling, by intelligent understanding of the forces back of a given act or by neglect of those forces. By hounding and espionage they can undo all the good that institutions may have accomplished upon recidivists. Policemen should make it a golden rule never to arrest ex-offenders without reasonable ground to believe that new acts of delinquency have been committed by them. The mere arrest "upon suspicion" of those whom society has already punished is one of the surest ways of stopping whatever process of reformation may have been begun.

The practical effect of having police forces that are trained in the scientific aspects of delinquency would be prodigious. A policeman, for example, who conceived his responsibility in terms of the broadest social interest and regarded himself as charged not only to protect society from the criminal but the criminal from himself, might with the proper training and encouragement set many a law-breaker back upon the path of moral conduct. Instead of sowing the seeds of an anti-social grudge by clapping his hand to a man's shoulder on slight provocation and dragging him off to jail, he might discover what conditions in the man's environment are causing his untoward behavior and try to remove them; or, if this proved impracticable, he might report the case to an agency that could make the necessary adjustments. During the unemployment crisis in New York City in the winter of 1914-1915 the police helped to find jobs for hundreds of discouraged workmen. This is doubtless no solution of an acute industrial situation, but it is in a measure a rational approach to the prevention of crime. Then, too, a policeman who knew something of the relation between feeblemindedness and crime might easily prove a valuable ally in the detection of mentally defective offenders. One who knew the elementary principles of evidence might show more discrimination in the manner and number of his arrests.

Some beginnings have been made in securing professionally trained police forces. Scientific police schools have, of course, been established in Europe for many years. In this country the lead was taken by August Vollmer, chief of police of Berkeley, Cal., in 1908, and the Berkeley school remains perhaps the most thorough yet started. For ten years the faculty of the University of California have been furnishing the police force of that city with required courses in the following subjects: elementary rules of evidence;

general principles of evidence; criminal law; elementary physiology, first aid to the injured and municipal sanitation; parasitology; elementary psychology and feeblemindedness in its relation to crime; psychiatry; physical defects and their relation to crime, and social causes of crime. Plenty of laboratory work in Berkeley itself supplements this professional training. Chief Vollmer believes that "the more intelligent manner in which much of the police work of this city is now performed by our officers"[1] is adequate proof of the value of the training. The example of Berkeley has been followed by only a few other cities, notably New York under the recent administration of Commissioner Arthur Woods. Several cities have set up compulsory thirty days' training courses for new policemen, but these are necessarily inadequate. Psychopathic laboratories in connection with courts (in New York City there is a psychopathic laboratory in connection with police headquarters itself) have helped to open the eyes of policemen to the intricacy of criminal causation. The morning "line-up" at police headquarters can be made an effective laboratory for familiarizing policemen with the material they deal with. When a policeman first discovers that the repeated arrest, trial and commitment to an institution of a defective or psychopathic offender is simply one way to insure the continuance of criminal conduct by him, a long step has been taken toward making that policeman not only a more discriminating agent in gathering and presenting evidence, but a firmer ally of treatment that shall seek positive reformative results.

[1] See *The Survey*, August 12, 1916, p. 503.

Chief Vollmer expresses a high ideal of police service in these words:

> "It has always been my opinion that the police officer should be trained for the profession in much the same manner as physicians, attorneys and other professionals are prepared for their life work. There should be established in every state university a chair of criminology, and no person should ever be appointed to do police duty until he or she has secured from such an institution the necessary degrees to qualify as an officer."[1]

As an ideal for the individual policeman this may not be attainable for some years, but it seems to be reasonable enough for commanding police officers. Why should not college men volunteer and train themselves for such positions, as they do now for similar ranks in the army and navy?

Judges are preeminently the persons who should know well the offenders they deal with. We are slowly getting rid of the old doctrine that judges, lawgivers and all others with power to affect the destinies of their fellow-men can shut their eyes to whole departments of life and give decisions based on theory and legal abstraction alone. We are breaking down the barriers that surround admissible evidence. The doors of the court room are being opened to the inmost secrets of human nature and we are gradually enlarging the sphere of what may be regarded as "material" and "relevant." No judge to-day is justified in passing sentence until he knows enough about the delinquent before him to be able to predict the probable outcome of any contemplated course of treatment. This is the lesson of the new penology for jurists. It means, among other things, that the diag-

[1] *The Survey*, Aug. 12, 1916, p. 503.

nosis of the offender should first be made by the court or its adjuncts. Judges should bear in mind Goddard's dictum that every wrongdoer is irresponsible until proved responsible, and should spare no effort to determine the mental and environmental causes of delinquency.

Every court, therefore, should have the services of a psychiatric clinic, of an investigative staff competent to look up the family, social and personal history of the offender, and of a medical examiner. The judge himself need not be a specialist, but he ought to know the uses of specialized information. He ought to be able to interpret the data given him. His equipment for his task should be such that he can intelligently direct the study of the individual offender. He ought to be familiar with the more intimate and personal causes of anti-social conduct and with the remedial and therapeutic measures that are available for each. He should never commit the blunder, for example, of committing a man to an institution for hard labor if the man has delusional insanity, or is mentally deficient, or has a valvular disease of the heart that makes hard labor dangerous. Neither should he sentence a drug fiend, or an offender in the initial stages of tuberculosis, to an industrial cell-block prison if a farm prison affording life in the open is available.

A new standard in criminal procedure was set by a verdict handed down in 1914 by a jury in the supreme court of Herkimer County, New York. This verdict read: "Not guilty as charged; acquitted on the ground of criminal imbecility." The importance of these words cannot be overestimated. The verdict recognizes, as Goddard has pointed out, "that *weakness* of mind, as an excuse for crime, is of the same importance as *disease* of the mind; puts feeblemindedness in the same category with insanity, and requires that it, like insanity, be considered in all discussions of responsibility." Because an offender is feebleminded, it does not follow, of course, that no further cognizance is to be taken of him or that he should be allowed to go free; the important point is that his problem should be recognized as distinct from that of mere criminality and that the court is precisely the agency by which this condition should first be discovered.

The judge is not the only participant in the trial, however, who should be familiar with the individual delinquent. The lawyer is another. How much would it not mean for a wiser administration of the criminal law if lawyers understood what that bundle of complex traits, unsuspected weaknesses and potential strengths that we call "the prisoner at the bar" really is! Our courtrooms would undergo a marked change in procedure and spirit. They would become less a battleground where opposing lawyers fight duels with human lives depending on the outcome and more a laboratory for the discovery of truth. It is reasonable to suppose that fictitious pleas of insanity would lose some of their attractiveness; that the glaring artificiality of "hypothetical questions," with their unscientific way of getting at the facts, would soon be banished; and that defender and prosecutor alike would unite in a cooperative effort to learn the truth and to give the wrongdoer whatever advantage the truth may hold. The springs of human conduct should be best known by those who spend their lives in defending and prosecuting that conduct.

One way of bringing this about is for law schools to give required instruction in mental types, in the causes of wrongdoing and in the fundamentals of social adjustment. We may be quite sure that the mazes of human conduct are as important and can be made as intellectually attractive as the mazes of civil suits and of legal procedure. Few cases in torts or real property, for example, are any more inherently interesting than the life history of the youthful Italian-American given in a preceding chapter. Here, one would suppose, is a problem quite worthy of the legalist's best powers. What is needed is to catch our lawyers, like our criminals, young.

A number of cities have sought to secure a juster treatment of law-breakers before commitment by establishing the position of public defender. The first office of this description was created by Los Angeles County, California, in 1913. The purpose of the public defender is to stand ready to defend all persons accused of crime. His duties are thus the reverse of the duties of the public prosecutor. Chief among the arguments advanced for the creation of this position is the fact that many people accused of crime are either too poor to secure competent legal defence or are so unfamiliar with legal procedure that easy advantage of them can be taken. This is undoubtedly a powerful contention. It may be pointed out, however, that it would help little toward the discovery of truth if public defenders were animated by the same spirit that animates many prosecutors and if, irrespective of the offender's guilt or his danger to others, they tried to secure acquittal at all hazards. If, on the other hand, they should raise professional standards and promote a scientific interest in the causes and treatment of wrongdoing, they ought to be encouraged.

Policemen, judges and lawyers do not exhaust the list of those who need to know something of what the modern study of crime is revealing. Probation officers, heads of temporary detention homes, teachers, physicians, pastors and, above all, parents, are others. Teachers, pastors and physicians often have it in their power to establish confidential relations with wrongdoers; if they understood more than they do of the springs of anti-social conduct, many a wayward course might be prevented or cut short. The case for parents is obvious: The home is the earliest training school for life. Many a beginning in delinquency is first seen, however, in the school, and this institution must answer to the charge of often failing to arrest such beginnings through neglect or misunderstanding of causes.

The probation officer has, of course, a professional interest in this subject. He is often the first public agent to come into close touch with the offender. While tact and ability to win confidence are necessary qualities in him, first hand acquaintance with causes and personal histories is of paramount importance. He should know fully the record of each offender in his charge. The first applyer, many times, of treatment, he must know what it is that he is trying to correct or his efforts may prove of no avail.

Probation is, indeed, one of the measures most

frequently taken in the preinstitutional treatment of crime. It has suffered from the common error of being regarded as only another name for judicial clemency or for letting offenders "down easy." In reality it is a positive method of treatment. Probation officers keep a close and sympathetic watch upon the habits and conduct of persons put in their charge and report periodically to the court concerning them. Probation is, thus, a method, short of actual confinement, of retaining control over the offender for the purpose of learning more about his delinquent proclivities and of exerting a wholesome educational influence upon him. "From a social point of view," say Flexner and Baldwin, in discussing particularly the relation of probation to the juvenile court, "probation may be said to be a process of educational guidance through friendly supervision. Mere surveillance is not probation. Probation is an intimate, personal relation which deals with all the factors of a child's life, particularly his home. Its chief function is to adjust the forces of the community to the child's life. Every social agency is called into play, the object being to surround the child with a network of favorable influences which will enable him to maintain normal habits of life." Often a suspended sentence, enforceable if the probationer fails to show progress or relapses into anti-social conduct, accompanies probation.

It is apparent, therefore, that the probation officer ought to be familiar with both the mental and environmental causes of delinquency. In the Boston Municipal Court the probation department is directly connected with the psychopathic service. Not infrequently the best recourse of the probation officer is to change whatever in the environment of the offender makes for a continuance of his delinquency. Sometimes it is possible to induce a whole family to move, if by so doing a demoralizing neighborhood and bad companions can be avoided.

Laws authorizing putting convicted persons upon probation have been passed in every State in the Union, in the District of Columbia, in Alaska, Porto Rico and Hawaii. A federal probation bill, applying to United States district courts, was passed by Congress late in 1917 but failed of Presidential approval. In fifteen States the law applies only to juveniles; the remaining States, except Wyoming, have both adult and juvenile probation; Wyoming has adult probation alone.[1] Not all of these laws, however, secure adequate or satisfactory probation systems. In some the number of probation officers is too small, in others their work is undervalued and underpaid. A "model" probation law has been prepared by the National Probation Association, whose offices are in Albany, N. Y. This association and others[2] who have studied probation in operation believe that paid officers are superior to those who merely volunteer their services, because of their greater professional interest in the work and greater amenability to supervision.

[1] "Annual Report of the National Probation Association," Albany, N. Y., 1917.

[2] See, particularly, "Juvenile Courts and Probation," by Flexner and Baldwin, pp. 117-119.

Treatment During Confinement

The treatment of the offender can never be wholly reduced to scientific formulas. Like teaching, it will always remain a great art. Skill in drawing people out, in appealing to the best in their personalities, in bringing tact, judgment and sheer divination to bear upon the intimate problems of changing the lives of others, will always be large elements in its success. The great prison warden will ever be a man with insight into strength and weakness of character and with an instinctive touch for the springs that control emotion and conduct. Treatment in the institution, however, is likely to become both more deft and more precise. There the environment can be artificially molded and controlled. Hence, as diagnosis becomes more accurate and we come to understand better the means of criminal therapy, institutional treatment will become more scientific and more resourceful.

The first thing to remember with respect to the institutional treatment of offenders is that a uniform regimen for all prisoners is worse than bad; it is futile and defeats its own purpose. Reference has already been made to the ridicule that would be heaped upon any physician who should prescribe the same remedies for every person who came to him; similar distrust would be felt toward any hospital that should treat all of its patients alike. Yet our prisons are for the most part built upon the principle of uniform treatment, and not only receive men for fixed sentences (imagine a hospital that should decide when a man came to it exactly how long he should stay!), but do the same things to them and expect the same things from them while they are there. The folly of this practice may be made still clearer by an analogy to a school principal who should refuse to make distinctions among children and should subject all of them to the same rate of progress, the same discipline, the same course of study. Too much of this is still done in most of our public schools, but even there individual differences have long been recognized and children who have not satisfactorily passed the work of a given grade are compelled to remain in that grade another year. This is, indeed, a species of educational indeterminate sentence. But in prisons we have only caught up with those crude devices of an earlier generation, the fool's cap and the dunce's stool.

Dr. Glueck has some pertinent remarks upon this subject in his study of Sing Sing recidivists.

"It should be obvious from the foregoing that it would be futile to expect any uniform machinery, no matter how perfect such might be, to be equally applicable to all of the individuals embraced within this group of 608 cases, and that a more hopeful solution of the problem might be expected from a more intensive individualization in the administration of it.

"To the student of behavior, a knowledge of the individual back of a given act is considered absolutely essential if a clear understanding of the nature of behavior is to be had. Nevertheless, one cannot escape the conviction that as far as the administration of the problem of crime is concerned, the man back of the act is largely lost sight of, and what is actually administered is the criminal act and not the criminal. Intimate contact with the problem of crime inevitably leads to the opinion that every agency concerned in the administration of this problem sees in its own work an end in itself, and seems to lose sight of the common goal or end, toward which all should be striving, namely, the readjustment of that badly adjusted individual, the criminal.

"That this cannot be expected to be otherwise under the prevailing attitude of the average community toward its problem of crime must be obvious to anyone who takes the trouble to look into the situation more closely. Just as long as a community will judge the efficiency of its police officers, its prosecuting attorneys, and its judiciary by the volume of crime they are able to detect and punish, rather than by the extent to which they succeed in preventing crime, an unnecessarily large number of what might be termed provoked crimes must be the result.

"The manner in which the problem of any individual criminal is handled before he is admitted to prison must, of necessity, affect the degree to which the institution will succeed in accomplishing what is perhaps the most important of its functions—the return to the community of a better man than it originally received. To expect any institution, penal or reformative, to accomplish this in all cases, in view of the constitutional makeup of so large a part of the constituency of the average prison, would be well nigh expecting the impossible. But if the reformative institution cannot accomplish this result, it loses very much of its usefulness as an agency for the administration of the problem of crime, and some other method must be resorted to in those cases in whom periodic imprisonment fails to produce the desired result." [1]

The institutional ideal toward which the conception of individual treatment points is a system of specialized prisons for giving appropriate care to each definable class of law-breakers. Separate provision ought to be made for every group that requires a particular kind of treatment or environment. The make-up of such groups will be determined, of course, by mental, physical, industrial and other classifications. In an ideal system of this sort the length of the prisoner's term will be unfixed, since no one can tell beforehand how long it will take to effect the desired change.

[1] *Mental Hygiene* for January, 1918, pp. 86-87.

What prisoners will be placed together in an institution will depend upon what ones can be adequately cared for in a single group or under a single management. The kind and diversity of institutions will in turn depend upon current knowledge of the nature, causes and therapy of crime.

This ideal is nowhere fully attained to-day. Some progress toward it has been made. Nearly every State in the Union, for example, has made separate institutional provision for the so-called "criminal insane," though the care given to this class is not always of the best. Several States, also, have separate provision for epileptics. A number have established farm prisons on wide acreage for prisoners who can benefit from life in the open. The reformatory, of course, is a commonplace in our penal system. So, also, are parental and industrial schools. Each of these institutions is intended to meet the need of a more or less specialized class. That they do not do so with uniform success is no denial of the fact that their establishment shows society's realization that specialization is necessary.

On the other hand, special provision for so clearly defined a class as the defective delinquent is almost wholly lacking. Massachusetts has recognized the existence of this class in recent legislation, but still provides for its commitment only to reformatories containing normal delinquents. Washington authorized in 1918 the erection of two new wings for defective delinquents at her state custodial school. Indiana, by a recent law allowing the transfer of inmates from one institution to another—provided this does not increase the severity of punishment—has probably opened the way for putting defective delinquents into the Indiana School for Feebleminded Youth or into the Village of Epileptics. Minors brought before a juvenile court in Ohio may be committed to the guardianship of the State Board of Administration and by it to the State Bureau of Juvenile Research; if found to be feebleminded or epileptic they may then be assigned to institutions for the special care of those classes. In Ohio, also, a minor who has been committed to one institution may be transferred to another whenever it appears that he ought to be in such other because of "delinquency, neglect, insanity, dependency, epilepsy, feeblemindedness or crippled condition or deformity."

California has taken the longest step toward special institutional provision for defective delinquents. By an act passed in 1917, $250,000 was appropriated for the initial expenses of establishing the Pacific Colony. To this institution not only non-delinquent feebleminded and epileptic persons will be admitted, but also boys and girls who have been brought before a juvenile court and found feebleminded; any person convicted of crime in any court if he be found feebleminded; any feebleminded boy who has been or may be committed to the State reformatory at Ione or the Whittier State School; and finally, any feebleminded girl who has been committed to the School for Girls at Ventura.

When it is remembered that approximately one in five of the inmates of penal and correctional institutions is mentally deficient, it will be seen that the slight provision above mentioned is wholly inadequate. Not even this provision, however, is made for the many kinds of mentally abnormal offenders other than the feebleminded. Dr. Glueck found the psychopathic delinquent to constitute 18.9 per cent. of his 608 Sing Sing cases. These he calls "beyond doubt the most baffling group in our classification." In spite of the fact, however, that the psychopathic individual "deserves much more attention at the hands of society than he has received thus far," almost nowhere is he recognized as distinctly abnormal, and no special provision for him is anywhere adequately made. Even our classification of the "criminal insane" is haphazard and unscientific. On the medical side, too, we are far from meeting the issue of classification and individualized treatment squarely. We still send tuberculous offenders to damp, ill ventilated, cell-block prisons; we frequently fail to segregate persons afflicted with syphilis; we make practically no special provision for alcoholics or drug addicts. On the side of personality and recidivism, also, we fail to distinguish adequately. First offenders are still housed, in many prisons, with adept and professional criminals, as well as young offenders with adults. Tramps and vagrants, who often present peculiarities of character and temperament all their own, are treated in much the same way as murderers and thieves. It is not contended that each of the groups here named requires an exclusive and separate institution. It is contended that the needs of each require to be more definitely recognized and that some degree of special institutional provision ought to be made for them.

New York has under consideration a plan for a diversified prison system that will, if carried out, be the farthest step yet taken in the direction of the ideal above described. This calls, first, for the erection of a new prison on the present site of Sing Sing, to serve primarily, if not exclusively, as a station for examining and classifying the entire prison population of the State. This new prison will be the clearing-house for diagnosing the individual offender. It will have a psychiatrical clinic, facilities for the medical, social and family study of delinquents, and departments of vocational guidance, education and religious or moral supervision. Every prisoner will go to it first and will there be observed for so long as may be necessary to discover the causes of his wrongdoing and to establish a profitable prognosis. Three or four months are expected to be the average stay of an offender in this institution.

From the clearing-house offenders will be sent to the other prisons of the State. These at present number four (excluding the present Sing Sing, which is to be replaced): two industrial prisons at Auburn and Clinton, an agricultural prison at Great Meadows and a hospital for the criminal insane at Dannemora. To them will be added *a special institution for defective delinquents*. It is expected by Dr. Glueck and his associates that the classification of prisoners at the new reception prison will, for purposes of administration, divide offenders into five more or less well defined groups. These do not include "the accidental offender who, before coming to prison, was well able to earn his livelihood by honest means." The five prisons can then be made to meet the needs of these groups. Following is a description of each group, with the institution to which it will be assigned:

1. The normal prisoner who is capable of learning a trade. This group embraces the normal young adults who are still in the formative period of life and who could be benefited materially by being taught a useful trade, should they possess no trade upon admission to prison.

This group will be assigned to the two industrial prisons at Auburn and Clinton.

2. The normal prisoner who is more or less advanced in years, whose occupation has been that of an unskilled laborer and who would make himself most useful to the state as well as derive the most benefit to himself by agricultural work.

This group will be assigned to the agricultural prison at Great Meadows. It will also be used in the housekeeping of the various institutions.

3. The insane delinquent whose presence in prison should be recognized as early as possible so as to obviate, on the one hand, the interference with the proper régime of the institution which is bound to take place as a result of his presence and, on the other hand, so as to afford the insane prisoner proper treatment as early as possible when therapeutic measures may have some beneficial effect.

The insane delinquents who require treatment of a more or less permanent nature in a hospital for the insane will be transferred to the Hospital for the Criminal Insane at Dannemora, while those suffering from transitory mental disturbances that promise recovery under proper treatment will be treated in a specially constructed psychiatric pavilion at the reception prison.

4. The defective delinquent. The presence of these prisoners among the normal population of the prison seriously interferes with the proper discipline of the institution, and they should be recognized on admission and segregated elsewhere. The defective delinquent is found in large numbers among recidivists. A certain number are unteachable and incapable of benefiting much from any form of procedure and will ultimately have to be kept under custodial care more or less permanently.

This group will be assigned to the special institution for defective delinquents to be provided.

5. The psychopathic delinquent. Prisoners of this type are the most troublesome element in a penal institution. They are subject to outbreaks of pathological emotionalism and excitement, and cannot be given proper care in the average prison.

Some psychopaths break down completely under the stress

of imprisonment and require treatment in a hospital for the insane; others will eventually have to be segregated more or less permanently [1] in the institution for defective delinquents.[2]

The accompanying chart shows this plan in diagram. The erection of the reception prison has been begun.

How such a plan, if carried out, will be handicapped by the necessity of using existing plants, built with the idea of giving uniform treatment to all inmates, remains to be seen; administrative expedients can overcome this difficulty to some extent. Two other factors will largely determine the success of the plan. One of these is the flexibility of commitment and transfer; it should at all times be easy to remove an offender from one prison to another if it appears that he will make a better response there. The other factor is the character of the administrative force in the various prisons. A force capable of making a great success in one of the industrial prisons might fail utterly if placed in charge of the institution for defective delinquents. From wardens down, each group of employees should be chosen with a view to its fitness for the particular situation it will have to face.

Interesting in this connection is a plausible contention recently made with considerable vigor[3] that none but physicians, or persons with the training of physicians,

[1] "So radical a procedure as permanent segregation," says Dr. Glueck, "should never be resorted to until a competent board of inquiry has so recommended as a result of thorough scientific investigation into the problem involved."

[2] Adapted from "Types of Delinquent Careers," by Bernard Glueck, M.D., in *Mental Hygiene* for April, 1917, pp. 171-173.

[3] See, for example, a paper entitled "The Desirability of Medical Wardens for Prisons," by E. E. Southard, M.D., in the "Proceedings of the National Conference of Social Work for 1917," p. 589.

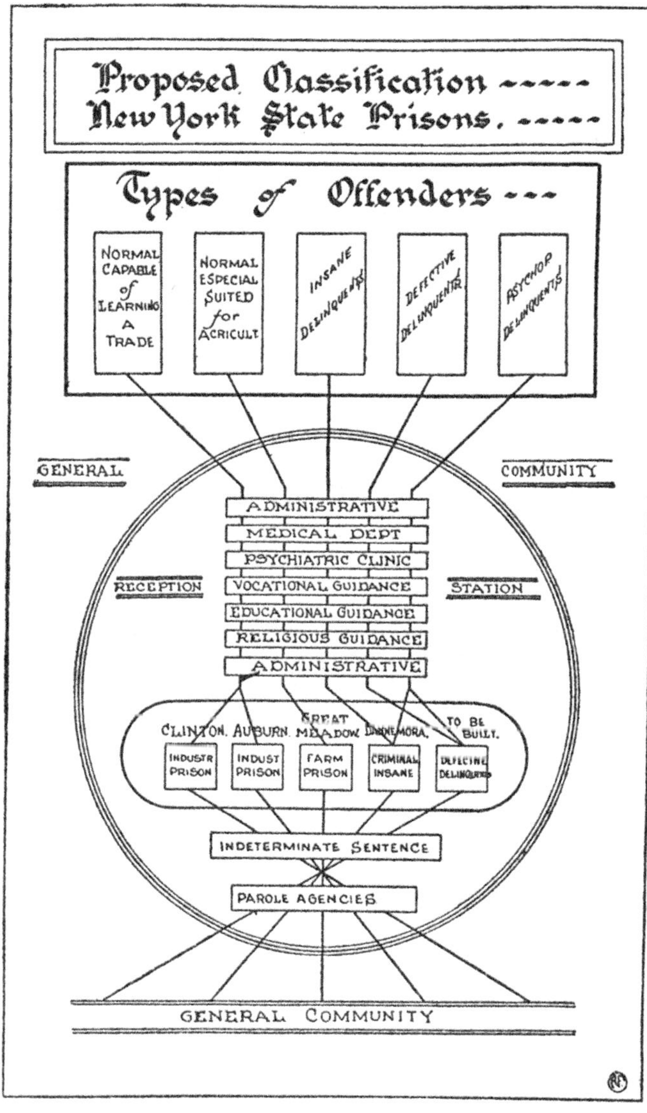
Proposed Classification
New York State Prisons.
Types of Offenders
NORMAL CAPABLE of LEARNING A TRADE
NORMAL ESPECIAL SUITED for AGRICULT
INSANE DELINQUENTS
DEFECTIVE DELINQUENTS
PSYCHOP DELINQUENTS
GENERAL
COMMUNITY
ADMINISTRATIVE
MEDICAL DEPT
PSYCHIATRIC CLINIC
RECEPTION
VOCATIONAL GUIDANCE
STATION
EDUCATIONAL GUIDANCE
RELIGIOUS GUIDANCE
ADMINISTRATIVE
CLINTON.
AUBURN.
GREAT MEADOW.
TO BE BUILT.
INDUSTR PRISON
INDUST PRISON
FARM PRISON
CRIMINAL INSANE
INDETERMINATE SENTENCE
PAROLE AGENCIES
GENERAL COMMUNITY

should be wardens of penal institutions. The chief argument brought forward in substantiation is that in the properly run prison to-day there is a constant recurrence of matters involving medical or semi-medical knowledge. Such problems as sanitation, ventilation, the prevention of epidemics, diet, the relation between the physical condition of the individual and work, and the effect of discipline are cited. To these are added, of course, the many problems pressingly brought forward by the study of individual delinquents, such as the treatment of epilepsy and the control of defective hereditary strains. Thus, both in the mass handling of prisoners and in their individualized care, it is evident that the medical viewpoint and medical knowledge are important. It does not necessarily follow that the warden himself must be a physician, though undoubtedly the prompt services of an adequate medical staff should be always available; indeed, for a prison of the customary size it may be regarded that a resident physician is indispensable. Nevertheless, one might as well argue that because mental factors play a large part in the etiology of crime, all prison heads should be psychiatrists, as to argue that they should be physicians. Then, too, if the plan of diversified institutions just outlined were put into effect, medical problems would tend to be more numerous and serious in some institutions than in others, and the desirability of medical wardens would be greater in some than in others. That medical technique will play a larger and larger part in the skilful administration of penal institutions may, however, be regarded as certain.

Next to a diversified system of institutions, the chief requirement of individualized treatment is a genuine indeterminate sentence. Most indeterminate sentence laws are half-way measures; they prescribe maximum and minimum periods of confinement and permit the release of the offender at any time between those limits, but they do not really allow his confinement until such time as he may be regarded to be no longer a menace to himself or to society. This is the test of the true indeterminate sentence. Obviously, the judge who commits a man to prison and decrees beforehand the exact time at which he shall be released is in no better position than the physician who sends a patient to a hospital and determines ahead of time the moment at which he shall come forth. The only consideration in favor of the judge is that he usually is compelled by law to do what he does. Yet, if the object of institutional treatment is to remove causes, one would suppose that treatment ought to last until causes have been removed; and it certainly does not lie in the omniscience of any human being to know beforehand how long that process will take.

The case for the indeterminate sentence has been set forth in detail by Dr. Wines in Chapter X. It is interesting to note that later studies of delinquent individuals enforce his view. Dr. Glueck's figures,[1] for example, are illuminating: Of 171 "intellectually defective" prisoners who constituted more than a fourth of all incoming prisoners examined at Sing Sing in a period of nine months, 85.7 per cent. were certain to be returned to society again in five years; of the 115

[1] See p. 297 *et seq.*

psychopathic prisoners who constituted nearly a fifth of the total examined, 82.4 per cent. were certain to be returned in five years. In other words, mentally defective and psychopathic prisoners to the extent of 39 per cent. of the total admissions were dischargeable in five years and could not be kept beyond that time. This meant, of course, that no matter what their condition, no matter how serious a menace they might constitute to the lives and property of others, forth they would go to wreak upon society whatever damage their stunted and deranged faculties would enable them to carry out. Such is the effect of fixed sentences. In spite of the seriousness of setting these persons free, the law regarded the *time* of their departure as more important than the safety of it. The law failed, too, to take into consideration the good of the inmates themselves. It would have been much better for them to remain in an institution where they could receive treatment and stand in some hope of ultimate improvement than to be allowed freedom to bring upon themselves further trouble at the first opportunity.

Although a diversified prison system is the best, much individualized treatment can be given in an undiversified one. The first requirement is that the prison authorities have a thorough understanding of the nature of the individuals who make up the prison population. Diagnosis, if it has not been made before, should be made within the shortest possible time after the inmate has entered an institution. It ought to reveal any striking factors in his make-up or record, and ought to contain a prognosis of his response to the institutional environment and to ordinary disciplinary measures; especially, it ought to classify him mentally. A record of the diagnosis should be kept in the warden's office.

In most prisons it is possible to follow the mental classification in the daily activities. A tier of cells, a wing or other structural division affords an easy mode of segregation by groups. Work can be carefully assigned in accordance with both the inmate's intellectual and physical fitness for it. For prisoners of dull mentality there is usually enough rough or unskilled work to afford an outlet for their abilities; many a mental defective has found his path to social adjustment made easy by interesting manual or finger work. Prisons have much to learn in this regard from schools for the feebleminded.

Offenders of normal intelligence can usually be encouraged to feel definite pride in their labor. This requires patience, educational insight, and close attention to personal peculiarities on the part of those in charge. To set a man at digging a ditch is one thing; to set him at digging a ditch twenty feet long and three feet wide, with straight lines and a uniform depth throughout, is quite another; and if, in addition, he be made to believe that not every man with a spade in his hand can dig such a ditch, a long step has been taken toward putting a new interest in that man's life. Tom Sawyer, with his facility for getting others to paint his aunt's fences, might have been a good person to be in charge of prison industries.

Vocational guidance can be made a solid aid in the individualization of treatment on its industrial side.

This should have back of it, of course, as wide a variety of occupations as the prison plant and the ingenuity of the warden can provide. To set a man with clumsy fingers at a task requiring high digital dexterity is only typical of what one has come to expect of our penal methods. An interesting demonstration of the possibilities of providing varied occupations and of fitting each man's work to his needs and capacities has recently been begun at Sing Sing. Vocational classes have been formed in sign-making, automobile repairs, hair-cutting and shaving, stenography, and a large variety of mechanical occupations. Many of these are taught by inmates. The assignment of men to work is largely in the hands of a vocational guidance clinic, participated in by the resident psychiatrist and others who are in a position to know the inmates well. A lesson may be learned here from the practice of the Gary public schools. Most of the maintenance and repair work in these schools is done by students in the vocational classes, under direction. While many prisons now utilize inmate labor for work of this sort, they do not always give it the constructive educational value that it might have.

Not only the mental and vocational peculiarities of prisoners, but the physical as well should be considered in assigning work. A man with a weak heart is not a fit subject for strenuous labor, nor is one with a poor stomach for work that will give him a ravenous appetite. Here, as elsewhere, common sense and careful medical diagnosis are necessary.

Prisoners should be studied individually by all officers over them. The diagnostic report ought to be read not only by the warden but by each official in charge. It is the practice of the warden of an Eastern prison to ask his officers to read the reports of men before the men are assigned to them. "Here is a man," he will say to an officer, "whose record shows him to be highly excitable. He will probably get along well enough with other prisoners until something goes wrong and then he will fly into a fit of temper. He is likely, too, to become a victim of a delusion of persecution. Ordinary disciplinary measures may have to be used discreetly. Do you want him?" The officer who takes him does so with full knowledge of the man's peculiarities.

Obviously this practice makes it desirable to have officers of different attainments and temperaments. There should be officers, for example, capable of directing the strong and the self-willed, officers with patience to handle the mentally inert, officers who understand the vagaries of the quixotic and the psychopathically inclined, and so on. The day when a strong arm and a fearless heart were the sole requisites of a prison officer is gone.

So far we have discussed treatment chiefly on the industrial side. Treatment may be divided under various heads—physical, psychological, educational, religious, etc. It should be a commonplace of criminal therapy that a sound body is one of the indispensable foundations for improvement in conduct. Whether physical defects be the cause of delinquency or not, reformation will obviously have a better chance if it have no physical obstacle to retard it. Many instances have been brought to light of the part played by bodily ailments or incapacities in producing or accelerating delinquent careers. One of these was a street car motorman who suffered from flat feet. Obviously flat feet seriously interfere with the comfort and even the efficiency of a motorman. In this instance depression and final incapacitation led to delinquency. The first measure of scientific therapy in such a case, one would imagine, would be to cure the flat feet or to fit the motorman for a job that did not require standing. Instead, the fact that flat feet had a causal connection with the man's delinquency was not discovered until after his third or fourth offence. Another instance was a man who had served five or six terms without anybody discovering that his vision was one-fifth normal and that his general physical make-up rendered him unfit for most labor. When the Juvenile Psychopathic Institute in Chicago found this man, society had merely "passed him along with the offenders of the day through the mill of the law, and that's all there was to it."

Treatment on the psychological side is the most baffling problem before penologists to-day. While ultimately psychiatrists will sail far voyages, to-day they stand on the edge of an ocean into which they have only begun to wade. The important thing, of course, is that penologists should be passengers on their voyages. Penologists ought to accompany them with sympathetic minds and ought to accept whatever guidance their explorations may afford. Already some facts of value have been obtained. One of these is that certain causes of delinquency having a mental basis can be removed by merely bringing them to the attention of the offender himself. Such, occasionally, are mental conflicts and mental imagery. Not infrequently a delinquent career has its causal inpulse in criminalistic imagery traceable either to association with other criminals, to things seen at moving picture shows, or to other sense impressions. Usually the offender has realized only vaguely, if at all, the bearing of these images upon his conduct. Once this connection is made clear, however, the spell is often broken and delinquent acts are more easily avoided. Somewhat the same thing is true with respect to mental conflicts. With both, a supplementary aid to cure sometimes lies in reconstructing the old environment or removing from it.

Of mental defect, or feeblemindedness, more is known and the main lines of treatment are better marked. For all except the higher or so-called "border-line" cases of mental defectiveness, permanent segregation is desirable[1]—both for the good of the individual and of society. The feebleminded is seldom able to lead a life of normal adjustment in the world at large. When he is able to do so, the reason is usually found in the care taken of him by friends or relatives—in the fact that his environment has been made comparatively simple. Segregation is therefore desirable in order to secure for him a greater degree of comfort and safety than he would otherwise have. It is also desirable for society because mental defect is highly inheritable and because feebleminded persons, while no more inherently vicious than others, are to a greater degree potential criminals. They are apt as Goddard

[1] For further discussion of this point see pp. 451 *et seq.*

has put it, to lack "one or the other of the factors essential to a moral life—an understanding of right and wrong, and the power of control." Under custodial treatment they can be carefully shielded from temptation and trained to do simple tasks suited to their intelligence. Institutions for the feebleminded can, under favorable circumstances, become nearly if not entirely self-supporting. Treatment of them in penal institutions should adopt as far as possible the well established methods worked out in the best schools for the feebleminded, such as those at Waverly, Mass., and Vineland, N. J.

Aside from the feebleminded, there remain large groups of the mentally abnormal in almost every unselected population of offenders. Among these are persons who can be recognized as mentally dull from physical conditions; the 12 per cent. whom Glueck found at Sing Sing to be "mentally diseased or deteriorated"; the 18 per cent. whom he found to be "psychopathic, or constitutionally inferior"; the mentally aberrated or insane; and those suffering from a wide range of hardly definable mental peculiarities.

For some of these, definite treatment can be prescribed. The treatment of the constitutionally inferior, says Healy,

"resolves itself down to very careful oversight and patient education, particularly during the years of adolescence. Permanent colonization is needed for many of them. We have seen very few, indeed, do well ultimately under merely family care, although in very favorable environmental circumstances, such as good country life, this regimen has succeeded. One trouble, as we have seen it, is that these individuals who are brought up amid the stimuli of city life, cannot be satisfied for long with 'country dulness.' . . . Along the same line is the need which this class feels for the ingestion of stimulants. Of course, any stimulants taken in excess markedly increase instability.

"One great difficulty which we and others have noted in the disposal of these cases is that their reactions may be satisfactory enough in institutional life, but quite inadequate to meeting the world where they have to assume at least some responsibility. A penal institution may, according to its record of good conduct, find them fit for parole, a hospital for the insane may declare them not out-and-out insane, and so discharge them. Then they return often straight to criminalism."

Minor as well as major deviations in mentality are important. It is easy enough to classify a man who goes through the streets killing every dog he meets or who presents himself in public naked. Judges and prison authorities should not insist upon such extremes, however, before they admit the existence of mental disease or give ear to the doctrine of partial responsibility. Neither is rigid classification in technical language always possible or desirable. The primary object of everyone concerned with treatment should be to discover the specific malady, whatever it is, and to apply adequate corrective measures if they are available.

With reference to the treatment of the emotionally unstable, Adler says:

"It would seem that by careful training based on an analysis of each individual—especially from the behaviorist's point of view, considering the past life and career rather than the self-explanatory, subjective statements—it should be possible to influence the future conduct of these individuals. While their fundamental equipment cannot be changed any more than that of the other two groups, these people suffer more from the effects of their conduct than from their subjective attitude toward themselves or their environment.

"Thus, as Kraepelin points out, alcohol is an important factor in producing the final downfall. Extravagance, profligacy, sex excesses, venereal disease, bad companionship, and so forth, are the factors which combine to cause the social difficulties. The suggestibility of these individuals, their intelligence and insight, which is usually quite adequate for their needs, can be made use of in acquiring and strengthening the habits which the individual would never be able to gain if left to himself.

"What is desired, therefore, is a system of mental and emotional exercises for the purpose of habit formation. This might be designated as *orthopsychics*. This term is further applicable in that a good many of those cases are instances not of disease in the sense of an acquired, deteriorating process, but rather comparable to physical deformities. For the present our experiences in orthopsychics is limited. We have had a few cases in which, after a preliminary survey at the Psychopathic Hospital, a course of training has been applied which has consisted above all in arousing the interests and appealing to the pleasure-loving side of the individual. It is a well-known fact, for instance, that in dealing with wayward young people, even under the most advantageous circumstances, and even with the most favorable and friendly environment, the individuals do not do well. This appears to be due to the fact that the emotional impulses are of short duration, and leave no strong impression behind them. Therefore, when the novelty of the situation has worn off, there is nothing to hold the interests of the delinquent and tide him over the tedious days of monotonous routine." [1]

It is apparent that treatment on the psychiatrical side merges at many points with treatment on the educational. Education has for a much longer time, however, been pursued by man, and educational highroads are well blazed. For normal prisoners of fair intelligence prison authorities can have no excuse, therefore, for not developing adequately this aspect of institutional therapy. Formal instruction is not enough, though it is useful in enlarging the outlook and en-

[1] "Bulletin of the Massachusetts Commission on Mental Diseases," Vol. I, Nos. 1 and 2, 1917, pp. 232-233.

riching the mental life of prisoners. Practical vocational training must play a large part in educational plans. An educational motive, too, should infuse as many activities of the prison as possible. Intensive individualization here, as elsewhere, is needed. Penal institutions may well be their own educational experiment stations. Such highly selected and diversified groups as they contain afford opportunities for devising new educational methods and ways of approach that are superior to the opportunities of almost any other place where human beings come together—superior even to the schools themselves.

In regard to the value of purely formal religious training and instruction, opinions will differ. This much can be said: If the type of such training that has heretofore prevailed in penal institutions is the best that can be offered, there can hardly be two views about its usefulness. This type is not the best, however. Undoubtedly an appeal to man's finer motives can be made by the religious approach. Indeed, there is ample evidence that religious experience or conversion has played a part in the reformation of some delinquents. Usually, however, this has been of an informal—what might be called a cataclysmic—nature. It has occurred more by accident than design. The laws of its operation have not been well formulated and for that reason it does not occupy as dependable a place in prognosis as it should, perhaps. Offenders are usually very pragmatic. They have lived in a world of facts, often very hard facts, and are apt to judge any teaching by its practical bearings. Religion, therefore, should not be made for them a matter of precept and authority merely. It should be fused with whatever else they learn and do, not remain a thing apart, a veneer. One reason why chaplains do not command more respect than they do is that they are so apt to be thinking and talking about release from this world, whereas what prisoners are interested in is release from jail. Religious teaching ought to identify itself to a greater degree with civic patriotism and industrial efficiency. It ought to supply motives that can be acted upon and ideals that can be approached. In short, it ought to cooperate with the other activities of the prison in helping inmates to a workable method of life.

There remain two aspects of treatment that deserve mention, recreation and participation by inmates in the conduct of their own affairs. The latter will receive more extended discussion in another chapter. Here mention is made of it only to include it in the catalogue of therapeutic measures. Recreation is as constructive an element in the life of a prisoner as in that of any person on the outside. It has to do, essentially, with the right use of leisure. It is precisely in their knowledge of how to use leisure that many delinquents are deficient. They have led narrow and constricted lives; faculties and aptitudes wholly desirable have been neglected or have lain dormant. The prison should aim to develop these. It should present a sufficiently varied range of activities to call every faculty into play. Like the college and the university, it should furnish social life in miniature and prepare its inmates for a rounded adjustment to conditions after discharge. It is in such a program as this that recreation plays its most important part. Recreation is both a diversion and a means of building up habits that will enable offenders to spend their non-working hours doing interesting and wholesome things.

Athletic activities constitute one of the most desirable forms of recreation for prisoners. Baseball games between different prisons and between different teams within the same prison are now common. Tennis courts are coming into use and are easily laid out. Bocci, an Italian game somewhat similar to duck-on-rock, is a favorite pastime in many prisons; so, also, is basketball. Field days are diligently encouraged in some prisons and the control and preparation of them given over to the inmates. Whatever sports are encouraged, they should present enough variety to meet individual abilities and tastes. It would be a good thing if gymnasiums should become more general in prisons. Running, jumping, trapeze work—the whole range of health-giving outdoor and indoor sports—constitute a desirable part of prison life.

The possible forms of recreation are manifold. Motion pictures are shown several times a week in some prisons, purely narrative or dramatic films—"thrillers"—being varied with educational ones. The possibilities of platform entertainments are unlimited. Institutions near large cities can often secure dramatic talent for "prisoners' shows," and performances by inmates themselves are a never-failing source of amusement as well as often being highly educational. The restrained use of the lecture or set speech, preferably by someone not officially connected with the prison, is also a wholesome diversion. Illustrations of recreation could be given without number. The important thing is that its constructive and therapeutic value as a builder of normal habits and adjustments be recognized. The administrative task and the devising of a program then become easy.

One advantage of recreation is that it aids discipline. It makes for contentment, mental alertness and self-control. In prisons of the old type, where the inmates are locked in their cells Saturday noon and remain in them until Monday morning, the first day of their deliverance is proverbially fruitful of infractions of discipline and of fights between prisoners. If, on the other hand, Saturday afternoon and Sunday have been days of wholesome relaxation, with athletic games and one or two good entertainments in the prison chapel, Monday becomes a day of increased orderliness and sobriety.

The place of punishment in treatment has not yet been touched upon. With educators and other students of youth still disagreeing over the precise value and methods of punishment, it is not likely that criminologists will entirely agree among themselves. The idea that extreme rigors must be added to incarceration and that offenders must at all times be made to feel the heavy hand of authority if not the actual rod of chastisement is fast losing ground. We seldom build prisons to-day, as Sing Sing was built ninety years ago, to fit the principle that "to make any impression upon convicts there must be suffering, and to make any adequate impression, such sufferings as will excite feelings of terror." This view is still occasionally defended in theory and has by no means died out in practice, but usually all that is necessary to give it a death-blow is the publication of a few vivid details of its application in a newspaper circulating near the institution where it is allowed. The day is not yet entirely gone by when a Congressman of the United States can openly plead for retaining that relic of barbarism, the public whipping post,[1] or when the governor of so presumably enlightened a State as New York, campaigning for re-election, can urge a régime of "iron discipline" for all prisoners; but it is a sign of progress that the defenders of these things do not speak out in public as often as they once did. We are emerging from the browbeating stage of prison treatment and are entering upon the therapeutic one. This does not mean that severity and even cruelty no longer exist in prisons. So recently as January, 1917, a reporter for the New York *Evening Post* found dungeons and wall shackles for hanging men by their wrists in the New Jersey State Prison at Trenton. Other prisons could doubtless show similar halls of torture. The ball and chain fastened to the legs of prisoners and causing festering wounds is still a not uncommon spectacle in Southern States. Indeed, if one could start at the front door of every prison in the country and go through them all from end to end and top to bottom, removing stone from stone if necessary in the search for secret chambers and hidden devices of torment, he would have a goodly collection of thumbscrews, head cages, paddles, wall manacles and various other instruments of cruelty to show at

[1] Delaware is the only State where the public whipping-post is still statutorily allowed.

the end of his search. It is a crying need of prison reform to get rid of these things. The very circumstance that they are now used so much more secretly than formerly is evidence of enlightenment, but it also renders more difficult their discovery and abolition. If the far-reaching hand of the federal government should be invoked to ferret out the places where these things are used, and to get totally rid of them once for all, one of the most damning barbarities of the twentieth century would at last be ended.

Imprisonment itself, except for people who have lost most of the interest and incentive of life, is severe punishment. Confirmed recidivists may snap their fingers at frequent terms, and mental defectives may be unchanged by mere confinement, but for a large number of offenders the closing of the prison door behind them completes all the punishment that it is in the power of the state to inflict. Additional punishment, in whatever form it may be given, should be regarded as simply one of the therapeutic measures available, not as the sole basis of discipline. Prisons should no more be built exclusively upon the idea of punishment than upon that of removing insanity, or teaching trades, or education, or curing disease; each of these is important in proportion to its success in restoring better men to society. Reasonable punishment (we are not now using the word in a physical sense) has an undoubted place in criminal therapy, for the contemplation of discomfort is a strong deterrent, especially for the man who possesses fair intelligence and foresight. One should always be sure, however, that the capacity to foresee discomfort is present. This is by no means always the case, as the statistics of mental defectiveness amply show. Healy quotes an unjailed expert criminal as saying: "The only way to stop us is to find out who and what we are, and what we're good for. Then you've got to make punishment severe enough or opportunities good enough for us. You don't do either of these now." This would perhaps hit nearer the truth if the "or" were changed to "and." What reason is there that good opportunities should not go hand in hand with punishment?

The desirability of bodily punishment, even in moderation, is a difficult question. There may be natures that respond only to such treatment, but, as a rule, it is extremely doubtful whether the infliction of physical pain by one adult upon another, except in a fair fight between equals, often accomplishes the end sought. When a prisoner is deprived of all resisting power beforehand, is strapped and fettered or so awed by fear or superior force that he becomes the mere passive object of blows, the resulting state of mind is not likely to be congenial to better intentions, whatever the outward conduct may temporarily become. Such discipline is not likely to lead to the formation of better habits or higher ideals. It is more likely to produce humiliation, which is the parent of anti-social grudge, or motives of revenge and sentiments of hatred. Few prisoners will think that they have deserved such chastisement or brought it upon themselves. They will be more likely to attribute it to the cruelty of persecutors. The best proof of all this is that the chastising system of discipline is notorious for its production of recidivism. Instead of keeping people out of prison, physical punishment has the paradoxical effect of drawing them back in.

One of the most effective forms of intra-mural punishment is deprivation of privileges. This avoids the humiliating and incalculable results of chastisement and yet constitutes real discipline. Instead of adding directly to the severities of life, to which prisoners grow used and toward which they soon acquire a stoical attitude, it subtracts from the pleasures and so attacks them at a very vulnerable point. For it is the small pleasures of prison life that make that life endurable. Take away a prisoner's expectation of occasional enjoyment and you have wounded him far more deeply than physical pain could do. But you have not embittered him or warped his mind by the indignity of personal attack. You have not destroyed his equilibrium. You have left him free to change his conduct as soon as the deprivation becomes irksome or intolerable. Men can stand harshness, which is short-lived, better than vacuity, which soon becomes interminable.

The intuition of a skilful handler of men is a better guide to the use of punishment than any set rules. Its very withholding in instances where it might reasonably be expected is sometimes the key to awakening a prisoner's better self. Where it is needed, its infliction should be immediate and certain. Nothing is more fatal to discipline or to an offender's formation of better habits than procrastination in exacting the penalty for misdeeds.

The arguments for and against capital punishment have been so often gone over that to repeat them here would be tedious. We may regard it as substantially proved that the deterrent effect of capital punishment is almost negligible. Louisiana has given a fresh hint of this by her law of 1918 providing that when sentence of death has been passed in that State, the hanging shall take place in the parish where the crime was committed and not, as heretofore, in the State capital. The demand for this law was based upon the belief that people in the neighborhood of the crime were often skeptical that the hanging ever took place, and so the moral effect was lost. Another consideration, of course, is the degrading and brutalizing effect of executions upon the mass of mankind. Finally, in view of what we know about the possibilities of diagnosis and of individualized treatment, the taking of life for crime seems to be nothing short of a confession of failure. In effect, society says: "I do not know what else to do with this offender, so I will kill him." The development of scientific criminology should put an end to such impotence.

Treatment After Release

Treatment after release bears a closer likeness to treatment before, than to treatment during, confinement. The most terrible moment in the life of an offender is not that in which the prison door closes upon him, but that in which it opens to permit his return to the world. He has lost his character and standing among men. He has suffered for months or years the deprivation of normal pleasures and associations. Usually he has little money and is without friends who will assist him to secure work or to get a new start in life. Thrust upon his own resources, his situation is critical in the extreme. If he meets a hostile attitude, relapse into crime is almost certain to be the result. His former friends and associates are waiting to receive him; they will literally ply him with arguments for resuming his old habits. Society, therefore, if it would save him from his new dangers, must surround him at once with counteracting influences.

It ought to become a working principle of penology that if an offender is ready to leave prison, he is ready to rejoin society on terms of reasonable trust and confidence. The public has often been scolded, of course, for its hostility to "jail-birds," especially that part of the public which controls the avenues to employment. It must be recognized, however, that to a degree this hostility is justified. The recidivist is altogether too frequent a figure in prison life for society to be wholly to blame for its skepticism. So long as men return to prison in large numbers, unreformed and guilty of fresh offences, prison administrators have no cause to take a "holier-than-thou" attitude and to put all of the censure upon society for difficulties encountered by prisoners after discharge. They should first remove the ground for society's aloofness. Nevertheless, progress does not come by justifying one's negative attitudes. Society must do its part. It must meet the prison half way. It must recognize that even when crime is the act of deliberate intention and a responsible mind, help and not obstruction is the key to reclamation. It should, therefore, cooperate in making the offender's fresh start easy. It should insist, first, that he be retained until the specific causes of his waywardness are discovered and so far as possible removed, and second, that when the prison door closes behind him it shut out of his life unnecessary suspicion, prejudice and an eager willingness to believe him as ready as ever to commit crime.

A prisoner can gain his release in any one of three ways: he can complete his term and so earn his unconditional release; he can be pardoned, which is the equivalent of unconditional release; and he can be paroled. Parole is the act of granting a period of probation in which a prisoner may test his ability to be outside of prison walls and to merge again into industrial and social life. It carries with it conditions, and the violation of these constitutes a ground for taking him back into custody. In an ideal prison system release would never be wholly unconditional, except perhaps for a man who had been found to be innocent of the crime for which he was being held. Instead, society would extend its protecting care over every offender for a longer or shorter time after discharge, in other words it would parole him, and since there would be no such thing as a fixed sentence he would be paroled at the moment when a board of specialists should decide that he was ready to try life again in the world outside.

Whatever parole may be in legal theory, in spirit it ought to be regarded not as an extension of the term of incarceration but as a period for friendly and sympathetic assistance toward rehabilitation. The following propositions have been laid down as underlying the theory of parole:

"1. That the prisoner ordinarily arrives at a period in his imprisonment when further incarceration will be of less service to him and to the state as a reformative measure than a like period passed in liberty under parole supervision.

"2. That in the determination of the proper time at which to admit the prisoner to parole, an exhaustive and painstaking study will be made of the individual case, in order that both the right of society to be protected, and the right of the prisoner to rehabilitate himself, may be preserved.

"3. That the supervision of prisoners while on parole shall be conducted thoroughly, and with efficiency and sympathy." [1]

In determining the proper time for granting parole, a careful record should be made of the offender's progress in the institution and a thorough reexamination of his physical and mental condition. For this the psychiatric clinic is indispensable. Its study will help to determine not only what effect physically, mentally, socially and industrially the period of imprisonment has had upon the individual, but also whether he is in consequence fitted to go out into conditional liberty. In general the following points should be considered in relation to every application for parole: First, the prisoner's physical health—whether, by being kept in prison a longer time, he can be restored to society in better physical condition and therefore better able to cope with the difficulties he will there meet; second, his ability to earn a livelihood—whether, for example, his habits of industry and knowledge of an occupation can be increased by longer residence; third, his prospect of immediate employment upon discharge; fourth, the whole record of his pre-institutional life as throwing light on the probable tendencies of his future; and fifth, his institutional record as showing the extent to which he has overcome the causes of his former delinquency.

[1] "Prison Progress in 1916, Being the Seventy-second Annual Report of the Prison Association of New York," p. 72.

The cardinal principle of good parole work, or of any effective care of prisoners after release, is the preparation beforehand of the environment into which they will go. This involves primarily the prisoner's relations with his family, with prospective employers and with his former associates. Intensive preparation of environment is now undertaken by few penal institutions. One of those that attempts it most systematically is the Westchester County Penitentiary and Workhouse at East View, N. Y. The subjoined quotations from the first annual report (for 1917) of that institution will suggest some of the possibilities of applying this principle. The report first recites that shortly after the arrival of each prisoner "a very full and comprehensive study is made by the psychiatrist, which gives us intelligent direction in handling the man. We know his mental twist, his temperament, his mental age or level, and what his probable reaction to discipline and work will be." With these things in mind, the report continues (pages 97-98):

"Our employment agent gets acquainted with the man and learns everything possible about his industrial life and wishes. The home conditions, if there be any, and, if not, the other conditions surrounding the man's life and work previous to coming to us, are investigated personally. The weekly officers' meeting gives light from time to time on the general progress of the man and his reactions toward the routine and discipline of the institution. The Tuesday morning Cabinet meeting, the Cabinet consisting of the Warden, Psychiatrist, the Deputy Warden, the Employment Agent, the Director of Child Welfare of the County, the Deputy Commissioner, and any officer or officers who may be called in for consultation, takes up in routine the case of every man who has entered the institution since the previous Tuesday, and the consideration of every man's case who is ready for parole or discharge within the next two weeks. The fullest possible discussion is undertaken to the end that the man shall fit as perfectly as possible into the environment we have selected for him after his discharge, and be able to function efficiently in the job he is to accept.

"The next step is to properly place the man in his work. This, we consider, a very personal matter. The Employment Agent meets the discharged prisoner in the office at the institution and takes him personally to his new job, introducing him to his employer, assisting him in finding a boarding place, if necessary, and doing any other act of supervision or consideration that is likely to lead to more comfortable relations between the man, his job, his environment and the community.

"Some notable work has been done. For instance, we have rehabilitated nine different families[1] which were hopelessly broken up, the children in institutions, the wife dependent or working, the husband and father in the penitentiary, the household furniture sold or pawned or in storage. In each of these nine cases the home has been completely reestablished, usually in an entirely new community, the children taken out of the institution, the husband and wife reconciled to one another, and the husband eager to support his family. The significant feature of this arrangement is that we continue, unofficially, the supervision of this man through a friendly, but non-inquisitive, attitude on the part of our Employment Agent, and with the cooperation of the local authorities and other interested people. There are several other cases of men who, while not married, had women and children or parents dependent upon them. Many of these we have succeeded also in reestablishing in their positions of protector and provider for those dependent upon them."

The following account of an individual case will further illustrate the principle of the preparation of environment:

"N—— B——, an offender who had formerly led a straightforward and hard-working life, got into trouble through gambling and intemperance. He neglected his home and was finally arrested for non-support, his wife swearing out the war-

[1] At the time this report was written, the work had been in operation only a few months. In addition to rehabilitating these nine families, many men had been placed at work.

rant for his arrest. Nothing could persuade the man after this that his wife was not really to blame for all that had befallen him; continual brooding in the institution only deepened his conviction. He refused to see his wife or to have anything to do with her. Meanwhile, two of his three children were placed in a child-caring institution and his wife, shortly after his incarceration, gave birth to a fourth.

"Parole officers called on the wife and got her story. She was as unwilling to see her husband as he was to see her. One day the warden said to the prisoner:

" 'When did your wife begin nagging you and getting irritable, "going back on you," as you say?'

" 'About four years ago,' was the answer.

" 'Wasn't that just about the time you began gambling?'

"So certain had the man been that his wife was the chief cause of his troubles that he had never made this simple chronological connection. Slowly he was led to see that his wife was not wholly to blame. Meanwhile the fate of his children was impressed upon him and his own knowledge of institutions, with which he had had some prior acquaintance on the outside, was drawn upon. Finally, he voluntarily asked to be allowed to see his wife. What was said at the interview is unknown, but when they parted both were anxious to try to live together again upon his release. This was the decision that the parole officers wanted. Through the intervention of the county children's bureau, the two children were taken out of the institution and restored to the mother. A job for the man in another part of the county was secured, he himself having expressed a disinclination to go back to his former place of employment. A house was secured and the family moved. When the man left prison, house, family and job were awaiting him—all in a new environment where he could start fresh. The man has now been out of prison a year, has made regular weekly payments on a small loan given him at the time of discharge, and to all appearances is living a normal, happy, family existence."

The parole period may be supervised and administered either by the institution itself, by another governmental department, or by private persons or associations cooperating with these. The initial granting of parole must, of course, lie in the hands of a public body, since only the state can decide when its prisoners may be released. Parole boards exist in most states. There is the greatest disparity, however, among their standards and methods. For the most part they are purely perfunctory bodies, automatically granting paroles upon the receipt of stereotyped reports, making no adequate investigation of individual prisoners and maintaining no sufficient staff of field agents to keep in close touch with released prisoners. An anlaysis of work done by the New York State Board of Parole in 1916, made by the Prison Association of New York, showed that of 1028 persons on parole Nov. 22, more than 91 per cent. had been released either immediately upon the expiration of their minimum sentences, or within one month after the expiration of those sentences. In other words, the minimum sentence represented practically the length of imprisonment to be undergone by the inmate. It is hardly possible, as the association pointed out, "that 91 per cent. of the men in prisons are sufficiently similar in character, training or other physical or mental condition to justify the almost automatic release of nine out of ten applicants practically at the expiration of the shortest term during which they may be held in prison." One of the causes of such poor administration, which is not limited to New York, is that the members of most parole boards are unpaid or paid only nominal amounts. As a consequence they give very little time—often only a few hours one day a month—to a consideration of their delicate and important task. Many of them, moreover, are political appointees, or at best have no special qualifications for their work.

The salaries of parole board members should be sufficient to attract competent, devoted men and women and to enable them to give full time to their work. Parole boards should sit as continuously as any of the higher courts of the state. The function of the board is, indeed, the counterpart of that of the court. The court decides when a man shall enter prison, the parole board when he shall come out. The court, if enlightened, seeks to know the causes of crime and the kind of treatment best calculated to remove them; the parole board is equally interested in causes and seeks to know whether the treatment given has been beneficial. Both are concerned with the past chiefly because of its light on the future; both take testimony, weigh evidence, pass judgment. In addition, the parole board has certain administrative functions, such as prescribing the principles governing parole, supervising the work of parole officers and determining when violation of parole has occurred. These, in themselves, are exacting responsibilities and only add to the need for permanence and continuity in the board's work.

Perhaps the best illustration of what a parole board should be has been afforded by the recent Parole Commission of New York City. This was organized under the Indeterminate Sentence and Parole Law passed in 1915. Under the provisions of this law, several thousand offenders annually committed to city institutions became subject to an indeterminate sentence that had a maximum but no minimum. A prisoner could, therefore, be released at any time after the first day of his sentence. The parole commission created by the law was intended to be a body of permanent character. Three members, including the chairman (who is the "parole commissioner"), are appointed by the mayor for terms of ten years (the initial appointments were for two, four and six years), while the commissioners of police and correction are *ex officio* members. The salary of the chairman is $7,500 a year, that of the other two appointed members $6,000 each. The members of the board give full time to their work and have appointed a secretary, who also gives full time.

The importance attached to the work of this commission is indicated by the appropriation made for it by the city, which in 1917 amounted to $85,902. In staff this provided for one chief parole officer, three senior parole officers, thirty-six parole officers, fourteen clerks and stenographers and a telephone operator. Not only is the commission thus equipped, but it regards itself as in duty bound to carry on intensive work among the prisoners subject to its jurisdiction. In reaching decisions in regard to the length of time inmates shall remain in the institutions, it has proceeded independently of the institutional authorities. Its work has, however, been based upon examinations by physicians, by the institutional school teacher, by the industrial department of the institutions, by the clearing-house for psychiatric study and by a representative of the commission itself. In its supervision of prisoners after release, it has secured employment for large numbers, has helped or obtained help for dependent families of prisoners, has done much to establish friendly relations between paroled prisoners and the police, has recognized the different classifications of prisoners and attempted to provide individual care for them, and has in general given effective application to many of the principles above set forth. For the time being, and until its methods are superseded by better ones, its work may well stand as a model for the parole boards of the country.

CHAPTER XIV

INMATE SELF-GOVERNMENT

I. The Theory of Inmate Self-Government

Self-government in penal institutions is merely an application of the educational principle that people learn by doing. It is based on no unusual and quixotic conception of the *rights* of prisoners—their right to vote, to take part in the government over them, to say what orders they shall obey and who shall issue those orders. Doubtless prisons will always be conducted on the theory that men and women who break society's laws forfeit many rights and privileges previously enjoyed; certainly it is no part of the theory of self-government that they do not forfeit them. Self-government is simply an embodiment of the idea that if prisoners are to improve in the ways of normal living, if they are to grow more self-reliant in dealing with other people, and if they are to acquire the social habit of living in accordance with certain "rules of the game," as well as to develop their own capacity to help make those rules, the time to begin is while they are undergoing punishment for their offences.

It is obvious that the great majority of people in prison have failed to adjust themselves to the social *milieu.* What better remedy for this is there than to train them to adjust themselves to the prison *milieu?*

Self-government is, or ought to be, the setting up of a miniature world in which relationships become normal, acts spontaneous and the power of choice, within limits set by the necessity of keeping prisoners confined, free. Its aim, like that of all other reformative discipline, is to fit the prisoner for a return to society. Its method is to establish on a small scale a society in which he can form the habits, accustom himself to the responsibilities and gradually acquire the mental attitude, that make normal life attainable.

Self-government is, therefore, more than a mere lesson in the machinery of citizenship. It is more than going through the form of electing one's own officers and sitting in judgment upon one's offending fellow-inmates. It is an effort to train persons in the art of living in concert. It implies a strengthening of the ability to exercise one's own faculties—something needed mightily in the world at large. It implies freedom to choose one's own friends, to dispose of one's leisure hours, to order one's own life in ways that do not interfere with the necessary routine and discipline of a prison's purpose. Under the autocratic system of prison government the faculties of inmates are kept in abeyance or killed outright. Under that system he comes in time to accept the grinding routine that he cannot escape. His whole habit of mind is altered thereby. He relies solely upon the officer's command, and leaves the very ordering of his life to forces imposed from without. A prisoner recently discharged from an institution of this type stood in front of the prison door and, though suffering from no infirmity and in the prime of life, was afraid to cross the street because a wagon, still half a block away, was coming slowing down the road toward him. The vehicle was drawn by a single horse and contained a load of bricks! Yet the power of independent action of this man had become so dulled by long conformity to the prison routine that he could not make this simple adjustment and permitted the wagon to pass first. Such is the effect of robbing prisoners of all power to exercise choice.

If it be doubted that the customary despotism of prison governments is such as here described, a sketch of the daily life at Sing Sing before self-government was started there will remove all skepticism.[1] Under the old régime,[2] the day began with the raucous clanging of a bell at 6:30 in the morning. This meant that each prisoner must rise and put on the uniform that for the next ten hours would render him indistinguishable from 1,500 other human beings. After dressing, he made his bed and swept the floor of his cell; not much inventiveness was required in corralling the dirt on a dead stone surface of twenty-three square feet.

Then the prisoner stepped to his cell door, ready for the morning count. For this he was required to stand in either one of two ways—he must grasp a bar of the gate with one hand or he must show the fingers of the hand thrust out between the bars. The rap of a stick at the end of the gallery announced that an officer was coming to take the count. The officer un-

[1] The facts in regard to this daily life are taken from an article by the reviser, published in *The Survey,* April 1, 1916.

[2] The rigor of this régime was slightly modified by Warden McCormick, who was warden for a short time preceding Mr. Osborne.

locked each door as he passed, and at the end of the tier drew the master lever that permitted the doors to be opened. Another rap told each prisoner to step into the corridor, bucket in hand and take his place in line. Places were assigned on the basis of height—the tallest at the head—so that even here regularity was carried to the extreme.

A third rap told the men to begin to march, and closely attended by guards they walked in military formation to the bucket-house. There, without breaking line, they emptied the excreta of the night, held their buckets for a moment under a running faucet, and placed them on a rack for the day. They then proceeded to the mess hall for breakfast. Filing into narrow aisles between the long board tables, each man stood at his place until a rap of the ever-sounding stick told him to pull out his stool. A second rap told him to sit down and a third to begin to eat. Seventy-five guards stood by during the twenty minutes allowed for breakfast. When time was up, a rap told the men to rise, push in their stools and face to the left; and two short raps, to march out.

As the men left the hall each clasped his cap to his left shoulder with his right hand, and held his knife, fork and spoon in plain sight in the other. Under the close scrutiny of guards, he dropped his knife into one compartment of a large box, his fork into another and his spoon into a third. Thus was he prevented from carrying away any article that might have been put to an illicit use later on.

If weather permitted, ten minutes was spent in marching around the yard after breakfast. This was called recreation, though the men could neither break line, talk nor smoke. From this exercise they marched to the shops. So far they had indulged in no act of their own, no choice of movement. They had conformed to an iron routine that gave little zest to the day's work.

In the shops there was no relief to this monotony. Each man was given his stint for the day—so many mats to make, so many soles to put on shoes, so many brush-heads to complete. Work was not assigned on the basis of the worker's aptitude or liking for it; the men living in one cell gallery were put in one shop, those in another gallery in another, and so on. A slight dexterity was required here and there, but the tasks were for the most part unskilled; they offered no variety, no new problems to solve. The same processes were repeated day after day—the same amount turned out. The fixed wage of a cent and a half a day comprised the prisoner's total compensation and gave no incentive to fast work or to the development of new methods.

A man could not move from his place of work. If he needed to go to the toilet, he secured permission from one of the guards by raising his hand. He could ask questions of the guard concerning his work, but he could not talk to his neighbor. From the moment he entered the shop until the whistle blew at 11:50, he was engaged in an empty, fruitless task. When the whistle blew for dinner, the men washed at a trough that served eight at a time. They then fell into line by height and marched to the mess hall. The same repetition of raps permitted them to begin to eat, the same display of caps on shoulders, knives, forks and spoons in air, accompanied their departure. No recreation was allowed in the middle of the day; the men marched directly back to their places of work. Here they remained until 3:30. In one or two shops those who finished early could sit at their places, or pace back and forth within a space of four feet, two feet on each side of their machines or benches. Men who had been in prison five years and whose records were good, could read expurgated copies of newspapers, but if they were caught passing these to a neighbor they were punished.

To most people the end of the day's work brings a moderate sense of satisfaction. To the men in prison under this régime it brought only greater wretchedness: it meant a return to the horrors of the cells. No afternoon recreation was allowed. After washing their faces and hands, the men marched to the bucket ground, took their buckets from the racks and without breaking line continued to the cell-house. At the entrance to the cells stood tables containing bread piled in thick slices. As the line passed these tables each man helped himself to his evening meal—three or four slices, according to his appetite. Whether he took one more or one less was one of his few opportunities in the day to make a choice.

Reaching his cell, the man found his cup filled with a weak solution known as prison tea, unless he had previously requested water. The privilege of having tea or water was another notable choice enjoyed by him. He could not turn to his supper at once, however. After entering the cell and closing the door, he stood for the evening count. When a gong announced that this had been taken and found correct, he could eat his bread and drink his tea or water. The tea was usually cold by the time he was ready for it. After supper, he could enjoy his first smoke of the day. Only pipes were allowed, though many a man injured his health with cigarettes made from smuggled newspapers. By 4:30 the men were usually locked in their cells and counted. From this time until seven o'clock next morning—a stretch of fourteen hours and a half—they remained there. They could go to bed any time they wished, but lights had to remain on until 9 o'clock. Then all were compelled to let down their cots and retire.

Such was the man-killing routine of a Sing Sing inmate six days in seven.

The week-end was a still more barren stretch. From 4:30 Saturday afternoon to 7 o'clock Monday morning—thirty-eight hours and a half—the men did no work, remaining continuously in their cells except for two hours Sunday morning spent at breakfast and in the chapel. After chapel they took to their cells the food that was to last until Monday morning.

This empty life could be broken into once a month by the writing of a letter; once every two months by a visitor from the world outside. The only other way of varying the monotony was by some infraction of the rules that brought punishment, and many men were driven to such infractions by sheer desperation. The régime was, of course, the worst possible preparation for a return to society. To most of us the thought of a day of such existence is unbearable; a month is more than the mind can contemplate. Let the reader imagine, if he can, what five years of it would mean, five years in which every normal relationship, every rational exercise of one's powers, every freedom of motion and of thought is utterly foregone. To many a man in prison who suffered it—and men are suffering it to-day in many prisons throughout the country—it has meant the degeneration of all useful faculties, the death of every impulse that enables men to adjust themselves to other men.

Self-government seeks to rescue the prisoner from this grip. It seeks to break the treadmill monotony that quickly advances from a slavery of the body to a slavery of the mind itself. More than this, too, is involved in successful self-government. Such a régime sets up a new fealty for the prisoner to guide his life by. The traditional fealty of the law-breaker is to himself first and then to his "pal." Often the fealty to the "pal" is the most inspiring thing in his life, his greatest spiritual asset. It is not based on any ethical code carefully thought out; it has been forced upon him by the antagonistic hand of society and the police. To replace it, therefore, requires no new philosophy. All that is necessary is a new attitude toward prisoners and the establishment of a new impulse among them. They need to be made to feel, first, that other people are genuinely—not sentimentally—interested in their welfare and are willing to be of constructive help; second, that their own interests embrace more than one or two of their fellows.

The new fealty at which self-government aims is loyalty to the whole body of prisoners. By its very operation it identifies each prisoner with *all* of his fellows, it involves him and them in the same gigantic, communal enterprise. If a prisoner has fair intelligence, he can be made to see this, or rather to feel it, for it is as much a matter of emotion as of reason. Then, too, if he has a normal range of mental interests, he quickly comes to enjoy the more varied life that self-government brings. He sees that this is better both for himself and for others. The mixture of selfish desire and social appeal existing in all of us is enlisted on the side of the new régime and the new allegiance. One of the most marked successes of self-government has been its ability to effect this substitution of one allegiance for another. When a prisoner has been brought several times into the self-government court, has been prodded and quizzed by his fellow-inmates in their effort to untangle the truth, and has been made to see that his refusal to tell what normally he would be expected not to tell is actually frowned upon by his comrades, his eyes not infrequently open with a new light. He sees that loyalty to a comrade may involve the greater body of all his comrades in injury that he had not intended. He sees, too, that it is making him unpopular. That is usually enough, for most prisoners are at bottom social animals and need only the right kind of opportunity to reveal their group impulses.

Two objections to this view of self-government will doubtless be made. One is that people who have been sentenced to prison have already demonstrated their lack of self-control. Therefore, it is held that to expect them to control themselves in an institution, self-government or no self-government, is simply absurd.

The answer to this objection is two-fold. First, instead of lacking self-control, some law-breakers have an extraordinary amount of it; they have simply used it for anti-social purposes. Self-government and all reformative treatment aims to substitute other and better purposes for these. With respect to law-breakers who do lack self-control, the important question is: Which system of government is more likely to remedy this deficiency, the autocratic or the self-government one? Certainly the autocratic system has failed so far, failed lamentably and glaringly. It, at any rate, must be abandoned. If, then, the self-government system holds out better hope of success, why not give it a reasonable trial? No system of government is by itself an adequate basis for reformative treatment. Under any system, the therapeutic measures described in the preceding chapter are indispensable and must find their place. Under self-government the whole atmosphere of the institution is more congenial for carrying them out and, more to the point, for the great majority of prisoners self-government is itself an additional educational measure of constructive value.

The second objection is not unlike the first. Prisoners, it is said, are where they are because no sufficient restraint has been exercised over them in the past. Lack of government, or of government that controlled them, has been precisely their difficulty. Therefore, to continue the policy of no restraint in prison, on the theory that they need opportunity to develop initiative and power of choice, is simply to perpetuate the condition that has brought them to their present state.

This objection is even less convincing than the first. Self-government is by no means the abolition of restraint; the continuance of prison walls should be sufficient reminder of that. And it is not only by confinement that restraint is exercised. Self-government itself exercises it by the collective action of the prisoners. This is a different kind of restraint, with a different origin and different methods, but it is none the less restraint. The prisoner is still liable to punishment. Forms of punishment may vary and standards of conduct change, but the fact that the inmate shares with others the opportunity to set up the restraint, to interpret it and apply it to individual cases is no denial of the restraint. Actually, it is not unusual for prisoners to be more strict in the enforcement of their rules of discipline than a humane warden. Moreover, if collective restraint falls down, the state may step in at any time and re-employ its own. Indeed, the prisoner's consciousness of this very fact often makes him exceptionally desirous not to overstep the bounds of the liberty granted to him.

It is, of course, apparent to one who has read Chapter XII. that not all inmates of penal institutions can profit from self-government. Many mental defectives and some of the out-and-out insane cannot do so. They should be excluded. Others are temporarily unable to participate, such as prisoners segregated for contagious diseases; this, however, is no more than is met with in the world outside. Still others may be deliberately excluded for disciplinary reasons. The percentage of those who cannot profit will vary. In some institutions where mental defectiveness runs high, it may reach as many as a fifth of the total population. Not all persons suffering from mental abnormalities, it must be remembered, require to be excluded; indeed, for some types of mental disease self-government may offer the very tonic that will best help to effect a cure. Administration is greatly simplified here, as elsewhere, by a careful classification of offenders.

One other characteristic of inmate self-government ought to be mentioned before we consider its history and administration. It is, of course, ultimately paternalistic, though its paternalism may be no more than that involved in all formal education. In this sense, the thing we have been discussing is not really self-government at all; a more correct designation would be "inmate participation in government." It is, and in the nature of things must remain, a grant from those having authority to those without it. The state, in order to provide its derelict members with a better preparation for their return to society, permits them to assume a larger or smaller part in the control of their affairs. It does not relinquish any of its own ultimate power or responsibility; it can revoke its grant at any moment. All this is doubtless obvious, but the term by which the innovation has become known makes it important to bear the point in mind.

II. Early Experiments

It would be difficult to say with certainty who was the author of penal self-government. A record exists that the idea was experimented with in a boarding school for unruly boys in England late in the eighteenth century. More is known, however, about two experiments conducted in this country forty or fifty years later. These were at the New York House of Refuge and the Boston House of Reformation, the first two reformatories for delinquent children established in this country. The New York experiment came first. This institution was founded in 1824. Its first superintendent was Joseph Curtis. Curtis introduced a modified form of self-government, under which the boys tried each other by jury, the superintendent himself being the judge. Each boy made his complaint, and if the one complained of was found guilty, the foreman of the jury announced the number of stripes and the superintendent administered the punishment. The system seems to have extended little farther than that. Unfortunately, Mr. Curtis's superintendency lasted only about a year, so that we cannot tell how far he might have gone.

The experiment at the Boston House of Reformation was more ambitious. The superintendent, Rev. E. M. P. Wells, was a young Episcopal minister whose ideas about juvenile wickedness differed considerably from those accepted at the time. Wells believed that bad boys were no worse by nature than others, and was convinced that a boy "can always be reformed while he is under fifteen years old, and very often after that age." He became superintendent in 1828 and first drew attention to himself by introducing an educational curriculum that was wholly unlike anything that the staid overseers of delinquents at that time had ever seen. Regulated play and gymnastics figured prominently in the program and Wells frankly admitted that the "mechanical" parts of education, such as arithmetic, writing and spelling, held a low place in his opinion.[1]

For a fairly complete picture of the experiment in self-government at the Boston House of Reformation we are indebted to Alexis de Tocqueville and Gustave de Beaumont, who visited the institution in the course of their travels in America in 1831-2. Their report upon it is a part of their volume on the Penitentiary System of the United States, written for the French Government.[2] The "rules" submitted by Mr. Wells to his board of directors and approved by them make clear that the inmates were given a voting participation in the administration of the school. Each new boy, immediately upon entering, was introduced by name to the others and received a copy of the laws, if he could read. He then spent a week in one of the lower grades on probation. If he behaved well during that time, the fact was so reported to the rest, who voted on whether he should be received into the community. If the vote was adverse, the newcomer was obliged to remain another week on probation.

The petty administration of the school was committed in part to monitors. A head monitor presided in the absence of the officers. There were two "keep-

[1] For these facts the writer has drawn upon an article entitled "Inmate Self-Government a Century Ago," by O. F. Lewis in *The Delinquent* for January, 1918.

[2] It was to make this report that these two gentlemen came to this country. De Tocqueville's celebrated "De la Democratie en Amerique," while far more important, was an incidental result of this trip.

ers of the keys," who rang the bells, opened and shut the doors and answered the door bells. A sheriff and his two deputies had charge of the second and third *mal* grades of inmates. There was also a steward who attended to the marketing and the boys' meals; a monitor of police, with two or three boys under him, who daily swept and arranged the boys' part of the house; a monitor of the chambers, a monitor of the wardrobe, three door-keepers, and other monitors "occasionally appointed."

The monitors of certain divisions and of the first grade were elected monthly by the boys under them. "Each time," say de Tocqueville and de Beaumont, "that it becomes necessary to elect among themselves an officer or monitor, the little community meets, proceeds to the election, and the candidate having most votes is proclaimed president. Nothing is more grave than the manner in which these clectors and jurymen of tender years discharge their functions."

The jury for disciplinary purposes consisted of twelve boys. These youngsters pronounced "the condemnation or acquittal of the accused." A book of conduct existed, in which each child marked his own behavior. "Experience has shown," say the two Frenchmen, "that the children always judge themselves more severely than they would have been judged by others; and not infrequently it is found necessary to correct the severity and even the injustice of their own sentence."

De Tocqueville and de Beaumont were impressed by the unusual character of what they witnessed. Here are some of their comments:

"In Boston, corporal chastisements are excluded from the house of refuge; the discipline of this establishment is entirely of a moral character, and rests on principles which belong to the highest philosophy.

"Everything there tends to elevate the soul of the young prisoners, and to render them jealous of their own esteem and that of their comrades; to arrive at this end they are treated as if they were men and members of a free society. . . .

"We need not say that we do not consider this an infant republic in good earnest. But we believed ourselves obliged to analyze a system so remarkable for its originality. There is, however, more depth in these political plays, which agree so well with the institutions of the country, than we would suppose at first glance. The impressions of childhood and the early use of liberty contribute, perhaps, at a later period, to make the young delinquents more obedient to the laws. And without considering this possible political result, it is certain that such a system is powerful as a means of moral education."

Pleased as they were with the theory underlying Mr. Wells's method and with its application, the authors discovered in it the same defect that later critics have found in more recent experiments of the same sort. Not that the Boston House of Reformation did not "appear to be admirably conducted, and superior to both the others [New York City and Philadelphia]; but its success seems to us less the effect of the system itself, than that of the distinguished man who puts it into practice." In other words, Wells was a "profound genius," and although his discipline was of a very "elevated" order, it was extremely "difficult in practice." "It is possible," say the authors, "to find superintendents who are fit for the Philadelphia system; but we cannot hope to meet often with such men as Mr. Wells."

Mr. Wells saw his cherished experiment break on

the same rock that shattered that of Mr. Curtis—distrust and suspicion by the authorities in control. He continued his work, however, in a private school for the "moral discipline of boys" in South Boston. Why these early efforts in self-government made no permanent impression is a difficult question to answer. Undoubtedly they were far in advance of the opinions current at the time in regard to the reformability of human character. Perhaps the remarkable thing is not that the seed failed to take root but that it was ever planted. How could a society that accepted unquestioningly the view that "the reformation of girls who have contracted bad morals is a chimera which it is useless to pursue"[1] be enlightened enough to appreciate the possibilities in Mr. Wells's scheme? Such a doubt seems to have raised itself, at any rate, in the mind of one of Mr. Wells's recent followers, Thomas Mott Osborne, who declares that "self-government, as a working system in correctional institutions, except as a temporary experiment, was not possible a century ago; public opinion had not arrived at a sufficiently clear understanding of the general principle involved."[2]

Recent experiments in inmate self-government have drawn their inspiration for the most part from the George Junior Republic, founded at Freeville, N. Y., by William R. George in 1895. Both Calvin Derrick, who introduced self-government into the California State Reformatory of Ione, in 1912, and Mr. Osborne, founder of the Mutual Welfare League at Auburn

[1] "On the Penitentiary System in the United States," by de Beaumont and de Tocqueville, p. 123.
[2] *The Delinquent*, February, 1918, p. 22.

Prison, New York, in 1914, have acknowledged their indebtedness to Mr. George. Each was for some years associated with the Freeville Republic, Mr. Osborne as member of the board of trustees and Mr. Derrick as general superintendent.

The nature and success of the George Junior Republic are too well-known to require repetition here. Mr. George began his undertaking with more than a hundred boys and girls from New York City who had, for the most part, led unrestrained lives on the street and had been regarded by the courts or by their parents as incorrigible. Under his sympathetic leadership, these young folk began life anew in a typical small village without walls or physical restraint. They gradually established a community modelled in many respects upon the larger republic of the United States. The government was divided into legislative, executive and judicial branches and these were under the control of the "citizens" themselves. Officers were elected and the whole political machinery, including police activities and courts, was conducted by the inmates. Those who violated the rules of the institution were tried and punished by juries of their fellows. Business enterprises were established and everyone was expected to work. In this way private property was established, and respect for the law, especially law that protected property, was a natural consequent. Schools were opened and the citizens themselves passed a law making attendance compulsory.

In a short time remarkable success was attained. Youths of the most untoward character were reclaimed to useful and normal lives. The name of the republic spread far and wide and attempts to copy it were numerous. In 1907 an association for the spread of the republic idea was formed and altogether six republics, besides the original, have been started in this country and one in England.

Not only have many of the republic's citizens gone through college and become successful in professional and business life, but a few have achieved distinction. The writer has before him an incomplete list of these, containing twenty-seven names. Among these are lawyers, engineers, journalists, teachers, leaders in boys' work, one missionary, a contractor and several large holders of agricultural interests. One young chap left the republic to become noted a few years later as the coxswain of a famous Cornell crew. Another was a candidate for Congress on the Progressive ticket in 1912. Several of them now hold commissions in the United States Army, one being an aviator in the overseas service. Among the girl ex-citizens are graduates of colleges and normal schools, nurses, social workers and others. It is probable that there is a higher percentage of professional men and women and successful business people among the graduates of the George Junior Republic than among those of any other correctional or semi-correctional institution ever founded. It would be extravagant, of course, to credit the whole of this achievement to self-government. Part of it is due to the assistance Mr. George received from people who took a financial interest in his work and in the after-careers of his charges. But this interest could have done little if the citizens themselves had not been stirred to the pursuit of normal and wholesome purposes. And it is worthy of remark that ordinary institutions of reformation do not enlist in any such degree the whole-hearted support of outsiders.

The conditions of this experiment, which is still going on, were, of course, totally different from those to be found in most prisons and reformatories. Not only are obstacles of brick and mortar and ancient structure to be met in most of these; the class of offenders is for the most part more sophisticated and mature.[1] Moreover, years of repression and autocratic administration have established traditions difficult to overcome.

It is not surprising, therefore, that when Mr. George first suggested "that the same principles which were working so successfully with young boys and girls might work with equal success in a prison," most of those to whom he spoke thought the idea "preposterous." Mr. Osborne, then a member of the Freeville board of managers, was one of these. His conversion to the practicableness of the suggestion is recorded in his book "Society and Prisons." The following passages from an address delivered by him to the National Prison Association in 1904 are not without interest:

"Mr. Gladstone once wrote in relation to Ireland's demand for home rule, and the idea that it must be kept back until the Irish had developed farther and were ready for self-government: 'It is liberty alone that fits men for liberty.' A golden sentence, which contains the very essence of democracy. If it is true of nations, it is equally true of individuals; and just here is the fallacy at the bottom of our present prison theories. . . .

[1] Some of Mr. George's charges were, however, over twenty-one years of age.

"The prison system endeavors to make men industrious by driving them to work; to make them virtuous by removing temptation; to make them respect the law by forcing them to obey the edicts of an autocrat; to make them far-sighted by allowing them no chance to exercise foresight; to give them individual initiative by treating them in large groups; in short, to prepare them again for society by placing them in conditions as unlike real society as they could well be made. . . .

"Outside the walls a man must choose between work and idleness—between honesty and crime. Why not let him teach himself these lessons before he comes out? Such things are best learned by experience. Some can acquire their lesson in life by the experience of others; but most men in prison under the present system cannot do that. They are in prison for the very reason that they cannot do that. But everyone who is not an absolute fool can learn by experience, and the bulk of men in prison certainly are not fools.

"So inside your walls you must have courts and laws to protect those who are working from the idle thief. And we may rest assured that the laws would be made and the laws would be enforced. . . .

"The prison must be an institution where every inmate must have the largest practicable amount of individual freedom, because 'it is liberty alone that fits men for liberty.'"

In this early glimpse of the possibilities of adult inmate self-government, Mr. Osborne presented no practical scheme for carrying it out. In 1912 Calvin Derrick became superintendent of the state reformatory for boys at Ione, Cal., called also the Preston School of Industry, and at once outlined a self-government program.

III. Self-Government in California

The Preston School of Industry is a semi-military institution giving military instruction and drill to its inmates. These are young men and boys ranging in age from nine to twenty-five years and in seriousness of offense from mere dependency to murder. Differing in regard to some matters of application from Mr. George, though agreeing with him on the main principle, Mr. Derrick at once placed two limitations on the scope of self-government. The first was that all who seemed unfit to participate in such a régime, or incapable of deriving benefit from it, should be excluded. Among these were the mentally inferior, those afflicted with venereal disease in a dangerous stage, moral perverts, and a small number of "unbalanced, defiant boys who could not live peaceably except under rigid restraint." The total exclusions comprised about one-tenth of the population.

The second limitation was a restriction on the activities to which self-government should reply. Here the principle adopted was that the activities normally left to the control of boys outside should be left to their control in the institution. These embraced, of course, social activities in general, the management of clubs, and the use and upkeep of playgrounds. They embraced also home study, certain minor affairs connected with the military life of the institution, the control of a few unskilled industrial activities, and a partial control of discipline. Activities not included in the scope of self-government were the medical work of the institution (since boys outside are not normally the arbiters of their physical care); the giving of mental tests and the study of vocational aptitudes; the control of classes, shops and work squads; and the management of the dormitories.

Mr. Derrick aimed from the first to let self-government come, if at all, as a thing desired by the inmates. There was to be no autocratic imposition of it from above. Sooner or later they would have to become enthusiastic about it, if it was to succeed, and this might as well be at the very outset. Accordingly, he put it squarely up to them whether they would have self-government or not. His first move was to try out the interest of some seventy of the older boys, forming Company A, by describing to them the life of the George Junior Republic at Freeville. He explained to them that self-government was a difficult undertaking and that it meant assuming new responsibilities as well as receiving new privileges. After a spirited discussion, the members of this company decided to adopt it for themselves. They proceeded immediately to a consideration of the particular form the organization should take, devoting one evening each week to that purpose.

Company A soon became propagandists. They liked the idea so well that they tried to persuade other companies to adopt it also. As a result, a general convention was called, consisting of representatives of every company, and a constitution, tentatively drafted by Mr. Derrick, was placed before them. This constitution was approved, but before it became binding was referred to each company, which then voted on two questions, whether it would accept self-government in general or not, and whether it would accept the particular form provided by that constitution. Four companies besides Company A voted to accept self-government in general, but one of these held out for a military instead of a civil form of administration. It was allowed to have its way and so was not associated with the others in the launching of the main self-government experiment.

Each company was thus at first an independent self-governing body. Like the thirteen original colonies, however, they soon showed a desire for union. The reasons were much the same as those that produced the United States of America, a belief that with union would come greater strength and greater benefit to the individual. A constitutional convention was therefore called and representatives of the different companies agreed upon a federal constitution. This was again referred to the constituencies. In due time it was fully approved, even the Rhode Island of the reformatory, the company that had held out for a military instead of a civil form of administration, changing its mind in a few months and petitioning for admission to the union. Thus was the Preston School Republic formed.

The constitution thus adopted is patterned closely upon that of the United States. Its preamble recites that "we, the cadets of the Preston School of Industry, in order to form a more perfect government, establish justice, promote the general welfare and secure the blessing of more privileges and liberty for ourselves, do ordain and establish this Constitution of the Preston School of Industry." From this one might infer that the chief aim of the inmate government was to win concessions and privileges from the officers of the state. There are provisions, however, that reveal traces of a different purpose. For example, candidates for president must secure the approval of the superintendent before they can hold office. No inmate who has been convicted of embezzlement or defalcation of public funds before coming to the school is eligible for office; neither is one who has been convicted of taking or receiving an election bribe in the institution itself. An inmate cannot be a member of Congress and hold any other office at the same time. All executive and judicial officers and all members of Congress are bound by oath to support the constitutions of the United States, of California and of the Preston School of Industry.

The constitution vests legislative, executive and judicial powers in appropriate bodies. The officers are a president, vice-president, chief justice, attorney-general, secretary of state and treasury, and secretary of military affairs. The three judges of the self-government court hold office during good behavior. The powers of Congress are thus defined:

> "To make a uniform rule of naturalization; to coin Preston School of Industry currency and to regulate the value thereof; to provide for the punishment of counterfeiting the current coin of the Preston School of Industry; to define and punish felonies and offenders against the laws of the Preston School of Industry; to make all laws which shall be necessary and proper for carrying into execution the foregoing powers and all other powers vested in the Government of the Preston School of Industry, or in any department or office thereof, by this Constitution."

The rights of the individual are safeguarded in various ways. Trial by jury is secured to all. In every criminal prosecution the party accused is given the right to have a speedy and public trial, to compel the attendance of witnesses and to appear in person and with counsel. No one may be twice put in jeopardy for the same offence, or deprived of liberty or property "without due process of law." The right of citizens "to be secure in their persons, papers and effects" is guaranteed, and "no warrants shall issue but upon probable cause, supported by oath or affirmation and particularly describing the place to be searched and the things to be seized."

In the practical carrying out of this constitution, a great deal of interest centred in the inmates' court. The control of discipline was apportioned as follows: Every complaint against an inmate, whether brought by another inmate or by the officers of the school, first passed through the hands of the superintendent's second assistant, who had made a special study of discipline. This assistant then retained for disposal by the officers all cases involving sexual perversion and those appearing to involve pathological features, as well as any others that in his opinion ought not, in the interest of justice to the boys, be referred to the self-government court. The remainder went to the clerk of the court and were disposed of by it. In practice this gave the great majority of cases to the court. Even runaways were usually handled by it. Occasionally, of course, friction ensued, the inmates thinking that the officers handled some cases that should have been referred to it, though usually the feeling of deprivation was on the other side. A person tried by the inmates' court could always appeal to the supreme court, which was presided over by the superintendent, but there was only one appeal during the first three years of the self-government régime.

All manner of new problems were constantly arising under this régime. The solution of these was an excellent spur to initiative. How new needs produced new instrumentalities has been concisely told by Mr. Derrick as follows:

"I wrote and placed in operation the first constitution and administered the first court, training the boys in a crude way. The constitution was intentionally faulty. A casual reading carried the impression that a great deal of liberty had been granted, but in the court the judge, and out of court the citizens, were very closely restricted when they came to study the document. This was intentional on my part. It was not long before I had a committee visiting me, asking for a more liberal constitution. This was what I was aiming at—the development of their initiative. I prescribed certain limits, territories and restrictions and told them to do as they liked within this field. They did so. Within eighteen months we had four constitutions, each a great improvement over the former.

"A difference of opinion as to the interpretation of the constitution gave rise to political parties; the confusion resulting in various courts by reason of each company having a different set of laws and penalties for the same offense gave birth to the House of Congress; disagreement among the congressmen as to which laws should be abolished and which retained resulted in the formation of a commission to draw up a code of civil and penal procedure, and finally in a body of uniform law. This commission developed, after its purpose had been accomplished, into a bar association, and thereafter all boys who became applicants for the position of judges, district attorneys, or clerks of court, as well as those who wished to practice law before the courts, were obliged to pass an examination before the bar association.

"The code of laws caused the formation of a prison to enforce the mandates of the court. Political graft by the warden showed the necessity of reform in the matter of appointments to office. A civil service commission and law were enacted by the succeeding congress. Because the government now had prisoners to care for, it had to have work to busy them with; therefore, a commissioner of labor was created and made a member of the president's cabinet, and a certain field of rough, unskilled labor put under the jurisdiction of the government.

"A certain politician among the boys, who was running for

office, was elected by crooked work in the receiving company, the members of which were not well versed in the politics of the place. The next congress created a board of naturalization and made it a part of the department of labor. All boys entering the school after that time had to be naturalized before they could vote, the naturalization calling for the completion of a three months' course of study.

"The civil service law and the recall made the officials much more careful and ambitious in the performance of their duties, but it took practically all of their time. The next congress passed the compensation act, which allowed these officials extra credits for their official duties.

"The third congress made application for the control of the military training of the school. It was granted, and a secretary of military affairs was added to the president's cabinet. He acts as an *aide de camp* to the military instructor. The congress then passed military inspection laws, by the terms of which every member of a company became responsible for every other member's inspection. That is, if one boy in a company lost a certain number of credits for an infraction, every member in the company suffered the same loss. In other words, they had arrived at a stage where they realized, as a group, that the liberty and safety of all depends upon each individual doing his part, while the individual had learned that he cannot do as he pleases without injury to everyone else in his group. I considered the passage of these laws a marvellous advance in social and moral responsibility and understanding of the boys.

"The government began to feel an interest in the possibilities of the new material arriving at the school, and asked permission to establish a night school in the receiving company. This, of course, was granted. Out of this grew the commission on social affairs. The commissioner met with the president's cabinet, though not a member thereof. He established clubs, organized orchestras and glee clubs, until there are now twelve such organizations, three orchestras and two quartets. The social commissioner is allowed to draw upon the commissary and kitchen for sufficient cocoa, sugar, cookies, sandwiches and other necessary material to make a real sociable time for the club he is visiting that evening. Needless to say, the social commissioner is the most popular man in the government.

"The present administration has placed before me a proposition to permit the government to operate a store for the benefit of the boys and to put into operation a system of coinage. I have agreed to permit it if *they* can work out a feasible plan that I can with prudence approve.

"In the three and a half years I have been at Ione, I have never once interfered in their field of government. If a company becomes lax in its citizenship or indifferent toward its obligations, so that its standards of citizenship fall below a certain fixed line, it automatically loses its constitution and goes under state control, thereby giving up a great many of its privileges. This has happened twice. It takes a company from six months to a year to regain its charter. There is little trouble in this respect.

"I have never vetoed a law, reversed a judgment, altered or set aside any proclamation of the president, adjourned a congress, or declined to consider any kind of proposition whatsoever, nor have I permitted any of my officers to do any of these things." [1]

Former Governor Hiram Johnson, of California, took a strong interest in inmate self-government at the Preston School of Industry. At the inauguration of the second president, he went to the school and placed the stamp of his official approval upon the experiment. Moreover, when Mr. Derrick became superintendent in 1912, it was agreed on the part of Governor Johnson, the Preston board of trustees and himself that he should have a free hand in the working out of his theories for two years. If at the end of that time the plan was rejected, he should retire; if endorsed, he should remain. He continued in charge until August, 1916, when he was granted a year's leave of absence to assist in the self-government program that had meanwhile been instituted at Sing Sing. The plan was, therefore, regarded as a success and was continued under Mr. Derrick's successor, J. L. Montgomery.

[1] From *The Survey,* Sept. 1, 1917, page 473.

California may thus be regarded as the first State to have endorsed inmate self-government officially.

IV. New York and Sing Sing

In their report for the two years ended June 30, 1914, the board of trustees of the Preston School of Industry said: "During the past year we have developed the scheme of self-government to a fair completeness. . . . The scheme has worked satisfactorily, although it is still in an experimental stage. One of the noticeable characteristics has been that the larger boys, many of them actually over twenty-one, though committed as being under, have been the ones with whom the scheme has worked best. It is our feeling that such a scheme is applicable to adult institutions, better even than to the juvenile."

Before these words of the Preston trustees were published, an opportunity was given to test their wisdom. When the Mutual Welfare League was formed in Auburn Prison, New York, in January, 1914, under the leadership of Thomas Mott Osborne, every preceding experiment in self-government had been among youthful or relatively young offenders. The significance of the Auburn and Sing Sing ventures lay, therefore, in the fact that they were the first attempts to carry on self-government among adult and what are commonly called "hardened" criminals. Both of these prisons received the most irreclaimable offenders known to the wardens of this country. Both drew largely upon the sodden and relentless life of the New York underworld. Among the inmates of both were men who had spent the greater part of their years in reformatories or prisons, recidivists who had served three, four and sometimes as many as seven or eight terms behind the bars, professional criminals who had begun their careers in childhood and knew no other life. With such, to be sure, was a sprinkling of first offenders—men who had committed crime but once under unusual provocation and would not be likely to do so again. But in general the population was the most terrifying to the conventional mind that could be found anywhere. In addition the management of both prisons was traditionally autocratic and brutal. The treatment of prisoners in both, except for occasional lapses, was founded on fear and a policy of repression. Sing Sing especially had for years been a corrupting influence in local and state politics, while petty graft and favoritism stalked unchecked through its corridors. It represented all that was vile in American penology. The very site of the prison breathed physical as well as moral contagion. Men contracted disease amid its dampness and went mad in the confinement of its cells. To add a further disadvantage, it was the most widely known penitentiary in the western hemisphere. Its name was a by-word everywhere. Reform had frequently attempted to improve its management and had as frequently failed. The state of mind of the inmates was consequently prejudiced against the very name of reform; any suggestion that a new humanitarian experiment was to be undertaken was bound to meet with ridicule, skepticism and hostility from the very people whom it was designed to help. So ambitious a venture as self-government seemed in these conditions doomed to hopeless failure.

Probably never has an experiment in humanity been started so inauspiciously, and probably never has it so quickly won confidence and cooperation that could not have been foreseen.

Mr. Osborne has fully told in two books[1] the story of how self-government began at Auburn. The idea that it was practicable first took definite shape in conversations between him and Jack Murphy, a prisoner then serving a life sentence at Auburn. These conversations occurred during Mr. Osborne's week of voluntary incarceration, Sept. 28 to Oct. 5, 1913. Murphy was an intelligent fellow whose long thinking about the problems of prison life became articulate under sympathetic questioning; indeed, Mr. Osborne has called him the real founder of the Mutual Welfare League. When Mr. Osborne left Auburn at the end of his week, he had decided to ask Warden Charles F. Rattigan, on behalf of the inmates, for permission to start a self-governing organization of some sort. It was not until the latter days of December and the first days of January, 1914, however, that the exact nature and functions of the league were outlined. This was done at meetings of elected representatives of the inmates, wholly unattended by the prison officials and presided over by Mr. Osborne. In entire freedom the prisoners discussed one detail after another of the self-government proposal. A sub-committee of inmates was subsequently appointed to draw up a series of by-laws, and on Jan. 11, 1914, these were unanimously adopted by the whole body of prisoners. The first general election

[1] "Within Prison Walls," D. Appleton & Co. "Society and Prisons," Yale University Press.

of delegates of the new league was held on Jan. 15, and three days later those chosen took a formal oath of office in the presence of all the prisoners. Thus was the Mutual Welfare League of Auburn Prison started.

Nearly a year later, on Dec. 1, 1914, Mr. Osborne became warden of Sing Sing and started a second Mutual Welfare League there.

The league was the framework of the self-governing organization.[1] It corresponded to the body politic in the world outside. To belong to it simply meant that one was a member of the self-governing group. Its motto, chosen by the prisoners themselves, was "Do good, make good." Under Mr. Osborne everyone could belong to it except prisoners under sentence of death (who were closely confined in a separate part of the prison), members of the "awkward squad" (i. e., those who had been in prison less than two weeks), and prisoners being punished by the league itself.

Under Warden Kirchwey members of the "awkward squad" were permitted to join. Each new prisoner was called on in his cell, a day or so after his arrival, by a reception committee from the league, which explained to him the nature and purposes of the organization. He could refuse to join if he chose, but then he was automatically excluded from its activities. A very few prisoners refused and these usually changed their minds when they saw the league at work.

To understand the vital part played by self-government in the lives of the men at Sing Sing, one must try to imagine the little community at work. The

[1] The following pages describe self-government at Sing Sing under Warden Osborne and his successor, Warden George W. Kirchwey. No account is taken of changes since introduced.

governing body was a board of delegates elected every three months. This was composed of from fifty to sixty members, the number varying with the population. Every twenty-five members were entitled to one delegate. Each company or shop elected its delegates separately. Both caucusing and preliminary arranging of slates were at first forbidden, but Warden Kirchwey later allowed them. Certain men were, of course, known to be candidates for office, and much electioneering was done in their behalf; voting was by secret ballot. The board of delegates elected a sergeant-at-arms and an executive board of nine members from its own number. The executive board was the main body for transacting business. It chose its own permanent secretary, who became the official head of the self-governing organization. He presided at all meetings, both of the board of delegates and of the executive board. He was relieved of all other prison duties and gave his full time to this work. An office was fitted up for him next to that of the principal keeper, and here he kept his records, interviewed his callers and dictated his correspondence. He was one of the busiest men in prison.

The executive board also distributed considerable "patronage" by appointing all committees, both standing and special. Membership on a committee was much prized by those who held no other office. As a result, committees were created on the slightest provocation. The number ultimately became so large that although it was originally intended that all committee chairmen should be members of the executive board, these soon became exhausted and drafts had to be made upon the membership at large. At one time over 200 prisoners were functioning as committee members.

The sergeant-at-arms was the chief-of-police of the prison. He appointed his own deputies who, with the league delegates, constituted the police force. It was the duty of this force to preserve order, to make arrests, and to bring offenders before the inmates' court.

The real instruments of self-government at Sing Sing were the committees. It was these that effectively expressed the wishes of the prisoners and took the initiative in getting things done. The warden's day was filled with appointments with committee chairmen who wanted assistance or advice. The chairmen quickly came to realize that a great deal of power lay in their hands if they knew how to wield it. Not only were they the trustees of the wishes of their fellow-inmates, but the prison officials came to regard them as responsible makers of institution policy. Some of them became adept in the art of getting what they wanted without appearing to ask for much. Aside from the specific things they accomplished, their activity was beneficial in two ways: it taught them some of the difficulties of administration, thus enabling them to pass that knowledge back to their constituents; and it enabled the prison authorities, by means of the understanding thus promoted, to rely upon cooperation where before they would have received only suspicion and distrust.

Some of these committees are worth looking at more closely. The judiciary committee was the prisoners' court. The spectacle of law-breakers sitting in judgment upon one another always attracts profound attention. The complaining witness was usually the sergeant-at-arms or a deputy. The accused prisoner could represent himself or be represented by a friend as counsel. Witnesses were allowed on both sides. There were five members of the court, chosen usually because of the reputations for fairness and *their intimate acquaintance with prison life.* At various times murderers, forgers, highwaymen and other "desperate" criminals dispensed justice from this bench. Under them, as will be pointed out later, infractions of rules decreased and orderliness prevailed. When necessary the court sat each day after working hours, but sometimes lack of business led to no sessions for two or three weeks at a time. Every kind of offence was handled by it except escapes and assaults upon prison officers. The only punishment that could be inflicted was suspension from the league, which automatically deprived the offender of the freedom of the yard during the recreation period, confined him to his cell in the evening and on Saturday afternoon and Sunday, and carried with it restrictions on visits, letters and attendance at evening lectures, concerts, moving picture shows and athletic entertainments arranged by committees of the league. A prisoner found guilty could appeal to the warden's court, composed of the warden, the principal keeper and the prison physician, whose verdict was final.

The athletic committee was perhaps the most popular of all. It not only had charge of the upkeep of baseball grounds and tennis courts, but of all arrangements for games and athletic sports as well. Boxing, hand ball, bocci, quoits and setting-up exercises were among the forms of athletics provided. This committee worked in close cooperation with the committee on grounds. The latter constituted itself a general board of landscape architecture and although the possibilities for this were not many in Sing Sing, the committee showed great ingenuity in transforming unused plots into flower beds and otherwise modifying the historic ugliness of the place.

The committee on education had charge of the educational work with the exception of the official prison school, a minor exception. Prior to self-government this school had been acceptable only as a release from the cells. Under self-government something came over the educational aridity of Sing Sing such as frequently comes over the immigrant portions of large cities when education for adults is made available for the first time. Men who had long been strangers to the thirst for knowledge felt it parching their throats again. It mattered little what rivulet of learning they pursued. The education committee was empowered to add courses to the curriculum whenever it found a demand for them. The chairman possessed many of the qualifications of a successful school superintendent. This erstwhile "enemy of society" developed a rich talent for curriculum-making. He could tell what the inmates of Sing Sing wanted to study before they themselves were aware of it. A kind of extension teaching developed under his leadership, whereby any prisoner with a special knowledge of some subject became of a sudden a professor in that subject and found himself the centre of a group of eager learners. Many classes were formed in this manner. A dozen trades were taught, as well as French, Spanish, German, English and other branches. In a few months the number of subjects grew from three to twenty and the voluntary attendance upon classes increased tenfold. At one time over 400 men were enrolled in the night or prisoners' school.

Lectures, concerts, moving picture shows and various other performances were arranged by the entertainment committee. These were held in the prison chapel. The chairman was permitted to carry on an extensive and uncensored correspondence with people outside the prison, and to interview visitors, for the purpose of procuring attractions. Occasionally the committee made use of "home" talent, several variety and minstrel shows being given by the prisoners themselves. The prison officials were entirely relieved of responsibility for these entertainments and if they attended them, as they frequently did, it was as guests.

Several committees enjoyed a close relation to the elementary functions of government. The sanitary committee overwhelmed the warden with recommendations for the cleaning out of drains, the abatement of nuisances and bad odors, the improvement of ventilation and the general hygienic bettering of the institution. Any administration at Sing Sing must work under severe handicaps due to the archaic structure, but the intelligent activity of the sanitation committee brought about real improvement.

One of the most effective committees was the employment committee. This rendered very practical service both by assisting the prison authorities to discover the aptitudes of men confined and by helping the outgoing prisoner to secure employment. An industrial survey was conducted to ascertain what work men had done before coming to Sing Sing. The committee also wrote letters to the men's families and former employers for their industrial histories. Contrary to the current view of what is to be expected from prisoners, the members of this committee consistently refused to recommend fellow-inmates to outside employers if they believed that the men would not make good. They rightly held that the success of self-government rested on trustworthiness and fair dealing.

Many other committees performed no less interesting and useful duties. One on family relief obtained money for the needy families of men in Sing Sing, thereby assuming a burden that the state ought to have assumed. A committee on Jewish holidays provided suitable entertainment for these. A negro committee looked after the interests of colored prisoners. A committee on the prison graveyard attended to the upkeep of that spot and decorated it on special occasions. A committee on Catholic burial occasionally arranged for interment in consecrated ground outside the prison. Other standing committees, and many special ones, added to the opportunities for activity that self-government brought.

Let us now look at some of the evidence tending to show that self-government actually produced a change for the better in the social attitude of men in Sing Sing. Not infrequently individual prisoners were put to the test in ways that revealed with dramatic clearness the reversal of the usual attitude between prisoner and official. Ordinarily this attitude is one of mutual suspicion and distrust, if not of positive fear and hatred. Under self-government it became one of loyalty and cooperation. During Mr. Kirchwey's wardenship an inmate once came to Mrs. Kirchwey and told her that a window bar in the prison had been nearly sawed through. So excited was he by his own unusual act in reporting such a thing that he forgot to tell where the bar was. Warden Kirchwey was, of course, informed. Under the old régime the procedure would have been for the principal keeper to make an immediate search. But the Mutual Welfare League had its own officer for such emergencies. Warden Kirchwey called the sergeant-at-arms of the league and told him that the responsibility of finding that bar lay upon him. The sergeant-at-arms accepted the commission. Accompanied by two deputies he set out to inspect every bar in the prison. In a short while he reported that the bar had been found. The depth of the cut had been somewhat exaggerated and, moreover, the damage was of long standing, so it was deemed unnecessary to put in a new bar. The league, however, felt that its integrity had been vindicated.

On another occasion a still more alarming report was brought to the warden. This was that a number of inmates were planning to escape on a night already selected. The prisoner who brought this story to the warden refused to divulge the names of the conspirators, saying that he knew the administration disliked "stool pigeons." What this would have meant under the old system was clear: doubled guards, with a probability that for several nights everybody would have been locked in his cell early. Warden Kirchwey again placed the responsibility where under self-government it belonged. "You know I couldn't stop those fellows from escaping if I wanted to," he said to his informant. "But you know who can. You can! The league can." The prisoner looked surprised. Such a rejoinder was unexpected. "Well," he said, "that's one on me, I guess we can." Whether the report was true was never known. There was no escape.

Other incidents, small in themselves, revealed the dominant sincerity of the league's approach to its new duties. There was no disposition to be easy with offending prisoners. For example, men awaiting trial by the self-government court were at first kept locked in their cells until their cases could be heard. This, of course, merely copied the custom on the outside, where accused persons are usually held in custody pending trial; doubtless most of the members of the league had tasted that experience. The justification for it outside is that the accused might otherwise disappear and so escape trial, but Mr. Kirchwey, soon after becoming warden, pointed out that this danger was reduced to a minimum in Sing Sing. There was little chance that a man would not be found when wanted! Accordingly, he suggested that this unnecessary confinement be eliminated. The men themselves had not thought of the matter in that light, but accepted his advice and thereafter accused persons were allowed the same liberty as others until proved guilty.

The matter did not stop there, however. The original plan of the league was that not even prisoners convicted of offences by the self-government court should be locked in their cells more than others, since the ostracism and the deprivation of privileges that accompanied suspension from the league were deemed punishment enough. Nevertheless, a practice grew up of adding confinement in the cell to the other penalties. Warden Kirchwey reminded the league's officers of the original plan. The men took his view of it and so not only accused prisoners but convicted ones as well were relieved of confinement during the daytime. This apparent leniency did not decrease the deterrent effect of the punishment administered by the league.

Statistical evidence of the improvement in discipline produced by the league is not lacking. The records of the prison physician showed the number of "emergency cases" treated in the hospital. The great majority of these were due to wounds, cuts and other injuries caused by fights between prisoners; only a few were due to accidents. During the year ended Sept. 30, 1913 (before Mr. Osborne became warden), 378 such cases were treated in the hospital; during the year following (still before Mr. Osborne became warden), 372 such cases were treated. If the same ratio of "emergency cases" to population had obtained during the ten months of 1915 that Mr. Osborne was warden and that self-government existed, the number would have been 347. The actual number was 86.[1]

Moreover, 44 of these, or more than half, occurred during the first month of Mr. Osborne's régime and only 42 during the next nine months, so that when the Mutual Welfare League got well started, the improvement in this respect was over eightfold.

[1] These and the succeeding figures were compiled by the Westchester County Research Bureau, White Plains, N. Y.

Nor does the evidence stop there. It was possible to separate from these emergency cases all due to "incised wounds" and stabs. These were almost certainly the result of personal encounters and disorderliness. The figures showed:

	1913	1914	Ten months of 1915
Incised wounds	197	215	67
Stabs	94	43	4

These figures assume a still greater significance when it is remembered that during the self-government régime prisoners enjoyed more freedom and less espionage than ever before, so that opportunities for fighting were increased.

There was another column in the hospital sheet that bore on the effect of the new system. The routine that obtained at Sing Sing under preceding administrations was, as already pointed out, of the kind that frequently produced insanity. How much insanity was there under self-government? Neither the numbers involved in the following table, nor the period of time covered, is sufficient to justify positive assertion, but on the assumption that diagnoses were made in the same way for five years running, the trend was unmistakably one of improvement:[1]

	1911	1912	1913	1914	1915
Number of prisoners who went insane	21	32	48	27	19
Percentage of population that went insane	1.27	2.1	3.3	1.8	1.17

[1] This improvement was not due to better methods of dealing with incipient insanity, because the psychiatric facilities of Sing Sing were, during the first year of self-government, the same as before.

IV. Two Failures

Such is, in general, the case for inmate self-government. The reform has been tried in at least two institutions where it has apparently failed. These are the state reformatories at Cheshire, Conn., and Rahway, N. J. The Connecticut experiment was begun in 1915 and was abandoned in the following spring. No adequate description of its working there has ever been printed. Mr. Charles H. Johnson, superintendent of the Connecticut reformatory during the last eight months of the self-government régime, has, however, written as follows about it:

"The reason for the dissatisfaction in the organization was that it lent itself readily to so much misrule and dishonesty that the inmates were tired of it. The young men in the reformatory were, to a large extent, foreigners from the industrial sections of the cities of the state. Many of them knew but little of the English language, some of them practically nothing. There were very few who knew anything about forms of government, and their ideas in such matters were extremely vague. When it came to the election of officials, the more clever inmates were able by threats, bribery and other similar means to secure their own election, and the more ignorant inmates had but a vague idea of what it was all about. In judicial matters it was extremely difficult to find in such a population inmates who had a mind which lent itself to judicial procedure and which could weigh evidence for or against the institutional offender. The result was that the judges were invariably those who had been selected by the inmate population because it was expected that they would be helpful to possible offenders in time of need. All kinds of adjustments and readjustments were attempted to overcome these conditions, which were inherent in the nature of the population of the institution, but without success. It was finally decided at a gathering of the inmates that the management of the institution should be placed with the superintendent and the officers appointed by law.

"There was then begun the development of a method of military instruction. It was found that the young men who came to the institution had done practically as they pleased most of their lives, had no respect for authority and had very little idea of obeying anybody when they were told to do so. Their physical carriage was just as slouchy as their mental condition and social attitude. A military battalion was organized, inmate officers were selected on the ground of merit and ability and not on the basis of purchased popularity, and beneficial results were quite noticeable in the physical appearance and the attitude of the inmates. It was quite evident that what the inmates needed was not more freedom, of which they had had an excess in their life, but direction and instruction in self-control and obedience to law and order."

The New Jersey experiment was begun in 1914 and abandoned at the end of a year. The explanation of its failure, as put forward by Frank Moore, superintendent, in his annual report for 1915, is very similar to the above:

"We gave the [self-government] plan a trial for one year and then put the question to a vote of the inmates as to whether or not they desired to have the plan continued another year. A feeling had grown that there had been more or less unfairness by 'The Council.' Politics to some extent had entered from time to time into the selection of the councilmen, so that the two plans of being governed by council or by officers of the institution were put squarely before the young men for a decision as to which system of government they preferred. The result of their vote was overwhelmingly in favor of being governed by the officers rather than inmates. This vote shows that the young man who has been unable to control himself aright realizes that he is incapable of controlling others. He sees that it is best for him to be under proper control. When that control is fair and administered with a spirit of sincerity and kindness, he feels it is for his good and willingly yields to it. Especially will he do this, if he feels that he can look up to those who are governing him. But he will rebel, if those who assume to be his superiors are only his equals, who take advantage of their position to secure special privileges, violate rules or play favorites. Realizing these facts after giving the question sober consideration the inmates of the Reformatory felt that it was better for them that the institution should return to the original plan of being governed by the appointed authority of the institution and hence the council disbanded."

In both of these accounts appear the objections to self-government mentioned on pp. 372-374. The answers there given need not be repeated here. One wonders if the right kind of official guidance was supplied in either the Connecticut or the New Jersey institution. Bribery, threats and arrogance did not interfere with the success of self-government in the Ione reformatory or the Westchester County penitentiary or Sing Sing. Lack of familiarity with governmental procedure would seem to be as strong a reason for continuing self-government as for abandoning it. Then, too, the inmate officers at Rahway who assumed to be "superior" and took advantage of their position to secure special privileges might have been quickly dealt with by the other inmates, one would think, if these had been sufficiently induced to regard self-government as *their venture*—as something that they could make or mar as they chose. Certain it is that such early pioneers as the citizens of the George Junior Republic had little difficulty in disciplining such of their leaders as put on arrogant airs. One suspects that possibly the remedy for the ills of democracy, inside prison as out, may be more democracy, and that what self-government needed at these two institutions was an arrangement for the "recall" of arrogant and recalcitrant officials by the inmates themselves.

Superintendent Moore's explanation did not appeal

to the members of the New Jersey Prison Inquiry Commission (1917) as final. Referring to the fact that this experiment was said to have developed "ward politics," the commission pointed out in its report that "that is an incident not unknown to self-government outside prison walls and, if it is a greater menace in a correctional institution than in the wards of a city, it is, on the other hand, more easily dealt with." Of all correctional institutions, it went on, Rahway seems, "both in the character of its population and in the strong and efficient government that it possesses, to be the one best adapted to work out such an experiment safely and successfully." It finally suggested that "another trial might wisely be made" before the method was wholly abandoned.

Perhaps the strongest argument against these alleged failures is the success that inmate self-government has attained in institutions so nearly similar to them as the Ione Reformatory and the Westchester County penitentiary. Other New Jersey institutions seem to be following the lead of other States rather than their own, for within the past year self-government has been inaugurated in the county penitentiary at Caldwell and has taken on new strength in the state reformatory for women at Clinton Farms. Even military penal institutions have opened their doors to it. A new Mutual Welfare League has been organized by Mr. (now Lieutenant-Colonel) Osborne in the naval prison at Portsmouth, N. H., and a modified form of self-government has been started at the United States Disciplinary Barracks on Governor's Island, N. Y., under the administration of Colonel John E. Hunt.

V. Self-Government and the Honor System

Undoubtedly the honor system, if that which exists under so many forms can be called a system, has done much to raise the standards and to heighten the sense of responsibility of many prisoners. In Great Meadow Prison, New York, squads of inmates, accompanied by guards (some armed and some not), engage in farming and other labor at considerable distance from the prison. In New Jersey inmates of the reformatory also work under a small guard on a farm some distance from the institution. Colorado prisoners are allowed to work many miles from the state prison. Occasionally spectacular uses of the honor system are resorted to. Governor West of Oregon recently permitted a life prisoner to come all the way from the prison to the state capitol unattended. Sometimes inmates are sent to look for their fellows who have escaped. Twice when floods threatened to destroy property and lives in Indiana, young men from the state reformatory at Jeffersonville were allowed to go out and help to fight the waters.

One effect of these measures has been to make it evident to the public that many prisoners are not so different from other people as has been thought and that they can be trusted, on occasion and if properly appealed to, to keep their word. Nowhere, however, has the honor system afforded that continuous opportunity for action as member of a self-directing group, and for the development of a sense of corporate and group loyalty, which self-government affords.

The distinction between self-government and the

honor system is easily made. At bottom, the honor system is based upon a relationship between two individuals, the warden and the prisoner. Self-government is based upon a relationship between the prisoner and the whole body of his fellow-inmates. The distinguishing feature of the honor system is the trust reposed in the prisoner when he is out of sight of, or not under the direct supervision of, the prison authorities, or (what is the same thing) when he is so loosely guarded as to make escape easy. This trust may extend all the way from the granting of a few minor privileges to sending prisoners on long errands to remote cities; the warden remains the personal source of each man's privilege. Under the honor system the prisoner is compelled to please only the warden. Under self-government he must please his own fellows. That the second of these is a moral force of a higher order than the first, few will question. Moreover, the temptation is likely to be strong under the honor system for the warden to say in effect to the prisoner: "You behave yourself and cause me no trouble, and I'll give you favors and privileges in return." It then becomes a way of making the warden's job easy rather than of improving the prisoner. Finally, the honor system tends to the creation of caste in a prison, since certain individuals are in a better position than others; whereas, under self-government, all or nearly all are on the same level to begin with, and are placed in positions of special desirability only through the suffrage of their companions.

CHAPTER XV

FURTHER CAUSES AND PREVENTION

I. Some Remarks on Environmental Factors

The mental factors contributing to crime were discussed in Chapter XII. We shall now consider briefly other aspects of causation and shall then turn to the important subject of prevention.

Writers on criminology have sometimes been careless in their use of the word "cause." They have not always employed it in ways that shed light on the real origin of crime and criminals. This has accounted for much loose thinking and failure to understand some of the problems involved. One set of writers has declared that any condition, act or circumstance that precedes the commission of a criminal act, without which that act could not be performed, is a cause of crime. Thus, war has been called a cause of treason, for obviously treason cannot occur without war or the existence of external enemies. The conflict between capital and labor has also been called a cause of crime, for without that conflict certain crimes would not be committed. City life, in this view, becomes another cause of crime, for city life makes necessary certain restrictions upon the liberty of the individual, and to violate these restrictions is crime. Banking becomes a cause of embezzlement, and religion of certain forms of criminal persecution. Indeed, in the last analysis, civilization itself becomes the arch cause of crime, for it may be said to comprise the sum total of conditions that necessarily precede all criminal acts.

Obviously such a conception has no value for the student of criminology. It reveals nothing as to the real nature of criminal acts. A second method has been to analyze crime into the conditions that must be present for its commission, such as a motive, an opportunity and the absence of adequate opposition or restraint. Whatever contributes to any one of these is then called a cause of crime. The extreme to which this method has been pushed is perhaps even more remarkable than that to which the former has been pushed. For example, since the opportunity to steal cannot exist unless there is something to steal, private property has been called a cause of theft. Lewd women are said to be a cause of licentiousness, and virtuous women of rape. Men, women and children have been called causes of the crime of murder.

Still a third method has been pursued, that of classifying causes as individual, social and cosmical. Individual causes are those rising out of the individual; social, those rising from the nature and structure of society; cosmical, those beyond the control of the individual or community. Among the last are various astronomical, geographical, climatic and meteorological conditions. Thus, the seasons and the weather are held to be causes of crime because they influence the nervous system of man; gusts of passion are said by some people to be more easily aroused in summer than in winter, and in torrid zones than in temperate climates. Crime upon the mountains varies both in form and prevalence, it is held, from crime upon the plains; that upon the seacoast from that in the interior; and that upon a river from that along a railway line.

Bizarre as these classifications are, they differ only in degree from many other and more familiar explanations of crime. Sociologists, backed by statisticians, have found causal relations between nearly every kind of social condition and crime. Poverty, insanitary housing, overcrowding, ignorance, idleness, density of population, unemployment—these and a host of others have been set down as causes of crime because the commission of criminal acts has in some way been shown to be related to them. We are not now denying the relation; we are only deprecating the inaccurate use of the word cause. A cause, if it is to have any meaning for the criminologist, must bear a fairly close and inexorable relation to the act it produces. Yet those who have reasoned in the above way have felt no inconvenience, from the fact that the opposites of many of the conditions enumerated may with equal truthfulness be held to be causes of crime. Sparsity of population, for example, is as congenial to some kinds of crime as density; one seldom hears of stage coaches being robbed in the city streets. Then, too, there are crimes for which only the possession of great riches can fit a man, others that can be committed only in the course of regular and continuous employment, and still others that are possible only amid cleanliness and sanitation. Another objection to this view is that there are plenty of people who have spent their lives in the midst of poverty, overcrowding, bad sanitation, ignorance and the rest and yet have not committed crime. Sometimes these are members of the same families as criminals and so have been brought up under almost identical circumstances. Causes, it would seem, ought to operate with more certainty. They ought to stand in a more direct and logical relationship to the results produced. Above all, they ought to shed some light on the origin of the criminal and the processes by which he has been brought to his state of criminality.

The futility of such studies as these lies chiefly in the fact that they tell nothing in regard to the operation of the supposed cause in a given instance. Take poverty as an illustration. The statement of the statistician that poverty shows a high correlation with crime tells nothing as to how poverty causes criminal acts. Poverty is not one thing, it is many. It is overcrowding, undernourishment, bad sanitation, a low level of companionship, inadequate protection from heat and cold, and sometimes squalor and disease. To say that poverty causes crime is to give the impression that poor people steal simply to alleviate their want of money. As a matter of fact the process is usually much more complex. Undernourishment, for example, may lead to other physical and even mental derangements that are the immediate and effective causes of the theft. Similarly, overcrowding or bad association may lead to mental imagery that is the real cause of the crime in question. Undoubtedly poverty often is the ultimate condition out of which the cause arises; nay, it may rarely be the operating and immediate cause itself. But too often another cause or series of causes intervenes. The point to be borne in mind is that although poverty and its attendant conditions may be more conducive to crime than plenty, the mere lack of economic sufficiency is seldom enough to explain the criminal act.

Every crime is the effect of a particular personality reacting to a particular environment. No one can be said to have discovered a real cause of crime in an individual who has not put his finger upon the precise point at which this anti-social reaction took place. All conduct, as we have already pointed out, is "an expression of mental life." The trouble with the kind of descriptive and statistical explanations of crime that we have been considering is that they do not show the way in which external and environmental circumstances affect mental life. Neither do they show the various ways in which differently constituted persons react to the same environment. It is not possible to know the causes of crime in a given instance until we know what defect, circumstance, or outward or inward peculiarity stands in the closest relationship to the delinquency involved.

Now, all of this does not mean that environmental factors do not play a large part in producing crime. It does mean that relative values should not be assigned to such factors on the basis of a mere general or statistical consideration alone. There should first be numerous and many-sided studies of individual offenders. These are as necessary in evaluating the environmental as the mental causes of crime. The truth of this is at once seen when we consider any practical program of prevention. For example, when

Bonger,[1] after a laborious search through all the literature of criminology, finds that economic conditions play a "preponderant, even decisive" part in causing crime, he appears to be justified in drawing the inference that to combat crime all that is necessary is to change such conditions. The trouble is that his study was made without reference to the individual criminal, and while he admits the existence of a small number of "pathological crimes," he does not realize that many crimes which seem on a superficial view to be due to economic conditions are in reality due to personal causes *which themselves explain not only why the persons involved became criminals, but why they fell victims to the economic conditions.* As soon as one sees that crime is the result of personality reacting to environment, that all sorts of environmental conditions may supply the friction necessary to anti-social responses, and that a great many personal factors may make individuals especially prone to such responses, it becomes evident that the problem neither of causation nor of prevention is so simple as Bonger and others of his school would have it.

To attempt to list all of the environmental factors that have been or may be shown to contribute to delinquency would obviously be impossible. Reference has already been made to Healy's method of enumerating, as major and minor factors, those personal and environmental traits and conditions that he found to contribute to delinquency in his study of 1,000 cases.

[1] "Criminality and Economic Conditions," by William Adrian Bonger, Amsterdam, Netherlands, 1905. Translated by Henry P. Horton and published in the Modern Criminal Science Series by Little, Brown & Company, Boston.

In his table on page 291 of this book, defective home conditions stand second in the list to mental abnormalities and peculiarities. The importance of other environmental factors is there shown.[1] Defective home conditions break up into such elements as quarreling in the home; poverty (where the lack of adequate income appeared itself to be a factor); lack of home control through ignorance; illness; mother working out; broken relations between parents; immoral home environment, etc. The group of factors called "defective or unsatisfied interests" includes such causes as school or vocational dissatisfaction, excessive interest in moving picture shows, the social life of saloons, exciting literature and lack of healthy recreational interest.

The fact is that criminologists are just beginning to approach the subject of environmental factors from the vantage ground of the individual delinquent. Little as is known about the personal causes of crime, it is perhaps true that more is known about them than about the factors of environment. This is partly due to the fact that the leaders in studying the individual have been, for the most part, psychiatrists, and it is natural for them to look for that with which they are most familiar. It is partly due, also, to the fact that personal factors are the more constant and that what is true of one environment may not be true of another. The study of criminology stands in great need to-day of an exhaustive inquiry into environmental factors. This inquiry should be on

[1] For a detailed analysis of these factors the reader should consult "The Individual Delinquent," pp. 126-157.

a large scale, should be conducted in various parts of the country and even of the world, and its method should be the evaluation of factors revealed by a study of individual offenders. It is not enough to say that whatever deviates from normal conditions of life contributes to crime, since in the first place it is probably impossible to define normal conditions of life satisfactorily, and in the second place many conditions regarded as normal provoke some personalities to crime.

That there is a causal relation between the use of alcoholic beverages and criminalism is matter of everyday knowledge. Alcohol may operate as a cause not only through its use by the individual offender, but also through the home and environmental conditions that spring from its use by others, perhaps through its effects upon the heredity of the offender, and through its effects upon him during his ante-natal period. A warning should be sounded against regarding alcohol as a cause every time it appears. An antecedent cause for both alcoholism and crime may exist, such as disease, mental defect, poverty and the like. This is true also of other habit-forming stimulants.

II. Prevention

It is amazing to note the comparative silence that writers on criminology have maintained upon the subject of prevention. One would suppose that to prevent crime, just as to prevent disease, would be an important activity of a self-conscious society really interested in its own betterment. Crime is an ugly thing. It eats at the heart of social wellbeing. Not only is it enormously expensive, but it is opposed to beauty, art, happiness, the service of others and whatever makes for the flowering of talent and the growth of self-respect. It is contaminating, for its example drags down many who would otherwise escape. Its expense lies not only in the cost necessary to arrest, convict and confine offenders, but also in the loss of ability and achievement of those who spend their lives in the pursuit and supervision of offenders.

Prevention may be regarded under the same two heads as causation: environmental and personal. Since crime is always the effect of a particular personality reacting to a particular environment, any comprehensive program for the prevention of crime would necessarily include every measure that so modifies either the individual or his environment as to decrease the kind of friction that results in anti-social conduct. One does not need to belong to the sociological, biological or any other school of criminology to accept this statement, though it may be better to speak of such measures as weapons rather than as preventives, since no one of them nor any considerable number together will ever completely prevent crime; each may in some degree help to diminish it.

In practice, too, it is sometimes difficult to distinguish between measures that attack the personal and those that attack environmental causes of crime. Eugenics attacks only the personal; raising incomes chiefly the environmental. A more wisely regulated school life attacks both. The distinction is not always important, since the chief object is to be sure that the measure in question is directed at a fundamental cause of crime.

Fundamental Social Forces: The Home

A large part of the task of preventing crime falls to those fundamental social forces that operate directly upon all young people. Among these are the home, the church, the school, and the larger community, especially through the opportunities it offers for recreation and the wholesome use of leisure. Preventive treatment, to be effective, must begin early. Most confirmed delinquents have their first anti-social flings in youth, some even in childhood, and a great many in the elementary grades of school. It is important, therefore, that incipient tendencies should be sharply noticed and measures taken in time. We cannot do better than to quote several paragraphs from Healy on this subject:

"The best treatment for adolescent troubles is preventive. The preemption of the field with healthy interests before the age of thirteen or fourteen forms the best possible safeguard against the development of dangerous social tendencies. The consideration of adolescence as a causative factor of criminalism is no longer a theoretical matter; it is of vast practical import. There is a great social need for carrying the individual safely into this period that during it he may not tend to form bad associations, mental and environmental, which stand in the way of desirable social development. Preventive treatment unquestionably involves the training of proper discipline which gives the basis for self-control, and also equipping the young individual with knowledge which shall forfend development of considerable amount of delinquency which is entered into as the result of ignorance or mental vacuity.

"There is little doubt in my mind, as I have elsewhere insisted, that much of the success of institutional work with young delinquents is to be attributed, not so much to the specific activities of the institution as to the fact that the individual is tided in a stable environment through the adolescent period. The need of just this thing being done appears so assured that to my mind there is no doubt of the value of placing all adolescents showing criminalistic tendencies in some environment that creates healthy interests and is free from stimulation toward misconduct—and this for a considerable share of the formative period of their life. Struggling, for instance, under probation in a bad environment, with adolescents who have deep-set tendencies to misconduct, is inviting social failure. That success can be had sometimes by placing the offender in a different home where there is a better range of interests, or where there is less friction, or in country life away from city temptations, as well as by placing in institutions, goes without saying. . . .

"In attempting moral treatment of the adolescent offender, the peculiar mental characteristics of adolescence must never be forgotten. For instance, the steadiness of purpose or normal desire for self-preservation found in an older person cannot be reckoned on. One comes to have little faith in the efficacy of the cry of danger to many healthy boys and girls during adolescence. At this feckless age the appeal to self-interest will often bring little result. We have noted it fail time and again. The irregularities, impulsions and emotions of this period are all to be considered in their true light as conditions to be struggled with, which with good care may later drop entirely away. Only too often do we hear, even from parents, character tendencies of adolescents interpreted as being the permanent traits of the individual." [1]

It is as important to reach the home with a definite program of improvement as it is difficult. Anglo-Saxon peoples look askance at any attempt to interfere with the sovereign parental right to control childhood. Nevertheless, many homes are not safe for children. Doubtless we shall have to abide the fruits of education and race culture, but there seems to be no necessity of compelling children to remain in homes

[1] "The Individual Delinquent," pp. 727-728.

that are plainly making offenders of them. Wherever the policy of finding private foster homes for children has been seriously attempted, even in the vicinity of New York and other metropolitan districts, desirable ones with their doors open have been found in abundance. Another means of decreasing the number of unfavorable home environments for children is to make the laws of divorce more amenable to the social utility of the separation sought, especially when the grounds on which it is sought affect the life and training of children.

An important possibility of immediate action is to bring into the home a scientific knowledge of the causes of youthful misconduct. Not only would this in time prevent much bungling interference in the lives of children by parents, but it would enable them so to interfere, when interference is necessary, as to give some assurance of success. Promoting the economic security of parents, also, will tend to surround the child with a more desirable environment. A closer relationship and joining of hands between parents and teachers should be striven for, too, for the good of the child.

It is not only the "bad" or "broken" home, however, that stands in need of guidance. We are only beginning to discover how little we know about the processes by which young children are "spoiled." "There is a growing conviction," says Frederic Lyman Wells in his recent book, "Mental Adjustments," "that all mental events of infantile life are of far more significance for adult personality than we had supposed, and that they deserve far more care than we have been giving them in proportion to the later years." In spite of a well-known historian's recent effort to trace his education through three-quarters of a century, there is some justification for Freud's contention that a boy's education, in effect, ends with his first trousers. It begins with his earliest adaptations to the environment around him. To what extent sentimental, indulgent, self-centred and egoistic parents contribute to the difficulties of their children in achieving harmonious relationships through life, cannot yet be said with certainty. It is clear, however, that undue indulgence may be quite as serious as severity and repression.

Some of the possibilities that spring from the relationship between parent and child are indicated by Dr. Wells in the following paragraphs:

"We may assume that no parents would knowingly injure the mental health of their children; yet there is a singular blindness in this respect that is more than mere lack of judgment. The parents who spoil their children do so in feeding their own self-admiration as parents of that child. If unbounded affection for the child often results in such harm to him, it is because his adaptation to life is not the underlying motive of the affection of his parents, to whom he is essentially an instrument for the living out of a particular group of feelings. They betray him to their own self-love.

"One may truly respect a boy of six who, when asked by his grandmother whether he was not sorry that she had hurt her foot, replied that he had tried to be, but couldn't. There is no easier way to damage a child's character than by artificially stimulating his emotions. It is an evil turn to a child, and an all too frequent one, to teach or allow him to lash himself into emotion because it appears to be the "right way to feel." If we try to act as we feel, we are apt to act only as we think we should like to feel; it is more honest to judge our feelings by our reactions.

"The emotional display of sympathy, in particular, is a thing that is blessed neither to give nor to receive. Those who ridicule our sufferings are better friends to us than those who merely pity them. The underlying cause of such displays is that it is easier to cry over our friend's hurt than to mend it; sympathy may injure the recipient by undermining his self-control, and by leading him to exaggerate his difficulties. Though such conduct is hard in the case of those personally dear to us, it is best to confine one's appreciation of another's suffering, so far as is humanly possible, to do something objective to lighten it." [1]

Fundamental Social Forces: The School

Nothing is easier than to bring an indictment against an entire institution. This is especially unfair if the indictment singles out some one function that has not always been regarded as among the duties of that institution. Nevertheless, recent studies of individual offenders justify the contention that the school can do more than it now does to check incipient delinquency.

Clearly the school is one of the most important agencies in influencing conduct. For many months each year the child is turned over to it for practically the whole day, from the age of six years to fourteen or sixteen. Although, as a recent writer, Mr. Charles L. Robbins, teacher of the history of education in the New York Training School for Teachers, has pointed out, the home has the advantage of an earlier beginning and the church has the important possibility of supplying a religious sanction, the school alone is under the direct control of the state. Consequently it offers opportunities for conscious direction in a man-

[1] The student who is interested in this subject will find much that is suggestive in Dr. Wells's volume, "Mental Adjustments," published by D. Appleton & Co., 1917.

ner quite different from other institutions. It is "*par excellence* the state's most available instrument of control." Whether or not the school willingly accepts this responsibility, society seems to have no alternative but to depend upon it as one of the principal agencies in the prevention of crime.

Studies of adult offenders have shown clearly that definite intimations of anti-social careers are usually given early in school life. Sometimes these are wholly unnoticed by the school authorities; sometimes they are recognized by the teacher or truant officer, but no steps are taken to ward off the fatal end. In many instances the school environment itself contributes directly to the delinquency. As Healy has pointed out:

> "We find the specialized defective, for instance, developing anti-social tendencies because he was kept with small children, although in many respects he had mental powers corresponding to his age. Others on account of nervous trouble or physical ailments, including uncorrected sensory defects, are irritated by the confinement of the schoolroom. Conditions of hearing, which are more difficult to correct than vision, may cause great irritability and recalcitrancy. Then we might cite the case of the boy who, as educationalists say, was not book-minded. His traits required that he do things with his hands; his delinquency was the result of impulsions which arose in this way. Attendance at a school where there was poor teaching and poor discipline, or where language was taught that was not the general language of the community, have all figured as causes." [1]

Glueck found in his study of 608 consecutive admissions to Sing Sing (see page 297) that the beginnings of delinquency could be traced back in many of these

[1] "The Individual Delinquent," pp. 295-296.

cases to the school period. For example, every teacher of elementary pupils will recognize familiar traits among the following:

"Aside from the fact that nine [of ninety-eight native-born defectives] never reached beyond the third grade, that five never reached beyond the fourth grade, and that twelve never reached beyond the fifth grade, many traits came to light which should have been properly evaluated. Thus, backwardness and inability to learn, which necessitated repetition of classes on one or more occasions, was manifested in thirty-four instances; excessive truancy in twenty-one instances; incorrigibility in five; extremely irregular attendance in eight; inability to get along socially in five; extreme dislike for studies in eleven; one case terminated in expulsion, and a number of them had to be transferred to reformatory institutions directly from school. In four instances school attendance was begun after the age of ten had been reached." [1]

Glueck put the responsibility of the school in these words:

"Whatever justification there may have been for the indifference displayed toward the many deviations from average normal behavior, which so many of these individuals manifested in their parental homes, surely the failure to appreciate these indications of a pathological state during their contact with the public school cannot be easily condoned. If our study of the adult offender were to demonstrate nothing beyond the extreme evil inherent in an unintelligent handling of these early manifestations of abnormality of behavior, it will have justified the time and labor expended upon it. Granted that there may be many difficulties in the way of adequately administering this problem while the individuals are still under the entire supervision of unintelligent parents, surely no such difficulty should exist in our school machinery.

"Perhaps the very significant fact that out of the ninety-eight native-born defectives 80.6 per cent. developed into individuals who are strongly inclined to behave in an anti-social manner,

[1] *Mental Hygiene*, January, 1918, p. 111.

may serve to convince our school authorities that the purpose of education reaches beyond the acquisition of the "three R's."

"At any rate, from the biologist's point of view education should have for its object primarily the fitting of the individual for proper living, and in this respect our school system has singularly failed, as far as these cases are concerned. Not that we believe that any large number of these ninety-eight defectives could have been restored to normality, but we do insist that in a great many instances they gave highly suggestive, if not unmistakable, evidence during their school life of being incapable of proper adjustment under ordinary conditions of life, and that some provision should have been made for placing them in a more appropriate environment."

Mr. Robbins, writing from the point of view of the educator, sees the school as an almost unused instrument of moral and social control. He defines moral education as "the process of building up attitudes, habits, desires, and ideas which actually enter into conduct and are in reality a part of it," and finds the school wofully deficient heretofore in choosing the proper means to build up such habits. To quote:

"It seems that the school as an institution has always shown a strong tendency toward specialization in intellectual activities. . . .

"Although the school in all ages and among all peoples has manifested a discouraging facility in separating itself from real life and in building up a little world of its own quite artificial in its nature, there seems to be no valid reason for permitting this condition to endure forever. Instead, it seems obvious that in the school there are and always have been most valuable opportunities and situations for emphasis of the moral in a practical way. The trouble has been merely a neglect of the possibilities that exist and must always exist where a group of children or young people are acquiring education. Every subject in the course of study and every school situation is rich in such opportunities.

"If the school is to operate effectively in bringing about proper moral development, it must provide an actual moral *milieu*. It seems clear that wherever human beings, whether adults or children, are working together there are inevitably conditions that afford the possibility of moral training. . . .

"An exceptionally important factor in providing a proper social and moral environment in the school is the cultivation of the right tone and spirit. . . . The orphan school which Pestalozzi conducted at Stanz is an inspiring example of the kind of spirit that is meant. He was father, mother, nurse, and teacher, pouring into the lives of the children his own love and sympathy and finding that spirit reflected in their conduct. The opposite type is found in many a city school of the present, where the teacher is a mere cog in a pedagogical machine and the pupils are but grist to run through the mill. . . .

"Such a subject as history offers a good illustration of the psychological principle which is here stated. If the teacher of history lays great stress upon the necessity of having material which is true and which is accurately stated, he may be able to produce in his pupils a development of habits or attitudes which reflect his own ideas so far as the work in history is concerned; but there is considerable likelihood that what he does will not be transferred to their work in other fields. If, however, instead of being merely a teacher of his own subject, he tries to raise the practice of seeking the truth to the level of conscious purpose, to connect it with other phases of life, then, if at all, there is hope that a wider range of conduct will receive the benefit of the work that is done in the history field. . . .

"One of the great reasons why student self-government, as exemplified in the school city or republic, has real value, is because the scheme of organization gives students something to do and something to think about in a way which is not obviously connected with the repressive force of teacher or principal. While a healthy amount of stress is laid upon that which is not to be done, a large amount of emphasis is placed upon the idea that certain qualities are necessary, that certain kinds of conduct are for the good of the school, not merely for the pleasure of the teacher. The duties of student officials, the necessity of occasional elections, and the making of laws or rules continually give the pupils something of a definite and positive nature to do; that is, discipline becomes a matter of doing in which the negative side of inhibition is set in its proper place of subordination to the positive idea of doing right."[1]

There are other ways, however, in which the school can effectively contribute to an environment and training that will be helpful in preventing delinquency. It has been often enough pointed out that too much education is still academic and literary in character and does not sufficiently fit young men and women for the work of the world. This is partly the result of tradition and partly the result of a belief still current among educators that the chief aim of education is cultural, or that it is to train faculties quite apart from the specific uses to which these faculties will be put later on. Psychology has lately thrown doubt upon the soundness of this assumption. At any rate, it is undeniable that large numbers of children drop out of school at the fourth, fifth and sixth grades, and that the school is unable to exercise any further influence upon them. Investigation has shown that for only a small part of these is economic pressure the real reason for the withdrawal. For the remainder the reasons must mainly be found in the surge and inquietude of youth, and in the failure of the school to hold interest during the years of adolescence.

As a result of this situation, much has been written about the need of more vocational and industrial education as a means of combating the exodus of school children. In the view of modern criminologists this is a wholly desirable development. Mr. Burdette G.

[1] Readers who are especially interested in the school as an agency for the prevention of delinquency should read the whole of Mr. Robbins's suggestive chapter on "The School as an Instrument of Control: Moral Education," in his book, "The School as a Social Institution," published by Allyn & Bacon.

Lewis, an experienced administrator of penal institutions, has recently argued for this change at some length.[1] Many school systems have already made long strides in this direction, but American education as a whole still clings to the old ideal. What is wanted, in order to give the school that kind of well-rounded environment that will make it the most effective agency of social control, is not so much two systems of instruction, one cultural and one vocational, as one system combining both elements in due proportions and capable of being modified to meet individual needs. The Gary plan of a work-study-play curriculum correlated to many other agencies in the community is an excellent illustration of what the student of delinquency would like to see more widely established.

There are still other ways in which the school can check individual tendencies toward misconduct: First, it can require teachers and principals to know something about the personal factors in wrongdoing, so that they will more readily recognize them and will be competent to take the necessary disciplinary action. This does not mean simply that teachers should acquaint themselves with the contributions of other people to this subject, but that they should make their own. Why should not the school help to discover the causes of misbehavior? Certainly it is the scene of much behavior, the one institution above all others that ought to be familiar with incipient tendencies toward delinquency. Criminologists have a right to

[1] "The Offender," by Burdette G. Lewis, Harper & Brothers, pp. 262-276.

expect much from it in the way of scientific additions to the etiology of crime.

A second way is to study truancy and its causes. At present too many school systems simply content themselves with trying to compel attendance. The machinery for even reporting nonattendance is not always efficient, as was shown by the discovery of Frank P. Bachman in 1911-1912 that although 90,000 New York City school children were absent during one-half year for at least one school month each, the attendance officers reported only 6,579 as having been truants for five days or more during the entire year. Truancy, in spite of the classic example of Robert Louis Stevenson, is the beginning of much serious misconduct, and until the school has found some way to solve this problem, it will not have made its full contribution to the prevention of crime.

A third step is to insure the earliest possible discovery of pathological and abnormal mental states, and to provide special training for those who need it, such as backward, retarded and slightly defective pupils. This is already being done to some extent in some cities.

A fourth step is to refer children who are clearly feebleminded[1] to the authorities who are charged with committing the feebleminded to special institutions. If there are no such institutions, or if the accommodations are insufficient, teachers are in a strategic position to agitate for more prompt and adequate care of this class. The carrying out of this step will require

[1] Goddard found that two per cent. of the children in the New York City public schools are probably feebleminded.

the services of a psychiatrist, for which an excellent precedent may be found in medical inspection, which is another desirable measure in mitigating the physical contributors to delinquency.

A fifth step is the reduction of classes to smaller units, the modification of the system of periodic and simultaneous promotion in all subjects—called by the somewhat inaccurate name of "lock-step" schooling—and more individual attention to pupils. Indeed, this is important enough to be placed side by side with the vitalizing of instruction by adding more vocational content.

Many progressive schoolmen are constantly calling attention to the desirability of some of these measures. Special classes for backward children are now found in many cities. Classes in some public school systems are tending to be reduced in size and more individual attention to be given, though an opposite tendency is also visible in some places. Very little is being done, however, in the way of assuming responsibility for the proper disposition of the feebleminded, and almost nothing toward training teachers in a knowledge of the personal factors in wrongdoing.

That delinquency is "fundamentally a problem for the public schools to handle" is the opinion of Ellwood P. Cubberley, professor of education, Leland Stanford Junior University. In a volume embodying the results of a study of the schools of Salt Lake City, he writes:

"Many boys and girls are now in our reformatories and juvenile institutions who might have been saved through vocational guidance and other provisions which the public schools should have made for them. It is generally recognized that the feebleminded child is a potential delinquent. The minds of these children will always remain like those of young children, and consequently they will have neither the ability nor the desire to resist the temptations which cause their downfall. Even some children of normal mentality are weak in will-power, or have emotional characteristics which lead to crime.

"In 1910 there were 25,000 children in institutions for delinquents. Of these, 14,000 had been committed in less than one year. Not less than one-third of these are feebleminded, and not less than one-half are mentally retarded to such a degree that this deficiency would account for their delinquency. There are fully 12,000 who do not belong where they have been placed, and for whom no form of punishment can be of great benefit. Many, when released, will again enter lives of crime, and will spend many of their later years in prison. Hence the responsibility of the public school in the classification and guidance of children who exhibit these tendencies."[1]

It will thus be seen that the responsibility to make the school a real agency of prevention has been accepted by progressive educators. What remains is to make this aspiration a reality.

Fundamental Social Forces: The Church

Throughout the ages the church has attempted to elevate man's moral conduct. Its purpose has perhaps been more to make the spiritual satisfactions of life real than to prevent actual delinquency. Primarily, its attack has been upon sin rather than crime; indeed, many religious people and not a few noted preachers have deliberately violated man-made laws in adherence to conscientious and religious mandates. While there may be room for discussion, therefore, in

[1] "School Organization and Administration," by Ellwood P. Cubberley. Vol. I. of the Educational Survey Series. World Book Company.

regard to the lengths to which the church ought to go in bidding obedience to the state, there can be none in regard to its opposition to the great mass of law-violation known as crime.

To play its full part in the prevention of crime the church must profit from what psychology and education have to teach it. As has already been suggested in these pages, the intimate relationship existing, or capable of existing, between ministers and children or ministers and parents may be of great preventive force. The minister must understand, however, the origin and nature of delinquency and the best ways to meet it. He must have some of the tact of the good teacher and the special knowledge of the probation officer, and must come to realize that conduct is an expression of mental life and that a spiritual approach can only be made through the vestibule of whatever mental habits and traits the individual may possess. Sunday School teachers, club leaders and other persons whose contact comes through the church can be similarly helpful if similarly equipped.

Particularly can the church do much to foster wholesome recreational habits. In rural and small urban communities, there seems to be a special opportunity for the church to become the centre of social life. A recent study of juvenile delinquency in rural New York, conducted under the auspices of the United States Children's Bureau, found striking opportunities of this sort wasted. To quote:

"Turning to the social side of country life, we find the church the only generally approved social institution for all ages. Its activity is seen to range from the performance of public worship, without other contacts, to hearty participation in the community life as a whole. The extent and nature of its activities seem to depend largely upon the personality of the minister. He is usually very poorly paid, is sometimes ignorant, sometimes indifferent, but often in the most discouraging surroundings is eager, devoted, socially minded, and laborious in trying to arouse church and community to a sense of their mutual relation and obligation. In part the tradition of a particular denomination determines the extent of the church's social activity. But whatever the cause—the minister, the denominational tradition, or the prejudices of the people themselves—in some communities the church appears as a positive hindrance to the development of a wholesome social life by its hostile attitude toward certain forms of amusement or indeed toward any amusement at all. In others it goes to the opposite extreme in its laxity. . . .

"At the two extremes in the matter of amusement are the church which holds its suppers in a road house of questionable reputation and the church belonging to a denomination which permits no socials and frowns upon women who wear ribbons or feathers and upon men who wear neckties.

"On the other hand there was the socially-minded minister who formed a boys' club following the rules of the Boy Scouts, which did a great deal of good and gave him a wholesome hold on the boys. This is the minister who wished to use the unoccupied church building for a community centre but could get no support from his parishioners." [1]

The organized church can be of great assistance in specific preventive work. In some communities, churches, both singly and through central bodies such as federations of churches, are strong allies of probation officers and afford constructive help in rescuing incipient offenders. Some, too, help in reconstructing the paroled law-breaker. Wherever the church has recognized social service as a part of its function, the

[1] "Delinquency in Rural New York," by Kate Holladay Claghorn. Publication No. 32 of the Children's Bureau of the United States Department of Labor, Washington, D. C. 1918.

care of criminals and the prevention of crime are among the first aspects of such service to appeal to it.

Fundamental Social Forces: Community Recreational Life

The formation of wholesome recreational habits in childhood and youth is one of the best safeguards against later trouble. The study of individual offenders has thrown much light upon the ways in which young law-breakers spend their leisure time. Many seem to have no idea that there is such a thing as amusement that does not lead to misconduct. The recreational desires of young men who have begun anti-social lives centre largely about gambling and its attendant excitement, the possession of women (not entirely for sex purposes but for the pleasure that comes from mere proprietorship), and the use of alcohol. Whether the failure to form more wholesome habits is due to constitutional defect in the individual or to defect in early training may be difficult to answer in some cases, but there can be no doubt that defect in training and lack of early advantages is all too often a causative factor. Too much emphasis cannot be laid, therefore, upon the importance of tiding over the period of youth with healthy mental interests.

The growth of cities is largely responsible for a cramped and misdirected recreational life. Innumerable forms of adventurous activity indulged in by youngsters violate one ordinance or another passed for the safety and comfort of adults. In 1914, the People's Institute of New York City published a report, entitled "The City Where Crime is Play,"[1] showing that a large percentage of the offences for which city children are arrested originate in the play impulse and have no moral significance whatever. The court records describe these offences by all sorts of names that cover up their real nature, such as disorderly conduct, creating disturbances, destruction of property, burglary and the like. In reality, they often amount to no more than throwing baseballs, pitching pennies, singing noisily in chorus, pilfering things needed in play (such as fishing tackle and baseball bats), upsetting garbage cans for amusement, etc. Even gang stealing in many parts of New York City has come to be a recognized amusement and to have a definite form of organization. This game is described by one of the authors as follows:

"A band of boys from three to six or seven in number will go from tenement to tenement on Saturday evenings, taking orders from the housewives for fruits, vegetables, groceries, light hardware and clothing, just as though they were delivery clerks. When they think they have a sufficient number of orders they go out on the street and by a series of organized raids secure the goods which the housewives have ordered. These goods are sold on a regularly established scale of prices, which in most parts of the city is arbitrary, with no relation to the market value of the stolen articles. After the boys get their money they retire to their 'hang-out,' where the money is divided into equal parts and the possessors shoot 'craps' until one of them has it all. This boy divides the winnings into two parts, one of which he spends in treating the other members of the gang. The other half he is permitted to keep and spend for himself.

"This is a regularly organized form of amusement, which has

[1] "The City Where Crime is Play," by John Collier and Edward M. Barrows. The People's Institute, New York. 1914. Price 10 cents.

existed to the writer's personal knowledge for a decade or more on the Middle West Side."

It is such amusements as these, indulged in largely in the exercise of normal play impulses, that often cause a child's first contact with the law. This first contact is frequently enough to open the door to a delinquent career. A child who is arrested at once becomes stamped by adults as a "boy who has been to the courts," and is very likely to be made a minor hero by his companions. His acquaintance with rough characters widens. Even if his first offence brought no punishment, the second is likely to do so, and at a house of correction or children's protectory he meets other and older offenders and is likely to learn new ways of committing crime.

The growth of organized recreation in American cities may be expected to do something to remedy this situation. Such recreation will have to be carefully thought out and conducted under skilled supervision. It will have to reach many children, not merely a few. It should aim to restore or supply substitutes for those elements of home life that are lost amid the divisive influences of a great city. It must make play both attainable and interesting. It must supply those wholesome mental interests that are so important in tiding over the period of early adolescence.

For this reason the mere building of playgrounds and other machinery of recreation is not enough. There must be competent supervision and direction. Illicit amusement can thrive as easily among a crowd of boys in a municipal playground as on the street. Figures showing the growth of supervised recreation are encouraging,[1] but one cannot tell from these alone whether the recreation offered is of high quality or whether its spirit is such as to combat influences making for delinquency. Moreover, many playgrounds and recreational centres are not open evenings.

School buildings are being opened in increasing numbers after school hours and throughout the evening for use as civic and social gatherings of both young people and adults. There is a growing tendency to construct school buildings so that they will be especially adapted for community use. Such organizations as the Boy Scouts, the Camp Fire Girls and others devoted to the recreational, physical, cultural and moral development of young people, afford a real help in establishing wholesome habits of recreation, if they do not err by too great a tendency toward ceremonial and military glamor. Supervised dancing and other forms of entertainment in which both sexes may join can also be used in building up right attitudes and habits that will make for good conduct.

The problem of combating evil play habits is by no means a city problem alone. The village tavern is likely to be the "catch-all for every sort of proscribed amusement." Here the gossip of the neighbor-

[1] Questionnaires sent to American cities by the Playground and Recreation Association of America showed that during the year ending November 1, 1917, 481 cities maintained 3,944 playgrounds and recreational centres under paid leadership. At least 23 other cities returned partial information, making a total of 504 known to have conducted recreation work in 1917. These reports indicate an increase over 1916 of 17⁶⁄₁₀ per cent. in the number of cities and 15⁸⁄₁₀ in the number of centres conducted. In the 481 cities, 8,748 workers were employed, an increase of 1,626 over 1916. During the summer months 422 cities reported a total average attendance of 737,519. An attendance of 230,897 was reported by 114 cities at winter centres.

hood is exchanged and here—in the bar, pool-room or bowling alley—may be found, legally or illegally, numerous young boys "who learn to drink, smoke, swear, steal, tell dirty stories and amuse the adult crowd thereby."[1] Even in villages that are "dry," the village store is often a club-house for men and boys where neighborhood matters are discussed, racy stories are told, matters of sex held up to indecent comment and a taste for gambling fostered. Habits of wholesome recreation need to be inculcated in country children as well as in their urban brothers and sisters. One hopeful remedy lies in the consolidation of several one-room school houses into a single, larger and better school, with more ample facilities for education and play.

Prohibition

Reference has already been made (page 420) to the several ways in which alcoholism operates as a cause of crime. It follows that to diminish the excessive use of alcohol is one of the tasks of prevention. The abstinence campaigns of Father Mathew in Ireland are a classic example of the success attending such an effort. This great leader apparently succeeded, by his speeches and the power of his personality, in making 1,800,000 total abstainers in that country in a few years (1837-1842), and in reducing the consumption of spirits 50 per cent.[2] Offences dropped in number from 64,520 to 47,027, and the serious crimes from 12,096 to 773—only one-sixteenth as many. Aschaf-

[1] "Juvenile Delinquency in Rural New York." See footnote p. 437.

[2] Baer, "Der Alkoholismus," p. 395.

fenburg points out that the transitoriness of this success proves that the method employed was not the right one and apparently most nations to-day agree with this, since the spread of compulsory restriction upon the use of alcohol is universal. Indeed, one almost feels that any discussion of this question is a little academic, since complete prohibition seems to loom so closely on the horizon.[1] The old question, "Does Prohibition prohibit?" is seldom asked nowadays. So, too, the old debate on the relative efficacy of local option, high license and prohibition is nearly dead. Prohibition in a small district, such as a county, may not prevent adjacent wet districts from sending liquor surreptitiously into the dry area, but when a whole state goes dry, jail statistics noticeably shrink. Even so small a region as the District of Columbia shows this. Mayor Pullman, in his 1918 report as superintendent of police of that district, attributes the falling off of 58 per cent. in arrests to the recent enactment of prohibition. Birmingham, Ala., built a fine new jail a few years ago and when the State went dry the only use for the jail was as a storehouse for hay.

Eugenics

One of the most hopeful methods of preventing crime in the long run lies in the practice of race culture. Writers on criminals have almost wholly neglected this subject. Nevertheless, if it be true, as the reviser of these chapters has attempted to point out,

[1] Since this was written, enough States have ratified the prohibition amendment to the Constitution to make it effective.

that a causal relation exists between criminality and certain defective or abnormal physical and mental characteristics, *transmissible from one generation to another,* then it is reasonable to expect that the progressive elimination of these traits will lead to a reduction in the ratio of criminals to the general population. The prejudice that has in the past attached itself to the name and study of eugenics is most unfortunate. Uninformed persons have assumed that eugenics means the breeding of human beings, as animals and plants are bred. Some have assumed that the aim of this socio-biological science is to level the human race up—or down—to some single uniform type, some species of superman. What jury, it has been asked, is competent to pass upon "desirable" characteristics, and who are the "unfit"? Such interrogators have taken it for granted that eugenists propose to weed out whole classes of the population on the mere basis of acts performed, such as murder, thieving and the like.

The truth is, of course, that eugenics aims at none of these things. It does not propose to experiment with human beings, but merely to learn the results of man's experiments upon himself and to induce him to accept the teaching of these experiments. It seeks excellence in all desirable types, not a uniform type. It hopes to proceed only so fast as the accepted proofs of science justify it in proceeding, and to adopt definitely restrictive measures only with respect to those persons who possess germinally degenerate traits and who are, therefore, demonstrably unfit to reproduce their kind. It has no interest whatever in social or economic classes, but only in hereditary classes, whose members are found in all ranks of society. It bases its proposals for action not upon the acts of individuals but upon their innate hereditary qualities, and for the most part desires nothing more than to be allowed to proceed by means of the uncoerced, voluntary and enlightened cooperation of mankind.

Obviously, it is impossible here to discuss the scientific bases of eugenics, involving the history and growth of the germ plasm, the laws and methods of heredity and environment in shaping human destinies, and the contention—now accepted by the vast majority of biologists—that acquired characteristics are not transmissible. These bases are fully set forth in books on heredity and biology. For a practicable eugenics program it is necessary only to know that men differ in their mental and physical characteristics; that these differences are inherited; that some of these characteristics are racially desirable and that some are racially undesirable; and that, therefore, "the make-up of the race can be changed by any method which will alter the relative proportions of the contributions which different classes of men make to the following generation."[1]

From this statement, it is clear that criminalism is only one of the aberrant manifestations of mankind in which eugenics is interested. The practical measures by which eugenics has so far proposed to improve the race are divided into two groups, called positive and negative eugenics, or constructive and

[1] Cf. "Applied Eugenics," by Popenoe and Johnson, page 99. Macmillan Company, 1918.

restrictive eugenics. We shall consider restrictive eugenics first, discussing briefly the classes to which it can be applied and then the methods open to it.[1]

Restrictive eugenics aims to prevent reproduction by parents whose offspring would almost certainly be undesirable persons, i.e., so mentally or physically defective as to become inevitable moral menaces or charges upon the common welfare. No one will deny that of these the feebleminded constitute one group. The defect of feeblemindedness is highly transmissible. Two feebleminded persons who carry the defect in their germ plasm, are almost certain to produce only feebleminded offspring, and the marriage of a feebleminded with a normal person is likely to produce a considerable number of feebleminded children. There are probably more than 300,000 definitely feebleminded people in the United States to-day. Of these not more than 40,000 are cared for in institutions intended for the feebleminded; a few thousand more are in jails and almshouses and a somewhat larger number in reformatories and prisons. The great bulk are free to reproduce their kind. Even many of those in jails, almshouses and prisons are sooner or later set free to do likewise. Then, too, it must be remembered that many persons not feebleminded carry the taint of feeblemindedness in their germ plasm and hence are capable of transmitting it to their offspring.

Another group to which restrictive eugenics can be

[1] For the general outlines of this discussion the writer has drawn, with permission both of the authors and the publisher, upon the book above referred to, "Applied Eugenics," by Popenoe and Johnson. Considerable information from other sources has, however, been used.

safely applied is the insane. The census of 1910 showed that there are 187,791 insane persons in institutions in the United States. It is estimated that the total number in the country is much larger, and that this number is increasing year by year. It must be borne in mind that the word insane means nothing biologically. No one should become the subject of restrictive eugenics merely because he is what is called insane. It must first be determined that he possesses an hereditary tendency or weakness. Say Popenoe and Johnson:

> "Two types of insanity are now recognized as especially transmissible: dementia præcox, a sort of precocious old age in which the patient (generally young) sinks into a lethargy from which he rarely recovers, and manic depressive insanity, an over-excitable condition in which there are occasional very erratic motor discharges with periods of depression."

Institutions for offenders contain examples of both of these types of insanity.

A third group to whom the methods of restrictive eugenics can be applied are epileptics It has been calculated that the number of the epileptics in the State of New Jersey will double every thirty years under present conditions. There are many epileptics in the general population who have not been discovered. Dr. David F. Weeks, president of the International Association of Epilepsy and superintendent of the State Village for Epileptics at Skillman, N. J., recently pointed out that the war had caused a considerable increase in the number of known epileptics, due in part to the discovery of unsuspected epileptic persons by companions occupying the same tent or barracks. Epileptics so discovered ought to be reported and, if necessary, subjected to the measures of restrictive eugenics.

Other persons to whom the methods of restrictive eugenics ought to be applied are thus described by Popenoe and Johnson:

> "In addition to these well-recognized classes of hopelessly defective, there is a class of defectives embracing very diverse characteristics, which demands careful consideration. In it are those who are germinally physical weaklings or deformed, those born with a hereditary diathesis or predisposition toward some serious disease (*e.g.*, Huntington's Chorea), and those with some gross defect of the organs of special sense. The germinally blind and deaf will particularly occur to mind in the latter connection. Cases falling in this category demand careful scrutiny by biological and psychological experts, before any action can be taken in the interest of eugenics."

Coming now to criminals, it is clear at once that the measures of applied eugenics cannot be adopted *en masse* for them. The greatest danger, both in wronging society and the individual, lies in any application to criminals that does not distinguish carefully between those who possess germinally degenerate traits, mental or physical, and those who do not. *There is no unit character of crime.* Nevertheless, to take care of all the hereditarily feebleminded, insane and epileptic will weed out many criminals and potential criminals. Whether there are any criminals outside of these groups who ought to be prevented from reproducing their kind is a matter for psychiatrists and biologists to determine, and to determine on the basis of a study of individuals. That many chronic inebriates owe their condition almost wholly to heredity, and are likely to leave offspring of the same character, is regarded as proved by biologists.[1] Even persons whose *present condition* cannot be said to be in any true sense hereditary, such as prostitutes, paupers and others, deserve careful study by the eugenist because of the possibility that they possess hereditary weaknesses. Persons in whose criminality heredity does not play a part or plays only a minor part should be excluded from the scope of eugenics, and in every investigation the benefit of any doubt should be given to the individual.

We come now to the *methods* of restrictive eugenics. Execution is perhaps the oldest way of preventing people from reproducing their kind. It is not a weapon included in the armory of modern eugenists. Eugenics is not a wholly cold science, pursuing a single aim inexorably in spite of all other considerations and riding rough-shod over humanitarian objections. It recognizes that execution does violence to many valuable instincts of the race, and that there is such a thing as buying a biological benefit at too great a moral or spiritual cost.

Castration is the next most drastic form of preventing propagation. This, too, is discarded by eugenists. A milder operation is that which takes the form of vasectomy in man and salpingectomy in woman. The effect of these is to render the subject sterile without affecting his sexual life in any other way. Eugenists are not wholly agreed in regard to the desirability of sterilization. From a purely biological standpoint it is effective and is not attended

[1] Popenoe and Johnson, "Applied Eugenics," p. 181.

by the changes in character that are likely to follow castration. On the other hand, it is extremely difficult to safeguard properly and has the disadvantage of admitting of no rectification if an error is found to have been made. In some States where it has been tried men have sought the operation in order to free themselves from the consequences of sex promiscuity.

More than a score of States in this country have at one time or another passed so-called "sterilization laws." Most of those have been poorly and unscientifically drawn, though it is to be said in their favor that they show the beginnings of a public awakening to the importance of eugenics. Twelve such laws providing for the sterilizing of certain classes of criminals stood on the statute books in 1916. These varied all the way from laws purely eugenic in purpose to laws purely punitive in purpose. Few of them have ever really been enforced. Operations were performed under the Indiana law, but Governor Thomas R. Marshall later prevented further enforcement. In Wisconsin the law has been applied to a number of feebleminded persons.

A "model" sterilization law has been drafted by a committee of the American Breeders' Association, which has taken much interest in eugenics. This committee was formed to "study and report on the best practical means of cutting off the defective germ plasm of the American population," and has been at work since 1911 under the auspices of the Eugenics Record Office, Cold Springs Harbor, Long Island. The following is a condensed statement of the principles which, according to the committee, ought to be embodied in any model sterilization law:[1]

1. Sterilization should be actuated by the strictest eugenical motives and should be ordered only by due process of law and only after expert investigation.

2. Inmates of institutions for the insane, feebleminded, epileptic, inebriate and paupers, and of all reformatory and penal institutions should be made liable to investigation.

3. The determination of the desirability of a sterilizing operation should be made by a commission composed of persons possessing expert knowledge of biology, pathology and psychology.

4 and 5. These amplify and enforce 2 above, specifically providing that no member of the aforesaid classes be released to society without examination.

6. If it be found for any given individual among these classes that he or she is the potential parent of defectives, the commission should report this fact to a state court of competent jurisdiction and recommend an appropriate type of sterilizing operation.

7. If, after a full hearing, the court is satisfied that the individual is a potential parent of defective offspring, it should order the head of the institution where the individual is confined to cause the operation to be performed before discharge and in a safe and humane manner.

The method of restrictive eugenics upon which eugenists, penologists and social students agree is segregation. We have already discussed in a previous chapter some of the practical aspects of segregation and its therapeutic side. Here we may add one or two general considerations. To be effective eugenically, segregation in institutions must be for a long enough period to prevent reproduction. It must be extended not merely to those who have already become delinquent or dependent, but to those who would

[1] The full text of this law is given in Bulletin 10B of the Eugenics Record Office. The title of this bulletin is: "II. The Legal, Legislative and Administrative Aspects of Sterilization."

be practically certain, if they had children, to pass on the taint of their hereditary defectiveness. The segregable classes are those already mentioned. Concerning one of these, the feebleminded, Dr. Walter E. Fernald, superintendent of the Massachusetts School for the Feebleminded at Waverly, said before the National Conference of Charities and Corrections in 1915:

"Indeed, the results of eugenic research are so impressive that we are almost convinced that we are in possession of knowledge which would enable us to markedly diminish the number of the feebleminded in a few generations if segregation or surgical sterilization of all known defectives were possible. But really, we have only begun to apply even our present knowledge of the causes of feeblemindedness. The only feebleminded persons who now receive any official consideration are those who have already become dependent, many of whom have already become parents. We lock the barn door after the horse is stolen. We now have state commissions for controlling the gypsy moth and the bollweevil, the foot-and-mouth disease, and for protecting the shell-fish and wild game, but we have no commission which even attempts to modify or to control the vast social, moral and economic forces represented by the feebleminded persons at large in the community."

The type of custodial care best suited to the feebleminded is that found at such institutions as the Vineland Training School, Vineland, N. J., the Massachusetts School for the Feebleminded at Waverly, and the New York State Custodial School at Rome. For some of the other groups that ought to be segregated on eugenic grounds, such as the insane and epileptic, excellent institutions have already shown the way. In earlier pages we have seen the beginning of a movement to place defective delinquents in special institutions. The pressing problem to-day is not how to care for these groups, but how to find all persons who belong to them and how to persuade legislators and the public that it is socially desirable to segregate them. Everyone admits that a hopeless idiot ought to be segregated, but not everyone knows that a feebleminded person of higher grade is just as considerable a social menace as an idiot—indeed, he may be a greater menace because of his greater capacity for misconduct—and that he ought to be effectively prevented from reproducing his kind.

Recently some specialists familiar with the feebleminded have come to believe that universal segregation is not necessary for that class. Segregation must be the cornerstone, say these specialists, of our social policy in dealing with them, but there remains a larger or smaller group of high grade feebleminded, carrying the hereditary taint of their defectiveness, who can still be helped to live happy, clean lives in their homes with safety both to themselves and to the State. A step in this direction has already been taken by one or two institutions for the feebleminded, notably the New York State Custodial Asylum at Rome, whose superintendent, Dr. Charles Bernstein, has established groups of feebleminded boys on farm colonies more or less remote from the institution proper, under the care of a farmer and his wife. These boys live nearly normal lives, produce enough to be substantially self-supporting and are even allowed to go to nearby towns for recreation without guardians.

More than this, however, is proposed in the policy mentioned. In 1915 Dr. Fernald outlined a plan for a state bureau that should be responsible for the supervision, assistance and control of the feebleminded at large in the community who are not properly cared for already by their friends. It was his contention that since a large number of feebleminded now run the gauntlet of the police, the courts, the penal institutions, the almshouses, the tramp shelters, the lying-in hospitals and even private societies and agencies, and since it is a matter of chance at any given moment what agency is caring for a particular feebleminded person, the protection of this numerous group might wisely and economically be entrusted to some single, official body. This body would be responsible for discovering who and where the feebleminded are. It would also be responsible for deciding which ones could safely be allowed to live, under supervision, in their own homes. Locally, supervision would be supplied by, possibly, local health boards or other specially qualified local officials, or perhaps by competent social workers already dealing with dependents and delinquents. Under this plan, the feebleminded would enjoy a species of continuous probation, which could be terminated at any time when it appeared that their liberty was likely to become socially undesirable. Such oversight would be conducted not on the principle of espionage, but for the development of the individual's highest usefulness consistent with community safety.

An argument often advanced against segregation on so large a scale is its cost. The answer is that the cost is trivial compared to the real cost of caring for these same persons at present, plus the cost of caring for their progeny in the future. What the public loses sight of is the fact that the waste and loss suffered by society and individuals through the mistakes and misconduct of the feebleminded and the insane, is enormous. When a million dollar munitions plant was blown up in New Jersey early in the recent war, it was on record in the office of a committee interested in the feebleminded, that three former inmates of a state institution for the feebleminded were at work in that plant. The origin of the explosion was never traced to them, but any one of them was perfectly capable of doing a foolish thing any day that might have wrecked the whole plant and killed hundreds of people. Unquestionably many minor disasters constantly occur due to the irresponsible conduct of such persons.

But this is only part of the bill they present to society. More calculable is the cost of arresting, trying and convicting such of them as get into court. Many a conviction rolls up a bill double, treble or quadruple the amount that would be required to segregate the particular offender for life. "One has known a trial," says Healy, "based on psychopathic accusations [this particular case did not involve feeblemindedness] and fairly estimated to have cost the State $15,000, which might have been wholly avoided through the application of scientific diagnosis." Everyone will readily recall the case of a distinguished individual, mentally abnormal, whose efforts to escape confinement recently set at naught the legal machinery of one State after another for more than a decade, and must have cost a total of hundreds of thousands of dollars. This individual is now at large and still capable of adding to society's loss on his account. Another element in the waste of present policy is represented by the talent and energy of those who spend their time in the apprehension and conviction of defectives who have violated the law.

A second answer to the argument that segregation costs more than society can afford is that it does not actually cost as much as at first sight appears. Many feebleminded people are capable of being self-supporting under proper institutional supervision. Moreover, the expense of institutions and farm colonies for them and other classes of defectives will be counterbalanced in a few years by the reduction in the population of almshouses, prisons and other expensive institutions.

So much for restrictive eugenics, that part of the science that has received the most practical consideration and application so far.

The chief aims of constructive eugenics are two: to bring about a decrease in the birth-rate of the inferior, and an increase in the birth-rate of the superior. No program having at once the practicability and unity of segregation for restrictive eugenics has been, or probably can be, worked out to achieve these ends. The justification for using the words "inferior" and "superior," and the somewhat complex arguments by which various specific measures are sought to be supported, must be left to the books on eugenics. In general, the "inferior" mean those who possess biologically undesirable traits, capable of being transmitted in sufficient quantity or strength to make them race enemies. The "superior" mean those who possess biologically desirable traits and are reasonably without undesirable ones. No social or economic class distinction can be allowed to cloud these words. Some eugenists, unacquainted with the abundant virtues that exist in the midst of unseemly surroundings, and tainted with the prejudices of a comfortable bourgeois social philosophy, have made foolish statements on this aspect of the subject. They are effectively answered by Caleb W. Saleeby, who wrote in "The Progress of Eugenics," in 1914:

"The people called eugenists must repudiate those who seek to identify them with the cause of class hatred. Surveying the whole disastrous field of sham eugenics, one is inclined to regard this as the most dangerous and menacing at the present time, not only on its own demerits, but because so many professing eugenists, including not a few whose position makes them influential, are to be found amongst the ranks of those who seek to increase class contempt and class hatred on the ground that the 'upper classes' are really upper in the vital and biological sense, and that increased attention to the needs, especially the children's needs, of the 'lower classes' means national degeneration. This spirit of class prejudice and selfishness, which underlies the so-called eugenic activities of many professing eugenists, is the worst of all the enemies that eugenics has to face."

The degenerate, the waster, the idler, the man with the psychopathic taint and the defective strain—in a word, the biologically unfit—are found in all ranks of society and in all walks of life. Those who, because of some constitutional and hereditary weakness, fail to contribute valuable services to the world, may be born in the midst of luxury or they may be poor. To the eugenist they are the same. Not even he who fails to keep his head above the current of economic self-support can, in this day of monopoly and wage slavery, be held to be *therefore* eugenically unfit, and it is equally true that he who succeeds is not to be accounted fit on that ground alone.

The measures of constructive eugenics are sometimes divided into coercive and non-coercive. Every measure should be scrutinized in regard to its capacity for achieving one or the other of the two aims mentioned, either the decrease of the birth-rate among the inferior or the increase of the birth-rate among the superior. Among the measures most frequently proposed are the following: the extensive collection of existing data, and the persistent search for new data, about heredity and racial history; the dissemination of such data in popular but scientifically accurate form among all people; the inculcation of a higher regard for parenthood; making marriage a more deliberate and discriminative act (for example, by surrounding it with greater, even compulsory, publicity, a revival of the custom of publishing the banns, etc.); some method of endowing motherhood that will place a premium upon eugenically desirable babies; the adjustment of income taxes to the end that they shall not penalize marriage and having children; inheritance taxes that will effectively keep the idle and the useless from finding it too easy to live (for example, placing the tax on the amount received by each beneficiary rather than on the total amount bequeathed); the abolition of certain non-eugenic customs, such as the prevailing requirement that women teachers may not marry; the dissemination of information about birth control, thereby making parenthood intelligent and voluntary and decreasing the number of undesired and uncared for babies; the elimination of racial poisons, such as alcohol and syphilis; the abandonment of all forms of charity, philanthropy and altruism that encourage or permit the free reproduction of defective offspring;[1] regulating emigration (for example, by making the country a more desirable place to live for the energetic and progressive); and back-to-the-farm movements (on the ground that the best families tend to leave the country and to "run out" in a few generations under city conditions).

One should remember that eugenics aims at the prevention of many forms of social waste other than crime, and that it touches criminology only where the criminal act is due to some transmissible personal defect. That this is true in a sufficiently large percentage of crimes to make eugenics one of the best hopes of the criminalogist is not to be doubted.

General Education

Coincident with all other measures for the prevention of crime, society itself must achieve a more informed attitude toward the problems involved. In so far as the discharged offender is concerned, this attitude has already been discussed. Something more is required, however, than an understanding of the ex-convict. We must understand the pre- or ante-convict. It might almost be said that effective prevention of crime will proceed *pari passu* with the diffusion of knowledge concerning the causes of crime and the

[1] It is here that the strictly scientific eugenist and the social worker most often clash; undoubtedly each has much to learn from the other; the eugenist must reckon with the humanitarian sentiment, in itself a racial asset; the social worker must reckon with the ultimate good of the race.

real nature of criminals. This diffusion doubtless will be greatly aided by the special training of teachers, judges, lawyers, physicians, ministers, social workers and other groups who come into close personal contact with potential offenders. But the diffusion must be more widespread than that. We do not regard it as sufficient, for example, that only physicians should know the fundamental rules of health; the individual himself must be equipped with an elementary knowledge of how to live. Doubtless an acquaintance with criminology will be of very little effect in keeping an individual from becoming a criminal, but it will enable him to take a more intelligent attitude toward crime in others. It will also lead to a readier acceptance by society and by legislative and administrative officials of specific measures of improvement. A committee of the American Institute of Criminal Law and Criminology believes that "the higher educational institutions of our land should do all in their power to advance the interest of research and teaching in criminology."[1] The committee recognizes that something is already being done in courses in sociology and political science, but it believes that by the pursuit of a vigorous and reasonable policy such institutions may assume a leading rôle in the attainment, or in the approximate attainment, of the following ends:

"1. A more intelligent attitude on the part of the bar and the judiciary toward the criminal as an individual with certain defined physical and mental traits; an individual who, under certain

[1] See the report of this committee entitled "On the Teaching of Criminology in Colleges and Universities" in the *Journal of the American Institute of Criminal Law and Criminology* for November, 1918.

definable conditions, commits a concrete act which is described as delinquent or as criminal, but who should be cared for as his condition demands rather than punished, in the narrow sense, for the one act.

"2. An open mind on the part of the public at large, such as will in time stimulate earnest and intelligent search for the most suitable legislative, educational, and other means for preventing the development of criminals and for controlling them when they do appear.

"To meet these ends it is the judgment of this committee that wherever it is feasible colleges and universities should establish in their departments of psychology or of education or in their schools of law or medicine psychopathic laboratories and clinics. Such laboratories, etc., will find their data in the public schools, in philanthropic institutions in their vicinity, in the courts, jails and other places of detention. The laboratory, therefore, will be a contribution to the equipment of several interests of the university: psychology, medicine, public school education, sociology and law.

"In addition the college and the university should establish professorships of criminology—not departments—within the department of sociology, economics, or political science (whatsoever the department may be called in a given institution) or in the department of psychology. Criminology is so composite a field that it is impossible to fit it into any one departmental organization of the university. The professor of criminology will bring together into a course of instruction, from the point of view of his special interest, pertinent matter from many fields of research and through the influence of his personality other instructors in other departments than his own will cooperate with him in their instruction. The professor of criminology may devote his full time to his professorship or he may employ a large or small portion of his time and energy in giving instruction in sociology, or in psychology, strictly so-called. He should so organize his course or courses in criminology that it may attract pre-legal and pre-medical students."

A tentative prospectus for the subject-matter, equipment and cost of a department of criminology in a college or university is contained in the committee's report referred to.

III. The Future

The complete elimination of crime need not be looked for by anyone now alive or soon to be born. Not only will there doubtless always be laws which, in the nature of things, not everyone can constantly obey, but the passions of men will ever be ready to simmer and boil. Under some conditions and among some people "the knife will ever sit loosely in its sheath," to quote Aschaffenburg's vivid phrase. One may add that the slanderous tongue will always hang loosely in the mouth and the covetous eye always roam wildly over other people's goods. Envy, greed, malice, lust, hate, the desire for revenge and sheer impetuousness of action will doubtless always be among the frailties of mankind. No program, however wise or effectively carried out, can ever wholly stop misconduct, as sacrifices to superstitious gods have now been stopped among the civilized portions of the race. Perhaps it is not even reasonable to hope that we shall ever see the last insane person, the last feebleminded, the last person suffering from a psychopathic abnormality.

Nevertheless, crime can be immensely diminished. He would be a bold man who would set the limits to its reduction. Lately, during the war, we have seen the effect of widespread opportunity for work, of attractive wages and conditions of labor and an atmosphere of national purposefulness and social homogeneity in reducing somewhat the volume of crime. When normal living shall have been made possible for all or all but a few, when the friction between society and the individual shall have been reduced, when men shall be reasonably able to satisfy their wants and to use their talents, when all shall know the ways of wholesome leisure and shall have the opportunity to embrace those ways, and when the racially undesirable shall have been reduced in numbers and protected from exploitation and temptation, then we may look for that reduction of crime that is the aim of criminology as it has been described in this book.

APPENDIX

Partial list of courts and penal, correctional and other institutions having clinics for the psychiatric and other study of individual offenders.

COMPILED FROM DATA FURNISHED BY THE NATIONAL COMMITTEE FOR MENTAL HYGIENE AND OTHER SOURCES

State	City	Institution
California	Ione	Preston School of Industry
"	San Francisco	Juvenile Court
"	Los Angeles	Los Angeles County Juvenile Court
"	Oakland	Juvenile Court
"	Whittier	Whittier State School
"	....	Pacific Colony (authorized but not built)
Colorado	Denver	Juvenile Court
Georgia	Savannah	Children's Court
Illinois	Chicago	Division of the Criminologist, State Department of Public Welfare[1]
"	Chicago	House of Correction
"	Chicago	Criminal Court
"	Chicago	Municipal Court
Indiana	Jeffersonville	Indiana Reformatory
"	Michigan City	Indiana State Prison
"	Plainfield	Indiana School for Boys
"	Clermont	Indiana School for Girls
"	Indianapolis	Marion County Juvenile Court
"	Indianapolis	Marion County Criminal Court
"	Crownpoint	Lake County Circuit Court
Kansas	Ft. Leavenworth	U. S. Disciplinary Barracks
Massachusetts	Boston	Juvenile Court (Clinic maintained by Judge Baker Foundation)

[1] The Division of the Criminologist at present consists of the Juvenile Psychopathic Institute, Chicago, and the physicians at the following institutions: State School for Delinquent Boys at St. Charles, State School for Delinquent Girls at Geneva, State Reformatory at Pontiac, Illinois State Penitentiary at Joliet, and the Southern Illinois Penitentiary at Chester.

State	City	Institution
Massachusetts	Boston	Municipal Court
"	Charlestown	Massachusetts State Prison
"	Concord Junction	Massachusetts Reformatory
"	Sherborn	Reformatory for Women
"	Lancaster	Industrial School for Girls
"	Shirley	Industrial School for Boys
"	Westboro	Lyman School
Michigan	Detroit	Children's Court
Minnesota	Minneapolis	Hennepin County Juvenile Court
Missouri	St. Louis	Children's Court
New Jersey	Rahway	New Jersey State Reformatory
"	Clinton Farms	New Jersey Reformatory for Women
"	Newark	Essex County Juvenile Court
"	Jersey City	Hudson County Jail
New York	Bedford Hills	New York State Reformatory for Women
"	Ossining	Sing Sing Prison
"	Elmira	New York State Reformatory
"	New York City	Children's Court
"	New York City	New York City Penitentiary on Blackwell's Island
"	White Plains	Westchester County Dept. of Charities and Correction
Ohio	Columbus	Bureau of Juvenile Research
"	Mansfield	Ohio State Reformatory
Pennsylvania	Philadelphia	Juvenile Court
"	Darling	Sleighton Farms
Rhode Island	Providence	Children's Court
Tennessee	Memphis	Juvenile Court
Utah	Salt Lake City	Juvenile Court
Washington	Seattle	Children's Court

INDEX

Printed in Dunstable, United Kingdom

91220130R00278